Cults and New Religions

Sources for Study of Nonconventional
Religious Groups in Nineteenth-and
Twentieth-Century America

*A collection of
reprinted books, pamphlets, articles, and ephemera
documenting the development of nonconventional religion in America*

Edited by
J. GORDON MELTON
Director
Institute for the Study of American Religion
Santa Barbara

A Garland Series

The Unification Church I

Views from the Outside

Edited with an introduction by
MICHAEL L. MICKLER

GARLAND PUBLISHING
New York   London
1990

Library of Congress Cataloging-in-Publication Data

The Unification Church / edited with an introduction by Michael L. Mickler.
p. cm. — (Cults and new religions)
Vol. 3 edited by James R. Lewis
A reprint of books, articles, and pamphlets.
Includes bibliographical references.
Contents: 1. Views from the outside — 2. Inner life —
3. Outreach.
ISBN 0-8240-4489-4 (v. 1)
1. Unification Church. I. Mickler, Michael L., 1949–   .
BX9750.S44U65 1990

289.9'6—dc20   89-49682

Printed on acid-free, 250-year-life paper.

Manufactured in the United States of America

Contents

Acknowledgments

Material from *Japanese Religions* © 1976, reprinted by
permission; *Rev. Sun Myung Moon* © 1978 by University Press
of America,™ Inc., reprinted by permission; "Ideology,
Conversion and Faith Maintenance in a Korean Sect" © 1977
The Association of the Korean Christian Scholars in North
America, reprinted by permission.

INTRODUCTION

Books, articles and other secondary works published on the Holy Spirit Association for the Unification of World Christianity (HSA-UWC), popularly known as the Unification Church (UC), can be grouped into several major categories. The first consists of responses to the Church in religious publications. A second consists of secular accounts. A third consists of scholarly, academic treatments. A fourth consists of government documents. This introduction will discuss the selections in this volume within the context of these basic divisions. (See *The Unification Church in America: A Bibliography and Research Guide* by Michael L. Mickler, Garland, 1986.)

Responses to the Church in Religious Publications

Although this sourcebook does not cover the full range of responses to the UC in religious publications, it does contain some helpful and hard to obtain selections. Of particular significance are three articles reprinted from the July 1976 number of *Japanese Religions*, a magazine issued by the Kyoto-based National Christian Council Center for the Study of Japanese Religions. These articles are useful in two respects. First, they exemplify the dominant response of "mainline" Protestant churches which have tended to view the UC as deviant and "non-Christian" on doctrinal, ritual or socio-political grounds. Second, they include relevant information on the UC's development in Japan and Korea. At the same time, the articles have significant limitations. Most obvious is their polemical tone. They also are dated. Beginning in the late 1970s and continuing in the 1980s, the UC has been able to engage a broad range of intellectuals and religious professionals (including clergy) in ecumenical and interdenominational dialogues. On the other hand, the UC has not gained recognition from either the National or World Council of Churches.

Notto R. Thelle's "The Unification Church: A New Religion," the lead article in the National Christian Council of Japan's series, defines the UC as "a new religious movement which has an obvious background in Christian traditions, but at the same time develops so many particular doctrines and practices that it separates itself from the traditional Christian churches"

(3). In support of this thesis, Thelle refers to the UC's "syncratist tendency" and terms Rev. Moon a "modern shaman." His article, while not useful for its discussion of UC theology, provides an informative listing of UC publications in Japan, critical studies published about the Church there, and some specifics about the background and recruitment of the UC's first generation Japanese leadership, information not readily available elsewhere.

Young Bok Chun, in "The Korean Background of the Unification Church" is more polemical than Thelle. Critical of the National Christian Council of Japan for not clearly denouncing the UC as a non-Christian movement in 1975 as several Korean church leaders had done earlier, Chun contends that the UC "should not be characterized as a Christian sect" (14). He asserts that it is more correct to call it "*Moon*-ism" rather than Christianity. Yin-yang philosophy, a Korean prophetic scripture called *Cheon Kam Nok*, ecstatic movements advocating the "restoration of Eden," and sects in which sexual rites were practiced, Chun maintains, are key elements in the background of the Church's origin and development in Korea. Holding that "Compared to Japanese Christians their Korean brothers have a much stronger sense of the uniqueness of Christ as the sole basis of salvation," Chun found it "strange that Japanese Christians do not take a much firmer stand against the Unification Church" (18).

Though he also considers the question of doctrine, Wi Jo Kang in "The Unification Church: Christian Church or Political Movement" writes that "the real danger of this movement is not its theological heresy, but rather lies in the area of its political involvement" (22). The appeal of the UC and its impact, Kang argues, "are mainly felt in the area of its political activities, and its followers are greatly attracted by its commitment to the fight again communism" (22). Whereas "Christian involvement in political activities should not work for a particular political ideology, party, nation, or block of nations," Kang asserts that the UC has closely identified with the political line of anti-communism, the security of South Korea and the destiny of the United States" (22-23). Further alleging that the Rev. Moon is not above advocating "Watergate tricksterism," Kang concludes that "Such unchristian political activities, however sincere . . . cannot help but alienate many of the followers of the movement, and with the eventual death of its founder it is quite possible that the impact of the Unification Church itself will die out" (32).

Following the Korean Christian documents in this collection there are a couple of significant Jewish documents. One of these is a three page transcript of Rabbi Maurice Davis' testimony before an informal, *ad hoc* panel of federal government officials in 1976, reprinted here in *The Unification Church: Its Activities and Practices* (37-40). A leading UC critic as well as the founder and then-leader of C.E.R.F. (Citizens Engaged in Re-uniting Families), Davis testified:

> [T]he last time I ever witnessed a movement that had these qualifications: (1) a totally monolithic movement with a single point of view and a single authoritarian head; (2) replete with fanatical followers who are prepared and programmed to do anything their master says; (3) supplied by absolutely unlimited funds; (4) with a hatred of anyone on the outside; (5) with suspicion of parents, against their parents—Senator Dole, the last movement that had those qualifications was the Nazi youth movement, and I tell you, I'm scared (40).

Davis' testimony garnered some publicity and reflected widely-held Jewish perceptions. The other significant Jewish document included in this volume is A. James Rudin's *Jews and Judaism in Rev. Moon's Divine Principle*, reprinted as appendix II (101-109) in Chong Sun Kim's *Rev. Sun Myung Moon* (University Press of America, 1978). Rudin's report, commissioned by the American Jewish Committee, charged that the UC's primary theological text "reveals an orientation of almost unrelieved hostility toward the Jewish people" (104). Citing specific passages, he asserted, "Whether he is discussing the Israelites of the Hebrew Bible or the 'Jews' of the New Testament period, Reverend Moon portrays their behavior as reprobate, their intentions as evil (often diabolical), and their religious mission as eclipsed" (104). This 1976 report was widely influential and helped further solidify Jewish antipathy toward the UC. Despite subsequent UC responses (including "official" repudiations of anti-semitism, pledges of support for the state of Israel, and the removal of "offending statements" in new texts), this antipathy has continued, in part due to Jewish misperceptions of a disproportionate number of former Jews in the UC. (Further Jewish materials on new religions can be found in volume 14 of this series.)

Secular Accounts

Secular responses to the UC, unlike responses in religious publications, do not fall into clear-cut institutional categories but rather into opposing camps in what has been a wide-ranging public debate over the Church's right to exist and propagate its beliefs. Within the context of this debate, a fundamental distinction emerged between the UC's opposition critics and its libertarian defenders. This source book includes on of the most significant documents ever compiled to attack the church in North America. Almost impossible to locate today, it having been superceded, it highlights the persaecution experienced in the pre-Jonestown era.

The most important subgrouping of UC critics in that they have supplied the raw data from which other critics have drawn, is made up of deprogrammed apostates. T*he Unification Church: Its Activities and Practices*, Vols. I and II (1976), reprinted in this volume, contains a representative and influential collection of these accounts. Published as an informal transcript of a February 18, 1976 meeting between some two hundred distraught parents of former or current UC members and Senator Robert Dole (R-Kansas) and a panel of government officials, Volume I includes oral testimony from eight ex-members in addition to other anti-UC activists. Volume II, "a sampling of letters of parents and victims," contains testimonial letters of fourteen ex-members along with those from families involved with the UC and other "cults." Consistent with what became a familiar litany of charges during the 1970s, their criticisms flayed the UC for alleged political and interorganizational authoritarianism. It was maintained, for example, that Rev. Moon intended his followers to fight for South Korea, if necessary; that the UC intended to set up a theocracy with Rev. Moon an "absolute dictator of the United States;" and that the UC was, in reality, a political front. On the intra-organizational side, ex-members alleged sensory and sleep deprivation, "mind control," slave-like work conditions, and deception. UC recruitment practices, particularly within its San Francisco Bay Area wing, were subject to more extended treatments. See "A Couple of Summers" by Eric E. Rolfes and "The World of the Cult" by Paul Engel, both reprinted in Chong Sun Kim's *Rev. Sun Myung Moon* (24-31).

Interventionists, a related grouping of UC critics who include relatives of Church members, deprogrammers and an assortment of journalists, psychiatrists, jurists and clergy, have used apostate materials to reinforce their efforts to extricate individuals from the UC. *The Unification Church in America: Its Activities and Practices* is an excellent example of a document assembled from this perspective. Including the testimonies of parents, relatives, selected health care professionals and educators among others, an important undergirding assumption of this perspective is that the UC is not a "true" religion but rather a pseudo-religion or "cult" utilizing manipulative tactics to induce sudden personality changes, the impact of which was thought to be the complete loss of an individual's free will. A second assumption naturally followed: once in, an individual was powerless to leave. Hence, the necessity for intervention. One important result of the gathering which led to this document was the formation of "a national organization to combat destructive pseudo-religious cults," the Committee Engaged in Freeing Minds (CEFM). Apart from removing individuals from the Church an important purpose of this "anticult" group and other similar ones was to agitate for a broadly-based government investigation of the UC.

Aside from lacking selections from the libertarian side of the debate, this sourcebook is limited in its treatment of UC critics. It, for example, has no representative selections from what might be termed UC resisters: those who do not favor intervention in UC internal affairs but who have sought to discourage outsiders, especially eminent scholars, from interacting with the Church. Nor does it give evidence of the UC's numerous debunkers: those who have depicted the UC as a passing, even laughable phenomenon unworthy of serious attention. Even the apostate accounts lack full development. Accounts of ex-members who were in the Church only a matter of months, as were most of those cited in this volume, tend to be sensationalized with stress laid on their "rescue" and stark contrasts between life in the UC and outside. Accounts of ex-members who had been in the Church for several years, lacking here, though frequently severely critical, note progressive disillusionment and areas of overlap between life within the without. Despite these limitations, source materials from *The Unification Church: Its Activities and Practices* are significant in that they helped coalesce anticultism as an ideology and led to the formation of a national coordinating body for all major anticult organizations.

Scholarly Treatments

In recent years, the UC has gained the reputation of being one of the most thoroughly studied of the new religious movements (NRMs). Most of these studies are easily obtainable, but this sourcebook contains one early, hard-to-obtain item which could rightly be termed scholarly: Byong-suh Kim's "Ideology, Conversion and Faith Maintenance in a Korean Sect: The Case of the Unified Family of Rev. Sun Myung Moon" (*Korean Christian Scholar's Journal*, Spring 1977). Kim's article has not been widely-cited or particularly influential. It does, however, nicely illustrate some important differences between academic and popular treatments mainly in the areas of motivation, methodology, and results.

Kim, a professor of sociology at Montclair State College, states in the introduction to this article that having noticed declines in other successor movements to the 1960s counterculture, his primary concern "is to explore some significant structural and psychological sources which may explain ... [the] unusually rapid growth of the Korean sect of World Christianity" (9). Thus, unlike the critics cited above, his motives are not to refute the UC's doctrines or to challenge its practices but rather to inquire why adherents joined, how they became converted and why they stay. This is not to suggest that all scholarly discussions of the UC are "value-neutral" (heated debates, for example, have raged over the propriety of academics attending UC-sponsored conferences and over "brainwashing").

Most academics studying the Church, however, tend to be more detached in orientation, viewing the UC's doctrines and practices through the lenses of their respective disciplines.

In terms of methodology, there are significant differences between Kim's approach and those approaches of the UC's religious or secular critics. Kim, for instance, exhibits a degree of methodological suspicion about accepting data at face value. Rather than uncritically accepting the claims of the movement's critics or adherents, Kim "utilizes the methods of qualitative analysis with an emphasis on participant observation as a major technique of data collection" (11). Connected to this is his use of multiple sources ranging from journalistic reports and UC publications to personal interviews, observation and competing sociological theories. All this adds shading and complexity to what in more polemical accounts is a stark portrayal of the UC as an unmitigated menace. Finally, rather than portraying his article as the final word or exhaustive, Kim terms his study an "exploratory case study."

Not surprisingly, given his motivation and methodology, Kim's conclusions are more balanced than those openly hostile to the Church. This is evident throughout. For example, though concluding that among Moonists, "there exists a conscious effort to misrepresent the self identity of Sun Myung Moon and a deliberate concealment of a certain portion of Moon's message from public disclosure (23)," he suggests on the basis of socio-psychological theory that such behavior "can be considered as a normal occurrence in our everyday life" and that it has significant functions for group life (27). On the brainwashing/mind-control controversy, he argues that although there is no evidence of coercion or compulsory techniques in Moonist training sessions, "any process of conversion to religion or political ideology employs ... latent techniques of 'desocialization' and 'resocialization'" (39). He similarly views participation in UC's mass wedding ceremonies as one of several ritual processes contributing to "communal solidarity."

Chong Sun Kim's *Sun Myung Moon* (1978), although published by the University Press of America and insightful as to the UC's Korean cultural and religious background as well as to political, social and intellectual pressures extant in American society, cannot be considered a scholarly work without serious qualification. The main problem is Kim's penchant for amateurish psychologizing of and personalized attack against the Reverend Moon. In addition, Kim seems to uncritically accept all, even the most blatantly sensationalized of the offenses charged to the Church by its critics. As a result, his work is not even-handed and appeals less to a scholarly than to a popular audience. Beyond these limitations, Kim's book contains a wealth of information and some good analysis. He is especially strong in his collation of anthropological studies related to shamanistic traditions in Northeast Asia and Korea (7-15, 47-59). He also is discerning in his sociological analysis of factors in the United States (chiefly alienation) which contributed to the UC's recruitment and visibility (79-93).

Government Documents

The UC has been embroiled in near constant litigation within the United States since 1975. Though costly and time-consuming, several decisions (won on appeal) have gained it gradual recognition as a *bona fide* religion with tax-exemption privileges, public solicitation rights and access to missionary visas. In addition, the UC has been able to extend constitutional protections to its members, press for action against deprogrammers and combat inappropriately-applied conservatorship statutes. On the other hand, the UC has been subject to legislative hearings, restrictive legislation efforts and investigative reports linking it to alleged abuses in the areas of recruitment, fundraising, child care and political lobbying. None of these led to actual legislation. They did, however, highlight significant levels of strain between the UC and major sectors of the American public.

Strictly speaking, *The Unification Church: Its Activities and Practices* is not a government document, but includes a transcript of an informal question and answer session between distraught parents and federal officials in the Dirksen Senate Office Building. This document, however, was published by a National Ad Hoc Committee of concerned parents, not the government. It is, nonetheless, instructive in two respects. First, Senator Dole convened the meeting both in response to "hundreds of inquiries" he had received during the previous years regarding the UC and in response to a petition with "signatures of over 14,000 parents from the State of Kanses and surrounding jurisdictions demanding to have their views heard" (5). Additionally, whether accurately or not, the speakers detail what they perceive to be the means employed by the movement to alienate "psychologically kidnapped youth" from their government, families, prior religions, eduction, and society.

Besides documenting strains between the UC and sectors of the public (chiefly relatives of members), *The Unification Church: Its Activities and Practices* also illustrates potential frustration between anti-UC activities and the world of "officialdom" personified by government bureaucrats. Sensitive to jurisdictional restraints, demands of confidentiality, and formal procedures, officials from the IRS, Department of Labor, U.S. Postal Service, Bureau of Consumer Protection and other federal agencies represented at the informal Dole forum listened politely but could not gratify demands for direct action. For this reason, some UC opponents sought recourse outside existing institutional networks through vigilante-style abductions, novel interpretations of guardianship laws and efforts in favor of legislation to block UC recruitment.

The Unification Church: Its Activities and Prac-

tices is helpful in understanding some of the dynamics of governmental response to the UC. Mention has been made of court rulings which, on the whole, have vindicated UC claims. To a certain degree, however, these organizational gains were overshadowed by the Reverend Moon's conviction on tax charged in 1982. Nonetheless, it is important to examine that case in light of unambiguous court affirmations of the UC's legal and religious status. Mention also was made of legislative hearings, proposed legislation and investigative reports. These frequently shed less light on the UC than on the social milieu within which it operated. The most substantive report followed mid-1970s disclosures of Korean influence-buying and attempted, with little or no success, to link UC officials with "Koreagate." A second Dole forum in 1979 and a legislative inquiry of the New York Assembly Child Care Committee resulted from pressures to link the UC and other groups to the People's Temple. During the late 1970s and early 1980s, several states proposed legislation designed to hinder UC recruitment and to facilitate removal of members by guardianship statutes. Only one such law passed—and this legislation was vetoed by then-Governor Hugh Carey.

Michael L. Mickler

*Notto R. THELLE**

THE UNIFICATION CHURCH: A NEW RELIGION

> ... for years I have been watching and waiting for all of you. I am fulfilling my mission all by myself. When you hear me speak, then you will feel that the world has become so small and that everything comes within the grasp of your hand. It is natural that you feel that. Three people are most fearful of me. First of all, Christians fear me, Communists fear me, and Satan, of course, fears me. Are you afraid of me? If I am Father, we are your True Parents, and you are the children, how can children be afraid of their parents?[1]

> There is one very important thing to remember. When Jesus Christ returns to our world, he will bring with him another Bible .... The most important thing that we must realize tonight is that Jesus Christ is not coming merely to repeat the New Testament. He is coming to reveal the new truth, which might be called the Completed Testament ....
> The time of the Lord's coming is near. Therefore God has summoned the modern-day prophet, the Reverend Sun Myung Moon, as a channel, to speak to the World, revealing God's word.[2]

The Unification Church, or The Holy Spirit Association for the Unification of World Christianity, regards itself as the beginning of the new humanity. It was started by the charismatic and eloquent Korean, The Reverend Sun Myung Moon, and has created confusion and criticism, not only in Korea and Japan, but also in the United

---

*   Associate Director of the NCC Center for the Study of Japanese Religions.
1.   Sun Myung Moon, "The Unification," *The Way of the World*, August 1972, p.20.
2.   Bo Hi Pak, "How is Christ Coming?" *The Way of the World*, No. 7/8, 1974, pp.87–88.

States and other Western countries, in which members of the "united family" are active.

It is not our intention here to give any extensive review of the teaching of the Unification Church, but rather to examine, against the Japanese background, its function as a sort of "Christian new religion," i.e., a new religious movement which has an obvious background in Christian traditions, but at the same time develops so many peculiar doctrines and practices that it separates itself from the traditional Christian churches.

Even though the Unification Church never tires of proclaiming the importance of making God the only center of one's life, and also stresses the central role of Jesus, one can easily recognize that its teaching is basically opposed to vital Christian doctrines. It tends to claim that it does not bring something old, but a radically new message, based on the revelation given to Sun Myung Moon himself. Consequently, Korean and Japanese Christians have clearly voiced their criticism against the movement, denouncing it as anti-Christian, non-Christian, heretic, or at least questioning the Christian character of its various doctrines.

The Divine Principle[3] is the basic scripture of the Unification Church. It is a peculiar mixture of Biblicism and evolutionary theories, quasi-scientific explanations, Eastern thought and anti-communism. It starts to demonstrate the dual nature of God, masculine and feminine, positive and negative, in terms closely related to traditional *yin-yang* philosophy. Then it goes on to depict the original state of man in the garden of Eden. The fall was caused by the sexual intercourse of Eve and Lucifer, the fallen angel. Thus the blood of Satan came into man-

---

3.   Written by Young Oon Kim. This article is based on the Japanese edition, *Genri kōron*, Tokyo: Kōgensha, 1972.

kind as the satanic lineage. Because man cannot himself cleanse this satanic blood, the Messiah (Jesus Christ) had to come to restore the relation to God by purifying the blood of man, marrying and getting children without sin. Unfortunately Jesus was crucified before he was able to create a family and fulfill his salvation. He brought merely spiritual salvation, but did not solve the basic problem and bring physical salvation. Hence the redemption of our bodies is yet to come, and the Lord of the Second Advent is now going to fulfill this purpose, purify the satanic blood and initiate the new era, the new family, the new state, the new world.

Just as Jesus was misunderstood and persecuted, so will be also the new Messiah. "However," as it was proclaimed in the film about Moon's crusade in the United States, "this time he will not die upon the cross. This time he comes to triumph!"

The whole teaching of sin and salvation is integrated in a view of history that leads from Eden to World War III (sic.) and the final unification of mankind. History develops through separating and unifying tendencies. Eden was the original state of perfect harmony. The Roman civilization, in which the Jewish and Greek cultures were unified, was the stage of the coming of the Second Adam (Jesus), and the final unification is now at hand through the Third Adam: all ideologies and faiths and political systems will be integrated through the complete unification in Him, the Lord of the Second Advent. World War III and the fight between democracy and communism (God and Satan) is included and gives the teaching a strong political colouring that sometimes tends to cover the more specific "religious" elements of the movement. The support by the Korean government, Japanese liberal democrats, and American conservative politicians, depends obviously more upon its fanatic anti-communism than its somewhat strange religious ideas.

Among other Unification Church-publications which give additional information about the movement we should mention the Japanese monthly *Shin-tenchi* (The New Heaven and Earth), and the weekly newspaper *Shūkan Shūkyō* (Religion-Weekly). The Korean branch issues the monthly *The Way of the World* in English. A collection of Moon's speeches during his crusade in the United States in 1974, *Christianity in Crisis—New Hope*, is also translated and published in Japan as *Kibō no tōrai* (The Advent of Hope). The small pamphlet *Tōitsu shisō no kosshi* (The Essence of Unification Thought) gives in the form of questions and answers a concentration of its views on vital issues of philosophy, ideology, education and unification. The small Hymnbook (*Seika*) gives an impression of strong devotion to the coming Lord (Messiah, Moon). The emphasis is on the return to Eden, and the importance of marriage goes together with a burning consciousness that the light comes from the East, brought victoriously to the world by the young vangards of unification.[4]

In addition to the publications issued by the Unification Church itself, one should also mention some easily available publications written by people who have done a critical study of the Unification Church. *Tōitsu kyōkai no machigai ni tsuite* (About the Error of the Unification Church), Tokyo: Kurisuchan Bunsho Dendōdan, 1966, is written by Mr. Moriyama Satoshi. His main purpose is to examine and reject the doctrine of the Unification Church, but he also points out its close connection with the anti-communist movement. A more recent publication written by Mr. Arai Arao, is entitled *Nihon no kyōki—shōkyō rengō to genri undō* (Japan's Madness—The Anti-Communist League and Genri Undō)[5], Tokyo: Kikuya Shobō, 1971. This is a much more thorough and critical treatment, not only of its teaching and relation to rightist and/anti-communist movements, but also gives the historical development

4. The above-mentioned books and pamphlets are all issued by the Unification Church and are available in its book store in Tokyo.
5. Genri Undō (The Divine Principle Movement) is a common Japanese name of the Unification Church.

of the movement and its founder. The author is concerned to
portray the real Moon, not the image that he is given by the
Unification Church, and describes his central role as the Lord of
the Second Advent. In this connection he depicts Moon's activities
in Korea, in which sexual rites played an important part in the
restoration of the new humanity. Not only an overwhelming mass
of documentation material, to which Korean observers and
previous members are important contributors, but also the correspondence between such rites and its basic teaching about fall
and restoration, seem to support the evidence of this epoch of the
movement. Several articles by other authors are also included in
the book, which gives an interesting insight into the Unification
Church. *Nihon no kyōki* is not written by an objective spectator,
but an active Christian opponent who aims at exterminating the
Unification Church. The book should be read with criticism; but
basically the material seems to be reliable.

A new report about the Unification Church is written by a
journalist, Yamaguchi Hiroshi, who walked in the steps of the
prophet and wrote his book *Genri undō no sugao* (The True Face
of Genri Undō), Tokyo: Eru Shuppansha, 1975. Based on a wealth
of material, interviews, and testimonies, he depicts "the true face"
of the Unification Church. His intention was not to oppose the
movement, but to make good journalism, and the result is an interesting and very readable report which supports most of the conten-
tions of the above-mentioned book.

Apart from these publications, Japanese newspapers and
journals carried quite a lot of critical reporting about the Unification Church during its campaign in major Japanese cities in 1975,
especially denouncing its propaganda methods, its rightist and anti-
communist campaigns and its questionable fund-raising activities.
Of articles published about the movement in English we could
mention: Lee Seaman, "The Unification Church—Blessing or
Monster," *Japan Christian Activity News*, Nos. 471–474, 1975,
reprinted in *The Japan Missionary Bulletin*, Oct. 1975; James A.
Gittings, "Genri Undo," *Japan Christian Quarterly*, XXXIV/3,
1968.

Most of the so-called new religions of Japan grew out of Buddhism, Shinto, and/or traditional folk religion, and can be traced back to the different traditions. But at the same time they developed new organizations and new teachings revealed to their respective founders, and were established as separate new religions. Just as there are new religions with a Buddhist or Shintoist background, the Unification Church could be characterized as a new religion with a Christian background.

Relation to Established Christianity

The Unification Church's attitude to the traditional churches is characterized by an ambiguous feeling of hate and love, rejection and acceptance.

On the one hand, it regards itself as the true continuation of Christianity. History has developed from Adam and Noah to the present, and the Biblical history and church history constitute the central historical development. Church fathers, reformers, missionaries, and Japanese Christians such as Uchimura Kanzō, are all included.

When the National Christian Council of Japan last year issued a statement about the Unification Church, in which the possibility of a critical dialogue with the Unification Church was mentioned, this was received with enthusiasm as a sort of official Christian recognition. Time and again—sometimes through somewhat dishonest methods— the Unification Church has tried to give the impression that they are accepted by the churches. The monthly *The Way of the World* reprints articles and essays of internationally known Church leaders such as Philip Potter and John Taylor. The German theologian Jürgen Molt- mann attended one of their conferences in England. Did he know who sponsored the conference? If a pastor or leading Christian has given a positive evaluation of the Unification Church, he may discover that he is quoted and presented as a supporter of it.

In this way traditional Christianity is positively affirmed, and the churches are regarded as elder brothers. Members of the Unification Church claim that their only hope is to be allowed to stay in the same house and belong to the same family. They are practicing true Christianity, and when they are driven out of the house, it is merely because the elder brothers are blind and authoritarian.

On the other hand, this effort to be recognized goes together with an even stronger rejection of traditional Christianity which is denounced as almost blind and dead. The Unification Church does not preach something old, but a radically new message. True salvation is not found in the Christ of the New Testament, but in the Messiah of the Completed Testament. The new in Moon's teaching is not a return to the New Testament, but a new revelation received by Moon himself and systematically developed in *The Divine Principle.*

In a discussion at the headquarter of the Unification Church in Tokyo, a spokesman of the movement agreed that in this perspective the strong reaction from Christian churches was only natural. The frequent appeals for "unification of world Christianity," therefore, sound rather hollow and propagandistic. One wonders whether the desparate efforts to be recognized by the churches they denounce merely expresses their intention to utilize the influence and goodwill of traditional Christianity, or whether there is any possibility for a "critical dialogue?"

Syncretism—Search for a Religious Synthesis

Several new religions are characterized by a syncretistic tendency to include several disparate religious traditions into a new synthesis. This also applies to the Unification Church. Apart from the Christian background of the movement, it is easy to point out the heavy influence of Oriental traditions, such as *yin-yang* philosophy, Korean shamanism, and folk religion.

In Japan the first generation of leaders was recruited from Risshō Kōsei-kai, a Buddhist "new religion." The present president of the Unification Church, Mr. Kuboki, was once the private secretary of the Risshō Kōsei-kai leader, Niwano Nikkyō. These members inevitably gave the Unification Church some Buddhist influence. An interesting, but unsuccessful, effort was made by one of the previous Risshō Kōsei-kai members, Mr. Komiyama. He wanted to integrate Buddhism and Shinto into the unification thought by harmonizing the Bible, the Lotus Sutra and the classical Japanese record, *Kojiki*. However, he had to give up, alledgedly because the unification of these ideas left no room for the central role of the Messiah, the Lord of the Second Advent.[6]

Spiritualism also seems to be an important aspect. Looking through one volume of *Shin-tenchi* (The New Heaven and Earth) one cannot but be impressed by the importance given to spiritualism and occult phenomena. This interest obviously goes back to the Korean origin of the movement, but there is no doubt that it also appeals in Japan, where spiritualism is a vital part of popular faith. At the headquarters I was told with some pride that *reinōsha*—men with special spiritual power—often were guided directly to seek contact with Sun Myung Moon.

These syncretistic or synthetic elements are not merely accidental phenomena that occurred during the development of the Unification Church. They are also given an ideological foundation. One aims not only at the "unification of world Christianity," but of all ideologies and

---

6. Cfr. *Nihon no kyōki*, pp.233–238.

religions. The original unity was lost in Eden. Through the Second
Adam the Greek and Jewish cultures were unified in the Roman culture
and medieval Christianity. The Third Adam will unify all the scattered
ideologies and faiths in a synthetic idea and a unified culture. Even
communism and democracy will be integrated in the system along with
religious faiths. Buddhist, Confucian, Hindu and Muslim cultures are
only given peripheral importance, but at the same time so-called "Far
Eastern thought," stemming from Buddhism, Confucianism and folk
religion, is in a peculiar way given a central role in the final stage of
development, leading to the advent of the Messiah.[7]

The Founder—A Modern Shaman

What most markedly singles out the Unification Church as a new
religion is the overall importance of the founder, Sun Myung Moon.
Members usually refuse to answer definitely the question whether
Moon is the Messiah or not, and emphasize that Moon himself has never
declared that he is. They tend to give vague suggestions such as, "Some
people believe he is the Messiah, some do not." Or, "Religion is an
individual matter of belief, and every man must find the answer for
himself." Or, "You will understand if you yourself join us," etc.

On the other hand, there is no doubt that Moon is regarded as the
promised Lord. In a recent conversation at the headquarters I got a
positive answer when I asked whether it was their idea that true salvation and the new era could not be initiated without the presence of the
Messiah. "But since the new era has already begun," I asked, "does
this mean that you know the Messiah, then?" The question was clearly
confirmed. This leaves us with the strange ambiguity: The new era has

---

7.   Besides *Genri kōron*, cfr. also *Tōitsu shisō no kosshi*, p.54.

already begun and we know the Messiah, but Moon himself has not declared that he is the Messiah. *The Divine Principle*, however, has clearly indicated the place, the time, and the circumstances of the birth of the Messiah, all of which point to the life of Moon himself.

By members Moon is called the One (*hitori no okata*), the Great Teacher (*Daisensei*), the Father (*oyabun*), the Prophet, etc., and the role he plays is very close to the role of charismatic founders and divine mediators of other new religions. In Moon's case this seems to be especially connected with his ecstatic experiences and his contact with "the World of Spirits," or "the Spiritual World" (*reikai*). In order to understand the more specifically religious element of the movement this point might deserve more attention than the preoccupation with the more doctrinal questions of heresy and perverted Christianity.

A comparison of two statements about Moon and about Deguchi Onisaburo, founder of the new religion Oomoto, might elucidate this point.

The preface of *The Divine Principle* depicts Sun Myung Moon as the One who was sent by God in order to solve the fundamental problem of man and the universe, in the following terms:

> His name is Sun Myung Moon. As the unique one in human history he wandered for decades through inconceivable shadowy invisible worlds, a way besmeared with blood, sweat and tears, which God only remembers. Because he knew that he could not discover the final truth which saves mankind without fulfilling the greatest trials that man must undergo, the Master alone fought with myriads of Satans in both the world of spirit and the world of flesh, and he triumphed. And then he had free contact with Jesus and the many saints and sages of Paradise, and through quiet communion with God he clarified the divine mystery.[8]

The experience of the Oomoto founder is described in the following

---

8.   *Genri kōron*, pp.37–38.

words:

> ... leaving its physical body behind in a cave on the mountain, his soul soared into the Spiritual World. During his period of separation of body and soul he learned the mysteries of Heaven and Hell. He also gained knowledge of the Universe and for the first time was fully conscious of his mission as the Saviour of Mankind?

There are several common features: the shamanic elements, the wandering to the spiritual world through hardship and austerities, the knowledge of the divine mysteries, and the strong consciousness of being mediator and saviour.

New Religons—Signs of Crisis

Sometimes one wonders whether it is really worth while for Christian churches to waste their energy to oppose a movement like the Unification Church, which has departed so far from traditional Christianity that it is rather a new religion than a Christian church. If one also considers the fact that such opposition merely tends to strengthen the consciousness among the members of the Unification Church that they are martyrs of the hatred and persecution from hypocritical, intolerant and authoritarian Christians, one might be tempted to do as little as possible. However, the basic reason for Christian opposition is probably the fact that the Unification Church has actively approached the churches and with a certain success appealed to unsatisfied Christians. It has also made use of the general goodwill of Christianity in its fund raising campaigns, often without being willing to identify itself. In addition, the problems connected with its aggressive propa-

---

9. Quotation from Clark B. Offner, Henry van Straelen, *Modern Japanese Religions*, Tokyo: Enderle, 1963, p.66.

11

ganda and blind anti-communism have made opposition from the churches nothing but natural.

However, one should not forget that the relative success of the Unification Church as a characteristic new religion is in many ways a warning for the established churches. For years Christian observers have—at a safe distance—followed the development of the numerous new religions in Japan. And as a matter of course they have interpreted the phenomenon as a dramatic expression of the deep crisis of the established religions such as Buddhism and Shinto.

It is easy to conclude that the Unification Church is a new religon and disclaim any connection. But the problem is not solved through proclamations. The fact that the Unification Church has appealed to a significant number of Christians is in itself a serious sign of inner crisis. Thousands of Japanese Christians find that church life is life-less and that the worship leaves them untouched. The church is established in a negative sense; it is there, and one wants to be loyal, but one does not expect a real challenge. A movement that creates a spirit of community and commitment, and gives challenging visions and a feeling of meaning —however perverted— is in itself a threat to the decent, boring and life-less Christianity experienced by too many Japanese Christians.

Therefore, the Unification Church should not only lead to self-defence and proclamations, but should also help the churches to realize the radical crisis of Christianity in Japan.

Young Bok CHUN*

THE KOREAN BACKGROUND OF
THE UNIFICATION CHURCH

Let me first clarify my own standpoint in the present discussion about the Unification Church. Last year several Korean church leaders issued a statement which clearly denounced the Unification Church as a non-Christian movement. Later the National Christian Council of Japan also presented its veiw on the movement, but it merely pointed out which parts of *The Divine Principle* differed from its own understanding of Christianity, and abstained from claiming that the movement was not Christian. I myself find this vague attitude somewhat unreasonable and basically agree with the Korean church leaders: The Unification Church should not be characterized as a Christian sect.

One has to admit that the Bible is an important part of its teaching; but Islam also recognizes and quotes the Bible and regards Moses and Jesus as great prophets. However, no one would claim that Islam is Christianity. Several of the new religions of Japan stress that their teaching is basically in harmony with Christianity, and often refer to the Bible, but none of them want to call their teaching Christian. The

---
*   田 永福. Secretary of the Evangelical Department of the General Assembly of the Korean Church in Japan. The article is compiled by the NCC Study Center, based on a presentation about the Unification Church by the Reverend Chun on Nov. 10, 1975, arranged by Kyoto Christian Council.

Unification Church claims that it is a Christian church founded on the Bible, but the Bible is interpreted through its holy scripture, *The Divine Principle*, which is the real basis of its teaching. I have had quite a lot of contact with members and leaders of the Unification Church, but the more I inquire and study their scriptures, the more I am convinced that it is quite unreasonable to call it a Christian sect.

Seen against the background of its origin and development in Korea, it is more correct to call it *Moon*-ism than *Christian*ity. For it is a movement based on the founder, the Reverend Sun Myung Moon himself. In order to understand the Unification Church, one needs to see it in the light of the general Korean religious background and specific developments in some Christian sects. I will briefly indicate four points: the *yin-yang* philosophy, the prophetic scripture called *Cheong Kam Nok*, the ecstatic movements which advocated the "restoration of Eden," and finally some sects which practised sexual rites as part of the establishment of the coming kingdom of God.

1. It is natural to point out the *yin-yang* philosphy as an important background for Moon's thinking. In many popular forms this idea has penetrated the religious life of Korea. Even the Korean national flag has the traditional symbol of the "Great Origin," which expresses the dual nature of the universe. The influence of this *yin-yang* philosophy is so obvious in Moon's teaching that it is sufficient just to mention it here. The basic idea of the dual nature of God and the harmonious unification of male and female forces, man and woman included, reflects nothing but traditional *yin-yang* philosophy.

2. Another important factor which has influenced the Unification Church and several other new religious movements in Korea is the old scripture called *Cheong Kam Nok* 鄭鑑録. It conveys both an indigenous form of the *yin-yang* philosophy, and also a sort of Messianic idea. It is a prophetic scripture and describes the apocalyptic catastro-

phies in a manner similar to the Biblical Apocalypse. In *Cheong Kam Nok* there is a prophecy that in the end period "the true man" will appear from the "Southern Ocean," which is nothing but Korea itself. Moon's understanding of himself is linked to this tradition. In his teaching there is a strong conviction that he himself is the elected prophet.

3. The idea of the "return to Eden" is another dominant factor in Moon's thinking. This is not developed by Moon himself, but was one of the central ideas in several Christian movements in the 1920's and 1930's.

It is said that Moon was 16 years old when he received the revelation that he was the prophet raised up by God. At that time (1936) there were several ecstatic and messianic movements in Korea, and especially a Methodist pastor called *Young Do Lee* seems to have influenced Moon. I often went to these meetings when I was young. The pastor was an enthusiastic and eloquent preacher and advocated a peculiar interpretation of the Bible. During the meetings he used to roll up a newspaper and go around saying, "Satan, get out! Satan, get out!" while the congregation was praying in a state of ecstatic shaking.

This movement advocated the socalled "restoration of the orginal state" before the fall of Adam and Eve. The congregation was dancing around and crying for the return of Eden. And when the pastor cried, "Adam and Eve were naked before the fall! Take off your clothes!" the men turned to the women and stripped off their clothes, and they danced around naked.

His doctor had predicted that Mr. Lee would die of tuberculosis within a short time, but he continued his evangelistic work for more than ten years and had a considerable impact on the churches in Korea. Moon came to him in 1936 and was deeply influenced by him and other charismatic leaders. The movement was suppressed and the leaders were scattered, but Moon, who was a member of the group, brought with him the idea of the return to Eden.

4. Finally I have to mention Moon's relation to some sects in which sexual rites were practised as a means to create a new mankind. At the age of 25 Moon engaged in this movement which practised the socalled "sharing of blood," *pi karim* (Jap., *chiwake* 血分け). These were rites of sexual intercourse between men and women. The idea was that the children who were going to be born through the "mixing of blood" would be without sin. Because of this "violation of social order" Moon was arrested in 1948 and sentenced to five years of imprisonment. He himself claims that a miracle occurred at that time: all the blood was extracted from his body, but he did not die. He was released during the Korean war in 1952, arrested again in 1955 for the same reason, but was later released.

When it was discovered that several femal members of Korean churches had been to Moon's center to receive *pi karim*, an increasing number of people started to protest against this movement as a heretical religion. However, Moon did not at this time draw so much attention as another much more influential movement called *Chun Do Kwan* 伝道館, led by a presbyter called *Tai Seon Park*. This sect had installed separate rooms in the basement of the churches in which men and women had sexual intercourse. These rites drew a large number of people to the movement.

In 1954 Moon's movement was established as a separate organization called The Holy Spirit Asscoiation for the Unification of World Christianity. In a later stage the political and anti-communist aspect of the movement has been more and more emphasized.

In 1958 the movement was introduced in Japan. While the practise of *pi karim* has been one of the central problems for the movement in Korea, the Unification Church in Japan seems to be extremely strict in sexual matters and it is difficult to trace any practice of sexual rites. But the idea of bearing children without sin is still central.

In 1960 Moon remarried, and called it "The Wedding of the Lamb." This year was proclaimed as the beginning of the new age, *cheong ki won nyon* 天紀元年, "The First Year of the Heavenly Era." All marriages had hitherto been the results of sinful relations, and in many cases people who were already married had to leave their spouses in order to marry according to Moon's will. Now marriage between the perfect men and women who were willing to follow Moon's command would initiate the new holy family and their children would be without sin. The mass-wedding ceremonies of the Unification Church are to be understood in this context.

It is often said that Moon himself has never declared himself as the Messiah. However, in 1968 he proclaimed that he was the Messiah, and later, when Korean pastors questioned whether Moon was regarded as the Messiah or not, a spokesman of the movement said that the one who should answer this question was not himself, but God. He himself, however, was convinced that Moon was raised by God to be the coming Messiah. If God had not recognized him, he said, he would not believe in him either.

Compared to Japanese Christians their Korean brothers have a much stronger sense of the uniqueness of Christ as the sole basis for salvation, and I find it strange that Japanese Christians do not take a much firmer stand against the Unification Church.

*Wi Jo KANG**

THE UNIFICATION CHURCH:

CHRISTIAN CHURCH OR POLITICAL MOVEMENT?

The Holy Spirit Association for the Unification of World Christianity, commonly known as the Unification Church, is a typical new religion. One distinctive characteristic of the "new religions" is a conglomeration of different religious concepts and doctrines. The unification Church officially acknowledges this aspect of the movement and writes: "A new religion, which will serve as the basis for the new civilization, would be a fusion of Christianity and Oriental philosophy."[1]

In advocating such "a fusion of Christianity and Oriental philosophy" the teachings of the Unification Church reflect the *yin-yang* thought of ancient China. According to this ancient Chinese thought, God always works through a male, positive force and a female, negative force in His creative activities and in all His works. As the *Divine Principle*, the official and basic book of Unification Church doctrines, states:

> A creation, whatever it may be, cannot come into being unless a reciprocal relationship between positivity and negativity has been

---

* Professor of Missions and World Religions, Concordia Seminary in Exile, St. Louis, Missouri.
1. Young Oon Kim, *Divine Principle and its Application*, Washington, D. C.: The Holy Spirit Association for the Unification of World Christianity, 1969, p.193.

achieved, not only within itself but also in relation to other beings. For example, particles, which are the essential components of all matter, have either positivity or negativity, or a neutrality which is caused when the positive and negative elements neutralize other[2]

Since all things are created and exist through "a reciprocal relationship between the dual essentialities of positivity and negativity," God created not only man but also woman. This dual harmony is expressed in His created order. But Eve had illegitimate relations with Satan and the stain of Satan's blood was transmitted to all the descendants of Adam and Eve. Thus the harmony was broken and the world of men became the place of Satan.

Such theological formulations involving a "fusion of Christianity and Oriental philosophy" are not inherently wrong. It is an imperative and positive task of theologians in Asia to utilize traditional Asian philosophy in developing an indigenous theology. Christian theology in the West also incorporated Greek philosophy and other cultural elements of the West.

However, the task of new theological formulations is not to distort the central message of Christ as revealed in the Holy Scriptures, but rather to affirm it. The weakness and error of the Unification Church rests precisely in its departure from the centrality of Christ as "the way, the truth and the life." The Unification Church teaches that God uses the power of male and female also in His redemptive activities as well as in His creative works. Jesus was God's chosen prophet to redeem mankind and restore man to his original sinless state. But Jesus Christ was murdered by the Jews and Jesus never had the opportunity to have a family. He failed to leave descendants through whom he could transmit pure blood to mankind. The Reverend Sun Myung Moon, the founder of the Unification Church, says:

---

2. *Divine Principle*, Washington, D. C.: The Holy Spirit Association for the Unification of World Christianity, 1973, p.20.

> When God created man, He placed Adam and Eve, man and woman, in the garden of Eden. They both united with Satan and became sinful, thereby leaving God isolated. In the process of restoration God must restore both Adam and Eve. Jesus came as the sinless Adam, or perfected Adam. His first mission was, therefore, to restore his bride and form the first family of God. Jesus came, but he was crucified. He was not given a chance to restore his bride. And this is why Jesus promised his second coming. Jesus Christ must come again to consummate the mission he left undone, 2,000 years ago. . . .[3]

Thus the redemptive work of Jesus and his mission to the world remain unfinished. But God now continues His work of redemption through the blood of the "true parents" of mankind, who "ascend from the rising of the sun, with the seal of the living God," just as is prophesied in Revelation 7 : 2–7. The true parents are The Reverend Moon and his young wife, who is honored as the "Mother of the Universe."

In 1960, when the "Mother of the Universe" was married, she was an eighteen year old high school girl, a very young age to be married by Korean standards, while Moon was forty-one years old and had had previous marriages. The children born between them are said to be children without original sin. To belong to the true family under the "true parents" is an important religious concern of every member of the Unification Church. The Unification Church emphasizes the importance of belonging to the "true family" to the extent that it degrades the Holy family of Jesus Christ. It is an unacceptable heresy and blasphemy to say that Christ's mission was left undone because he failed to have a wife and have children to transmit pure blood to mankind.

3. Sun Myung Moon, *Christianity in Crisis: New Hope*. Washington, D. C.: The Holy Spirit Association for the Unification of World Christianity, 1974, p.27.

According to the teachings of the Unification Church, the death of Christ was untimely and even unnecessary, for "Jesus did not come to die on the cross."[4] Therefore the Unification Church is not a Christian movement but Moon's movement, or a new religion with a certain Christian coloring. For the followers of the Unification Church Moon is superior and more important than Jesus. A Korean Professor of sociology in a prominent Korean University, who was a follower of Moon in his early years of developing the Unification Church, demonstrates this point eloquently:

> Moon, therefore, is superior to Jesus Christ, because he fulfilled the mission which Jesus could not accomplish. Jesus is no longer one of the Trinity, the Holy Son, because of his failure in his original mission. But Moon is not only the founder of the Church but also he is the Messiah of the Second Advent, one of the Trinity, a living God.[5]

Hence no Christ-centered theologian or Christian can take the Unification Church seriously as a Christian movement. However, the real danger of this movement is not its theological heresy, but rather lies in the area of its political involvement. The appeal of the Unification Church and its impact are mainly felt in the area of its political activities, and its followers are greatly attracted by its commitment to fight against communism. Of course all Christians should be concerned about the influence of Marxism and communism in the modern world as a challenge to the expansion of Christianity. But Christian involvement in political activities should not work for a particular political ideology, party, nation, or block of nations. Christian participation in political activities in witness of Christ's truth in the world against injustice, poverty, ignorance, oppression and unjust war should rather

---

4. *Divine Principle*, p.143.
5. Ch'oi Syn-duk, "Korea's Tongil Movement," *Transactions of the Korean Branch of Royal Asiatic Society*, Vol. XLIII, 1967, p.175.

be the expression of Christian conscience and love toward fellow man transcending any political party lines and national boundaries.

Thus Christian participation in political activities is not for the sake of politics, but for the cause of Christian truth prompted by the love of Christ. In this sense, Christianity is for politics and against politics. In other words, Christianity should not use any one political line. Christianity has lived under all kinds of government and political systems in its history. Whenever Christianity has identified exclusively with any one existing political power, it has weakened the real meaning and purpose of Christianity: to be true salt and light to shine in the darkness of the world.

The Unification Church, however, has closely identified itself with the political line of anti-communism, the security of South Korea and the destiny of the United States. An offical declaration of the Unification Church, published widely in Korean newspapers, stated the following:

> The Unification Church movement is a movement of national (South Korean) survival. Communism is the enemy of mankind and the enemy of God. The communism that denies the existence of God should be defeated by the Christianity that believes in the existence of God. The principles derived from the teachings of the Reverend Sun Myung Moon prove the truth of the existence of God and the falsehood of the materialism originated by Marx and Lenin. The precious unification thought provides the truth and the confidence of the people of the world for the victory over communism. This is why the communists throughout the world are afraid of the Unification Church. The Unification Church is playing the leading role in the fight against communism in the free world. This movement is, within the nation (Korea), a movement that directly contributes to the national defense and national survival. Externally it is a movement to save the world and give hope in this world of chaos.[6]

---

6. "Declaration of the Unification Church," *Hanguk Shinmun*, May 3, 1975, p.6.

Therefore the Unification Church teaches that the greatest task in which the Christian Church should engage in this world is the fight against communism, which it explains in these words:

> Communism is a providential ideology which emerged at the end of the world to take the Cain position of thought in the dispensation of restoration. Human history started with the struggle between good and evil. Cain, who represented Satan, slaughtered Abel, who represented Heaven. Therefore, according to the law of indemnity and separation, God is going to conclude the evil history by separating good and evil worldwide. God (Abel) will subjugate evil (Cain). Communism appeared in this sense as the Cain ideology.[7]

Then why does God allow such evil ideology to exist and even to advance? The Unification people explain that God allowed the trend of thought leading to Communism to develop "for the sake of restoring the human environment in the dispensation of restoration." The official source of the Unification Church reads:

> God allowed the expansion of the communist ideology as a chastisement to warn the democratic bloc, which is the Abel side, and to direct it toward good. In the Old Testament Age, to awaken the rebellious tribes of Israel, God chastised them through the Gentiles. Today, in order to awaken the Christian nations which stand in the position of the modern Israel, God allowed Communism to emerge in the role of the modern "Gentile."[8]

Now, however, Communism is doomed to fail, according to this church movement. But the doom and demise of Communism from the world must come from a vigorous fight against the Marxist movement. Therefore, the followers of the Unification Church go out into the streets and preach the "evil ideology." Typical preaching one hears in

---

7. Song Hun Lee, *Communism: A Critique and Counter Proposal*, Washington: The Freedom Foundation, Inc., 1973, p.233.
8. *Ibid.*

the streets of the United States is:

> In North Korea, school children are required to bow down to statues of
> North Korean dictator Kim Il-Sung, and are given their choice of praying
> to the statue or praying to God. If they pray to God, they get no rice for
> lunch, but if they pray to Kim Il-Sung, they get a full portion. Children
> who consistently refuse to bow to Kim Il-Sung and call him their
> "beloved" Father have been shot, along with their entire families, as
> examples to the "bourgeois and un-proletarianized elements in North
> Korean society."[9]

The Unification Church's many organizational fronts in fighting
against Communism are the International Federation for Victory over
Communism, the Collegiate Association for the Research of Principles,
the Freedom Leadership Foundation, the World Freedom Institute,
the American Youth for a Just Peace, the International Cultural
Foundation, the One World Crusade, the Project Unity and the Little
Angels Korean Folk Ballet.

Among them, the Freedom Leadership Foundation and the One
World Crusade are the most vigorous of those organizations engaged in
the anti-Communist movement in the United States. The official
publication of the Unification Church explains the Freedom Leadership
Foundation:

> The Freedom Leadership Foundation (FLF) is a nationwide, non-profit
> educational organization, established in 1969 by a group of young men
> and women who were deeply concerned about the influence of Marxist
> thought in America and the consequent erosion of national purpose and
> will. It is the American affiliate of the IFVC, (International Federation
> for Victory over Communism), which was founded by Sun Myung Moon
> in 1967.[10]

The Freedom Leadership Foundation identifies with such political

---

9. Young Whi Kim (ed.), *The Way of the World*: Seoul, The Holy Spirit Association for the Unification of World Christianity, 1972, p.103.
10. Sun Myung Moon, *The Unification Church*, not dated, p.9.

activities to oppose Communism in terms of its "religious ideals." One
of the main goals of the foundation is "to proclaim that the materialistic, anti-democratic doctrines of Marxism-Leninism constitute at
present the greatest single barrier to the fulfillment of world
freedom."[11]

The members of the foundation are in the forefront of the campus
movement throughout the United States and conduct rallies, demonstrations and prayer vigils. The foundation also publishes a bi-monthly
newspaper, *The Rising Tide*, intended to offer "a nationwide youth-
orientated alternative to the left-wing underground press." The "Rising
Tide Bookstore" is situated in the nation's capital in Washington to
provide "students, educators, researchers and congressional aides with
the latest books, magazines and newspapers dealing with the problems
of Communism."[12] The foundation also sponsors foreign students
studying in the United States, and young visitors.

The most visible mark of the presence of the Unification Church
movement in the United States is made under the name of "One World
Crusade" which was organized by Moon in 1972. The crusade units
travel with groups of young people from Europe and Asia and conduct
many rallies, give lectures, appear on local and national media for the
cause of anti-Communism throughout the cities in the United States.
"One World Crusade" teams are working at this time in practically all
fifty states.

The Unification Church groups believe that the United States is
the specially favored nation of God, chosen to play the leading role
in the Unification Church movement and to oppose Communism. In
one of his talks to an American audience, Moon asked: "Have you ever

---

11. *Ibid.*, p.11.
12. *Ibid.*

thought which nation should be restored first? The leading nation (the United States)! If we restore your nation, one sixth of the globe will be restored."[13]

The United States is, therefore, important for the special fulfillment of God's purpose on earth. The Unification Church talks about America with favorable words of praise:

> America's existence was according to God's providence. God needed to build one powerful Christian nation on earth for His future work. After all, America belonged to God first, and only after that to the Indians. This is the only interpretation that can justify the position of the Pilgrim settlers.[14]

The Unification Church further argues officially that

> God has a definite plan for America. He needed to have this nation prosper as one nation under God. God wants to have America as His base, America as His champion. And America was begun in the sacrificial spirit of pursuing God's purpose. America may consummate her history in the same sacrificial spirit for God's purpose. America will endure forever.[15]

America will endure forever because "America is the center of those God-fearing free world nations. America has been chosen as the defender of God . . . ."[16]

America's destiny is inseparable from the destiny of the world. America's well-being affects the plan of God. "This is a country that loves God." God, who loves the United States so much and who frequently encountered Moon since he was sixteen years old, appeared to him again on January 1, 1972. God told him "to go to America and

---

13. Kim, *op. cit.*, p.57.
14. *Christianity in Crisis*, p.55.
15. *Ibid.*, p.59.
16. *Ibid.*, p.61.

speak to the American people."[17]   With this sense of mission and in obedience to God's command he came to the United States and established his headquarters.

On another occasion he told his American audience:

> I know that God sent me here to America. I did not come for the luxurious life in America. Not at all! I came to America not for my own purposes, but because God sent me .... The future of the entire world hinges on America. God has a very [big] stake in America.[18]

The effects of this type of preaching were soon evident. A *Newsweek* magazine of October 15, 1973 issue reported:

> Dr. Moon has recently shifted his international base of operations from three rented rooms in a poor section of Seoul to a lush 22-acre estate in Tarrytown, N.Y...., which his disciples purchased last year for $850,000. The estate includes a luxurious mansion for Moon ... (p.54).

Despite the recognition of the importance of the United States and God's favor on her, Moon and his followers were aware of the political crisis concerning Watergate. To seek God's help in solving America's "Watergate" problem, Moon went back to Korea in November, 1973, where he spent much time in prayer and meditation in search of an answer.

God gave him the answer, which was "to forgive and love President Richard Nixon." And he wrote a statement, "Answer to Watergate," which read:

> I bend my head and place my ear upon the heartbeat of America. I hear no one seeking the solution from above. We keep on criticizing, and the nation sinks — we criticize some more and the nation falls even further, deep into greater peril. Now is the time for America to renew the faith

---

17. *The Unification Church*, p.1.
18. *Christianity in Crisis*, p.64.

expressed in her motto "In God We Trust." This is the founding spirit
that makes America great and unique. God blessed America because of
this spirit. Furthermore, America is fulfilling a vital role in God's plan
for the modern world. God is depending on America today. Therefore,
the crisis for America is a crisis for God.[19]

The statement further read:

> I have been praying specifically for President Richard Nixon. I asked
> God, 'What shall we do with the person of Richard Nixon?' The answer
> did come again . . . God spoke to me . . . It is your duty to love him.
> We must love Richard Nixon. The office of the President of the United
> States is, therefore, sacred. God inspired a man and then confirmed him
> as President through the will of the people. He lays his hand on the word
> of God and is sworn into office. At this time in history God has chosen
> Richard Nixon to be President of the United States of America.

In support of Nixon the church sponsored frequent prayer meetings
and demonstrations. A headline in *Washington Post* on December 18,
1973, gives a good indication of this — "Watergate Day of Prayer
asked by the Unification Church." Another headline in *Minneapolis
Star* on December 1, 1973, read "Korean Preacher Urges U.S. not to
'Destroy President.'"

According to the followers of the Unification Church, President
Nixon was the greatest President to be known as ardently anti-
Communist. However, the Communist-influenced politicians are
destroying the President with the Watergate issue. At the national
Christmas tree lighting ceremony in 1973 over 1000 followers of the
Unification Church turned out to "cheer President Nixon," carrying
signs like "God loves Nixon" and "Support the President." Not long
after this "cheering of the President," Moon was invited to the twenty-
second annual National Prayer Breakfast at the Hilton Hotel. On the

---

19. Moon, *Answers to Watergate*, not dated, p.3.

following day the President invited him to an unscheduled meeting.

President Nixon further appreciated Moon's effort to support him in the following text of a letter from the White House, dated December 11, 1973.

> All the words of encouragement I received are deeply heartening to me, and I am particularly grateful for the prayers and good will that you and members of the Unification Church have expressed at this time.
>
> I have read news of your efforts, and I share your belief that it is vitally important for this Nation to attain a sense of unity — unity that can come only from sharing our concerns about our common ideals. If we keep faith in ourselves and our faith in God, I am confident that America will remain a great symbol of hope for millions around the globe, a Nation with a rich heritage, and an even more promising future.[20]

Despite such an expression of gratitude by Mr. Richard Nixon, and the efforts of the Reverend Mr. Moon and his followers to save the President, the latter had to resign from office. The resignation of the President, however, did not weaken the office of the Presidency of the United States or destroy the office as the people of the Unification Church had predicted. On the contrary, the United States demonstrated to the world the strength of the democratic government and political process of the United States.

After the resignation of the President this writer frequently asked the followers of the Unification Church about the downfall of President Nixon. The usual answer was: "Our Master, The Reverend Moon,[21] urged President Nixon to hold on to his office and not resign. But President Nixon was not strong enough and not patient enough to hold his office." In any case, contrary to the hopes and desires of the Unification Church movement, the President had to leave his office.

---

20. *Ibid.*, p.8.

In such contradiction lies the dangers and weaknesses of the Unification church movement.

In spite of such contradictions and weaknesses, however, the Unification Church appeals to many frustrated people in a time of economic depression and political uncertainty. The leaders of the Unification Church strongly argue that the greatest task of Christians is to fight against communism, especially in Korea. The high ranking officers of this church explained to this writer when he visited the home office of the Unification Church in Seoul, Korea, a couple years ago that God in His providence divided the peninsula of Korea so that it could be the testing ground of Christianity against Communism. After Korea was liberated from Japan, the northern half of Korea was destined to be ruled by the Communist regime and the South Korea to be ruled by "democracy."

So South Korea is a special country, not only as the land of the "true parents," but also as the sacred battle-ground of Christianity in its struggle against communism. In fact, Moon claims that he would send one million Christian soldiers from throughout the world if South Korea were in danger of a communist take-over. According to *The Christian News,*

> Joan Meyer, a former member of the Unification Church, said that she was expected to be "willing to go to South Korea to fight, if necessary." One of Mr. Moon's avowed objectives is to unify Korea, "the holy land," and there is fear among those who oppose his movement that he might plunge thousands of the youth into this "holy war" eventually.[22]

Such fears may not be so alarming yet. However, the political involvement of the Unification Church does raise some serious concern. A

21. All those members of the Unification Church who answered this writer's questions also confessed that they truly believed that Rev. Mr. Moon is the Messiah.
22. *The Christian News*, February 10, 1975, p.13.

newspaper in America reported:

> Mr. Moon purportedly has said that if necessary he would give the command for hundreds and thousands of his followers to move to certain areas at certain times to effect political and other objectives. Mr. Moon was said to have asserted that even with only 500 full dedicated workers in each of the States some of the objectives of his theocracy can be put into force.[23]

It should be noted, however, that the political activities of the Unification Church are not universally considered as ethical or desirable. *The St. Louis Globe Democrat*, for example, recently reported:" ... Moon is not above suggesting Watergate tricksterism, such as using beautiful young girls to try to influence senators." Indeed Rabbi Maurice Davis of New York recently testified in the United States Senate that "... Mr. Moon has said that he wanted 300 good girls for the Senators — so watch out, Senator."[24] Such unchristian-like political activities, however sincere the members of the Unification Church may be in their opposition to communism, cannot help but alienate many of the followers of this movement, and with the eventual death of its founder it is quite possible that the impact of the Unification Church itself will die out.

---

23. *Ibid.*, March 1, 1976, p.16.
24. *St. Louis Globe Democrat*, December 13–14, 1975, p.11.

PART ONE

A SPECIAL REPORT

THE UNIFICATION CHURCH:
ITS ACTIVITIES AND PRACTICES

A Meeting of Concerned Parents

A DAY OF AFFIRMATION AND PROTEST

Dirksen Senate Office Building
Washington, D.C.
Wednesday, February 18, 1976

CONTENTS:

PART ONE: UNOFFICIAL TRANSCRIPT
(42 pp.)   GOVERNMENT PANEL
              CITIZENS APPEARING

PART TWO: LETTERS OF TESTIMONY
(80 pp.)   FROM PARENTS AND
              EX-MEMBER VICTIMS

Compiled by National Ad Hoc Committee,
A Day of Affirmation and Protest

(Not Printed at Government Expense.)

Preface

The following unofficial recrod (pages 5-41) of
the meeting was taken, for the most part, from a transcription of a cassette tape recording. Some corrections
have been made and some material was deleted to improve
readability. Supplemental material, which did not appear
on the tape because of the lack of time to present it in
Washington, has been added to provide a more complete
record of the evidence prepared for the meeting (less
than 3 pages).

FOR INFORMATION

After the DAP meeting, representatives of various
parent groups met for the purpose of forming a national
organization to combat destructive pseudo-religious
political cults. This resulted in the formation of the
"Committee Engaged in Freeing Minds." At this time, C.E.F.M.
is fund-raising and has engaged a professional firm to
make an objective survey of the cult problem in America.

We invite everyone to join our efforts to awaken
our citizens to the national and international dangers
posed by the cults, this pehnomena of the 1970's.

The temporary address is P.O. Box 5084, Arlington,
Texas 76011. We invite anyone wishing to join to contact
us. If you wish to help in any way, financially or with
volunteer service, or if you desire information for yourself or to educate others, please let the committee know.

June 1, 1976

George M. Slaughter, III
Interim Coordinator
National Committee Engaged
in Freeing Minds

(See part two of this Special Report for testimonial
letters.)

REPORT OF THE MEETING
A DAY OF AFFIRMATION AND PROTEST
Washington, D. C. - February 18,1976

On Januar y 30, 1976, an ad hoc National Committee was set up to organize the
captioned meeting. The committee's position was stated, as follows:

We AFFIRM: 1. our love for our youth;
              2. our loyalty to our government;
              3. our support of our families;
              4. our belief in time proven religious faiths;
              5. our confidence in American education;
              6. our trust that our society can and will respond
                 to human needs.

We PROTEST: The destructive cults and their strategy of alienation--the
              alienation of psychologically kidnapped youth from their:
              1. government;
              2. families;
              3. prior religions;
              4. education;
              5. society and its viable values.

The meeting between a panel of government officials and concerned parents and
citi zens was held in the Senate Caucus Room of the Dirkson Senate Building.
Arrangements were made by Senator Robert Dole of Kansas who had been peti-
ti oned by 14,000 Kansans to investigate the activities and organizations of
Korean Sun Myung Moon's movement, "The Holy Spirit Association for the Unification of World Christianity," commonly called "Unification Church", and its
fifty or so front organizations and recruiting arms. Three hundred and fifty -two parents and ex-members of cults registered for the meeting, coming
at their own expense from 32 states, to present their experiences with and
testimony about Moon's pseudo-religious political cult. The attendees had
been quickly organized by an interim national committee created for this
specific purpose through Citizens Engaged in Reuniting Families, Inc., of
White Plains, N. Y., Rabbi Maurice Davis, President. Dr. George W. Swope,
President-elect of CERF, was appointed Chairman of the committee, whose voluntary membership was selected according to geographical regions from the
various representative citizens groups.

The Committee met in Washington, D. C. the day before the panel meeting with
ten persons appointed to ask questions of the government officials present:
they selected the most pertinent areas to be covered, questions relating to
illegal activities of Moon's movement and the subsequent alienation of youthful members of Unification from their government, families, prior religions,
education and society and its viable values. Statements of facts and per-
ti nent information were presented to the government officials as a basis for
asking the questions; eye-witnesses and participants in law violations were
introduced and gave their accounts of the wrong doings; and, because only
two hours were alloted for the meeting, each attendee was asked to submit a
one-page "testimonial letter" of his or her experience with cults, which
would be made available for any duly constituted government authority which
investigates the cult. A sampling of these letters appear in this report; all
are on file with the national co mmittee.

35

Page 2 - Report of the Meeting - A DAY OF AFFIRMATION AND PROTEST

This booklet contains Senator Dole's opening statement, names of the government panel, the anti-Moon speakers and witnesses and the National ad hoc Committee, excerpts from a tape transcription of the meeting, the statements and questions presented to the panel, and the testimonial letters of ex-members and families involved with Unification and other cults.

Names are being withheld from many of the included letters at the writer's request because of the real danger to the family or its cult member-victim, not only through fear of physical harm but fear of the almost certain final separation of the member victim from his family and also to protect them from those who, through lack of understanding of the mind-control phenomena and as-.pect of modern day cultism, could further disrupt the family. However, the writers of these statements will divulge their identities and make th emselves available for an approved and qualified investigation. Those who spoke and otherwise identified themselves have passed the stage of the necessity for secrecy to protect someone and are willing to take the chance of personal reprisal.

'Most of us realize that only by publicly coming forward with our personal factual knowledge will the whole gamut of illegal, dangerous, and mind-controlling activities of the cults be proven to the authorities satisfaction so that an investigation will begin. Our Government is the only power large enough to stop Moon now. We incur whatever risks there are as responsible c i tizens who value our American Freedoms above all else and who know beyond doubt that unless the growth of pseudo-religious political cults is stopped, those very same freedoms will be destroyed.

For these reasons and this purpose, our booklet was assembled. We, the Committee, as patriotic citizens, expect our appointed and elected off icials to act on this information--enough proof is here.

No portion of the information and letters contained herein may be reproduced or used for any purpose without the written permission of the publisher.

Publisher:

National ad hoc Committee
A DAY OF AFFIRMATION AND PROTEST
P. O. 5084
Arlington, Texas 76011

Addendum (at press time, April 20, 1976):

Here is an ironic development. The Committee has just learned that the U. S. District Attorney for New York is about to subpoena our National Committee Chairman and several other parents and ex-Moonies who appeared at the D. of A. & P. Meeting in opposition to Moon to appear before the Federal Grand Jury to support charges made by the Unification Church against them (our members).

We call your attention to the fact that a Justice Department representative is not listed among those government officials who participated in the D. A. P. Panel discussion.

3

A DAY OF AFFIRMATION AND PROTEST
<u>Senate Caucus Room, February 18, 1976</u>

The following government officials were members of Senator Dole's panel:

Mr. Charles Rumph
Special Assistant for Exempt
  Organization Matters
Internal Revenue Service
Room 3404, IRS Building
1111 Constitution Avenue, NW
Washington, DC 20224

Mr. Lawrence A. Callaghan
Special Assistant to the
  Assistant Attorney General for
  Legislative Affairs
Department of Justice
Room 1133
Ninth & Constitution Ave, NW
Washington, DC 20530

Mr. Ronald J. James
Administrator, Wage and Hour
  Division
Department of Labor
Room S3502
200 Constitution Avenue, NW
Washington, DC 20210

Dr. Julius Segal, Director
Division of Scientific and
  Public Information
National Institute of Mental
  Health
Public Health Service
Department of HEW
Room 15105 Parklawn Building
5600 Fishers Lane
Rockville, Maryland 20852

Mr. Donald M. Thayer, Director
Office of Policy Control
Social and Rehabilitation
  Service
Department of HEW
Room 5229 HEW South
330 C Street, SW
Washington, DC 20201

Mr. Paul Coe
Assistant Chief Inspector
Office of Criminal Investigations
U. S. Postal Service
Room 3565
475 L'Enfant Plaza, West
Washington, DC 20260

Ms. Margery W. Smith
Assistant Director for Evaluation
Bureau of Consumer Protection
Federal Trade Commission
Sixth and Pennsylvania Avenue, NW
Room 482
Washington, DC 20580

Mr. David O. Bickart
Deputy Assistant Director for
  National Advertising
Bureau of Consumer Protection
Federal Trade Commission
Room 6117 Star Building
414 11th Street, NW
Washington, DC 20580

Mr. Morton M. Kanter
Deputy Commissioner
Office of Youth Development
Office of the Assistant Secretary
  for Human Development
Department of HEW
Room 1651 Donohoe Building
400 Sixth Street, SW
Washington, DC

Mr. Joseph A. Tedesco, Director
  Exempt Organizations Division
Internal Revenue Service
Room 6411
1111 Constitution Avenue, NW
Washington, DC 20224

NATIONAL COMMITTEE
DAY OF AFFIRMATION AND PROTEST
February 18, 1976

Committee Members: (Dr. George W. Swope, Chairman)

Region	Name	State
New England Region:	Mrs. James Goldsmith (CERF)	Rhode Island
	Mrs. Jean Merritt (RPC)	Massachusetts
Middle Atlantic Region:	Rabbi Maurice Davis (CERF)	New York
	Dr. George W. Swope (CERF & RPC)	New York
Southeast Region:	Dr. Thomas Scharff (CERF)	Kentucky
Southern Region:	Col. Richard Feiden (IF IF)	Texas
	Ms. Cynthia Slaughter (IF IF)	Texas
	George M. Slaughter, III (CFF)	Texas
Central Region:	Dr. Arthur Devine (FM)	Iowa
	Mrs. Jean Tuttle (FM)	Kansas
	Glen Amundson (CERF)	Minnesota
Middle West Region:	Larry Trimble (FM)	Minnesota
West Coast Region:	Mrs. A. Crawford Greene	California
	William Rambur (CFF)	California

Panel of Questioners:

GOVERNMENTAL AND POLITICAL LEVEL - Mrs. A. Crawford Greene, Calif. and
                                   Honorable James J. Sheeran, New Jersey

FAMILY -   Mrs. James Goldsmith, R. I. and
                                   Ms. Cynthia Slaughter, Texas

EDUCATION-COERCIVE PERSUASION -   Dr. Frederick Bunt, N. Y. and
                                   Mrs. Jean Merritt, Massachusetts

SOCIETY AND ITS VALUE SYSTEM, -   Dr. Thomas Scharff, Kentucky
     HEALTH AND DRUGS   Dr. Arthur Devine, Iowa

RELIGION   -   Rabbi Maurice Davis, N. Y.
                                   Dr. Samuel A. Jeanes, N. J.
                                   Rev. Dr. Ki-Bum Han, N. Y.

Witnesses (Ex-victims):   Joan Meyer, Kansas
                                   Ford Greene, Ca.
                                   Cynthia Slaughter, Tx.
                                   David Geissler, Ohio
                                   Paul Engle, N. Y.
                                   Peter Tipograph, N. Y.
                                   Marina - Peru
                                   Martha Lewis, N. H.
                                   Ellen Rosemara, N. Y.

At 1:40 p.m., in room 1202, Dirksen Senate Office Building, the Honorable Robert Dole, a Senator from the State of Kansas, called to order a meeting of approximately 400 persons convened to discuss before a panel of Federal officials the activities and practices of the Unification Church.

Assisting Senator Dole in presiding over the session at various points throughout its two-hour-and-fifteen-minute duration were Senator James L. Buckley of New York and Representative George M. O'Brien, Congressman from the Seventeenth District of Illinois.

In addition to former, as well as present, associates of the Unification Church, the gathering was attended by some fifty staff assistants from both Senatorial and Congressional offices, and numerous members of the media.

Government officials participating, and their respective agencies, were: Mr. Charles Rumph, Special Assistant for Exempt Organization Matters, and Mr. Joseph Tedesco, Director of Exempt Organizations, Internal Revenue Service; Mr. Ronald James, Administrator, Wage and Hour Division, Department of Labor; Dr. Julius Segal, Director, Division of Scientific and Public Information, National Institute of Mental Health; Mr. Donald Thayer, Director, Office of Policy Control, Social and Rehabilitation Service; Mr. Morton Kanter, Deputy Commissioner, Office of Youth Development, Department of Health, Education, and Welfare; Ms. Margery Smith, Assistant Director for Evaluation, and Mr. David Bickart, Deputy Assistant Director for National Advertising, Bureau of Consumer Protection, Federal Trade Commission; and Mr. Paul Coe, Assistant Chief Inspector, Office of Criminal Investigations, United States Postal Service.

Senator DOLE. The meeting will come to order.

If there are any more chairs available, please indicate their location to those who are standing so that everyone possible can be seated.

- - - - - - - - - - - - - - - -

Let me say at the outset that in, addition to his role as a legislator, every Member of Congress wants to be genuinely responsive to the needs and concerns of his constituents. When those he represents have problems they believe to be of legitimate interest to their government, he tries to make every effort to assist them in communicating directly with the appropriate Federal agencies.

I have personally received hundreds of inquiries during the past year regarding the activities and practices of the Unification Church. More recently, I have been presented with a petition bearing the signatures of over 14,000 parents from the State of Kansas and surrounding jurisdictions demanding to have their views heard with respect to this and related organizations.

This afternoon, I am providing them that opportunity. Individuals representing some 30 States have come here at their own expense to talk face to face with officials from those Federal Departments they feel should have an interest in what they have to say.

39

I should stress in that regard that the members of the Executive Branch who have come here at my request are really themselves the audience. Their answers can, understandably, be phrased only in the most general of terms -- but certainly, any disappointing limitations on the substance of replies should be more than offset by the satisfaction of knowing those giving them care enough to listen.

Every Senator has the privilege of requesting space within our Capitol buildings to accommodate activities he deems to be of significant importance to those he serves. So just as an individual Congressman made the Caucus Room in the House of Representatives available for the Reverend Sun Myung Moon to give an address two months ago this date, I have arranged this gathering to give those who feel adversely affected by what he advocates a chance to speak.

The nature and format of this proceeding are not to be misconstrued by those present as anything other than what it is. I wish to emphasize that, contrary to distorted representations that may have been circulated prior to this meeting, it is not a Congressional hearing; it is not any kind of investigation; it is not a public speech-making forum; and above all it is not a debate between opposing points of view.

It is, very simply, an informal question and answer session involving two predesignated panels of participants whom I have brought together to discuss subjects of possible mutual concern. While it could very appropriately have taken place in my own private office, the widespread interest among both the general public and the press led me to select a larger and more open facility.

Since there may be those who disagree with what is said or done, I want to remind all in attendance that this room is under my control and that the open seating is made available as a courtesy to those desirous of acting as observers. Accordingly, everyone should be on notice that one of the ground-rules will be to recognize for questions only those who are now seated at, or who later come to, one of the microphones on the front table.

Along with the privilege and discretion to sponsor an unofficial forum such as this goes the responsibility and authority to see that it is conducted in a smooth and orderly manner. I have every intention of doing precisely that and solicit your cooperation.

Before going any further, I would like to introduce and welcome those Federal agency representatives who are here with us, seated to my left and right: Mr. Ron James from the Department of Labor; Mr. Charles Rumph and Mr. Joseph Tedesco from the Internal Revenue Service; Mr. Paul Coe, United States Postal Service; Mr. Donald Thayer, Social and Rehabilitation Service; Dr. Julius Segal, National Institute of Mental Health; Mr. Morton Kanter, Office of Youth Development, Department of HEW; and Ms. Margery Smith and Mr. Dave Bickart of the Federal Trade Commission.

I think it might also be helpful to those present -- whatever their views may be -- to know that there has been a considerable degree of Congressional interest expressed in this event. Without speculating as to what the nature of that interest might be, I would just note for the record that we have had inquiries from Senators Allen, Biden, Buckley, Cannon,

Chiles, Curtis, Domenici, Durkin, Goldwater, Griffin, Philip Hart, Hartke, Hatfield, Helms, Humphrey, Javits, Leahy, McGee, McGovern, Mansfield, Mondale, Montoya, Percy, Schweiker, Bill Scott, Stone, Taft, Thurmond, Tower, Tunney, and Williams.

Thus, there have been some 31 Senate offices in touch with us prior to this meeting. In addition, we have had inquiries from 42 House members. Congressman Richardson Preyer of North Carolina was here a few minutes ago, but had to return for a vote.

I will turn the program over now to Dr. George Swope, Assistant Director of Guidance Services at Westchester Community College, Port Chester, New York, who will act as moderator for the parents and other speakers. In doing so, however, I would remind everyone one more time that we are not taking any testimony and no one is under oath. Moreover, nothing that is said or done is to be interpreted as a prejudgment or stamp of approval by the legislative branch on anything.

Again, I will be in control of the room and may have occasion to determine that certain questions are inappropriate or cannot be answered in the time we have. If that is the case, such inquiries will be referred to the relevant agency for a more complete, written response.

Obviously, there are some areas that simply do not lend themselves to open discussion. Moreover, there are others that might require extensive deliberation before a meaningful reply can be offered.

Many of the questions you may desire answers to have only come to the attention of these Federal officials within the last couple of hours, so we should all be understanding of the need for thorough processing and the inability to be candid in those instances. Your main purpose is to make these problems and concerns known, in any event, and it is in that framework that we should proceed.

Dr. Swope, please begin.

STATEMENT AND COMMENTS OF DR. GEORGE W. SWOPE, ASSISTANT DIRECTOR OF GUIDANCE SERVICES AT WESTCHESTER COMMUNITY COLLEGE, PORT CHESTER, NEW YORK.

Dr. SWOPE. Senator Dole, we appreciate your response to the petition with 14,000 names of Kansas people, asking that an investigation into the Unification movement and other similar movements be launched. You have provided us with our day in court. We also appreciate the presence of officials with important government agencies to receive our questions and hear our statements. We are also pleased that there has been this great response from Senators and Congressmen and their offices.

I must say first for myself that I come from a long tradition of religious freedom. This is a heritage of my family. Members of my family, my ancestors, have died that men might be atheists or agnostics or Christians or Jews or Moslems or whatever else. Thus, with deep mental anguish, I have wrestled with the question before us today: When should there be careful investigation of a nonreligious ideology that uses the terminology of "religion" and is basically subversive to our government, destructive of our homes, and is

channeling the creative potential of wonderful young people into drab
and nonproductive morasses?

The others of these more than 300 concerned citizens have wrestled
with this same question. This spiritual wrestling has brought us to this
day of affirmation and protest. We affirm our love of your youth, our
loyalty to our government, our support of our families, our belief in
time-proven religious faiths, our confidence in American education, our
trust that our society can and will respond to human needs. I indeed
protest those destructive movements and their strategy of alienation;
the alienation of psychologically kidnapped youth from the government,
the alienation from their families, prior religions, education, society
and its viable values.
This is our Day of Affirmation and Protest.

As you already know, it has been estimated that there are in America as many as 5,000 cults and movements that have in their grip two to
three million young people, ages 18 to 28. A number of these ideologies
are represented in our gathering today. This is a serious matter.

We are citizens, concerned citizens, with deep, controlled anger
resulting from psychological havoc in our homes, and a deep fear about
the future of this nation we love. This deep anger and this deep fear
will carry us unted for months and for years, if need be, in corrective
action until a cure has been found for this cancer in our national body.

I read to you without comment, except to explain one word, excerpts
from the words of Sun Myung Moon to his inner circle of leaders, reproduced for study in Unification centers in each State. His addresses to
his leaders are entitled "Master Speaks," and several of these "Master
Speaks" have come into our possession when young people have been rescued out of the cult by their families and have brought copies with
them.

"You can trust me as your leader...I am a thinker, I am your brain...
You must call to the nation, 'Come on, U. S. and the whole world. I will
attack and win over you. Come on, State of Wyoming, State of Texas!'"

"If you are dedicated enough to work at the cost of your lives, we
are going to be of tremendous strength, and we are going to be victors
at the last."

"If teams of 40 members each are stationed in each of the 50 states,
that means 2,000 people. In the future, in each state four mobile units
will be the ideal number; that means 160 in each state, and in 50 states,
8,000. If that number of members are working in 50 states, we can do
anything with senators and congressmen; we can influence them. Even
senators representing that state will have to beg the help of our (Unification) State Representative."

"Then the Republican Party will want to have you on their side,
while the opposition party will want to have you on their side. You
must say, 'Come to me.'"

"The (Unification) State Representative is only 23 years old now;
but after three years or more, perhaps senators will come to take him
to their place in a luxurious car, and they will put themselves at his
disposal. That's what is happening in Korea."

"If the U. S. continues its corruption, and we find among the senators and congressmen no one really useable for our purposes, we can make senators and congressmen out of our members. (The female members-) Would you want to be wives to senators and congressmen? The male members--wouldn't you like to be senators? If you have confidence, you will make it possible, and I will make you that."

"I have met many famous - so-called 'famous' - senators and congressmen, but to my eyes they are just nothing; they are weak and helpless..."

"If our foundation has been laid, are we going to be confident persons or not? Then we will win the battle. This is our dream, our project - but shut your mouth tight, have hope and go on to realize it."

"My dream is to organize a Christian political party including the Protestant denominations, Catholics and all the religious sects."

"We must have an automatic theocracy (direct rule of God - through Sun Myung Moon) to rule the world. So we cannot separate the political field from the religious....We have to purge the corrupted politicians, and the sons of God (members of the Unification Church) must rule the world. The separation between religion and politics is what Satan likes most."

"I am not going to send you into the political field right away (May, 1973), but later on when we are prepared."

"If we have 500,000 members all over the country under one command from Master, if they are told to come and live in New York. What would happen? Upon my command to the Europeans and others throughout the world to come live in the U. S., wouldn't they obey me? Then what would happen? We can embrace the religious world in one arm and the political world in the other."

"The present U. N. must be annihilated by our power...We must make a new U. N. Then, I must be able to make out of you world-renowned personages. Wouldn't you want to be trained for that? You will have to go through training of such type that history has never seen."

"You may have to die or be killed. There may be casualties by tens of hundreds and thousands. But if you are not ready to die for the cause, you cannot live and save the world."

"The whole world is in my hand, and I will conquer and subjugate the world."

"Those who judge me will be judged by me in the future. They will fall into misery."

"The time will come, without my seeking it, that my words will almost serve as law. If I ask a certain thing, it will be done. If I don't want something, it will not be done.

"Let's say there are 500 sons and daughters like you in each state, then we could control the government. You would determine who would become Senators and who the Congressmen would be. From the physical point of view, you can gain no faster success than in this way."

"Our strategy is to be united into one with ourselves, and with that as the bullet, we can smash the world."

This is what concerns us. Not only what happens to our children, not only what happens to our homes, but we happen to be patriotic Americans from the west coast to the east coast, from the north to the south. We love this land.

And now I call on a group of people from various walks of life, a cross section of our country. And these people will speak to you from their hearts and their interests. We have organized this information into the five areas of alienation, and the first we touch upon is the alienation from our government.

I call upon Mrs. Daphne Green, recently resigned after five years as Chairman of the Board of the Graduate Theological Union in Berkeley, California--now a director of the Institute of Ethics, Society, and the Life Sciences in Hastings, New York--and the honorable James Sheeran, Commissioner of Insurance of the State of New Jersey, a member of the Governor's cabinet.

Senator DOLE: Before you go ahead, I do want to acknowledge the presence of Senator Buckley.

Mrs. GREENE: Thank you Dr. Swope, and thank you, Senator Dole.

The first thing I would like to touch upon is capitalized by the attendance here today. But yesterday when we were darting around from one building to the other and getting continuously lost, I realized for the first time in my life that I really had some action or some say-so or some feeling of a vital part of my government. Today, that is kind of hard to find. It is a very exciting experience to feel. So, I thank you for that experience, even though I came here not under the best of circumstances.

Before I say anything, I would like to state categorically that in no way am I questioning the rights given to all of us by the First Amendment. And because we are dealing with kind of a hairy subject, that's very easy to get confused. I am here to point out that there is a strong possibility that the American taxpayer is being deceived and tax laws may well be broken. I don't know. That's why I'm here.

I would guess that all of us present have worked in some way for nonprofit tax exempt organizations. I for one was chairman of the board of an educational institution that fell into that category. We were meticulous in every area of fund raising and were vitally aware of our responsibility to the law, to the faculties of the schools, and especially to the donors. I have strong evidence that the game playing and "mickey mouse" surrounding the fund raising activities of the Unification movement requires more than my homework. I am not a detective, although I found out that I'm not bad. I should have chosen that a long time ago.

When I started putting together all the particular sects of the Unification Church in San Francisco, Calif., in the Bay area, I came up with what looks like an ecological flow chart that is all backed up with facts and documents. We have been involved in a maze of craziness.

In my judgment as a private citizen and one that has worked with non-profit organizations, we shouldn't be involved in a maze of craziness.

In one year I have been able to search and ferret out some 60 front organizations of the Unification movement. When asking members of the movement in the San Francisco Bay Area if they are members of the movement, I get a flat denial or an evasive, "Well, we follow some of the teachings of Rev. Moon." When soliciting for funds they avoid using the names of Moon or Unification. The purposes, aims and goals are ~~neither~~ stated openly and in many cases directly denied. For these reasons there is a grave possibility that the American public faces what I can only see as a misuse of their tax dollar. In some cases, I would have to call it fraud.

The question I ask you, Senator Dole and ladies and gentlemen, is a serious one that should be looked at very carefully. Can a political ideology or movement receive in good faith and under the laws of our land a non-profit status in this fashion? If the answer is Yes, then I suggest that the American Nazi Party proclaim Hitler a God and the KU KLUX KLAN proclaim themselves a Church and their fund-raising problems will be over.

I have done my homework as a private citizen. I ask my government now to take over, for you have the resources to do so.

I would like to call on an ex-member of the Unification Church, Joan Meyer, who is sitting right behind me. Joan will tell her own story. I think it is better that it come from her:

Ms. Meyer: I was a member for three years, and during this time, I went to Japan and Korea. And then while in Korea, we had a rally. And it was at this time Moon made a statement that all Unification Church members throughout the world should be willing to go to South Korea and fight, if necessary. I believe they had a list of all the names of members in the Unification Church at this time. And they had a list of members in other parts of the country.

And life wasn't too good. What about my American citizenship? What's that stand for? Is it something that allows us to go to work in his army in order to go overseas?

Senator BUCKLEY: Mrs. Greene, I wonder if I might ask a question at this point. You spoke and showed us that chart and talked about some "mickey mouse." Is it my understanding that these are organizations that are tax exempt and soliciting money that actually ends up with the Unification Church and does not identify the true backing?

Mrs. GREENE: Senator Buckley, some of them are and some of them are not. It is a very unusual situation in San Francisco and in the Bay area where these front groups appear. To my knowledge they were legal until about two weeks ago. They will say that they are creating a drug center. Try to find it; you can't. This is what this represents. It is identical to the maze I went through when our daughter, Catherine, joined the Unification Church, and when I asked to see her as a member, they said "no."

Not until two weeks ago was I able to come up with the form from the State of California that states, "The International Re-education

Foundation is a religious organization, members of which are also members of the Unification Church International." This absolutely staggered me, because I had been working for a year trying to figure out what all' these different groups meant. You are almost at a loss in California to find out which ones are part of the Unification Church and which are not. Until I had this piece of paper, there was no way I could prove anything. I could think they were liars, but I couldn't prove that they were. Now, I can verify our account.

I asked Joan to speak because this is what I mean by playing detective. And this is why we have to come to the very people that can do the job for us. We can't do this incredible amount of investigative work. I can have Joan call me up and say, "Mrs. Greene, what do I do before I lose my American citizenship?" What's my answer? "Call the Governor. Call your Senator. Call...I don't know what to do." Now you get this continuously from the different members who call them up for help or friends who call for help. And we should be answering their questions.

On front groups, I think a good example of that appeared in San Francisco about three weeks ago, and that was something called, "Judaism: In the Service to the World." There were two members that we know of, that we have affidavits from, who were in the movement with them. One answered the Rabbis in San Francisco and the Jewish civic leaders and said that they were working to help out Israel. When they were asked if they were members of the Unification Church, they said, "No, we are not." Now, this is frustrating. I think this is what you are really dealing with. You are dealing with a mammoth amount of people in this country that don't know what to do, because they know they are being lied to, they know they smell a rat, but they don't know how to get it out.

And the front groups, especially in the Bay area--I am not speaking except of the west coast because I don't know and haven't done that much investigative work--but that is the problem we are dealing with. And the question that obviously cannot be answered today is a crucial one for me, because it is the one I have come to wrestle with. And that is, can a political ideology or a political philosophy get a tax exempt status in this country? And I think it is a crucial question to ask, and I know it can't be answered, but I hope we can research it and it can be thought out and somehow get the public that answer.

STATEMENT AND COMMENTS OF JAMES SHEERAN, COMM. OF INSURANCE, STATE OF New Jersey:

Mr. SHEERAN. I think I would like to start by first explaining that I am the father of three daughters who are involved with the Unification Church. And that has caused great pain to our family. But I also have been involved in our political structure in America and understand the movement. I feel I know these people well enough to know that what is here is far bigger than any individual. Far bigger than, probably, our own personal lives to consider it factually.

Of all the people that are here--and I look out there and find them from all parts of the country, and I might say that we all pay taxes--we paid to be here. We pay with our dollars. We pay with money that we earned. I think, among other things, that the people of America are being ripped-off by cults--political organizations such as this--who deal in the name of religion.

As for Sun Myung Moon, there is no question that he lives in splendor: a large mansion, well furnished, probably close to a million dollars; limousines; yachts; owns business and property holdings which probably are derived from tax exempt organizations. And I would like to know, among other things, whether or not his private ownership of industrial properties, both here and in Korea, are taxable to him as an individual. For example, in Korea, there is a pharmaceutical company; an industrial company that produces shotgun and rifle parts; there is a stonework and titanium company; there is a Ginseng Tea Company which I would like to stay with for just one minute because the Ginseng Tea Company sells its products through the young people who are in the Unification cult. And they sell it out on the streets to the public. I understand that Moon himself owns a part of that company as an individual. I would like to know, for example, as far as the Labor Dept. is concerned, can these young people go out and sell those products, work in companies that are actually business corporations—particularly out in the California area—and are not paid, whether or not they are in violation of our labor laws and whether or not they are in violation of our fair standards and labor practices.

Senator DOLE: Mr. James, from the Department of Labor, can comment on that.

Mr. JAMES: I can comment in general. When complaints are brought to our attention—and we do have some now, we are investigating those complaints—we have traditionally interpreted the word "employee" very broadly. And I look with suspicion on those "volunteers" who spend substantial—or all—of their time in "voluntary" activities. As you are probably aware, there is an exception, additional exception, for lay or religious organizations or charitable institutions. When we have attempted to go into this area, First Amendment questions have been raised, and sometimes those questions have been raised successfully. As cases are brought to our attention, we will go back to give further evidential review to the facts and situation.

Mr. SHEERAN: Perhaps I was not clear. I'm talking about the business corporation, competing with businesses of America, where Moon followers are working without pay in a business corporation.

Mr. JAMES: Well, sir, the question again is, are the volunteers employed? If they are not in fact employees, they are not covered by the Fair Labor Standards Act.

Mr. SHEERAN: May I just follow that one step further. Is it traditional that you look at the employees to determine it, or would you chance looking at the entire business to see whether it was just made up of a series of volunteers who are avoiding our laws and responsibilities and are competing with industry and labor in this country?

Mr. JAMES: We would look at that as well as the more subtle features then. And in addition to the kind of business, in addition to the number of hours worked by the volunteers, in addition to the number of people in the organization-corporation, we try to see if there were in fact more volunteers than paid employees.

As far as the companies you are talking about right now, I cannot give you a specific answer, just general guidelines. And I can indicate that there are some investigations underway, but I am not privileged to discuss those in any detail. In particular, I cannot discuss the matters which may come up for investigation by the Dept. of Labor.

Senator DOLE. Was there an earlier question addressed to the IRS, the Internal Revenue Service?

Mr. SHEERAN. If you are referring to my remarks, I will refer to the issue of whether or not one who owns foreign investments and is here on permanent resident status and receives monies from those investments, whether or not those investments are taxable.

Senator DOLE. I don't know whether the IRS can comment on that or not.

Mr. RUMPH. I don't know whether we can comment on that type of question with the limited number of facts that we have. I'd like to say, though, that we can make a very brief announcement regarding the Internal Revenue Service.

Let me point out that the Service maintains a regular program of auditing tax exempt organizations. This program is adopted to ensure that these organizations continue to qualify for treatment as tax exempt organizations. In this program, if we receive information from any interested individual which is appropriate for consideration in this program, we will collect that information, study it, and use it in determining our final action in regard to the particular organization.

However, I would like to point out that we, as we explained to the Senator's staff, from the IRS are prohibited from discussing any particular organization or industry when it comes to tax matters. I would like you all to understand that, so that if we indicate that we cannot answer your questions at the present time, you will understand our situation.

Now if you have information which is pertinent to a tax exempt organization, I would suggest you send that to me and I will see that it gets to the proper channels for evaluation.

Mr. SHEERAN. I think we appreciate your position. What we are doing is really raising the questions. And I would like to stress that we are simply working people, citizens paying taxes. We can't be the investigators.

I started with the FBI, and I know that we didn't deal with small cases. We got information that led us to go further.

And I'd like to identify some corporations that, with literature, I would indicate that Sun Myung Moon as an individual owns substantial interest in And the question was, if he does, is he taxable as an individual through those investments, even though he is a so-called head of a tax exempt organization?

Mr. RUMPH. Sir, that's exactly the type of question that I prefer not to get into, because of the complexity of it. I would want to treat it fully and fairly. And if you would write to me and give me the facts that you have, I will make sure that it gets to the proper branch in our office. And then they will prepare a reply.

Mr. SHEERAN. Thank you.

Senator DOLE: I'd like to introduce Congressman O'Brien from the State of Illinois who just came in. We understand you may have to return to the floor to vote, George, but appreciate your attendance.

Mr. SHEERAN: There is one other question. If there is a tax exempt organization, can that organization then invest those monies in legitimate organizations through their individual members? And I refer to the Diplomat National Bank in Washington, D. C. which was recently chartered with approximately 17 very close followers of Moon--his top lieutenants--as investors.

Senator DOLE: I think that's another question . . .

Mr. RUMPH: I Can't possibly answer that, Senator.

Senator DOLE: I think that I indicated at the outset that you can pose the question but that they're not in the position to provide specific answers at this time. You are welcome, however, to submit them directly in writing.

Mrs. GREENE: We have asked some of the young members in the Unification movement to speak of their own experience on the subject of fasting. (Ed. note: Fasting is used as a spiritual condition for a rebirth, lasting anywhere from one day to two weeks.) I would like to introduce our son, Ford Greene.

Ed. note: The following testimony has been excerpted due to the limitations of space in this booklet.

Mr. GREENE: Senator Dole, Senator Buckley, distinguished gentlepersons and members of the audience.

I heard that my younger sister, Catherine, had joined the Unification Church. Since its founder was accused of being an exploiter of young people's spirituality, and this accusation was undocumented, I decided to see for myself. A friend and I drove to the Ideal City Ranch in Boonville, California.

When I asked questions about what they studied and did, I received unclear answers but was told that I definitely would get my answers at the weekend training session.

Eventually, I was able to talk with my sister alone for about half an hour. I asked her if she felt she knew how to love people. With tears in her eyes, she said that she felt that she didn't and thought this was the place for her to learn. I felt reassured because I had reached her. And after hearing Reverend Moon speak at the Opera House in San Francisco, I noted a general sense of peace. I felt that if it meant I could be happy, even I could join this group.

My brother and a friend and I went to Boonville for the weekend, where we played games, sang songs and listened to lectures. I was inspired by a hope of greater understanding and a higher quality of life.

We were divided into groups which stayed together for discussions and meals. In the evening, each group entertained the others. It was fun.We went to bed about 11:00 p.m. My brother and my friend didn't like what was happening but I did. On the whole, I felt that the people around me seemed pretty harmless and I couldn't see any justification for any accusations.

Dr. SWOPE: I'm going to have to ask that we go onto the family unit now.

Senator DOLE: Unfortunately, we don't have time for anything but a summary.

Senator BUCKLEY: You can put it in whatever record may be kept of this.

Mr. GREEN: O. K., we can wind it up. One evening, the oppression of hard work, little sleep, insufficient food, intense emotional turmoil, and little communication drove me to express rather desperately some of my fears to my Center director. His reply, "I understand, I understand." I guess it was decided that the Satanic pressure of the city was aggravating my spiritual difficulties because the next day, I was told to go to Boonville for more training. I welcomed this because it meant I would get to sleep 8 hours at night rather than 4 or 5.

The story goes on and on. Finally, when I said, "God, if you are God, you are the same for me and them. Is Reverend Moon the one? Is he the Messiah?" Hours later while I was listening to the lectures on predestination, I had the experience which I could only construe as God answering my prayer affirmatively, "yes".

Reverend Moon's teaching of absolute validity depends on whether or not we can establish that he is the Messiah, the person upon whom the world must depend for guidance. Members of Unification admit if our fabric didn't lack something vital, there would be no need to follow a Rev. Moon. They also say, "you show me a higher standard, I'll follow that."

Regardless of Moon's status, the membership of his organization speaks clearly to a lack in America. Most of us probably have something we would like to hide from, but it is our responsibility to try to bring that out. The more we hide, the more covertly or blatantly harmful we become to others and ourselves.

Will the Unification Church come up front and state its business? If Rev. Moon and the Unification Church can aid any flaw of ours, let them com forth freely under scrutiny so that we can be convinced that they truly have something to offer, are not trying to exploit the vulnerability of the United States of America, and make it clear that they do not intend--with no regard for America's people--to infiltrate a weakening society and overthrow the government. Thank you.

Dr. SWOPE: Thank you very much.

Senator BUCKLEY: Before we move on, I would just like to say that Ford Greene's full statement will be part of the record, and because I have a certain amount of ESP, I know that part of what he omitted described being required to work, or being asked to work, very long hours at a gasoline station in San Francisco with most of the proceeds being turned over to the movement. Is that correct?

Mr. GREENE: That is correct.

Senator BUCKLEY: I know all this because he is my godson.

Dr. SWOPE. We come now to the areaof the family and the two who are raising questions are Miss Cynthia Slaughter and Mrs. Marion Goldsmith. Mrs Goldsmith has a wide range of activities in the State of Rhode Island with national responsibilities as well.

STATEMENT AND COMMENTS OF MRS. JAMES GOLDSMITH.

Mrs. GOLDSMITH: Senator Dole and honored guests, it is difficult and really not possible to direct my questioning to any one single agency representative or Congressman here today, because my questions and concerns relate to each of us.

I come before you as one parent, representing the thousands of parents unable to be with us today. At this very moment, there are parents across this country who are angered, frightened, confused. In despair, because a strange and dangerous phenomenon is happening for which most American parents find no previous experience to turn to for guidance.

How can parents cut through the invisible barrier that isolates their children from free and open contact with their families? How can parents combat an atmosphere that combines isolation, curtailment of letter writing or telephone calls, fear, and a breakdown of trust in parents? This breakdown of trust is accomplished by indoctrination in Unification centers of a constantly repeated concept of everyone out there being influenced by a Satan and a threat that if they leave the Unification cult, they or someone in their family will die a terrible death. What a horrifying instrument of fear, guilt, and superstition to implant in a person's mind!

Who can parents turn to when they realize their children have been instantly enslaved by Moon and his well-paid army to sell peanuts, flowers and candy for 10 to 19 hours a day, lying to fellow Americans by pretending the money goes for nonexistent social welfare purposes?

And what can they do when they learn that their sons and daughters are being psychologically and emotionally manipulated by the intangible techniques of brainwashing, too little sleep, an inadequate diet,isolation from family and friends, and excessive church pressure to conform? To this point, frightened and bewildered parents could only turn to each other and share their experience with hopes.

But at first, a parent wonders if it is really possible that in the United States of America, a so-called "religious cult" can arbitrarily manipulate the will of your child to move from one city to another or even out of the country without your knowing it; to dare not openly express their negative views and concern about the goals and philosophy of the Unificiation cult. Other parents tell you of their experience that this can and does happen, and how long it has been, many times months or years, since they have seen or heard from their child. And you feel immobilized with fear for your son or your daughter.

You call your lawyer or legislative representative and learn that this evil man, Moon, has, on the surface, totally kept within the law. The umbrella of religious freedom serves his founding church, and he carefully only admits those over 18 years of age. He uses our government's law to protect himself, but the law fails to protect the rights of our dear ones against a cult that demands total control of their bodies, minds, souls, lives. Surely, we must ask you to examine what can be done about this distortion of the issues of rights.

And how can you comprehend a man who arranges marriages between young people who have never met each other, and then charges $400 per person to bless these marriages in mass wedding ceremonies? Surely these parents must ask, what legal protection is there against Reverend Moon's license to arrange marriages to countless Americans and non-Americans, specifically to provide citizenship via marriage and then move these strange married couples, who are prevented from living together, around the world at his will for his political purposes? What can our immigration laws provide to protect against this breakdown of our traditions of the sanctity of marriage and family?

Any relationship, friendship, identity, or tie that exists outside of the strict confines of the Unification cult and the sole missions of fund raising and witnessing are forcefully discouraged or even settled by the direct order of a central figure in a particular center of one's capitol. This is accomplished through intimidation and guilt. All natural feelings of love, respect or identification of the individual are subverted to only serve the purposes of Moon. Can injustice of this slave labor be tolerated in this country? We, who have raised our children with the values of our Judeo-Christian heritage, taught them to respect all men and have a sense of responsibility as citizens of this country and of the world, now find our brightest, most idealistic sons and daughters the most vulnerable to enslavement to the distortion of these values by the self-proclaimed Messiah from Korea.

I have here articles telling of parents in Paris and parents in Japan who are also alarmed at Moon's insidious destruction of family bonds. His political power and future depends on this fanatic loyalty, just as Hitler succeeded in doing in Germany with the youth there. We all remember too well what that meant and what his policies and ambitions cost the United States and the entire world. Parents in this country and countries around the world are fearful of the rise of another Hitler-like power.

The time is now to investigate the rapid and mysterious growth of Moon. And I and many thousands of parents come to you today to ask your help, advice, concern, and action to help us to find crucial answers, solutions, and protection to fulfill the most basic responsibility of parents: to protect their children from destruction. Thank you.

Senator DOLE: I'm sorry, I had to run over and vote, but I understand you made several comments about immigration policies. We have, I think, some responses that might be helpful in the form of a February 17 letter from the Department of Justice, and these will be made available following the meeting.

Dr. Swope introduced Miss Cynthia Slaughter, a graduate of the University of Texas, and English major, and a former member of Unification, who said:

As was mentioned, I was a member of the movement. And I was deprogrammed, and I'm out now. And I'm here to help expose some of the things that go on inside. Because, you know, parents can say that these things happen and people just say, "well, these are overprotective parents," etc., etc. But I was in there and these other members were there, so we have certain areas that we have questions for. And we have something to back up why we are asking the questions.

I would like to establish a bit of communication, because I know that people don't understand how people like myself and other people here can come out and say things against the movement. Were they traitors? Were they dropouts? Were they horrible members? What were they? But I can tell you when I was deprogrammed, I was the top fund raiser. I had been accepted in the theological seminary.

The Unification family in Boulder told me that I had been accepted to the theological seminary after I was deprogrammed. Perhaps they just said this to try to get me back. I don't know if that was really true. My reason for saying this is because I was highly devoted to the movement as were the other ex-members present here today. I had to be deprogrammed because I was brainwashed. Edward Hunter, the man who coined the term "brainwash," is here today and I have taken my case to people like him. Very soon we will have credibility on this level.

Now we are talking about the alienation of the family in particular. My first question is: Are the mass marriages that were performed by Mr. Moon in Korea, are these valid according to American standards? Mr. Moon is not an ordained minister. Can anyone answer that, or could we just put it up for further research?

Senator Dole stated that this was a problem for the Immigration Service, which was not represented.

The reason that I ask this is because I have personal knowledge from a spiritual leader from Austria who told me that his visa ran out in October and I asked him what he was going to do. This was while I was still in the movement and he said, "Moon was going to marry him to an American to get American citizenship."

We have a list of at least seven or eight hundred foreigners who are here under illegal visas and it is a fact that they are marrying off Americans to foreigners to legalize citizenship.

Also, I was told that we must even be prepared to marry a Communist in the end. Since I was in such a short time, I would like to call on David Geisler to comment on that, because he heard Mr. Moon speak about this.

My name is David Geisler. I was a member of the Unification cult in Columbus, Ohio. I am referring to the lecture that I heard on September 7, 1975, with Mr. Joseph Stein of the Unification cult.

It was in the lecture.....Well, I'll make a supportive statement -- Unification as a front claims to be violently anti-Communist. If anyone were to investigate the ideology to any extent, he could see that it is very definitely a very strict, socialist state, centering on a totalitarian dictator.

Cont'd - Statement by David Geissler:

They call it automatic theocracy when Moon is God. It's very obvious what they are up to.

They told us that in preparing us for the future that, if necessary, we would have to marry a woman who might be high in the Communist party in order to convert her. After all, who can better persuade a person than her spouse?

We were also told that when we march, the big thing was the march on Moscow. It was a big slogan. They told us that the day may come when we would have to control these countries. They said it would take up to seven generations to bring the world under total subjugation. They said, for the time being, it might be necessary to control these countries forcibly, militarily, much the way they are being controlled now. In other words, we would be taking over the role of their Communist masters now. I think that is very close to what they are trying to do themselves.

If they are in cahoots with the Communists, I don't know. In my opinion, they are.

Ms. Slaughter:

They live communistically. They promote Socialism, which is closely related to Communism.

I'd like to introduce the best people that we have to stress the way that they are alienated from their families, through the use of a fairy tale. Anybody that opposes the movement is Satan. I have been overcome by Satan right now.

And there is a big difference between physical and spiritual parents. Now Moon and his wife were our spiritual parents. My father down here is just an old earth parent who brought me into the world to be born. Now, I would like to ask Paul Engel to speak.

Senator Dole asked how many young people had left the movement. Rabbi Davis replied that he knew of at least 95 people. He asked the ex-Moonies present to stand.

Ms. Slaughter: To continue, we will work through the court system now so we don't have to resort to kidnapping.

Statement by Paul Engel:

I'm from Westchester County, not too far from Moon himself. I was in the movement six and 1/2 weeks out in California. And I would like to just relate a short segment of what happened to me in terms of the family.

After three weeks of continuous indoctrination at the lectures, I was confronted with a situation where my mother was ill and my father had called but I was not permitted to speak to him at the time.

Before I was allowed to speak to him, my group leader talked with me for about ten or 15 minutes, explaining the reason for my mother's sickness. She told me that Satan had invaded her and it was because Satan was working through my family. The general idea is that Satan works through your loved ones to get you away. In fact, anyone who tries to get you to leave the movement is Satanic. And, so, therefore, I was asked to go against my own emotions toward my family. And she actually told me what to say over the phone.

Cont'd - Statement by Paul Engel:

My family was very upset about that. My father and my sister thought at that time that I just didn't know what to do. I was very poor. And later, before I was able to meet my father, I was told again not just that Satan had invaded my mother, my father and the family, but that my family was satanic and evil. Luckily, I was able not to accept that when I saw my father and how loving and understanding he was.

Ms. Slaughter:

I would just like to back that up by saying that one of my old boyfriends wanted to take me out to dinner one time. My leader called me in for a conference and told me that was Satan, that was Lucifer, pulling me away from God. So, you may think that you are stupid to believe that in the first place. Well, obviously, an intelligent young woman would have to be brainwashed to be influenced in this way. But I was afraid. I felt I had found the truth and that I had found God and that Satan would work through my parents and friends, and in fact, would pull me away. So, I did cut myself off from them and several friends and phone calls. My leader helped me do this.

Next, I would like for Peter Tipograph to explain something about deceitful letters. They coached us on how to write our letters home. Peter, could you come up here and also speak of the experience of your father when he took your letters to a psychiatrist, and what did he say?

Statement by Peter Tipograph:

Well, one aspect of the closed system is that usually there is complete censorship of information. The Unification Church, from most of the experiences of people in there, systematically censors the information that comes into the different communities it has across the country. The same is true of information that goes out to families of members and other people.

What happens a lot of times is that the young people in the different cults are coached that their parents are going to be hysterical, that they will be persecuted, and that in order to pacify them, a certain form of letter must be written. It must be very subtle, very passive, very pleasant, very soft, not really telling them what your experiences are.

I know some people have written letters home telling their parents the different places that they are fund raising, different places that they are living than where they are actually residing in order that the parents do not have a great accountability of where their young people are.

What happens is that the letters, if you read a lot of letters to parents, are very standardized. And in my particular case, my parents took certain letters to a psychiatrist to check them in comparison to the letters I had written throughout the years before I had joined the movement. And it was his judgment from reading my letters that my attitudes, my behavior, my thought patterns, were all altered in the sense that I was speaking not of my own free will but from a very standardized way. That happened in a lot of other cases.

Ms. Slaughter:

Here is Marina, from Peru, who was instructed to open mail and read it to the leaders.

Statement of Marina from Peru:

Well, my name is Marina, from Peru.

One afternoon in Tarrytown, after I finished talking on the phone with one of my friends, Mr. Garvis--Dale Garvis, one of the lecturers--called me to his room. I didn't know why. I felt very nervous, as though I did something wrong.

So, I went to his room. It was on second floor at Tarrytown in the house. He asked me to translate a letter, because it was in Spanish. So, I really felt very disappointed, because, I say, "Well, how can I read a letter when the person it was written to is not here?"

When I was reading, it was a private letter, a love letter from one of the members. Actually it was from a husband to his wife. And when I say to them, "This is a love letter," I couldn't translate at all because I was very nervous.

Terry Patrick, I mean Patrick Hickey, came in so I have no chance to read the letter to translate. Well, they were to meet some place and she is supposed to call him any time. That's all. It's a love letter and I could not sleep until I translated it.

Miss Slaughter:

Now that is tampering with personal mail, isn't it?

Mr. Coe stated that the responsibility of the Postal Service ends when the mail is delivered to the address of the individual.

Ms. Slaughter:

I have one question for the IRS, and I know you can't answer it right now, but...For instance, are organizations that are against brainwashing but don't have anything per se to do with deprogramming -- is this apt to jeopardize our tax-exempt status?

If not, then why do we apply this in the opposite direction. Is it legal for an organization to be tax-exempt when it uses mind control and brainwashing techniques in holding its members? Is that a general question?

Mr. Rumph stated that the question could not be answered because of the many ramifications and the many different things to look into before hazarding a guess. He asked that questions be directed to him in writing.

Rabbi DAVIS questioned Mr. Coe about mail:

You answered the question concerning ordinary mail. What is your answer, sir, if the mail is registered mail?

Mr. Coe: Well, certified and registered mail are individual. A registered or certified article, of course, requires a signature on delivery. The article is delivered to the addressee or to his or her agent. Now, there is a provision for restricted delivery when the proper fee is paid. In that event, we would deliver the letter only to the addressee upon proof of identity.

Rabbi Davis: That is called what, sir? Restricted mail?
Mr. Coe: Restricted delivery.

Meeting of Parents and Other Citizens from Thirty States with Senator Robert Dole, Kansas, in the Senate Caucus Room on February 18, 1976.

During the testimony and questioning session the following questions were asked by: Dr. Thomas G. Scharff, Louisville, Kentucky; Dr. Arthur Devine, Waterloo, Iowa; Miss Martha Lewis (ex-Unification member), New Hampshire; and Miss Cynthia Slaughter (ex-Unification member), Grand Prairie, Tx.

(1) What can be done by the Federal Government to bring about an investigation of the Unification movement in the matter of alienation of the Unification member from societal values through Unification indoctrination techniques? Is the Unification leadership inducing its members to practice deceit, to defy the law, to abrogate their important responsibilities to the Society?

(2) Will the Federal Government investigate the Unification movement for practices which either lead to neglect or to actual harm to the health--mental and physical--of its members?

(3) What can be done to prevent continuing deception and cheating of a generous American public by the Unification movement?

(4) Time was not available for Dr. Scharff to disclose to Senator Dole that Gary Scharff, son of Dr. Scharff and a member of the Unification movement, no longer feels that it is "important" to pay his debts to Princeton University, to his parents, to his sister and brothers, to the New Jersey telephone company or to the Princeton Bookstore. Gary feels that he is too occupied with saving the world to allow such minor matters (total debt of about $5,000-$6,000) to interfere. Dr. Scharff sent a letter to Mr. Moon reminding the latter that he--Mr. Moon--must take some responsibility for Gary's delinquency in paying his debts, since he--Mr. Moon--was employing Gary full time, without pay, for Mr. Moon's purposes. Dr. Scharff never received a reply from Mr. Moon. Question: How can Mr. Moon be made accountable for a complete personality change, a complete change in ethical values, when he takes young people into his cult?

Summary of Reasons for Asking Questions:

(1) Ex-members told of relating to the public the names of fictitious charitable causes in order to extract donations from the public for the Unification "Church."

(2) A dwelling zoned for one family contained 30 Unification members and conducted commercial sales from there.

(3) Martha Lewis of New Hampshire, at seventeen years of age, was illegally selling articles for Moon. This fact was known by her leaders.

(4) Dr. Scharff obtained from the Director of the Department of Consumer Affairs of the City of Louisville a letter in which is described the direct violation of laws (against peddling without a permit) by Unification cultists.

(5) Cynthia Slaughter of Texas was sent into bars at eleven o'clock at night to sell Moon's products. She was told by her leaders to use her "fallen nature" (charms) in order to get men to buy the products.

Dr. Thomas Scharff, Professor of Pharmacology at the University of Kentucky, introduced Martha Lewis of New Hampshire, an ex-cultist who spent two years and eight months in the cult, who testified:

In the Unification cult, two wrongs make a right. Because in the Garden of Eden, Satan deceived God's children. Now God's children--that is, the Unification Church members--are justified to deceive Satan, that is the Satan-controlled world.

This is called "heavenly deception." And I practiced this personally in my daily fund raising. I averaged $150 to $200 per day for a year and a half. This wasn't very good. Many people make much more. I sold candy and dried flower arrangements for nonexistent drug centers and programs for under-privileged children.

Now, how can our innocent and generous American public be protected from such deception? I think this is an important question.

Also, the fund-raising center in West Newton, Mass. is an example which housed over 30 young people. It was a house zoned for a one-family dwelling. It is a business, with offices inside and fund-raising products in the basement, and probably still in the garage. I lived there for almost one week before I was rescued by my parents.

I first became involved with the Unification movement when I was studying in West Germany. And I came back to the states after five months. But throughout my total involvement, 32 months, I was involved with the German movement. And it was common understanding that the leader of the German Unification Church is planning on becoming Chancellor. He is working to get political influence towards this end. I think that might interest you.

Senator Dole asked if she meant working towards becoming Chancellor of Germany.

Ms. Lewis: Yes, West Germany

Dr. Scharff then requested permission to question Miss Slaughter about the cult members and their ability to tell lies.

Dr. Scharff:

Cynthia, could you just comment on this?

Ms. Slaughter: Yes, I just want to say it briefly. As I said, I fund raised 18 hours a day. And before I went in there. I never lied. I was kicked out of office buildings three times and came back bragging. And we really got a lot of reinforcement from our leaders, because that showed that we were dedicated enough not to quit and give up until we were thrown out of the building. I tell you, my parents didn't raise me to do things like that!

I also fund raised in bars at 11:00 at night. I was told to use my "fallen nature" to get money. I'm sorry if I sound this way, but I just feel I was exploited. And I did do deceitful things, which is against my general character.

Mrs. Jean Merritt, Assistant Project Director of the Boston Childrens' Service at Boston University, Boston, Mass., introduced Ms. Ellen Rosemara, who said:

My name is Ellen Rosemara. I was introduced to the Unification Church in the summer of 1973. I was an honor student in high school in Brooklyn, New York, and I was hoping to go on to college in New York.

Statement by Ms. Rosemara - Cont'd:

I was approached at 22nd Street and Fifth Avenue by a young man. I was on my way to the library to do a term paper for school. I was invited to go to lectures. I was, at the time, sixteen years old. I went to lectures and it was a process for two or three months.

I became a member later on. We were sent illegally fund raising at the age of seventeen to California. The $9,000 that I raised in a two and a half month period was shipped to New York directly for Madison Square Garden on Sept. 18.

I was sent home by the state director of New York, because I was slightly ill. My parents were contacted, and my mother thought maybe I had a slight cold of some sort. When she came to pick me up, I was in a state of shock. I couldn't walk. I was held up by two people. I couldn't hold my suitcase. My belongings were not shipped to my house. When I went home, my parents realized that they would have to do more than just care for me at home, so I had to be taken to a mental institution where a further breakdown took place. And I spent 6 months in the mental institution, paying $75.00 a day. The bill came up to $20,000. The Unification Church takes no responsibility for my condition at all.

During the time I was a member, I did two seven-day fasts, which I was told I had to do. That's not to mention three or four other day fasts that I had done. I was kept without sleep for several days. My feet had no sensitivity due to the fact that I was fund raising for so many hours a day. And while I was in the hospital, my parents were contacted. And they had to have legal help in order for them not to come to the house.

Senator Dole inquired as to what she meant about illegal fund raising.

Ms. Rosemara: At the time, I was seventeen years of age. You are not allowed to fund raise in any state at that age and my leaders were aware of this.

Senator DOLE. I think Miss Smith can comment, in general terms, on the Consumer Protection aspect, and then Dr. Segal might want to address himself to the question you asked. Margery?

Ms. SMITH. Congress has given us, the Federal Trade Commission, authority to investigate the questionable commercial practices or unfair methods of competition or unfair deceptive actions and ʼactices affecting commerce. Our jurisdiction includes advertising and sales practices. With commercial products and services, our jurisdiction is limited to organizations for profit.

I couldn't answer the question without having the facts before me, but the Commission would be interested in receiving the facts from any organization and would look at them all equally.

We are here primarily to listen to all these facts, and we are open to all sides.

In addition, of course, due to the jurisdictional restraints involved here, we are concerned about the First Amendment protections (indistinguishable).

If you have any facts, would you please submit them in writing to the Commission?

Senator DOLE. Dr. Segal?

Dr. SEGAL. Your question, I believe, is what can be done to increase our understanding of the dynamics of alienation?

Dr. SCHARFF. Yes, but I would like to, if you don't mind, Dr. Segal, if you wouldn't mind this, I would like to present some more instances of alienation from the societal values and then come right back to you, if you don't mind.

Senator Dole, there have been a number of reports that have circulated among parents and people who are interested in cults, concerning the actual direct violation of laws by the Moon organization in the United States. I am going to read you very shortly a simple small single incident here, but completely validated, concerning a misdemeanor, or whatever it was, with the City of Louisville in Jefferson County, Kentucky, by the Moon cult. I have asked the Director of the Department of Consumer Affairs, Mrs. Minx Auerbach, to please give me a letter concerning her experience and the Consumer Affairs Department's experience with the Moon movement. This is the letter, and I will be very happy to provide the Senator with a copy of this after I read it.

"Dear Dr. Scharff. At your request, I am outlining a very brief history of the Unification Church's efforts to obtain a charitable solicitation permit in the City of Louisville.

"On 7/21/75, the Unification Church applied for a permit to solicit in the City of Louisville, their application for a permit stating that the previous year $4,000 had been raised. We were doubtful of this, and asked for their records, which they very willingly provided.

"Upon examination of their records, it was determined that $30,000 had been raised. When questioned about this discrepancy, they indicated they thought only $4,000 of it had been raised in the city of Louisville, and the remainder had been raised outside the city, although they could in no way document this.

"Also, their records revealed the majority of the money raised was used to support people living at a home located at 1402 Cherokee Road. Expenses included health care," -- And I might interject something here. This health care, to my knowledge, never comes from the top. If you are going to get health care, you get it yourself. -- "food, and so forth. It appeared to us that this violated the ordinance, which requires that the cost of a charitable solicitation campaign not exceed more than 15%. On this basis, the permit was denied.

"The Unification Church was notified that there was a process of appeal open to them. Many months went by with no response to our letter. We then heard they were soliciting in several locations within the City of Louisville, and a warrant was taken out against them. Several more weeks elapsed before the warrant was signed. At this writing, David Hoxtat, against whom the warrant was issued, cannot be found. We will probably take out another warrant against Frances Talkingham, who we understand is now the new leader here.

"We have found that there has been great mobility among the leadership in this community." -- That's the leadership of the Unification movement. -- "They move in and out very swiftly, but nevertheless seem to be going stronger." -- I imagine that should be 'growing stronger.' -- "There have been many reports of violations of soliciting without a permit, but it is very difficult for us to apprehend them. In order to arrest them, we need to catch them in the act. And generally, by the time we receive the report that they are soliciting, when we send someone there, they are gone.

"You should know that according to the ordinance, they have also lost their right to appeal, because they must do this within 20 days. Therefore, they are in violation of the ordinance, and that ordinance takes effect for a full year from the time they made their first application.

"I assume this is the kind of information you wanted. If I can be of further help, please let me know. Sincerely, Minx M. Auerbach, Director, Department of Consumer Affairs, the City of Louisville, Kentucky."

I might like to add two other instances here. Personal friends of mine, one at his home and one at a shopping center, were accosted by these cultists recently and in direct violation of the ordinance. And the one excuse for collecting money through selling whatever it is they were selling, was that they wanted to help families for delinquent children.

We have with us today . . .

Dr. SWOPE. Pardon me, Dr. Scharff.

I am going to ask that all of us from this point on may have to keep faith with the Senator and these people who are here. So, if we can limit our remarks to the most pertinent parts, I would appreciate it.

Dr. SCHARFF. Well, this is in direct violation of the law. The leadership certainly knew that the permit was not issued months ago. These things have happened very recently.

Senator DOLE. I might indicate, with respect to the charge of violating a loca ordinance, that there is no one on this list who would have any jurisdiction on it.

Dr. SCHARFF. No, but the point, Senator, that I am trying to bring out here, is the violation and the removal of these people from the normal ethical standards of the society.

I think maybe I'll cease here. Thank you very much.

Dr. SWOPE. Dr. Devine, did you wish to make a comment?

Dr. DEVINE. No. I'll relinquish my time.

Dr. SWOPE. All right.

Senator DOLE. I wonder if Dr. Segal might comment at this time on the initial question.

Dr. SEGAL. I believe the question that you stated originally was philosophical that is, what can we do to understand more than we do today about the procedures, the methods, the dynamics by which this alienation process that we have heard about today works?

The fact is that a considerable amount of research by sociologists, psychologists, psychiatrists, and foundations is devoted today and has been in recent years to study exactly this issue. Much of this research is supported by Congress and the federal government -- for example, the Department of HEW.

The problem, however, is that unlike the interaction between physical phenomena. . .

The problem, I am afraid, is that the issues are extraordinarily complex -- Much more complex than the interaction between two physical phenomena. And I believe it's safe to suggest that almost everyone who has experienced this phenomenon has their own individual hypothesis as to what it is that triggers a change of attitude and values. And probably every such variable that the parents here might suggest is under scrutiny. I can just name a few: the social upheaval in our country; the wars that we have endured; the quality in the parent-child interaction; the vulnerability and susceptibility of the individual. And so, I simply want to say that this is a complex issue -- one which deserves and is getting an extraordinary amount of attention. There are researchers who are devoted just specifically to this question.

Dr. SWOPE. We come now to another area of alienation. This has to do with the field of education. These young people are caused to drop away from their colleges. And then into the area of coercive persuasion, mind control.

Dr. Frederick Bunt, Dean of the School of Education, Case University, New York, and Mrs. Jean Merritt, Assistant Project Director at the Boston Childrens' Service, a psychiatric social worker and field instructor at Boston University.

Summary Outline of Statement by Frederick Bunt of New York: DAP - February 1°, 1976

Topic: Unification Church as an Educational Institution (p. 29)

Questions: 1. What standards does the Federal Government apply in determining whether
               an organization is eligible for funding as an educational institution?
            2. What type of investigation might be undertaken by the Federal Government
               if the Unification Church applies for funding of its so-called "educa-
               tional activities"?

Remarks: 1. Unification Church seeks to be known as an Educational Institution
               1.1 Front Organizations
                   1.11 CARP - Collegiate Assn. for the Research of Principles
                   1.12 NEDS - New Educational Development Systems
                   1.13 CCP - Creative Community Project
               1.2 Other Educational Activities
                   1.21 Day Care Centers in Bay Area, California
                   1.22 Seminary in New York
                   1.23 Plans for University in California

            2. Education as defined by Unification Church . . .
               2.1 Pure and simple indoctrination
               2.2 Democratic education considered illusory
                   2.21 Separated from reality
                   2.22 Citizens do not possess infallible, philosophical base
               2.3 Subject-Object Relationship
                   2.31 Democratic education faulted on all persons wanting to be
                         subjects instead of objects (servants)
                   2.32 Democratic education makes individuals too concerned about self

               2.4 American Education according to Unification Church
                   2.41 Materialistic learning, atheism, realism
                   2.42 Citizens have no direction, are confused
                   2.43 Individuals are not made "perfect."
               2.5 Unification Theory
                   2.51 Goal - to be like God and make God happy
                   2.52 Perfection - Making God happy
                   2.53 Love of God on Earth precede's Man's rights and freedom

            3. Moon is considered to be God
               3.1 Goal of education - make Moon happy
               3.2 Children to become like MOON
               3.3 Love of MOON should precede rights and freedom

            4. No right supercedes all others
               4.1 Freedom of religion does not have a "more equal" status to freedom of
                   thought and of education and to life, liberty and security of person.
               4.2 Utopian Society according to Unification Church places submission to
                   the "Subject" or MOON of greater importance than traditional democratic
                   rights and freedom

            5. Unification Church Theory of Education Antithetical to Democratic Education
               5.1 Deserves no support from Federal Government
               5.2 Should be investigated by the Government as an organization seeking
                    to gain power in the United States through undemocratic and extra-
                    legal means.

63

STATEMENT AND COMMENTS OF DR. FREDERICK BUNT, CASE UNIVERSITY, NEW YORK.

Dr. Bunt: I'm Fred Bunt from New Paltz, New York. My concern is that the Unification Church could become eligible for federal funding as an education institution. That is, eligible for grants, scholarship money, insured loans to students, and so forth. I'm concerned about what the standards might be that the federal government would apply to determine whether such an institution can be considered an educational one, can be considered eligible under the various higher education acts.

On numerous occasions Unification Church has sought to identify itself as an educational institution through such front organizations as CARP (Collegiate Assn. for the Research of Principles) and NEDS (New Educational Development Service). These names have changed from time to time. In the Bay area of San Francisco, they had been starting day care centers. And my daughter was actively engaged in beginning a university, or at least she was led to believe that.

In my home state of New York, we have become alarmed over the fact that he, Reverend Moon, has established a theological seminary in Barrytown, N. Y. He is asking for approval by our New York State Regents. The seminary is already in operation even though certification has not been forthcoming from the regents. Hopefully, it will not.

Secondly, church members recently entered a school in Tarrytown, N. Y., sat down with the children at lunch tables and began to proselytize. I think these are very serious matters to all educators.

Considering the Unification Church an educational institution is to pervert the word "education" To consider it an educational institution in the democratic tradition is to laugh in the face of democracy. Education is a process designed to enlighten the individual and cultivate his talents. A good democratic education opens new windows on the world, whets kids' appetites and helps them develop their rational powers--an especially critical thing.

Education in the Unification Church is none of this. Lecture after lecture, there is no question permitted until it is over. Gross repetition with indoctrination as the sole purpose is exactly what education is for the Unification Church. Questions after the lectures are asked and answered in isolation, are perhaps vaguely answered or not answered at all, or treated as negative or evil feelings coming forth from the individual. Questioning the authority of the Church is the work of Satan, as the young people will attest.

Now what does the Unification Church think of democratic education? Here's what they think of it. It's called "Theory of Education from the Text of Unification Thought," edited and reprinted by the Unification Thought Institute in Barrytown, New York:

"Current democratic education is not much better than a fantasy. It's imaginary and exists only in the mind, separated from true reality.
p. 2
"Democratic citizens who have received a democratic education do not have a firm infallible philosophic base." p.3. What is this base? The base according to the Unification Church theory grows out of subject-object relationships, master-servant relationships.

Again, I quote from this document. "If all the people are masters or rulers, then there are no servants or people being ruled." p. 3

"We can see that the system of democracy tends to make people assert their rights of rule from a self-centered point of view. To be self-centered is to be. . ."

And what does the Unification Church say about American education? It is an education "that is geared to materialistic learning, atheism, and realism," quoted from here. "Democratic citizens are like grasses floating on water." Supposedly, they have no direction, views isolated, despairing and lacking in self-confidence.

"To make us perfect, we need a new kind of education. Such an education would have as its goal to reflect the image of God and, there-fore, make God happy." (Applause from Unification sympathizers in rear.)

For them, individually, this means that each person as an individual should reflect the perfection of God. What this perfection means, "It means that God is a perfect being." Now every Moonie knows whether he is in or out, that there is only one perfect being in the world right now and that is Sun Myung Moon. So, with every quotation, we may substitute Moon. "To reflect the image of Moon and, therefore, make Moon happy is the object of education."

"The education is a means to guide children through their growth period to enable them to fulfill three blessings." So, in other words, it is to educate them more, then, to allow Moon to enjoy happiness, not God, by the resemblance of Moon's perfection, multiplication and dominion.

Finally, the document concludes, "Education from now on should be one which realizes the love of God" -- remember it is now Moon -- "on the earth. One that precedes man's rights and freedoms." That is stated right in this document. The Unification Church sees education as advocating their model of human behavior--a mimicking in entirety without any question or creative thought, a mimicking of Sun Myung Moon.

Rights and freedoms so dear to the American way of life, so cen-tral to a democratic education, are secondary at best and more than likely expendable in the grand scheme of human rights and utopian soci-ety designed by the church.

Are we going to permit the destruction of human and civil rights by the brainwashing and programming of your young people? No civil liberty can be considered so important that it takes precedence over all other civil liberties, that it supersedes other civil liberties of greater or equal validity. Freedom of religion cannot be used to destroy life and liberty in our democratic type of education. Thank you very much.

STATEMENT AND COMMENTS OF MRS. BRUCE MERRITT, BOSTON, MASSACHUSETTS: (Mrs. Merritt was accompanied by Ellen Rosemara, whose testimony appears earlier in this booklet, alongside that of other ex-member victims.)

Mrs. MERRITT: Senator Dole, I would like to begin by thanking you for having this open meeting. I represent a group of professionals that have had no relative involvement. Our objective was exactly to be objective and clinical and diagnostic in what is going on. We are,

Statement of Ki-Bum Han

- 34 -

Senator Dole and the distinguished governmental officials and friends, I was born in the land of Korea and in the city of Busan where Mr. Moon first began his "operations" on January 27, 1951. And I am presently a United Presbyterian Church minister. Strange though it may sound, I am a total stranger to the people of Mr. Moon's present followers in this room just as they are to me. I am equally a stranger to practically all the young people, parents and concerned adults who are supporting this "Day of Affirmation and Protest", just as they are to me.

The reason I am taking my stand has nothing to do with an infringement upon anyone's religious freedom which is guaranteed by the Constitution of this land. It is up to any individual or group to foster any kind of belief. But once such a freedom tramples upon the freedom of others in the name of the same Constitution then the government needs to fulfill its obligation of protecting the law-abiding citizens of this land. To be more descriptive, when we see a tip of an iceberg we should begin to take the precautionary measure of finding out what is below the surface in order to avoid the disaster called a shipwreck. When we smell an obnoxious odor drifting in the air we should nose around to locate the source. We should not ignore it or let it be. Perhaps we should call the sanitation department for help. The smell could be poisonous and fatal. Or, when we see puffs of smoke here and there we should make sure that they are investigated to prevent hazardous fire. It is better still if we call the local fire department. It is important to be on guard because Prevention seems to be much better and less expensive than Cure. Pearl Harbor damages could have been minor if there had been a coordinating effort of checking, communicating and investigating the available presented information.

The fact that these ex-Moon followers and their parents and other concerned citizens are vocal in "affirmation and protest" at least suggests that there is something to be looked into and investigated surrounding the activities of Mr. Moon and his followers. The stories which an increasing number of young people, who were once part of the Moon group, are telling surely seem to deserve a careful investigation into whether the Moon practices warrant the legal protection and governmental permission.

Man is a religious animal. Therefore he can do so many things in the name of religion. Besides, the term "religion" can be applied very loosely and broadly. An individual and an organization wearing the cloak of religion can engage in economic exploitation of young innocents and in political demagoguery by means of deceit, fraud and manipulation. If the Moon group is suspected of such economic exploitation and political subversion with ample evidence the government should never ignore the suspicion but should check into it. I observe a prevalent fear in the minds of many law-abiding citizens, both parents and others, regarding the activities of Mr. Moon's group. The young people are "forcibly" cut off from the family and community relationships they once enjoyed.

Come to think of it, it is certainly strange to discover that in Korea, as I witnessed so many times, it is a Christian convert who is cast out by his own parents and disowned by his family, while here in the U. S. A. it is the recruitees of Mr. Moon's group who denounce the family.

There is another matter that baffles me personally, too, that while Mr. Moon's group claims the privileges and exemptions of a religious organization it at the same time advocates its political nature and intentions. Mr. Moon's "Master Speaks" contains the following statements: "We must have an autocratic theocracy to rule the world. We cannot separate the political field from the religious...The separation between religion and politics is what Satan likes best," or "The present U. N. must be annihilated by our power;" or "Come on U. S. and the world, I will attack and win over you."

66

It is also known that despite the efforts of Mr. Moon's group, no Christian church in Korea or in the U.S.A. has accepted it into membership. In the New York area its membership was denied by the New York City Council of Churches and the New York Korean Ministers Assoc. In spite of the fact that the group takes a name such as "The Holy Spirit Association for the Unification of World Christianity," Mr. Moon has spoken thus: "The three greatest enemies of the Unification Church are Communism, Christianity and members of the opposite sex." Furthermore, an official statement by the Unification Church of America issued in the N.Y.Times (1/11/76, p. 41) has the following words: "Because the Unification Church proclaims a new world ideology to overcome Communism, avowed Communist groups in the U. S. and elsewhere have openly organized to discredit and destroy our movement, and have even terrorized our friends and members. Communism is more than just a political, economic or military system - it is a false idea and an atheistic religion. Only a living faith in God can effectively oppose it. We accept this as our Christian duty and responsibility." (the underlines are mine) What material evidence of political persecution has been submitted? Why the word "Church" if the group vents an anti-Christian slogan? In fact the group has been called a "pseudo-religion." Why the "Christian" duty and responsibility when Christianity is branded as one of the three greatest enemies? Furthermore, who is "God" Mr. Moon speaks of? From all the evidence of his own writings, "God" is no other than Mr. Moon himself, who claims to be the Brain.

What the same statement charges against some parents who have tried to "de-program" their own young people interestingly fits the description which all ex-Moon followers suffered. The statement reads: "Members have been subjected to vicious techniques including indefinite physical incarceration, obscenities and other verbal abuse, forced sleep deprivation, lack of food, and complete contempt for the person. The Church condemns such activities as violations of the First Amendment, which protects religious freedom and basic human rights." The fact of the matter is that the same charges can be, with substantial evidence, hurled back at Mr. Moon's group's actions. The group's "violation of the First Amendment, which protects religious freedom and basic human rights" should be investigated.

Senator Dole, words can be easily uttered, but it is hard to substantiate the words by actions. If a group in the name of religion acts differently from the accepted practices of religion, as the so-called "Unification Church" seems to demonstrate, then at least an investigation should be in order.

Please just look at the parents and adults and young people who are deeply concerned as law-abiding and conscientious citizens of this country and please respond with actions to their affirmation and protest. I am concerned about that which they are concerned, and strongly believe that a Congressional investigation should be undertaken to see what is under the tip of the iceburg, to determine the source of the smell, and to check the cause of the smoke, before any major disaster strikes us.

I thank you for your patient attention.

Respectfully submitted,

Ki-Bum Han

Statement of the Rev. Dr. Samuel A. Jeanes
Pastor of the First Baptist Church
Merchantville, New Jersey 08109

DAP - February 18, 1976

Re: The Unification Church

(p.36)

Though it is not within the province of our lawmakers to apply either a spiritual or theological yardstick to any religion, we cannot help but call attention to the fact that the Unification Church movement has repeatedly endeavored to identify itself with the terminology of Christianity. It has appealed to the general public under such names as the "Sun Myung Moon Christian Crusade", "The Celebration of Life and Christianity in Crisis". However, the movement is not accepted by any body of Christian churches and its interpretations of Scripture would not be accepted by any reputable Christian theologian.

However, reports that have appeared in the media indicate that its adherents can be found on the streets of our cities peddling wares of different varieties, and that the receipts for such sales have reached substantial figures. The media further indicates that such monies have been invested in large estates and mansions. The people of America have always associated religion with the simple definition of the New Testament as found in the Epistle of James. The glory of religion is to be pure and undefiled. It is not mixed with the inventions of men nor with the corruptions of the world. False religions may be known by their impurity and uncharitableness. Since the early days of our nation we have associated the churches and temples of our land with charities expressed in more recent years under such titles as Catholic Charities, Jewish World Relief, Church World Service, Care, The Salvation Army, The Volunteers of America, The Rescue Missions, and many others whose charities are made possible by the generous support of their various constituencies. Some of our States are moving toward legislation that requires credibility confirmed as to whether it offers the kind of charity which characterizes the established churches which Mr. Moon says 'God is leaving...' This is within the province of government. The people must be protected against solicitation of funds in the name of religion or in the name of good causes such as campaigns against drugs and pornography that may or may not be launched. America has 'Truth in Advertising Laws' as well as laws which deal with fraud which might be perpetrated on the public in the name of religion.

The government of the United States through its lawmakers as well as through the courts has always acted for the public good while at the same time giving respect for religion. Religious practices, however, must stay within the confines and boundaries of what is good for the citizens. Hence, the courts have ruled that blood transfusions may be given if a life is in jeopardy, even though it might conflict with a religious tenet. Polygamy was also banned in the early days of the republic even though it had been practiced in the name of religion. And more recently the courts have ruled that in spite of their respect for a religion, a practice such as the handling of deadly poisonous snakes in the name of religion would be illegal because the safety of human beings was in jeopardy because of such a practice.

Certainly, there is sufficient evidence in hand regarding the influence of the Unification Church on the minds and practices of young people that would justify government investigation and intervention. Whenever a leader says to people as the spokesman for the Moon movement is quoted as saying, "I am your brain" and "Out of all the saints sent by God, I think I am the most successful one already" such a movement requires some authoritative surveillance.

The fact that young people have been lured from their college campuses under the guise of a "Christian" movement to find themselves under some form of mind control or manipulation that interferes with their educational pursuits, alienates them from their families, their religion, and even jeopardizes their physical and emotional well being should be a concern of government.

Dr. SWOPE: Our final witness is a man who has led a long drive against the Unification movement. He is President of Citizens Engaged in Reuniting Families and Rabbi of the Jewish Community Center in White Plains, New York.

STATEMENT AND COMMENTS OF RABBI MAURICE DAVIS OF WHITE PLAINS, NEW YORK.

Rabbi DAVIS. My name is Rabbi Maurice Davis of White Plains, New York. I am active in constantly learning about this movement and speaking of it in the past few years. Thank you.

Senator Dole, there is a statement in Judaism to the effect that "the last is the most beloved." I don't know if that's true, but the last is sort of tired. And he has heard almost everything he wanted to say already said. And he is the most beloved because when he gets through the program, it will also come to a conclusion.

Dr. Han said that he is a stranger to the Unification Church and to its members and to those who have been rescued out of that movement. Senator Dole, I am a stranger to none of them. And I've heard today that you, Senator, are about to take my place as the number one Satan in America. And I am delighted to turn it over to you, (laughter, applause) along with the midnight phone calls threatening my life, which seem to go as part and parcel of the whole thing.

Senator Dole, I have been working on this for two and a half years. In that regard, we founded an organization called CERF. We represent an awful lot of parents. We are not, and I am not, at all desirous in any way to impinge upon the civil rights of any movement or of any people. Nor do I question the right of any group to the use, the proper use, of the First Amendment of the Constitution. I do question whether or not the Unification movement is in reality a religious organization and, thereby, is in reality entitled to the rights and protections afforded the religions, the great religions, of America and of the world. And to that degree, I would like to make a few statements.

The first question is: Is this movement a Christian movement as in so much of its literature it pretends to be? Dr. Han has already spoken somewhat to that, from another statement of "Master Speaks," I quote: "We" -- meaning the Unification movement -- "are the third Israel, the first Israel of the Jewish people, the second Israel of the Christian people, and now we are the third. Therefore, the first Israel and the second Israel must become united with us. After we restore the Christians, then the restoration of the first Israel will come." In every way, there seems to be a distinction made between the Unification movement and Christianity.

In regard to the Unification Church attitude towards Jews and Judaism, the Master said, in one of his speeches: "How many Jewish members are there here? In the olden days under the Jewish law, they were supposed to have stoned the adulteress people to death. Under our law, in the Divine Principle, it's going to be more strict."

The Moon movement teaches that the six million Jews who died in the holocaust were paying their just indemnity for having killed Christ -- part of the teaching of the Unification Church. These are the Jews and Judaism. Nonetheless, sir, the Unification Church has no compunction about opting for itself the word "Judaism."

A movement was begun, as Daphne Greene mentioned, called "Judaism in Service to the World." This movement is run by (indistinguishable) of the Boonville branch of the Unification movement which is called variously, the New Education Development Corporation, and once we exposed that, changed to the Ideal Creative Community Corporation. Nonetheless, this movement is an attempt now to infiltrate the Jewish community. To that extent, they announced that they were going to bring Judaism to the world. They announced they had the approval of the Executive Director of the Jewish Welfare Federation in California, which in fact they did not. They announced that they had the support of Benjamin Sweed, which in fact they did not. They continually lied, and letters that I have received from California state that the Jewish community there is up in arms: "Can an organization, simply because it wishes to opt a name and call themselves Judaism, simply for the purpose of infiltrating into the Jewish community?" It uses the name "Christian," and many of its front organizations have now used the name "Judaism."

Is it a religion, sir? Is it a religion when it sends its young men and women out into the streets, as you have already heard, to raise money by whatever guise, under whatever deception they wish? I would point out to you, Senator Dole, that in the 90 to 95 young men and women whom I have interviewed and from records which we have received from the Unification headquarters, we have never found a kid yet who brought in less than $100 a day selling his peanuts, flowers, candy, candles. Oh, he was told not to sell candles by Moon any more, because whereas if you sell flowers, they will die in a day, if you sell candles, the owner, the purchaser may not use them for a week.

They say that they have 30,000 members. We think they have somewhere between 3,000 and 5,000 members. We know that they raise between $100 and $500 a day. But, Senator, if they only had a thousand members on the street, and if they only brought in $100 a day, that would be $36.5 million a year. And I suggest that somewhere in the government of the United States this ought to be researched to the extent that, is such money taxable? Is it even required that the government be made aware of the enormous sums of money which are coming into the Unification Church. You may be aware, sir, that in the City of Tarrytown, the Unification Church, with its money, has purchased not one piece of property or two, but on this map of Tarrytown, everything that is shaded now belongs to the Unification Church -- something in tl area of $8.5 to $10 million. And I would be happy to give you this material, sir, for your own investigation.

I am told that a great many of the Unification parents are happy with their kids being in the movement. We have received almost a thousand letters, sir, from parents of young men and women in the Unification Church. The letters are heartbreaking in the deepest degree. And they are, in fact, the reason why I have found myself into this movement.

There was one woman who pleaded with her daughter to come home because the mother, herself, was dying of cancer. And for a year, she pleaded with her daughter to come home. And the daughter could not leave the Unification Church. Her work was too busy, too important. I will not read any of the letters that I have received. They are available, however, to your office or any concerned citizen. Well, Ruth White died Sunday. And she died alone. And her daughter wasn't home. And I wonder what kind of a religion it is that tells a daughter that her work for "God" is more important than being with her mother the last days of her life.

Is it a religion, sir, or is it a political movement when the master speaks and says, "We have fifty states. And within 120 days, all the state representatives can be changed. That means we finish three terms and then all the state representatives can have our training."

Is it a religion, sir, or is it a political cult when it says, "Master needs many good-looking girls. He needs 300. He will assign three girls to each Senator." Senator Dole, be ready. "That means we need 300. Let them have a good relationship with them. One girl is for the election; one is to be the diplomat; and one is for the party," whatever that means. "If our girls are superior to the Senators in many ways, then the Senators will just be taken by our members." Are these the words of a religion, sir? Or are these the words of a political cult?

The 45 organizations which go under different names, all of which belong to Moon, and all of which, incidentally, have been authenticated on television by a man in the back row -- I saw it on television -- these are the front organizations of Moon. I have prepared several kits filled with these materials, and you will be handed those kits to save time to peruse at your discretion.

This is a movement without clergy, without elders, without ministers. This is a movement with 300 pretty girls. This is a movement in which the leader lives in Oriental splendor, while these kids eat peanut butter and jelly, and go out on the streets. This is a movement, sir, that talks a great deal about Satan.

I have no right to discuss the theology of any other religion. Every man is entitled to his own theology. And if a religion wishes to be satanic, then I suppose that's their right. But you see, Senator Dole, I had occasion to talk to the mother of a boy named William Jeffrey Daley.

William Jeffrey Daley belonged to the Unification Church. And he was filled with the concept of Satan. And William Jeffrey Daley one day got rid of Satan. He took off all his clothes, and he put his head on a railroad track, and he was decapitated. And I called Mrs. Daley on the phone to offer my condolences, my sympathy, and my heartbreak. And she said to me, "What did they do to my boy? He was a normal human being. What did they do to my boy? Why is it that when he went into that movement, he continued to write letters to me and he continued to say that he loved me, but he began signing the letter, 'Sincerely yours, William Jeffrey Daley.'" And finally when they brought his possessions home, the picture of his dead father was no longer in his wallet. And William Jeffrey Daley had never, from the day his father died, had never left the house without the picture of his father in his wallet. I spoke to representatives of the Unification Church, and they said this is nonsense. They said they spoke to the parents of William Jeffrey Daley. I wonder how they could when the father was already dead.

Here is a movement whose followers are willing to lie and to cheat, and told it is a proper thing to do. This is a movement, sir, in which 35 youngsters have already told me that had they been told to kill, they would have killed, because it was in the name of God, or Moon, take your pick.

Senator Dole, I could go on for hours, as I have for years, on the kind of material we have come across, this so-called "Heavenly Deception." But, Senator Dole, I don't know whether this is a question or not. Sure, I have

- 40 -

questions. Can a man who is not ordained, self-ordained, perform marriages
in America? That's a question. I don't know the answer to it. In Korea,
he performed 1,800 marriages on a single day and told the parents that he was
saving America. I know that the kids who get married don't know who is
marrying whom. There's one from column A and one from column B. But I don't
know whether or not he has the right to perform marriages in New York, not
having been ordained.

Here is a man, here is a movement, sir, that has been denied membership
in the National Council of Christians, or National Council of Churches,
because they say it's not Christian. Here is a movement that has been denied
membership in the Korean National Council of Churches, because they say it's
not Christian. Here is a movement that has been denied membership in the
National Evangelical Association of Korea. Here is a movement led by a man
who was thrown out of the Presbyterian Church, who is himself a self-ordained
minister. And I question, sir, their right to call themselves a religion.

Senator Dole, I am a Jew. And my people have known religious persecution.
And I certainly would be the first person to defend everyone's right to that
First Amendment. It's a matter of life and death to me and to my people.
But it's also a matter of life and death when any political cult   can cloak
itself in the garments of religion, this pseudocult, using the vocabulary of
Christianity to hide its basic designs of world and American power. I question,
sir, whether or not this movement belongs to the First Amendment and it's coterie
of defense.

Senator Dole, I got into this thing because two and a half years ago, two
kids in my congregation got caught. And I went out to rescue them and saved
one and I failed in one. And I will never forgive myself, because if I had
known then what I know now, I could have saved the girl, too. And I've lived
with that, that she is still in it and I failed.

Along the way, 95 to 100 kids have come out. And the more I look at
this movement, and the more I interview the kids and their parents, I have
this final sentence to say:

Senator Dole, ladies and gentlemen, the last time I ever witnessed a
movement that had these qualifications: (1) a totally monolithic movement with
a single point of view and a single authoritarian head; (2) replete with fanatical
followers who are prepared and programmed to do anything their master says;
(3) supplied by absolutely unlimited funds; (4) with a hatred of everyone on
the outside; (5) with suspicion of parents, against their parents -- Senator
Dole, the last movement that had those qualifications was the Nazi youth
movement, and I tell you, I'm scared. (Standing ovation)

Dr. SWOPE. Be seated please. I would like to read to you, Senator Dole, a note
that one of the girls sitting at the front desk sent up to me regarding
our attitude.

Senator DOLE. I have a couple of comments to make, but maybe I can do so
after you finish -- go ahead.

Dr. SWOPE. "Please recognize the young persons in the back who are Moonies now.
We love them, but not what they are doing." And this is our attitude, gentlemen.

Thank you so much for attending.

72

Senator DOLE. I want to thank those members from the different federal agencies, departments, who have appeared here today. Do any of you have comments you would like to offer at this time? . . . There are none.

I would also indicate, as I did earlier, that if you have questions that were not specifically answered, you may submit them in writing to the appropriate agency, to those present. Those who are not represented, I think, will also provide answers to any questions referred to them.

I would also like to recognize at this time the parents of those who may be members of the Unification Church. If the parents would stand. . . .

(Someone in the audience). What was the question?

Senator DOLE. Could we have the parents of either present or ex-members of the Unification Church please stand? (Approximately 150-200 parents stood)

Because this meeting was for the parents, I want to get some idea of how many are in attendance.

I would recognize at the back of the room, I think, members of the Unification Church. Is that correct? How many parents? Would you raise your hands? (Approximately 30-40 parents responded)

I want to thank those members of the church, as well as the parents on both sides for the courtesy extended. I think the purpose of this meeting has been essentially fulfilled. I wouldn't want to be overreacting to your remarks, Rabbi Davis, but am interested in the comments you made about threats on your life and may want to talk to you later.

In any event, I also want to especially thank Mrs. Jean Tuttle of Manhattan, Kansas, who first made the inquiry of my office as to whether or not the parents in our State could get together and visit with those federal officials who might have, or should have, in her judgment, an interest in this matter. At the same time, we appreciate her own efforts and those of others in Kansas and elsewhere who have driven such considerable distances to be here. I thank all of those participating.

Since there was some reference made earlier to a "record" of this proceeding, I wish to make it clear again that there is no such official account being kept. There has been a tape made of the various statements offered, however, and that will be transcribed for the benefit of all who are interested. Beyond that, I would be happy to receive any documents you wish to submit to me for personal examination.

Again, I want to indicate as I did at the outset that this was not a Committee function; it was not a hearing; and no one was under oath. It was simply an opportunity, I hope, for those parents and others who are concerned about the Unification Church -- and what its goals may be -- to express themselves.

Dr. Swope, do you have any concluding remarks? We still have some time if you want another five minutes.

Dr. SWOPE. We just want to thank you and would like to express our appreciation the way Americans always do. (Applause)

Senator DOLE. Thank you very much. The meeting will be adjourned.

PART TWO

A SPECIAL REPORT

THE UNIFICATION CHURCH:
ITS ACTIVITIES AND PRACTICES

A Meeting of Concerned Parents

A DAY OF AFFIRMATION AND PROTEST

Dirksen Senate Office Building
Washington, D.C.
Wednesday, February 18, 1976

CONTENTS:

PART ONE: UNOFFICIAL TRANSCRIPT
           GOVERNMENT PANEL
           CITIZENS APPEARING

PART TWO: LETTERS OF TESTIMONY
           FROM PARENTS AND
           EX-MEMBER VICTIMS

Compiled by National Ad Hoc Committee,
     A Day of Affirmation and Protest

Explanation of Part Two

        Part Two of this booklet is a sampling of
letters of parents and victims being presented
to Senator Dole's panel. The 80 letters reproduced
herein are typical of the   experiences of hundreds
of victims from families caught up by the cults.
Some of the letters are unsigned in order to protect
the identity of those who are still in the cults, but
which names will be released to duly constituted investigative authorities. Likewise, hundreds of other
letters in our files are available for investigative
purposes.

        No portion of the information and letters con-
tained herein may be reproduced or used for any purpose
without the written permission of the publisher.

                    Publisher:

                    National ad hoc Committee
                    A DAY OF AFFIRMATION AND PROTEST
                    P.O. Box 5084
                    Arlington, Texas 76011

                    For Information

        As a result of the Washington meeting the
Committee Engaged in Freeing Minds has bee formed.
The purpose of CEFM is to create a national office
or organization to coordinate the efforts of all
citizens--parents, ex-members, and supporters-- to
unite us in the battle against cults generally described as destructive pseudo-religious political cults.
Anyone wishing information on how to help the Committee's
cause, financially or with volunteer services, should
contact:

                    Office of the Coordinator, CEFM
                    (Committee Engaged in Freeing Minds)
                    P.O. Box 5084
                    Arlington, Texas 76011

My 15-year-old son and I went to the Barrytown center of the
Unification Church on 25 January, 1975 to see his 18-year-
old first cousin, Ann Gumpper of Flint, Michigan. Ann had
dropped out of her first term at Goddard College to attend
a 45-day workshop, which was about to end. We went to find
out what was happening, after Ann's behavior had begun to
puzzle her parents.

In one afternoon, we found that Ann would not be allowed to
be alone with us. When I finally insisted at the end of the
day that some family matters had to be discussed privately
with her, Ann's group leader, Leslie Eliot, suggested that
my son stay with her while I spoke with Ann. Fine hostage
arrangement, I thought, but I agreed.

Ann was not thinking for herself. She hadn't even been able
to decide about going out to lunch with us. She was smiling
a lot but seemed distant, not like the person we had known
before in the family. I suspected that I would get nowhere
by arguing my own feelings about Moon and his indoctrination.
So when we were alone, I gave her the Moon article in the
May, 1974 issue of AD Magazine instead. I asked her to read
what it said about Moon and the questionable aspects of his
so-called church. She read it in front of me, but all she
had to say about it was, "Since I'm actually in the movement,
I think I know more about it than the author of that article
does."

We met Leslie right after that, and Ann said to her in front
of me, "He showed me an article." When she did that, I realized
that Ann was telling Moon's people everything and her family
very little. It was an odd sensation, to see such a quick
change in a forthright person.

My impression of the Barrytown facility was that it was being
run like a Marine Corps boot camp, not an honest place of
religious study. I found a barracks, not a school. There
were no books to be seen or places where one could sit down
and talk comfortably with his friends. The bulk of the trainees
were at a lecture, I was told. If that's where they were,
they stayed the whole sunny afternoon. However, I did see a
number of the staff around the halls and in the lunch room
talking to recruits on a one-to-one basis. As I passed one
pair, I heard the leader counseling the recruit about the
latter's concern with suicide. I was introduced to the young
man afterwards and have wondered since whether he was the
lad who a few months later lay naked on the nearby tracks
and let a Penn Central train decapitate him.

My conclusion from one afternoon at Barrytown was that Ann
was acting like a non-person with no control of her destiny,
bland and unreal in relation to the spirited girl I had seen
two months before. I advised her parents to be on hand at the
close of the workshop at all costs. That seemed to me like the
the only time they would have the chance to persuade Ann to
leave Barrytown.

H. B. Bullard RD-6 Guilford, Ct. 06437

TO WHOM IT MAY CONCERN:

I, Janis Feiden, was a member of the Unification Church cult for 13 months.

When I completed my 120-day training session at Barrytown, New York, I was given a manual which included the lectures that Mr. Ken Sudo, the head of Barrytown, had given in this 120-day session. I, as well as each graduate of that session, was told to guard that manual with my life, not to show it to even another Unification Church member. We were strongly cautioned that the press and the police would not understand it.

When I was rescued from this cult, I was home a week before my parents brought in a deprogrammer. In this period I kept this manual in a locked suitcase and had told my parents that the suit-case contained winter clothing. I lived in fear that someone might see this and was trying to decide on a safe place to hide it.

When I was deprogrammed and could see that I had been deceived by this so-called "Church", I brought out this manual for my de-programmer and my parents to see.

Since then I have had many nightmares in which the cult was trying to kill me for having brought this manual out of the cult and having shown it to others.

My parents in a recent trip to Washington, D.C. gave a copy of this manual to the Justice Department, in the hope that it will encourage them to investigate this cult. I believe this manual to be an excellent example of the "brainwashing" or "mind-control" techniques used by this Unification Church cult.

I have never known such terror as I did the moment I came to the realization that I could not control my own mind, that I had been given a new pattern of thinking.

Janis Feiden
Janis Feiden

To Whom it May Concern:

From April of 1973 until October of 1975 I was a member
of the Unification Church, an organization established by
Sun Myung Moon of Korea in 1954. For over two years I
helped in fund-raising, recruiting, and teaching activities
for this organization, as well as in public relations projects
setting up large, expensive banquets honoring Moon and gaining support for him from prominent citizens throughout the
United States.

In August of 1975 I was sent to Washington, D.C., at
Moon's personal request to do public relations work on
Capitol Hill for him and for South Korea. The Washington
P.R. Center has approximately 20-25 young men and women
working full-time in this capacity. I, like all the others,
was assigned a list of Senators and Congressmen which were
to be my own contacts exclusively (a copy of this list is
in the possession of Daphne Greene). P. R. members were to
make gradual acquaintances and friendships with staff members
and aides and eventually the Congressmen and Senators themselves, inviting them to a suite in the Washington Hilton
rented at $54/day (although the normal rate should have been
around $120/day), where dinner and films or short lectures
on Moon's ideas and "accomplishments" would be presented.
All this effort is sort of an on-going program by Moon to
get political support for himself and the Park Chung Hee
dictatorship in South Korea. Moon uses the guise of
"Christian anti-communism", but his tactics are not at all
ethical and his teachings are merely Marxist-Maoist platitudes
veiled in different terminology.

Moon is using 1st Amendment protection for freedom of
religon to cover his political activities. We (the P.R.
members) were told to be "somewhat" vague when dealing with
Capitol Hill contacts in order to protect our presence there,
but we were to try to influence our contacts to support
Moon and South Korea. Since I have been out of the Unification Church, I have read a State Department communique about
the U.S.'s need to continue protection for South Korea and
thereby for Japan - in nearly the same exact wording we were
told to use to influence our contacts on this issue.

The July 1974 Prayer and Fast for the Watergate Crisis
was engineered solely for political publicity for Moon.
Members' contacts with Senators and Congressmen at that time
were carefully recorded and followed up by the P.R. team.

P 2 ⌀ 3 PP

This is only one example of Moon's ploys to gain political advantage in this country.

I do hereby attest that the foregoing is my own statement and opinion.

s/ Ann Gordon

from the Bay Area of California

March 9, 1976

Addendum

P. R. Members now working in Washington, D.C.

Mitziko Matsuda)
Yoshiko   )   Japanese women-leaders of P.R. Center

Nina Zedehov Bergman - married Dr. Wm. Bergman 2/75
Susan Bergman - sisters of Dr. Wm. Bergman
Pam Lee
Bernice Rechlis Cowan - married James Cowan 2/75
Lorna Skaaren
Olga Silva
Betsy O'Brien (her sister Mary O'Brien Cordill - married
              to Perry Cordill - 2/75 - he is in U.S.,
              Mary is in Ghana)
Tolise Mize
Lori Anteloch
Chio (Japanese girl)
Christina Ziegler
Marilyn Cohen (husband Barry Cohen is in Africa somewhere)
Jim Gavin
Bob Sullivan
Rosemary Deddens (married Steve Deddens 2/75)

Susan Bergman is assigned to Carl Albert. When he toured Europe in summer 1975, she sent postcards ahead to each hotel on his itinerary, which she had gotten from his secretary. When Albert returned, he called her long distance to Barrytown, New York, to ask "Where is my friend, Susan?"

Bob Sullivan is assigned to Hubert Humphrey, I believe.

In December of 1973, during a national Unification
Church conference in Chicago, Col. Pak (Moon's interpreter)
received a call from Pres. Nixon's secretary at the White
House. The gist of the conversation was that if "Rev."
Moon's people would appear en masse at the White House
the night of the Christmas tree lighting, the (former)
Pres. Nixon would appear himself at the public ceremony,
despite low public opinion of him at that time. So the
national Un. Ch. leaders were instructed to return to their
states, pack up their members, and all to to Washington within
three-four days' time, which they did. In all, about 1500
members were present at the ceremony to cheer the beleaguered
President.

The following month "Rev." Moon was invited to
the annual Prayer Breakfast with other religious leaders
like Billy Graham, and to a 30-minute private session with
Nixon himself. Both invitations were engineered in the main
by Dr. Joseph Kennedy, a psychologist from North Carolina
who met & became involved with Moon's group at Moon's Atlanta
Day of Hope program in November 1973.

This is my sworn statement.

/s/ Ann Gordon
March 11, 1976

To the honorable Senators and Congressmen and whomever else it may concern:

I was a member of Rev. Moon's movement--called the Unification Center at 6502 Dana St., Oakland, California, and New Ideal City Ranch, Booneville, California--from August 7, 1975, to January 16, 1976. I was one of the countless number of people who experienced the Booneville Plague, constant diarrhea probably due to the poor plumbing which always seemed to be in need of repair. In any event, I soon found that almost all disease and injury is considered as "spiritual problems". Unity is constantly stressed as the only way to feel "heavenly Father's heart," Father being Moon himself and not God as the initial training indicated. I heard dozens of members pledge to do anything - including die for Moon. A similar loyalty was expressed for Onni and Dr. Moses Durst who are considered to be the True Parents of the United States by Jeremiah Schnee, Michelle Tunis and the rest of the leaders and followers in the Bay Area houses.. "Unity" was supposed to be accomplished by following "the higher standard of love" that my "center person" or leader had. "Don't worry about externals" was the common response to my request for warmer clothing and repair of broken glasses that were giving me headaches. There were no doctors at either Booneville or Oakland, so when I felt really ill, I ignored their suggestion of extra rest and went to a doctor who treated me for pneumonia.

I finally left the cult, unable to accept their assertion that Jews have been paying indemnity throughout history--the slaughter in Nazi Germany is often cited--for not following the will of God. Members are told the best thing they can do for their parents is to stay at the center. When my mother was about to have an operation, I asked to see her and was denied that request. I was told my parents would have to pay a terrible indemnity in the spirit world.(heaven) if they ever influenced me to leave the movement.

Looking back, I can see it was the poor health and intense pace and isolation at the Booneville training center that makes people believers of Divine Principle, because it doesn't stand up to any logical religious or ideological scrutiny. I hope that, at the very least, an effort can be made that would allow cult members to see what's really going on in the world, not with another member, but for themselves, and then decide what is right.

Respectfully yours,

David L. Needle

614 West Eleventh Street MV-P-1
Willmar, Minnesota 56201
February 14, 1976

Dear Sirs: MV-P-A-1

I was a member of the Unification Church, founded by Sun Myung
Moon, from 2-16-75 to 11-22-75. Before I joined, I was lied to—told
many times that I would be helping people throughout the world, and
especially in the United States. I was told the Unification Church
was feeding starving people, growing things in fields in New York. I
was told that people were being taught practical applications of Jesus'
teachings. (This last could, in part, be true, but only of those
members who joined as full-time members). At the introductory week-end,
at a retreat several hundred miles away, intense psychological pressure
was applied to me; I was surrounded by only Moonies, only Moonie literature (mental and physical isolation, the first step in any brainwashing situation), and told over and over that God had chosen me, that
I had to do a lot to save the world and make my way back to God, and
that I had to make up my mind immediately, or else Satan would probably
claim me. I was told to stay at the retreat center, not to dare to go
back to school and work. In the face of lots of objections, I went back
to work (at a hospital) for a week, to quit, and also to drop out of
school.

I moved to the South Dakota center. For several months I was the
bookkeeper. The group made much more money fund-raising than we put
down on our monthly statements (official documents—they had to balance
out in case the IRS looked at them). It was unofficial policy in the
Unification Church to report as little money made as looked reasonable.
I only wrote down as few bills paid as necessary (rent, utilities), and
then wrote down as much money made in fund-raising to cover the amount
of money going out.

After 6 months there, I was sent to a national fund-raising team
(MFT). I travelled throughout several states, for about 3 months. I
slept less than 4 hours a night. We were also told to give all our
energy for God. For those two reasons, I was always tired. I was never
alone, uniting together was the only way to get to God, so I was made
to feel guilty if I ever wanted to be alone to think.

I knew that my mother was working against the Movement, and I
didn't want her to damage herself spiritually by working against the
Messiah, so I went home for a 3 day visit, to convince her that I wasn't
brainwashed. Going home is something that all Moonies should sacrifice;
a Moonie is told that his/her parents will be very glad sometime in the
future (maybe even after they die) that their child was working for the
Messiah, so the present didn't matter.

I was very definitely brain-washed; Pavlovian techniques were
clothed in religious terminology and concepts: isolation, lack of sleep,
tiredness, hunger, tension, all put on the convert for religious reasons.
There were other things done for religious reasons: we had to learn to
follow orders blindly, and not to use one's own thoughts and judgement,
because the Divine Principle was above any human being's judgement. My
parents had me deprogrammed, where I proved to myself that my mind
had been played with, and very subtly lied to.

I really am very grateful to my parents for rescuing me, and I a-
gree with Judge McGovern (California) who said that parents can do no less
than rescue their children from these mind-manipulating cults, if they
really love them.

Thank-you.

Janice Ruchie

MP-P-A!

To Whom It May Concern:

Our daughter, Janis, was a member of the Unification Church cult for thirteen months. We rescued her from this cult in August, 1975.

In January, 1976, a Mrs. Gardiner who is a collector for the Southwestern Bell Telephone Company in Houston, Texas, called our home trying to locate our daughter, Janis. We inquired as to what her purpose was. She then informed us that Janis had an overdue telephone account in Houston. We assured her there must be a mistake as Janis had never lived in Houston. Mrs. Gardiner said the Unification Church had opened an account in Janis' name; so she contacted the Yonkers, N. Y. office and a Kevin McCarthy gave her Janis' home phone number. Since Janis was totally unaware that such an account had been opened and had never given anyone permission to charge calls to her, Mrs. Gardiner has since written a letter exonerating her from this liability. Mrs. Gardiner did inform us that this was the way the Unification seems to operate--they open telephone accounts in the name of members with telephone accounts in good standing. This was not the first such experience the telephone company had had with the Unification Church.

We requested that the telephone company write us a letter stating this but, because of having nothing written, no signatures, they would not as they did not want to become liable for a suit from the Unification Church. Their records would be open for investigation only under order of a subpoena--should any government agency decide to look into such matters.

We feel that this constitutes a conspiracy to commit fraud or theft and that it also constitutes slander or defamation of character against our daughter.

Jean M. Feiden

Richard S. Feiden, Lt. Col. (Ret.)

I would like to ask the Congressmen and senators of the
United States to try to experience in their imagination what some of
us have unfortunately had to experience in real life:

To imagine what it would be like to have their son or daughter
take a trip across the country after graduating college, planning to
return home at the end of a stated time, to resume the life and career
for which they had been preparing... and then to receive a phone call
from an unspecified place three thousand miles away, from someone who
sounds only vaguely like the son (or daughter) they knew so well only
a few months before, but whose voice is the voice of a ventriloquist's
dummy, who speaks to them only in the stilted phrases of a religious
pamphlet, who seems to have no recollection of the twenty-odd years of
mutual caring and struggling and tears and laughter that makes a
family... and who cannot answer the simplest question without consult-
ing some unknown person standing beside him:

> Parent: "-But when are you planning to come home?"
> (A PAUSE. SOUND OF A STRANGE VOICE MURMURING.)
> Son: "I'm not sure. When I'm ready and strong enough."
> Parent: "Strong enough for what? What do you mean?"
> (A PAUSE. MORE MURMURING FROM THE STRANGE VOICE)
> Son: "I'll write to you".
> Parent: "Why can't you answer my question? Why can't you talk
>   to me? Who's standing there telling you what to say?"
> SON: "I can't tell you."

Would this frighten you, Mr. Congressman, Mr. Senator? Would
the idea that your child was not being allowed to communicate with
you except in the words of a leader of a fanatic religious sect, send
chills down your spine?

This - and worse - happened to us, until our son realized that
his mind was slowly being poisoned against his parents, his sister,
his friends, and in fact against all the human world which did not
pay homage to 'Reverend' Sun Myung Moon. As he and hundreds like him
will tell you, he was being given massive injections of FEAR AND
HATRED of the non-Moon world.

22 Abington Ave., Ardsley, N.Y.   Herbert & Lucille Engel

Center City, Minnesota 55012
February 6, 1976

MP-P-AI

To Whom it May Concern,

Two years ago our son informed us that he was leaving his childhood faith and joining a new church, namely the Unification Church. Since that time he has become more and more deeply involved in this religious cult.

He is a graduate of the University of Minnesota Institute of Technology with a degree in Mechanical Engineering. He has had several opportunities for employment in his field, but has turned them all down to work with the C.A.R.P. organization on the University Campus.

We know that he and the people living with him support themselves by asking for donations and selling a variety of products on the street. They do not identify themselves as Unification Church members and therefore we believe they are gathering funds under false pretense. They pay no income tax and pay no sales tax and yet they sell hundreds of dollars worth of merchandise each month.

We know that they are using food stamps to help buy their groceries, and when our son was ill and needed medical attention he went to General Hospital in Minneapolis and the city paid the bill. This is going on all over the United States and is a gigantic rip-off of the American public.

The political aims of the Unification Church are frightening. Rev. Moon has stated that if they cannot make Unification Church members of the present legislators, he will make legislators of the Unification Church members. He wants control and power and has said that some day his word will be law. He has the intelligent, well-educated followers he needs to train to do the job.

Most of the Unification Church members are between the ages of 19 and 30. They are not allowed dating or freedom to marry, and all normal sexual desire must be removed. Even when marriages take place as arranged by Rev. Moon, couples are often kept apart. This is not normal and is a form of sex perversion as much as free sex which is allowed in some cults.

We strongly urge an investigation into all Unification Church activities -- their mind control techniques, fund raising, occult practises, and subversive political ideology. If allowed to go unchecked they could destroy our country and our freedom.

Sincerely,

Mr. and Mrs. Louis Anderson

11

To   New York Senators and Congressmen
      New Hampshire Senators and Congressmen   MP- P- A!

Our family experience has taught us that the Holy Spirit Association for the Unification of World Christianity (Unification "Church") is not a spiritual, supportive religion but an Association seeking political/economic/social and, ultimately, military power through deceit and ruthlessness.

Our daughter, Winnie, was recruited through the deceit of Mary Bizot, pre-medical drop-out from Boston University: "This is not the Unification Church", "We are going to have a rap session on how to improve the world (through ecological means)." Later, when Winnie was a victim/member, she was taught to use deceit, "heavenly deception", in her dealings with the public. As the one keeping the Boston Center books, she observed deceit used by her Center leader, Anthony Guerra, and the Regional leader, Mike Smith, toward other Moonies. She was aware of deceit through impossible fund-raising goals and through non-payment of bills: parking tickets ("throw them all in the waste basket"), telephone bills, medical bills, rent, etc. It is logical and inevitable that when "heavenly deception" is practiced toward outsiders "for the success of the Unification Church" there will also develop "heavenly deception" between various levels within the movement "for the success of the Unification Church". Thus, the entire power structure becomes corrupt, untrustworthy, deceitful.

We observed the basic ruthlessness of this Association when twice the leaders "encouraged" Winnie to break dental appointments we had made for her following a serious root canal, and twice to break appointments with the ophthalmologist we had made because she complained of some sight impairment. Although she asked her leaders several times to keep these appointments she was asked (told), "What is more important - to keep a medical appointment or to learn more about God in the lectures?" After the third denial she came to the conclusion "of her own accord" that it was more important "to learn more about God." Result? February 1, 1975 she underwent an emergency operation for a "massive tear of the retina". Today, one year later, her sight is very much limited in that eye. The explanation given by the Association? "One of your ancestors was a peeping Tom."

This same ruthlessness has been experienced by victim/members suffering from severe bronchitis, pain in the legs, diabetes, severe headaches, and other physical ailments. "You do not need medical attention. You are merely paying indemnities for yourself, your family, your ancestors".

This ruthlessness was expressed toward our daughter, and the other victim/members, in the overall schedule and procedures: 5 hours sleep per night, 78¢ worth of food daily, high starch/low protein diet, 12-16 hours begging on the streets with goals of $125-250 per person per day, lectures of 2½-3 hours without breaks, sanitary facilities that were so inadequate as to fail building codes and make impossible proper personal cleanliness (many Moonies develop a personal odor), the snarling meanness of Moon when crossed, improper clothing on cold days and nights, the embarrassment felt by young women when they were forced to "blitz bars" at night time and use their "fallen nature" to solicit gifts from drunks, the excessive male chauvinism that relegated women to "dirt beneath the feet of the men", the whole philosophy and methodology that destroyed personal worthfulness to create peons for Master Moon.

This Association should be investigated by several agencies of the government - perhaps, by Congress itself - and exposed as the non-religious, personality-destroying danger to America it is.

                   George and Winifred Swope

MV - P - A

To the Honorable Senators and Congressmen and to whomever it may concern:

I am a former member of the Unification Church and wish to inform you of this destructive militaristic and political movement (under the guise of religion) that practices deception, brainwashing and mind control. This is a strong statement, but here are a few facts of my own experience and the words of Sun Myung Moon himself.

I was told at first contact with this organization that it was not the Unification Church. In fact, it was. I was told by the leaders to decieve and lie to new members (especially concerning Moon as the Messiah), my family and friends, and to the public. I was told to deny any connection with Moon or the Unification Church and to use any means of deceit necessary to obtain either people or money.

The Unification Church under its front names N.E.D. and C.C.P. (presently E.A.T.) told me that I must be willing to fight for South Korea against North Korea. By this time I felt impelled to accept this condition. Moon talks of war, fighting, and victory in his talks to his followers in what is called Master speaks:

I have a master strategy to win America, and they [the leaders] did not know or truly understand my entire strategy. Therefore, when I as commander and chief landed in America, there should have been troops to join and engage in the greatest battle ever. But that order was not there. So, in the entire year of 1972, instead of engaging in the outward battle, I had to re-establish our own ranks myself.[1]

On the U.S. government, Moon speaks:

If the U.S. continues its corruption, and we find among the senators and congressmen no one really usable for our purposes, we can make senators and congressmen out of our members.... I have met many famous-so-called "famous"-senators and congressmen, but to my eyes they are just nothing; they are weak and helpless before God. They are scared to think it might be possible that they will not be re-elected.[2]

Moon instructs his followers (on the same page):

This is our dream, our project- but shut your mouth tight, have hope and go on to realize it. As it now stands, forget about those things, and try hard to lay the foundation for those things.

Also on that page:

But I am not going to send you into the political field right away-but later on when we are prepared.

With a degree in psychology, I was able to see some of the manipulation used during the process of brainwashing and use of mind control. But that did not stop me from losing more and more of my thinking and decision-making ability as I became more and more involved. Also, as time progressed, I recieved a low-protein diet with decreasing amounts of food, decreasing sleep time to four to five hours a night, and less and less time for myself. There were also many hours of repetitious lectures that never ceased.

Brainwashing is a science developed from Pavlov's work and used most successfully by the Communists on American POW's in Korea. In his own words, Moon discloses the method:

In order for you to be a dynamic lecturer, you must know the knack of holding and possessing the listeners hearts. If there appears a crack in the man's personality, you wedge in a chisel, and split the person apart.[3]

Let me add that most of the members are not to be blamed. They are good people but they have lost their free will and are psychological slaves.

1-Fourth Director's Conference- 7/1/73, p.5
2-Third Director's Conference- 5/7/73, p.12
3-Ibid., p.11

Sincerely submitted,

Paul Engel
Westchester County, n.y. Paul Engel

To whom it may concern:

As a high school and junior college guidance counselor who has served on state advisory committees and helped write legislation to aid young people, I believe in the responsibility of parents to provide their youngsters with good, strong values along with the ability and confidence to make independent decisions.

My story?...They're all alike. The victim is approached, then invited to a house where he meets bright young people who talk his language, (philosophy, literature, etc.). The victim is never left alone, given a low protein diet, kept constantly busy, is involved in chanting, singing and allowed very little sleep.

The ultimate goal is to develop willing slaves who are told their sole purpose is to make a better world, and with these seeds of reason, a dehumanizing process evolves.

The victim gives up all feelings of self worth. He sustains enormous physical exhaustion, personal sacrifice of family and private possessions, and relinquishes his right to free choice. Free choice and the normal process of decision making is replaced with a total obedience to the Messiah, without questioning. (In our case we asked our Moonie son which restaurant he would like to go to for Thanksgiving dinner, to which he replied, "Why don't you give me graham crackers and donate my share of the bill to Unification?").

Self sacrifice and charity are wonderful and rewarding. Working for mankind's betterment is noble, however none of the sacrifices of these young people has made any changes for the betterment of anyone, save Sun Myung Moon. A person who must pay indemnity or flagellate himself for kissing a girl or buying a candy bar, (using 15¢ of the money he earned), has given up the very subtle quality that separates human from beast or slave from free man.

If my dog doesn't want to go out in the rain, he stands his ground. A Moonie cannot make this choice. He responds as programmed by his leader. ONE SINGLE FORCE CONTROLS ALL THIS HUMANITY AT ALL TIMES!!!!

In the 50's, as computers came to the forefront, many envisioned a perfect robot, a steel, computerized mechanism with man's dexterity, who would be programmed to do all menial tasks, scrub floors, etc., without question. A simpler machine was invented which surpassed all the expectations of even the worthiest scientist. It involves taking a human with all these capabilities (and more), and manipulating his mind to achieve a selfless, mindless robot.

Obedience and discipline are encompassed in many phases of life, religion and otherwise; but they are not so all-encompassing so as to lower the quality of human life below the minimal standards which allow for questioning and reason.

Pinocchio's Candyland has become a realization, except the enticement is aided with a subtle, continuous force from which one cannot extricate himself without outside assistance. Nobody can give up willingly, a force that is all consuming, that answers all questions and fills all voids, because at that point the individual gives up his very being.

DEPROGRAMMING is a misnomer. The terminology which more aptly describes what must be done to give a Moonie back his mind is REHUMANIZING. A life of servitude should only be selected with a CLEAR FREE MIND, TOTAL KNOWLEDGE, (which means total disclosure), and with no coercion from any quarter.

Respectfully submitted by a grateful mother of an X Victim who shares the heartache of the families of other victims.

(mother of Reid Heller)
10517 Barrywood Drive
Dallas, Texas 75230

MV-P-A

To Whom it May Concern:

I have been asked to submit a statement about my involvement with the Unification Church.

While on vacation, I met some Unification members who talked about universal love and had a plan to effect a positive change in the world. I attended a 3-day workshop, at their invitation, in a converted sorority house in Boulder, Colo, and never left. I was told that after this weekend, I would never be the same. This was true. During the weekend, which could be compared to a "sorority rush," I was coerced into staying through fear and guilt. I joined "the family" after attending a seven-day training session in Noble, Okla. During that time I was never left alone and the days were filled with constant singing, praying, working, and hearing lectures.

After I returned to the Boulder center, I had a schedule of fund-raising on street corners, businesses (I was thrown out of several office buildings and establishments for breaking solicitation laws) for 14 to 16 hours a day. There was constant singing and praying and I was very fatigued all of the time. I frequently took cold showers which were supposed to drive out evil spirits and I sprinkled holy salt on my food and bed to ward off evil spirits. After three weeks in the movement, I did not know what day it was to the next and my only concern was overcoming Satan. Satan had become anything that disagreed with my belief or anyone who tried to take me out of the movement. On two occasions, I was forbidden to be with my brother and boy friend because I was not "spiritually prepared" to go out into the old world. I was told that Satan works through family and friends to pull me away from God.

I never had time to write my family or phone them. I had a planters' wart on the bottom of my foot; and instead of being given proper treatment, I was told to go to the emergency room of the hospital and have it cut out. If my parents had not remembered that I had this problem and sent me the money to have it taken care of, I could have developed a serious infection.

I said at the time that I was happy and doing God's work, but after being deprogrammed, I realized that Moon was just another fake prophet and I learned about some of the activities that I would have to participate in at a future time and they did not sound like commands from God.

I now have a natural love relationship and am able to make my own decisions and pursue my education. Before, I would have been married off to a man I didn't even know in a mass wedding ceremony and would have remained in a brainwashed state, severly limiting my ability to readjust to a normal life.

In a period of seven weeks of living in constant battle between God and Satan, not making any decisions and emotionally divorcing myself from all that I loved, I became a robot - completely devoid of spontaneity. In just this short period of time I was left disoriented and disorganized.

After being out of the cult five months, I can finally think for myself and can look at the movement - its activities and its beliefs - in an objective way.

                                        Cynthia Slaughter

2906 El Camino
Temple, Texas 76501

15

February 14, 1976

Dear Mr. Slaughter,   MP-P-A

In late July, 1975, our daughter, Sandra Lou Dysart, was
invited to a retreat of the "Unification Center" family on the
campus of the University of Texas where she was attending summer
school. She called us long distance to inform us and I went
to this Center in Austin and was given information about an
organization called C.A.R.P.(Collegiate Association for the
Research of Principles). I could not determine any harmful
influence but still I was uneasy. She returned vey early(6 A.M)
Monday and I was frantic calling her apartment and the Center.
She assured me she was all right but they had gotten a late
start home Sunday evening. The next weekend she called us to tell
us whe was quitting school to join the Unification Church and live
in the family. All plans for career and school were to be abandoned.
We went to meet her in Oklahoma where she was on a farm in Noble, Ok.
and spent the weekend listening to lectures and although we were
allowed about 30 minutes with her alone we were not allowed to take
with us to Austin to close her apartment. We did get her to return
home long enough to return her car to us but she was accompanied
by 2 women at all times. The next day she was flown to New York to
Barrytown training center and for the next 3 months she was in and
around New York handing out pamplets, selling candy and taking the
21-day and 40-day training. She continued to call us each week as
had a telephone credit card but she gave the Unification Church all
of her remaining money in her checking account. Her letters and
phone calls became increasingly disturbed and even when I, her mother,
had a mental breakdown and was confined to the hospital she would not
or was not allowed to return home. She was allowed to return home
finally in Oct. following completion of the 40-day training and we
were able to keep her long enough and convince her, with the help
of Ted Patrick's workers, that she had been misled and duped and she
finally broke with the "family". She had not been given proper attention to medical problems while she was away - she had not worn her
contacts, she had not had any menstrual periods, she had developed a
yeast infection, and because of improper diet she had gained much
weight and she lost the feeling in her toes from standing 24 or 36
hours preaching and selling candy on the street for the church.
While she was gone many of her possessions were stored with the
"family" in Austin and some of these things were taken and used by
other members and were never returned to us. She did not give these
things to them. She thought she was to return to the University of
Texas to go to school and live with the "family" at the Austin center.
After the break with "Rev. Moon family cult" she informed them,
and we, her parents, also informed them that she did not wish to see
any of them again. We had a legal paper drawn up to this end. In
spite of this attempts were made by mail and by phone to contact her.
Members came to our home asking for her and they have also tried to
contact her at her apartment in Waco where she is now attending a
commercial college. She, and we informed the Waco police of these
disturbances and she has signed a complaint with the police about
this. Since this, about 2 weeks ago now, she has been left alone.
Sandra is happy now, is like her old self, and we hope she
continues this way.

Sincerely,

Dr. and Mrs. Donald N. Dysart

91

1311 Gamma
Carlsbad, New Mexico 88220
9 February 76

George M. Slaughter, III   MP-P-A
Citizens Freedom Foundation
Arlington, Texas

Dear Mr. Slaughter,
We are eager to supply the following "case history" of our son's involvement with the
"Unification Church" in the heartfelt hope that it may be of service in exposing the
activities of the organization and its leader, Sun Myung Moon.

Our son, Chris D. Elkins, was psychologically kidnapped and brainwashed by representatives of this sect in June, 1973, while he was a senior at the University of Arizona
in Tucson. He subsequently dropped out of school, and has abruptly left a half-dozen
jobs, at the beck and call of Mr. Moon's group. His physical health deteriorated at
an alarming rate, but the most dramatic change was in his personality. He underwent
a radical change, from an honest, responsible, Christian young man, to one that lied,
cheated, stole, ignored financial obligations, and avoided all responsibility in general. He explained his lack of moral fiber by saying that traditional religion had
failed, Christ was one of God's "mistakes", and that Moon was the answer to all the
world's ills, both political and religious.

Using misrepresentation and false information, this organization hoodwinked Chris
into believing that its aims were charitable services to other youths. None of these
"charities" materialized, however. They use the same tactics to solicit donations
from a gullible and generous American public. Masquerading as a religion, they collect
millions of dollars in donations each year, while calling themselves a "non-profit"
organization and mailing their literature postage-free. This is an insult to all
intelligent citizens and a shocking misuse of the franking privilege.

Chris worked at various positions in the "church" for about two years. He was manager of the Ginseng Teahouse in Washington, D.C., editor of the "Rising Tide" and
similar organs of the sect, and tour coordinator for the One World Crusade Choir,
an offspring of the "church". At no time did he or any other follower/worker receive
wages or remuneration. My husband and I think it would be most enlightening to
discover where the millions of dollars in donations are going. Another aspect of
the group's activities needing investigation is its frightening rate of accumulating
property, presumably under the guise of "non-profit" acquisitions that would be un-
taxed.

Our son is attempting to break away from the organization, as he has twice in the past.
But, as always before, harrassing phone calls, emotional pressure, and suggestive
"guilt" persuasion will begin. There is apparently some hidden motivator...we believe
it to be post-hypnotic suggestion...that eventually wears down his resistance. Then
he will sneak away without warning, secretly removing his clothing and other belongings from the house, and we will go through the agony of not knowing where he is,
whether he is alive or dead, and when or if he will ever contact us again. We realize
that we are not the only parents who have suffered thus. But we earnestly request
the exposure of this cult and an investigation of its procedures. My husband and I
would gladly attend personally this meeting, but since we cannot obtain leave-time
on such short notice, we implore all interested people to intervene on our behalf.
Many thousands of families will be forever in your debt for this service.

Sincerely,

Mrs. Merle G. Elkins

Merle G. Elkins

92

17

LLOYD W. WESTERLAGE
ATTORNEY AT LAW
511 NO. AKARD
SUITE 1105
DALLAS, TEXAS 75201

February 16, 1976

To National Committee
Day of Affirmation and Protest   MP-P-A

Re: Unification Cult

The following is a brief summary of the experiences of my daughter, SHERILL ANNE WESTERLAGE , as a prisoner of the Unification Cult.

Sherril Anne is a graduate in music of the University of Indiana. Her studies included one year of studies in Vienna.

During the summer of 1973 after finishing undergraduate work at Indiana She was working temporarily in Dallas to earn money for additional studies in Europe One day she was invited by a young man from Austria to attend some lectures being given at the First Baptist Church in Dallas by a new religious organization' dedicated to the ideals of world peace. She attended several lectures during her lunch hour for a week and then was invited to a week-end retreat. When she told her Mother and I of this we were disturbed and we decided to find out all we could about the organization . I personally called upon a member of the Staff of First Baptist Church to question him about the organization. He assured me that the staff had investigated the organization and they were convinced it was a Christian movement and espoused a traditional Christian doctrine. Upon hearing this we agreed to permit our daughter to attend the retreat. When she returned from the retreat on Sunday evening she announced that she had become a member of the Unification Church, was going to quit her job, attend a training center in Austin, Texas for three weeks and then work for the Church full time. This was the first time we had heard the name of the organization . We attempted by various means to persuade her not to do this but were unsuccessful.

When she returned from Austin she worked in an office in Dallas for several months assisting in the promotion of a three day speaking engagement of Sun Myung Moon. Moon did come to Dallas for three days but no one attended his speaking engagements except for those who were already members of his cult.

After Moon left my daughter spent several weeks on fund raising campaigns and then left for a period of approximately ten months and worked throughout the United States on a promotion team headed by Ken Sude. She returned home in December, 1974 and told us she was leaving the Cult. However in January, she received a telephone call from Sude and immediately left for Barrytown where she was employed as a pianist for the Cult.

In August of 1975 we heard of Ted Patrick and his work, met and talked with him and decided to have him de-program our daughter. We succeeded in getting her home in September, 1975 and had her de-programmed by Ted Patrick. THERE WAS NO DOUBT AFTER THIS EXPERIENCE THAT SHE HAD BEEN BRAINWASHED. We did believe and had very good reason to believe that the de-programming was successful. However, about ten weeks after the deprogramming the first time that she was allowed to leave home to go out of town she rejoined the Cult and is still with them . She has now been gone for three months, and she has written two brief letters to her Mother and I.

Lloyd W. Westerlage

93

18

From: Mr and Mrs George G. White
3604 Country Club Cir.
Fort Worth, Texas, 76109

To: National Committee,
Day of Affirmation and Protest,
Washington, D. C.

MP-P-A

Subject: Our personal experience with the Unification Church.

Our son, Richard, was in the Unification cult for sixteen months. He was completely alienated from his family and friends, including brothers, sister-in-laws. On the few occasions he came home he was restless, withdrawn and uncommunicative; whereas in the past he had been very loquacious.

His older brother was the first to notice and commented on the glassy-eye stare and the smile with the mouth only.

He compaired himself to the twelve apostles, especially, St. Paul, when we would comment on his rigorous way of life. He lost allinterest in girls and finally gave away all his possions, including his car and other expensive articles, keeping only bare necessities.

When asked about his Naval Reserve drills, he said,"Mr. Sudo has taken care of it. He got me excused from drills because of my religious mission." when we picked him up at the International Airport, Houston, Texas, almost the first thing first thing he did was to hand his dad a packet of letters from the U. S. Naval Department. There were several letters dated June 4 thru Oct 4, 1975. All this in a Certified Letter, dated Oct 4, 1975. Richard stated that this Certified Letter was the only letter he got. Apparently the others were sidetracked. He was behind 17 drills and a two week cruise. The Navy was looking for him. His father was able to get the Navy to hold off until we could get his head screwed on. He is now in good standing with the Navy.

My husband and I visited the center in Austin within the week he dropped out of school. The Director promised us that he would see that Richard finished school and regularly attend the church he was brought up in. All lies, he had no intention of doing this.

Richard was "deprogramed" the week of Oct 6-10, 1975 by Ted Patrick. He has come a long way since, however, he will not discuss the cult of his feelings about real religion. He knows he is through with the cult though.

Richard was three days into his Senior semester as a Pre-Med student, University of Texas, Austin. He had a 3.989 gradepoint average. The cult got him almost on the spot. At this time he has no ambition, no aims. This is the young man who was to be an MD and the PRESIDENT OF THE UNITED STATES by the age of fourty.

Signed: Mr. G. G. White
G. G. White

Copies to: Senators John G. Tower
Lloyd Bentsen
Representatives Olin E. Teague
Jim Wright
Barbara Jo

94

(19

March 1, 1976

To Whom It May Concern: MV-P-A

I am an ex-cult member. From July 22 to November 1, 1975, I was employed to win money and converts for the Unification Church through successful indoctrination into the mechanics of 'ripping off society.' Training for street peddling includes a "never turn back" policy which states that a cultist must not regard warning signs prohibiting entry, even when enforced by law.

In Tarrytown, N. Y., I was informed that illegal aliens were to peddle Unification 'articles" in the N.Y.C. area exclusively since the city's overworked customs agents would be unlikely to discover their whereabouts there. These illegal aliens are Japanese, Austrian, German, Korean, French, Mexican and are all encouraged by Top Leaders to continue their activities under 'God's auspices'; I have observed that centers are always able to anticipate the arrival of Immigration officers by 20 minutes or more. The same period of warning holds true for the Board of Health.

All reported events I have observed and will swear to.

Signed

Reed Heller
10517 Barrywood
Dallas, Texas 75230

February 16, 1976

MP-P-A

To Whom it May Concern:

In mid-November, 1975, my husband and I were dumbfounded to receive a lett er from our son, Douglas, who was then in Munich, Germany, revealing that he had re-nounced his D. A. A. D. scholarship for graduate study (in journalism) at the University of Munich and had become a full-time missionary for Korean Sun Myung Moon's Unification Church; that he had, in fact, moved into their Center in Munich. We continued to hear from him about his work and various "spiritual experiences." In early December, when friends tried to contact him at the center, they were told that Doug had been transferred to Paris, France.

Doug wrote to us from Paris, announcing that he would be there about three months. However, shortly after Christmas, he wrote that he was being transferred to Japan on January 16. By then, we had checked-out Moon's movement and knew that we had to attempt a "rescue."

Our daughter, Lucy Jacobsen, and Cynthia Slaughter (a former member of the Moon movement) accompanied me to Paris in early January. We were there for two weeks and succeeded in getting Doug out of the cult. Through an organization of French parents, we were able to get the help of two French journalists and a Catholic Priest in the actual "rescue." De-programming took place in a Paris hotel room.

When we got Doug, he had no identification and has yet, so far as I know, to receive his passport and other papers from the center near Paris. We asked the leaders to send his passport and other items to the U. S. Embassy but they did not do so. They told my daughter, by telephone, that Doug's passport had been sent along to another town where the group going to Japan would be receiving "orientation." We were able to get some of his clothing and luggage from the center through our friend, Father Paul.

Only a few weeks after Doug joined the U. C., he reported that his billfold had been "lost" on a Church bus traveling from Munich to one of the weekend re-treats. He lost his American Express card, about $350 in cash and his press cards.

There is no way to describe the torment of the "rescue" operation. I do not believe that anyone can fully understand that these kids are "brainwashed" without a personal experience with a family member. The intense indoctrination convinces the converts that family and friends represent Satan if they talk against the "Church." I noticed many physiological changes - voice - posture - eyes - and felt that my son's thought patterns had changed. The wonderful sense of humor was gone. The Moonies do not use drugs, do not drink, smoke, or mix "romantically" with the opposite sex. Their purity is almost unreal.

Our son is still in France and we very much fear that he will rejoin the movement. Since we left, he has "floated" mentally into the thought patterns of the Moonies. We tried to undo in one week what they had spent three months doing!

Sincerely,

Helen G. Burton

Helen G. Burton

3-30-76
MV-P-A

As a former victim of the Unification Church I believe whole-heartedly that Moon's various organisations are exploiting and deceiving young people who sincerely desire to work for the betterment of mankind. Although Moon's organisations claim to believe in democracy, freedom, and christianity (This is what attracted me to the Unification Church) they in fact have nothing but contempt for these beliefs. They only use this as a cover and a way to get converts. Their ultimate goal is to make Moon an absolute dictator of the United States.

Believing the sincerity of Unification members when they talked about promoting a more peaceful and loving world, I was persuaded to join CARP, which is the Unification Church's organization at colleges. New members are given only a superficial exposure to the organization's beliefs. At the beginning, they are led to believe that it is a legitimate christian organization. It seems to be fun and games and smiling faces. It is only later, after members have given up everything they own, that they become informed of Moon's plans for a new order.

Not until I was sent to their training center at Barrytown in New York did I realize how evil and utterly insane the organization is. At Barrytown everyone was coerced to share with the other members all thoughts and concerns, there is absolutely no privacy. Members who showed even the slightest doubt about what was going on were harassed and derided by the other members until they learned to at least hide their feelings. If their skepticism continued members were told to fast from one to three days to receive the "truth". Managing to suppress your doubts and rational way of thought was called "having victory". This is just one example of the doublethought used by the organization. Also we were forced to attend lectures constantly, sometimes hearing the same thing over and over again. Since I and many others were hundreds of miles away from home and had no money, we were virtually prisoners.

In the lectures we were told that Jesus had failed his mission, that Moon was the messiah, that destruction here on earth and eternal damnation awaited those who refused to totally support Moon, and many other outrageous, heretical things. Mr. Mazumbar, one of the lecturers, told the 21 day seminar that all members must continually strive to lose their identity and become one with Moon's will. Members were supposed to surrender completely.

Fund raising was routine for members. Unless specifically asked we were told to tell avoid telling people that we were with Moon's Unification Church. It was alright to deceive people as long as it would help Moon. For example, my group of about eight people was told by the group leader, Jim Garland, to tell people that the money was to be used to help young people with serious drug problems. Though the Unification Church takes in millions of dollars to my knowledge not one drug center has been built by them. Apparently most of the money goes into Moon's pockets since he is a multi-millionaire. However, since most of the kids who fund raise are being coerced and lied to, they sincerely believe that the money is being used for a good purpose.

After a month of Barrytown's insanity, I was able to escape on my own. It was entirely my decision. After I became aware of the evil nature of Moon's organization I could not morally stay. I believe, though, that many of the young people who go to these seminars at Barrytown and other places are put under such heavy coercion and mind manipulation that they are unable to leave on their own free will. Most truly desire to help bring about a better world and they love this country, but their admirable ideals are being exploited by Moon and his henchmen for their own personal gain. It is the selfish leaders of the organization that are to blame, not the exploited young people, who have good intentions. These young people are being deceived, cheated, and victimized by Moon.

This is only a brief account of my experiences with the Unification Church. My advice to anyone considering joining the organisation would be to turn and run away as fast as their feet could carry them.

Sincerely yours,

Larry Marey

LARRY MAREY

Mr. & Mrs. Alvin J. Troyer   MP—P- A
3216 Kentucky Ave.So.
Mpls, Mn. 55426
929-5220

Son - Ronald J. Troyer
Born- 5/11/54

Our son joined the Unification Church in August 1973 at
Eugene, Oregon. Since then he has been home 2 times. He had
said Sun Moon wanted them to keep a good relationship with
their family. His last visit, July 1975 was anything but
enjoyable. He arrived at noon by plane from New York (for
a funeral) and wanted to leave in the evening, because he
was missing out on the last lecture concerning "selling this
$25.00 tea."

Fund raising in the bars in Philadelphia goes on until 3 and
4 in the morning. He was having trouble with his legs. The
doctor told him to stay off of them, so instead of staying
down, he took to driving the van, claiming he was following
the doctors orders. He is on the go constantly, with as little
as 5 hours of sleep a night. His dad visited him in Philadelphia, he was given a smelly sleeping bag and pillow - Ron slept
with his clothes on all night, ready to go the next day. The
house where he stayed had a kitchen table - no beds or chairs.
When he calls he talks so fast - he sounds like he is going on
nerves. I've told him to come home and we both would get
deprogrammed and find out who isn't thinking straight. He said,
"if it takes more than 3 days I can't spare the time."

At one time Ron said, Sun Moon would let everybody go home for
awhile, if the parents gave him to much trouble, to prove to
the parents they weren't doing anything wrong. When I think
back to all the things Ron said he would be doing (pottery
school, etc.) nothing has materialized - nothing but fund
raising.

Sure it is true, they don't smoke, drink or use drugs. There
are 30,000 young adults in the United States working long
hours, yet they don't need to file income tax - they work for
Sun Moon. No social security is building up for them - what
security is Sun Moon promising? If our government thinks the
welfare role is high now, what will it be like in years to
come?

Mrs. Mary Troyer
(Mrs.Mary Troyer

Our experience with Unification Church - Mr. & Mrs. Arthur Roselle
4581 Regina Dr. Utica,Mi. 48087

MP - P - A

Our son, Skip, now 27 years of age, joined Unification Church Dec.,1974
and was told not to tell anyone because they wouldn't understand. After
one week of his three week probation we found out and called him. He
said that he was in a school studing history, science and religion.

His director promised if he decided to stay they would house him, feed
him and assume his debts. We begged him not to become too involved right
away and to come home and discuss it but he would not. After two months
we could see the personality change and his dedication to follow Rev.
Moon to the ends of the earth if necessary.

Skip was always a loving, caring person, but suddenly he was very condemnng
with any family member when we showed concern about his personal will
being.

Our attempt to de-program him failed when Skip attacked the two deprogrammers and his brother-in-law and got away. The next day Skip filed
a complaint against his family for assault and battery and Unification
Church hired Ivan Barris (a well known Detroit lawyer) to represent him.
The family then found it necessary to hire a lawyer and after a meeting at
the Prosecuting Attorney's office they decided not to seek a warrent.
Later, after a radio series about our story and Unification Church, they
brought Skip back from Barrytown, where he had finished a 40 day training
and had hoped to start his 120 day braining, and he filed another complaint
against the entire family. Again the family was burdened with lawyer costs
and again the Prosecuting Attorney decided not to seek a warrent.

Skip's director, John Schuhart, will not meet with us to talk about
our son or hangs up the phone when we call to talk to Skip and leaves
orders not to except any messages from Skip's family, and not to call again.

POINTS OF INTEREST: Each time Skip visits the family and seems to show love
and concern the following day he calls very upset with us and highly
emotional and comdemning. U.C. didn't assume debts of Skips and bills
collectors call the family. Skip can not attend any family gatherings,
even funerals. Tells mother she will never see her son again if she does
anything against U.C.

To whom it may concern,   MV-P-A

My name is Carl Waranowski, age 23 years, reside in Ipswich, Mass. and was a member of Unification Church for four months. Previously I had graduated from an engineering school in Boston with an Associate degree and was travelling west. In Berkeley, Calif., I ran into two front organizations of the Unification; the New Education Development and the International Ideal City Project. I joined what I thought was a good thing. There was an article in the Oakland Tribune praising NED as a government funded, community action-plan experiment. The people in the group seemed very happy, hard working, and very moralistic. An attractive young girl Poppy told me that Dr. Durst was a special guest lecturer later I discovered he lectured virtually every day. No mention was made for a month of Sun Myung Moon and or Unification Church. I found out quite by accident.

During my stay with Unification Church I was fed an infrequent high starch, low protien diet consisting of peanut butter and jelly sandwiches, brown rice and powdered milk. During the initial month I contributed my life savings of $3,000.00. I was involved in a truck accident due to physical and mental fatigue. I was deprived of sleep getting an average of 5½ hours. I had a bout of dysentery diagnosed by Onni, the west coast leader, as being a spiritual problem. I lost 40 pounds of weight. I worked 10-14 hours a day for no pay. I was instructed to deceived the public making an average of $100.00 a day selling flowers. I was constantly drilled with the philosophy of the Principle and was under both psychological as well as physical duress. I was encouraged to get money from my family which I lied to get. Since being out of the movement I've been threatened and harassed through the mail and telegram.

Yours Sincerely, Carl Waranowski

1633 Rydalmount Road
Cleveland Heights, Ohio   44118
March 12, 1976

MV - P - A

To Whom It May Concern
Box 5084
Arlington, Texas   76011

To Whom It May Concern:

I am an ex-cult victim of the Unification Church. I had
spent a year and a half as a hard core member of this
organization.

My first aversion to this group began when I was told
support was possible through established businesses in Korea and
Japan. I was also told to "cut" all ties with my employer, my
friends, my family, my church and my country, until I was
strong enough to convert them. This was God's will because
these establishments had been taken over by Satanic rule.
My mission was to teach the Divine Principle and restore
mankind back to being God's children.

During this time I had no access to news media. Mail
seldom reached me. All my time was spent in group activities
centered on Rev. Moon and his teachings. No time was ever
allowed for individual reflection.

Weekly I found myself soliciting funds to open the
people's heart and bring them closer to God. This was the means to
strengthen my own spiritual power. Also, the money supported the
center and excess given over to Moon.

I took part in support of former President Nixon. I
myself - being myself- was opposed to his administration. But,
by coersion, I was convinced I was doing the right thing.

Being raised a strict Catholic, I was told many falacies to
break down my former belief. The cross became a symbol of the
failure of Jesus to be destroyed.

I believe this movement is wrong because lies and deceit
are being used to ackomplish righteousness.

Sincerely,

Ricka Shea

Ricka Shea

(Alias: Mary Schafrik)

February 14, 1976

26

Mr. George Slaughter
2401 Greenwood Drive
Grand Prairie, Texas   75050

MV-P-A

Dear Mr. Slaughter,

I would like to relate to you an incident that happened on February 2, 1976. This day was the culmination of a series of events that Lucy, my sister, and I had with a Unification member whom we later found out was named Kathryn Gonen.

The first event was Thursday, January 29th at an apartment house. She recognized me right away, though it took me several minutes to realize who she was. She told me her name was Kathy and asked if I were living there. The manager showing me the apartments told her not yet, and as we walked away told me what a nice girl that "missionary" was. It was then I realized who she was and decided not to get an apartment there. Later that day I leased an apartment at a different complex.

Still later that same day she tried to find me at my sister's dorm room. Even though I was not there, it shook both Lucy and me up, because I had not told her my full name, yet she had traced me there.

The third and last event before the final, frightening incident happened on Sunday, February 1st in the dorm parking lot. Kathy approached Lucy and I as we were getting in the car, asking Lucy if she knew where a room was and asking me if I had found an apartment. I told her I was not living with Lucy anymore.

The next day, Monday, February 2nd, Kathy knocked at my apartment door. Not opening the door, I told her to go away and never come here again or I'd call the police. She left, but a minute later Mayumi Fujii, who had been my "spiritual mother" and whom I had believed to be in Houston, knocked. I was stunned and bewildered and was thinking hysterically that they had come to capture me. I had no phone to call the police and I imagined wildly that they would break the door down. I found out later from my apartment manager that Kathy had called asking about me two times before and from my neighbors that Kathy, Mayumi and two boys had sat outside in their van for three hours that day. To this day I still do not know how she found where I lived.

Mr parents Dr. and Mrs. Dysart, came up that evening. They went to talk to the managers and ended up calling the police. Three patrol cars and two unmarked police cars arrived at the apartments to talk to Mom and Dad. It seemed like a more-than-necessary showing of police, but we found out later that they had had more than enough trouble with the Unification members soliciting illegally in Waco. All they could do, though, was warn them and were very interested that we wanted to file Disorderly Conduct complaints against Mayumi and Kathy. I signed the complaints late that night for their arrest Tuesday morning and have not been bothered since.

Sincerely yours,

Sandra Dysart

102

To Whom It May Concern,   M P - P - A

My experience as a parent of a son who was recruited into the Moon organization
without "FULL DISCLOSURE" was frightening and the following is an attempt to
describe it.

Reid Heller was recruited into the Unification Church, a fund raising business
with apparently no purpose other than the personal aggrandizement of it's
founder, Sun Myuong Moon, a Korean Evangelist. The recruiting process did not
include the ethical disclosure required that Reid would be required to convert
to a new religion. Rather, this was disclosed only little by little, only
after those in charge felt that he was ready to accept the "True Meaning." By
this time he was "hooked" and thru techniques very similar to "MIND Manipulation"
he was ready to accept anything.

By his own admission he had raised thousands of dollars to support the religious
works of the "True Parent, Moon" and also converted others to the religion of
Moon. (Also without FULL DISCLOSURE.) My attempts to discern what the "Good
Works of Moon were lead me to believe that indeed, they weren't "Good Works at
All" but simply ways that Moon used to gain credibility in the U.S. To my
knowledge, no money has been provided for any charitable works that could even
remotely be described as charitable.

During the time that Reid was "Hooked" by the "MOON CULT" I am certain that he
did not receive most of the letters his mother and I wrote to him and what contact we were allowed to have with him convinced us that he was not operating
with his own free will. He seemed strange and preoccupied with the communist
threat to this country. He talked like he was programmed and indeed he sounded
very much like a tape recorder. He constantly equated South Korea with the
highest ideals of the U.S. and he admitted that if asked by Moon to fight and
die for South Korea he would do so with question.

Finally, we lured him home and engaged the services of Ted Patrick, a deprogrammer, to release his mind and allow him to think for himself. The deprogramming effort was successful and when Reid actually realized the enormity
of the fraud that was perpetrated upon him he became outraged and has since
been assisting in the deprogramming efforts of other victims of Cultism.

I am glad to report that the fright that overtook his mother and I is now over,
and I am further glad to report we now have a son who is again ready to assume
a position in society at large.

The Moon organization represents itself as a religion and as such, enjoys tax
free status while operating a highly profitable business that in no way deserves
tax free status. As a tax payer I insist that he open his books to the I.R.S.
for investigation and that he makes FULL DISCLOSURE in his fund raising activities and his so called RELIGIOUS CONVERSIONS. Any activity conducted by him
or any of his myriad of front organizations should be openly identified as contributing to the establishment of a new religion and he should cease and desist
at once from hiding behind these many fronts.

As a taxpayer I insist that he be brought under the laws governing corporations
and that his tax exempt status be immediately denied. He lives in Baronial
splendor and does not pay taxes to the host nation that affords him so much
luxury.

His organization, in my opinion, offers no service to mankind and certainly no
product. His profits are huge. With the millions collected he is not even
required to pay a minimum wage to his willing workers. His organization presents a danger to the well being of our nation and because of his hysteria
about anti communism and the well being of South Korea he should be required to
register as a lobbyist or perhaps even an agent of a foreign power.

                                        SELWYN HELLER
                                        10517 BARRYWOOD
                                        DALLAS, TEXAS 75230

Signed statements given to Cynthia Slaughter for presentation at Senator Dole's panel on February 18, 1976:

They (Unification Church) sent a member to our house one night to check on us. My son called when the member was there and we know our son told him on the phone--"better leave now, Jack--they are waiting in the van for you at the corner." (This was taped and we have that at home.)

My son told us last night--"if you go to that Washington meeting you will lose your son!

> Mrs. Arthur Roselle, Mich. Chapt.,CFF
> Box 228, Utica, Mi.

When I landed in the hospital, the Moonies told Arthur to say he could not come home because he had no shoes. When Arthur argued with them, they said, "Let the dead bury the dead. You stay here and pray."

> Dr. and Mrs. Jack Rubins
> 1721 Whitehall St., Allentown, Pa.

In the spring of 1975, two Moonies came into the playground of Saint Joseph School, Kingston, N. Y., while our primary school children (grades 1-4) were playing at lunchtime. They went around shaking their hands and talking with them. They were with a group from Barrytown and they were "witnessing" on our city streets. Our parish priest came from the rectory across the street and made them leave the property.

> Kay Begley, Secretary, St Joseph
> School, Kingston, N. Y.

I was a member of Unification "Church" for 7 months, spending 5 of those months in the Oakland, California center, including San Francisco and Boonville. While in Boonville, I was aware of several cases of separation of young mothers and their small children, mainly between the ages of birth to five years. The children lived in a separate trailer which was about a five-minute walk from the rest of the living quarters and activity area. "Church" members were periodically rotated to take care of these children. For the most part their mothers were not included in the rotation.

At least two of the mothers were sent to live in the Berkeley center for a period of at least several weeks while their children remained on the farm. While the mothers were on the farm, they were too busy to see their children more than once or twice a week, at most. The children would often cry hysterically when the mothers would leave after a short visit. In one case, a young divorced girl with a two and 1/2 year old daughter wanted her child to join her on the farm but was denied the request. She was, therefore, in effect, forced to choose between Unification cult and her child. She chose the cult, leaving her child with her parents. She used to cry about this often, but always decided, with the help of several people, including myself, that the child would understand when she grew up that the mother had given her up to work for the Messiah (Sun Myung Moon) and the building of the Heavenly Kingdom.

I have chosen not to mention the names of the people involved to prevent retribution against them, but will reveal the names if necessary.

> Barbara Wexler

In Chicago in October of 1975, Moon spoke, informing us that we must be prepared to marry a Communist Committee woman (to convert them) or a black American (said with derision) to produce a beautiful tan race that everyone will desire a black-white marriage by Moon. Several hundred were present.

In Unification cult, due to the programming, I received justification for, the motivation for, and decided "for myself" that if my family proved to be a threat to "the mission of the Messiah," I would murder them. This logic became a part of me after two months. At my deprogramming, I wanted to.

David Geiszler

I was refused permission to go home for a wedding on May 12, 1975.

G. M.(Mike) Egart, Jr.

Our son has been in the Moon cult around six months. He invited us to see him in Manhattan, New York. My daughter, son-in-law, son-in-law's nephew and I went to see our son in New York. We took my son to dinner along with another Moonie. The other Moonie was 2 years in the cult. The cult would not allow our son to come with us by himself.

Our son's personality has changed. He was in a daze. We know he is being brainwashed. How can America allow this to happen?

Yours truly, ██████

THE REPORTER DISPATCH. White Plains, N.Y., Sat., March 27, 1976

Would-be Moonie says Church plans to kill,

By BARBARA ROSS
Staff Writer

A New York City judge isued a warrant Thursday for the arrest of a Sun Myung Moon disciple who is accused of trying to physically bar a Hicksville, L.I., girl from leaving a Unification Church center in Brooklyn.

Judge Jerome Vail acted after the Hicksville girl, Helayne Ordover, 18, and Dr. George Swope of Port Chester told him "there is more involved here than just a case of harassment."

Miss Ordover said she decided to leave the Brooklyn center after Elizabeth Williams (the woman charged with criminal harrasment) allegedly told the recruit that Moon's Unification Church will start issuing guns next year for members to "kill" opponents of the cult.

Miss Williams did not appear in court Thursday and repeated efforts to reach her failed.

In an interview, Miss Ordover said she was attracted to Unification after reading about it in Long Island newspapers.

"I LIKED the idea of a bunch of young people living together," she recalled. Miss Ordover said she was living at home, working "odd jobs," and studying hard to take an equivalency exam to get a high school diploma.

Miss Ordover said she attended several lectures at Unification's Hempstead center before deciding to participate in one of the group's weekend workshops.

On Thursday, Feb. 19, she said she spent three hours selling candy "to help retarded kids" for an interlocking Moon group called One World Crusade. The girl said she collected almost enough money to pay the $15 fee charged her for participating in the weekend seminar.

Friday evening, Miss Ordover left home against the advice of her parents and Rabbi Maurice Davis of White Plains whom the girl had contacted earlier.

The young woman said

she was taken to Unification's Brooklyn center, at 3235 Nostrand Ave. and attended long hours of lectures by group leaders.

"By Saturday afternoon, I was really starting to believe it. They have answers for everything," she said.

Sunday morning, however, Miss Ordover said she was "shocked" when her team leader, Miss Williams, said that starting next year, "We would have to be prepared to kill anyone not a believer of the Rev. Moon."

"I REALLY couldn't believe it." she said. "It really scared me."

Soon after that, Miss Ordover said, she quickly departed leaving her suitcase behind.

A few hundred feet from the center, Miss Ordover continued, she met Miss Williams who she said "held onto my coat and told me to go back now and repent for my sins."

"I told her I didn't believe in her religion and that Rev. Moon is full of crap, but she wouldn't leave me alone. For four blocks she walked with me, holding onto my

sleeve.

"Then," Miss Ordover continued, "she pushed me against the wall of a building, held my arm and asked how dare I walk away. I punched her in the face and ran for the police."

At the 61st Precinct house, Miss Ordover filed a complaint. She also persuaded the police and her father who had been called in from Hicksville to return to the center to retrieve another weekend recruit who had wanted to leave Saturday but had been persuaded to stay longer.

Miss Ordover said she has received several threatening phone calls since pressing charges against Miss Williams.

"They said I'd be a 'sorry girl' if I went through with it," she declared, adding:

"THEY PREACH love and goodness but they just want to take over the world and they don't care, who they hurt in the process."

SEQUENCE OF EVENTS WHICH OCCURRED

TO MY SON _____ IN HIS

INVOLVEMENT WITH THE UNIFICATION CHURCH

MP-SL-A

████ was approached last summer on the steps of the New York
Library, while studying for his Law Boards, by members of the
Unification Church who induced him to go to their 43rd street
headquarters. _____ visited there several times, unbeknownst to
his mother and myself and later, instead of going back to school at
████ College, where he had two semesters to go, went to a
seven day indoctrination program into the Moon Movement.

He emerged from this a totally changed person, disregarding his
schoolwork to a great extent, alienating himself from his friends
at school, as well as his family. ████ now spouted gibberish
as, "Six million Jews perished in Europe due to the fact that they
were responsible for the death of Jesus Christ". A few months ago,
prior to his involvement with the Moon Movement, ████ would have
been shocked at this association.

Upon his completion of his next to last semester at ████
████ has quit school and entered full time into the movement.
He has lost all contact with family and friends. He was kept
physically from speaking to his mother when whe went to Tarrytown
to see him and, at present, his whereabouts are kept secret from
us so that all communications have stopped.

He is a total stranger to his entire family, to his friends and to
all his former beliefs and has totally withdrawn and been brainwashed by this insipid movement which is avowed to take over the
U.S. as well as the rest of the world.

In Mr. Moon's manifesto he states that his is the Messiah, that he
must become the richest and most powerful man on earth, in order to
control it, and can use any means whatsoever to obtain this end.

████ we understand now, is "fund raising" which means he is
selling flowers or candy in the streets, being moved from town to
town. The money he raises goes tax free to enrich Rev. Moon.
All of ████ ambitions, hopes and aspirations for the future
have been taken away from him and he is no longer master of his
own destiny.

NAME WITHHELD

To Whom it May Concern: MP-S4-A

On ▓▓▓▓▓▓, 1975 I entered the Unification Church Barrytown Training
Center shortly before 8 AM for the purpose of visiting my brother, ▓▓▓▓▓
I had not seen my brother for over two years. He had been in the Orient
since early 1975, and was at that time just recently returned to the states.

After driving to this Barrytown Training Center, I was stopped at the entrance by a young man who told me he was the night watchman. He told
me I would have to wait for ▓▓▓ and he took me to a room to wait for my
brother.

My brother arrived at approximately 9:00 AM and he said we would eat
breakfast, and after we were finished he would like to show me around
the grounds of Barrytown. We ate some breakfast, and then I followed him
to the kitchen with the soiled dishes. When coming back through the dining
area, I noticed three Caucasian children, dressed rather poorly, scrubbing
the floor. I would approximate the ages of the children to be between seven
and nine. One boy stood up and looked at me and smiled. The only thing
I really noticed about this little boy was that he had long hair--compared
to my brother and the other Unification male members.

No other particulars about the children stand out in my mind, as I was rather
preoccupied with the noticeable change in my brother's voice and the juvenile enjoyment about a play he said they had put on that entailed climbing
in and out of windows.

                                Name withheld

March 22, 1976

MP-S4-A

To Whom It May Concern:

Our son joined Moon's group in late 1971 and was coaxed to join by a room-mate. Our son was taking graduate courses. He was a Phi Beta Kappa graduate of a U.S. University in mid-west. He was definitely idealistic, because he quit his job in his hometown because he felt the institution he worked for charged exorbitant interest rates to under-developed countries.

Mike (this is not his name) has never been home since he joined the group, because we told him we felt he was wasting his life working for Moon. We believe he has been in practically every state in the union, even Alaska, but not Hawaii. We had cards from many places. However, we did visit him twice. We noted the houses were clean where he lived. But I thought the food was not adequate. Both places had an open jar of peanut butter sitting on a table and a loaf of bread. Coffee and tea seemed to be available, but we saw no fresh fruit nor vegitables.

Mail from Mike has been infrequent and short, usually cards. However the very first letter was frightening--rambling and 10 or 12 pages long, trying to tell why he joined this movement. He talked about the drug problem, the race problem, poverty in the world, etc. And he implied that those who joined this group had all the answers. He never mentioned the name Unification Church nor Moon for over a year after he was in the group.

We seemed to get no Christmas or Easter greetings. One Christmas we got a Christmas greeting with a snow scene. Our family always sent religious cards at Christmas. But Christmas 1974 we got no word at all. Then in February we got word Mike was married by Moon in a mass wedding in Korea. He was married to a German girl we never heard of. He said he worked with her in the group for a year, but our daughter, a nurse went to hear one of Moon's talks the November before and met all the young people with him and this girl was not one of them. So we feel Mike lies to protect Moon. Later (in March) we received a letter from "our daughter-in-law". She said "I know you must wonder about your son who went out into the world and married someone you never met before". But she gave no explanation of this.

Then later we received a letter from our son's father-in-law from Germany. He and his wife are very good Christian people and they went to the trouble to find a student to write us in English. They wanted to know about the family now related to their daughter. We immediately told them we did not approve of the Moon Movement and they too said it has been the heartbreak of their lives. She, the daughter-in-law, was still being held in Germany after being flown from Japan in December. They are having visa problems we hear.

Our son was taken back to the states in early November--Barrytown, N. Y. The father-in-law of our son told us about this and we called for several days before he finally called us back. Then we took a chance on going up to see him, my other son, an ex-Moonie and I, Mike's mother. The ex-Moonie told him the Movement was a big rip-off. We talked to him for over 12 hours and he was shaking and vomiting. It was terrible to see him so programmed that if he broke in the middle of an explanation, he would have to start all over again just like a record. He told us he just read that Franco of Spain died that morning, after we told him he does not read nor listen to TV or radio. Franco, in fact, did not die for several days. Anyway, I stepped into the bathroom for a minute and he fled, because his brother fell asleep. He left his coat and ran out into the rain. We looked for him for a while and then called the ex-Moonies mother and she told us to get out of New York quick or we would be arrested. We left and I was so shaken from this experience, I spent 10 days in a mental hospital for my nerves. After witnessing the fear and vomiting, I was relieved to see him go, but later and still I cry for what has happened to my intelligent son.

I want to add here too that my son gave Moon $1,400 he had in a local bank. And when he married he defaulted on a state school educational loan. I received a letter about this in January 1975 and I gave the state all the recent addresses I had for my son. My son told me when we saw him November 1975 that he thought Moon paid off his loan. We heard also from a reliable source that Moon charged each person he married $400. Moon now is sending out booklets "Way of World" to presently active Moonie's parents to make us more understanding. The NERVE he has--we now never get a letter from our son at all. I cannot understand why the U. S. government lets this terrible thing happen to us the tax paying citizens and this foreigner with a permanent visa makes fools of us. Someone must be getting paid off. The First Amendment we need, but our judges and law makers administer the law.

To whom it may concern;

    I was a member of the "Unification Church" for 6½ months. During this time I was indoctrinated into a set of beliefs called the "Divine Principle" and put under a state of mind control. I entered the cult with the purpose of visiting my older brother who is still a member. After two weeks we were seperated.

    During the time I was there I had no contact with any type of media or other outside activities. Whenever I made a telephone call to my family an older member would stand by me and coach me. I was not allowed to visit my aunt alone and I was told that by staying I would be helping my family the most because I could restore them. I was instructed to lie and deceive my family as well as others.

    After attempts to get my brother out failed, he was put underground for over two months. During this time we lost all contact with him and our attempts to talk to him over the phone were in vain. We were told time and again that they did not know where he was. I feel very strongly that my brother is being abused mentaly as well as physically by this cult. I hope and pray that he and all of the beautiful young adults in this cult will have their rights and freedoms restored soon. Thankyou for your concern.

        Sincerely, ███████████

▓▓▓ was an achieving, loving person with a great sense of humor. He earned one-half of the cost of his college education, in a highly accredited and expensive college. He worked as a paper boy and a gardner during his high school years which enabled him to be active in sports, in which he earned many honors. During his college years he worked in factories and in construction. He held leadership positions in High School and in his Fraternity in college. He graduated from college with a high adverage in June of 1976.

Because of the recession and the fact that very few businesses were interviewing students for jobs, ▓▓▓ did not get a job. So he started across the country with two of his friends.

In Jackson, Washington he ran out of money and had to find a job. He worked in the Olymic mountains as a choker with a logging company, it was a very dangerous job which required excellent physical condition....it paid $6.25 an hour.

▓▓▓ was very impressed with the people he met in his travels. They gave him rides, asked him to have dinner in their homes, helped him to find jobs, and emmitted great friendship and love.

He had a great sense of security and wellbeing when he stepped off the train in San Francisco. He was going to see the city, go by Los Angles to see a school chum and head home for Christmas. Instead he was accosted by several young intelligent clean cut young men from The Unification Church. ▓▓▓ did not know that these young men were affiliated with a so called religious cult. He only felt them to be pleasant and took them up on their offer to have dinner with them.

▓▓▓ has not been the same person since. I'm not saying ▓▓▓ was perfect, or that he had not encountered any problems in his adolescent years, he had indeed. I'm sure he was seeking a goal in life, and I do know that his morals and values in life were very high, and that he was disenchanted with the social ills that he may have been a part of in his college years.

Now ▓▓▓ is tormented, depressed and very unsure of himself. He has talked with leading clergymen, psychologist, ex-cult members and their families who have told him of the dangers involved with this cult, yet he cannot decide what to do with his life. ▓▓▓ spent four weeks in this cult and he was so programmed into their teachings that he cannot believe the press, his family or the others that I have mentioned above. I'm afraid that he may go back into this group because of the frustrations involved in just making a decision: Because of the deep programming and the very great young people involved it is very difficult for him to believe his parents and friends.

NAME WITHHELD

To Whom It May Concern: MP-513-A

Our daughter, an intelligent, idealistic, moderately active girl,
was introduced to the Unification Church at age 21. This was
during a period of disillusionment with herself and the world. She
had completed two years of college.

After leaving home against our strong objections to follow "The Lord
of the Second Advent", we observed a distinct personality change in
her. She became a zealous disciple of Mr. Moon. Her manner of
speaking changed and she had the glassy, far-away look in her eyes
seen in many of the Moonies. Her experience of indoctrination into
the cult was similar to that of others which have been reported in
the press.

For more than a year she worked six and seven days a week for no
salary on various fund-raising teams of approximately 10 people.
Following are some quotes from the few letters we received during
the first few months of her life in the movement:

> "Never have I worked or pushed so hard. ... We've grossed over
> $3000 in 3 days & nights of selling and have a profit with
> all bills payed of $2100."

> "There's never enough time to do what you want to do."

> "I haven't been finding much time to look at what's happening
> in the world and I really want to."

> "We're using Mr., Miss, or Mrs. to address our directors
> now. It was strange at first. Mr. _____ is 19! It's
> part of starting to look at them as leaders, not on the
> same level as we are."

> "Yesterday I made $39.45 in 5 Hrs. That's not too good
> compared to what we did in N.Y. Today we'll be leaving
> about 9:30 and selling till 9."

After the few letters, our only contacts from her were collect phone
calls from scattered areas. In almost three years she has been
allowed to come home twice; once for five days at Christmastime and
one weekend. Other times we have had to travel a distance to visit.

She believes that most American young people are corrupt, that our
government and the organized churches are failing in their
responsibilities, and that Satan has a large influence on all of us
outside the Moon movement. She believes that the leaders of the
opposition to the Moon cult are evil and selfishly motivated.

She has given up her freedom and is willing to go wherever Moon sends
her, to marry whomever he chooses, to do whatever he asks, even if he
considers violence necessary to thwart Communism. She believes that
if she should leave or fail to succeed in the Unification Church,
there is no hope for her, that she will "fall into the Pit".

AS PARENTS OF A DAUGHTER INVOLVED IN THE UNIFICATION "CHURCH" CULT, WE BELIEVE THIS ORGANIZATION SHOULD BE IN-VESTIGATED, AND NOT ALLOWED TO OPERATE IN THIS COUNTRY.

OUR DAUGHTER WAS IN GRADUATE SCHOOL, JUST A FEW HOURS FROM HER MASTER'S DEGREE. ONE OF HER PROFESSORS PERSUADED HER TO ATTEND SEVERAL MEETINGS OF THIS CULT, AND AS A RESULT, SHE BECAME A DEDICATED MEMBER, DROPPED OUT OF SCHOOL, MOVED INTO THEIR COMMUNE, HANDED OVER HER BANK ACCOUNT, AUTOMOBILE, ETC. SHE CHANGED FROM A PERSON EXTREMELY METICULOUS IN HER APPEARANCE, THOUGHTFUL AND CONSIDERATE OF FAMILY AND FRIENDS, TO A PERSON COMPLETELY OPPOSITE. SOLICITING AND PEDDLING UP TO EIGHTEEN HOURS A DAY LEFT HER NO TIME FOR PERSONAL GROOMING, PROPER REST, OR NUTRITION. SHE WAS MADE TO FEEL THEIR MISSION WAS URGENT, AND EVERYTHING ELSE UNIMPORTANT.

TOTAL COMMITMENT IS EXPECTED OF EACH CONVERT, WITH NO TIME FOR FRIENDS OR FAMILY, EVEN ON SPECIAL OCCASIONS. ALTHOUGH IN THE SAME CITY FOR ALMOST TWO YEARS, WE SELDOM SAW OR HEARD FROM HER. NOW SHE HAS BECOME MORE FANATICAL IN HER BELIEF THAT MOON IS THE MESSIAH, AND IS DISTRESSED WHEN THE FUNDS SHE SOLICITS ARE INADEQUATE FOR THE "GREAT CAUSE", WHICH FURTHERS MOON'S EMPIRE.

WE FEEL THAT CONTINUED EXPOSURE TO THIS SUBVERSIVE GROUP IS DAMAGING TO OUR DAUGHTER'S MIND AND HEALTH, AND WE ARE FRUSTRATED BECAUSE THERE SEEMS TO BE NOTHING THAT CAN BE DONE TO END THIS MENACE.

NAME
WITHHELD

We have not seen our daughter since January, 1975. She finished her first semester of college and then left to live in a Unification cult center. She had gradually been drawn into it in high school by a family of young adults in our church. At that time not so much was known about this organization, and it did not appear ominous, as we now consider it -- even so, we did not encourage it, and allowed her to go to the center with friends only sporadically, and then never permitted her to stay overnight. Our daughter was affected by the extreme warmth and friendliness of all the people at the center. This 'total acceptance' is very flattering in contrast to the ups and downs of normal relationships outside, and it is well known now as a very clever way to entice young people in the uncertain teens and early 20s to join with what on an intellectual level they probably would not accept at all. To us it is a well-baited trap. We did not know about Mr. Sun Myung Moon 'calling all the shots' at that point, and we could not have believed that our daughter would ever give over her mind and body to anyone.

On the last weekend of summer before college (and she chose a col-lege with a U.C. center just off campus) she, an honest, dependable girl, deluded us for the 1st time, starting out to go to a workshop in one place and ending up far away from where she said she was going, and then staying overnight for the 1st time. Upon her return she in-formed us that she had formally joined the U.C. -- this despite all we had argued in the way of exposing oneself to education and to matur-ity-forming experiences before getting too involved -- even then we did not realize what a one-way path these cult kids take.

Our daughter's 1st weekend in college was spent at a far-away Unifi-cation workshop. She never gave college life a chance -- much of her time was spent at the U.C. center. Soon she called to tell us that she wanted to move into the center. We rushed out and persuaded her to stay in the dorm thru 1st semester. We talked with the center leader, who vowed that no pressure was being put on her to move (we found out differently later and know that there was plenty of pressure). Later came a call telling us she had moved, and upon considering our protests of broken promises, another that she had moved back to the dorm. There was a real struggle going on between pressures of those leading her away from school and her basic loyalty to her family. The U.C., always there and clever in its conscience-pressuring tactics, at last won out. It must have been a torturous time to our daughter, as it was to us. She did stay in her dorm until the end of the semes-ter, and then informed us that she was leaving school. This she did, and stayed in that center only a short time before being shipped to Barrytown, supposedly for a 40-day course, but actually for 1-2 weeks, and thence all over the country (always far away from her home), where she has been 'fund-raising' ever since. We are not able to contact her directly, but are at the mercy of the U.C. office in Tarrytown for all mail, etc.(we suspect some of her mail doesn't reach her). We never know where she is. She was a loving daughter and sister -- we were a close family -- but now she is not free to see us or we her. When she calls she tells us always that she is "about to move" or to join a new selling team the next day, we feel to keep us confused as to her whereabouts. The result is that even were we in the same locale we would not see her. It has been a heart-breaking experience for the rest of the family, as we fear so for her freedom of mind and her mental and physical health. Her voice on the phone is no longer the same, but a high-pitched, fading-away tone. Her experience at this young age (19 - we feel the 18 majority law was a bad one) is 24-hour obeissance to the whims of this movement.

Our daughter has been robbed of her right to mature naturally, and we have been robbed, after many years of devotion, of seeing our daughter grow to full dimension.

MP-816-A

Subject: "Moon" and his Unification Centers.

First, I want to thank who ever is responsible for getting cult information into the many magazines and papers and the possibility for our local radio and T.V. stations to be able to speak out and allow the public to be aware of what is happening to our young people.

People were thinking of me as a religious fanatic, overreacting mother whenever I opened my mouth about my son and Moon. Now, I can help people to be aware that these articles are to be read and realized that it's everywhere and happening to young people all over. Every-one can help by being concerned in who they contribute money to when they buy things on the streets.. Nephew located in Korea confirms the magazine article findings.

My son was contacted on a street in ▮▮▮▮▮▮▮▮▮▮ He called me within three days of his involvement to tell me about his "Messiah", that he wasn't with a Jesus freak group. Very concerned about getting his younger brother and sister in and didn't want me to talk with them. Was selling his beloved ▮▮▮▮▮▮▮▮ auto he had just purchased to give to his religion. I saw him at ▮▮▮▮▮ Center where he was out contacting youth on 4th Street (after one Month in cult) to come and listen to this divine principle. I dissagreed when I heard it there also. My son has become a very persuasive speaker with his capacity to use his full mind power; not the 5% capacity used by most of others, so he has explained to me. I was unable to reach him and get him to come home.

The center there was a duplex house and at Albuquerque, New Mexico it was a ranch style home. Both had the same similarity; no furniture, except a few chairs in one room and inexpensive table or one like a rough lumber outdoor table covered by sheet. Never saw a bible in either place. No beds, just sleeping bags and luggage. Live out of suitcases. The "Moon" Center at Albequerque was the second location with another move pending. Why??

My son has been selling for "Moon" walking streets 7 days a week from 8:00 A.M. to 8:00 P.M. and has even been kept out till almost midnight at times. Averages over $100 daily obtained from donation and sales. The day four of his buddies went to see him in ▮▮▮▮▮▮▮▮(week of Christmas) they kept him busy away from center till Midnight. His friends saw him only about 15 minutes after driving about 200 miles to see him.

I believed my son might have it better than some because he traveled and stayed at motels at times. I asked last time he called(collect always) if he was one of group that slept in beds. He said,"most of time the beds were not slept in." Slept on floor with feet proped up. .Found it more restful; wasn't easy to get up when in bed "bothered the backs". He is 15 lbs. less weight than before Moon involvement. Looks tired and dreamy eyed. Can't . come home - even when as near as 100 miles away. Working doubly hard because the yankee stadium is needed soon for "moon" to speak. Also told of a planned Mass Marriage to take place at Washington Monumental soon. What can we do about these plans of his(Moon)? I have hopes throu Gods will and other help to regain my son from this sort of controlled service for this Moon.

Moonies have been in ▮▮▮▮▮▮ here three times, selling. Possibly now, due to the publicity, it can cause people to think first before buying or donating to these cults; also warning parents and public to help inform our youth to beware of these cults that want to Control.

Please — Could we ask for help from our Government to be concerned about the protect-ion of our youth and the possible infiltering of these cults into our Government? We want to be a free country to be governed by the people for the people.

Our twenty-two year old daughter Anne was a devout practicing Catholic who
dreamed for years of being a public health nurse in Appalachia. She even
visited the town in which she would be trained after her graduation. Her
dreams and ours were shattered suddenly last January 1974 when Anne came
home unexpectedly and announced she was quitting nursing college and was
joining the unification Church.

Her experience with the Church was a weekend at Tarrytown after which the
church members promised to drive her back to school for a Monday morning
class, but kept her with them until Monday evening. Anne was angry. After
more pressure from a persistent smiling Moonie, Anne returned to a second
weekend workshop after which she made her startling announcement to us.

Within a week she withdrew her bank savings and gave them to her new church.
She moved in with the Moonies. Because of our violent opposition to Anne's
leaving college, her superior, Joseph Tully, gave her permission to complete her schooling.

Now Anne has a new father, Moon; a new mother, his wife; and a new family,
the Moonies. What a blow to us, her God-given parents and her ten brothers
and sisters!

We sincerely tried to learn more of this new religion which hurt us so.
We found that Anne does no nursing, she begs on street corners while selling
flowers, candles, etc. She talks of God when she is assigned to "witness."
Prospective converts are told nothing of Moon's connection with the "missionary" until they are in a position in which they can't argue or walk away,
eg. at a weekend workshop away from home and transportation.

Anne reads no newspapers, sees no T.V. and hears no radio. She tells us the
adverse publicity we see and hear concerning Moon is all lies. We visited
her many times at the church headquarters at 71 St. in New York but were
rarely left alone with her. She asked permission even to go around the
corner with us for a dish of ice cream. We experienced many lies and much
secrecy surrounding Anne since she joined the church. It is difficult to
get a Yes or a No answer. A promise made to us by Joseph Tully that Anne
could attend a family reunion was broken. Anne's personality has changed.
Her compassion toward an elderly invalid aunt living with us is gone. At
one time Anne confided in her uncle, a Capuchin priest. Now she claims he
cursed her, which could never have happened. She even distrusts us now,
although we have done nothing to deserve that distrust. We are convinced
that she is incapable of using her own judgment at this time.

Anne wears an I D card with a tax exempt number stating she is a missionary
of the Unification Church. A missionary of what? We can find no social
welfare programs sponsored by Moon anywhere in the world. Where does this
money go that Anne turns over to her superiors? She doesn't even have
medical coverage.

Moon must not be underestimated in his power to control the young idealistic
youth of our country for his own purposes. In "Master Speaks," a compila-
tion of Moon's sermons given to the "elite" of the church, he says,"Let's
say there are 500 sons and daughters like you in each state; then we can
control the government." Another quote"----we can make senators and congressmen out of our members." The power which Moon can wield through his
total thought-control of his many young followers is as frightening as when
he says, "The whole world is in my hand and I will conquer and subjugate
the world."

Our daughter, ███████ was 20 years old when she joined the "International Reeducation Foundation" four and one-half years ago in San Francisco. She had completed her sophomore year at the University of Michigan. Although we now assume that she knew about the Unification Church and Rev. Moon very soon after joining the group, this was kept from us for a long time, and the movement was represented to us as being non-sectarian, committed to "teaching everyone to love each other". Gradually we learned about Moon and about some of his ideas -- seemingly religious but with a strong political overlay -- and of ████ belief in him as the messiah.

Her commitment is total. On the few occasions when we have been together, both in Detroit and on the West Coast, she is constantly on a treadmill, always running, busy with many "duties " and "obligations", and always fighting fatigue. She has vague, memorized answers to all our questions. When we point out to her that we feel tht Moon lives a life of luxury on the sweat of his "family" while he preaches moderation and abstinence in everything for them, she gives us pat answers and incomprehensible explanations. Her "discussions " have become parrot-like repetitions of the prescribed "line" of the Unification Church. The articles and broadcasts about the movement which appear from time to time she denounces as totally untrue. It is obvious to us that her decisions are made for her by the "family". This is a marked change from the independence of thought and freedom of action which has always been characteristic of her behavior.

Eve has been home three times, each visit approximately two days, and we have seen her twice in California. She writes very seldom and calls (always collect) sporadically, sometimes every other week, sometimes once a month. After the usual amenities and family news, generally she attempts to convince us of the validity of Moon's principles and we attempt to make her stand back and take a good look at what she's doing -- both futile. The calls always end with mutual assurances of love, and we remind her that we are always available should she want us or need us.

TO WHOM IT MAY CONCERN: 41   March 16, 1976

MC-S-19-A

Bill_____, who is still be^ing rehabilitated
after escaping from the Barrytown, N.Y. Unification Church training
center was ~~physically restrained against his will.~~

A full description of his experience with his notarized signature
is in my possession and the possession of Eric Schuppin, Jericho,
Vermont. Because Bill is still fragile from his experience at
Barrytown I will describe what he has both written and told to me
in front of a witness (Jeanne Arnold, Times Union, Albany, N.Y.)
and told to me in private.

Bill was approached by a Japanese girl in New York City during
February, 1975; he accepted invitations to a "three-day workshop,
and then a seven-day seminar at the Barrytown Center."[1]

"'The Barrytown days were full with lectures, studies, praying,
singing, exercising, and the hours of sleep but four or five
a night. At no time, waking or sleeping, was Bill alone to think.'"[2]
"He was told the world outside the church was 'full of Satanic
~~influences.'"[3]~~

On the sixth day of the seven-day seminar, Moon himself appeared.
When Moon reportedly left by the basement, Bill and others rushed
down there to get a closer look at him again.

"'A strong feeling of fear overcame me in the basement.'" In the
dining room the same feeling of "doom" overcame him. "'I knew
I had to get out of there right away. This was evil. I felt I
was in danger.'" "Feeling faint he ran out of the building. The
leaders caught him and brought him back, telling him he had a
'spiritual experience.'" They took him upstairs to the dorm and
when he gain tried to run, they encircled him. It was while he
encircled, he said, 'I fell to the floor writhing.'"

"He was then carried to a small room where a leader sprinkled
'holy salt' on him and left with a 'guard' watching him all night.
When he awoke the next morning - the seventh and last day of the
seminar- 'I realized that the Unification Church was not a
religious group but a political and military group hiding under
religion.'" "The leaders sat at his table at breakfast. A 'burly
fellow I had never seen before' joined the group. As he entered
the classroom for the morning lecture, he was 'called out.'"
"Bill was told he was 'too exhausted' to attend the lecture. He
said he was 'pushed against the wall' and was too weak to resist.
Other men appeared...one carrying a billy club. He said they
pushed him downstairs into the basement as he resisted, and told
him to 'obey' and that he was 'detrimental to the spiritual
atmosphere of the group.'" "A woman told him not to be afraid
and to cooperate. He was then taken to the third floor and left
with a 'guard' in a small room. When the guard was not looking
he went down the hall as though to go to the shower room. Instead
he went out a window onto a ledge. He vaulted down onto a pine tree
and climbed down. He ran across the open fields back of the
building in a heavy rainfall wearing only shirt trousers and
shoes. Rexford Maine of the police received him when some people
in a house took him in, gave him a coat to put on and drove him
into Red Hook police station.

Bill was subsequently hospitalized and under the care of a
psychiatrist. He is still recovering. Jeanne Y. Fisher

Footnotes: Times Union, November 30, 1975, Section B

117

April 3, 1976

MP-S32-A1

To Whom It May Concern:

My son became involved with the Unification Church when he made a
bicycle trip to California. This was about the first part of September
in 1974. He stayed with them for a whole year and left to return home
in September 1975. He left of his own accord because of his many
questions that the church could not, or would not answer, and also
because he knew his family was quite upset about his association with
the cult. The church made every effort to pursuade him to stay, even
transferring him to their mountain camp near San Bernardino, California
and making him a "teacher". My son now says that he believes his year
with the Unification Church was one of the worst things that has ever
happened to him, and the worst part of it, he feels, is that he pursuaded
other young people to join it. He wants to completely forget the experience,
but states that if anyone wanted to have him answer any questions about it
he would do so.

There are three things in particular that my son observed while with the
cult which he feels should have some investigation.

1. During his entire time with the Unification Church, my son saw no
sign of any charitable work being done by the church. It is true that
the young people often earn hundreds of dollars a day selling their flowers
and candy, but apparently all of the money is being spent to meagerly
support the young people, to support the church leaders in a lavish fashion,
and to buy property for the church. My son feels that a full investigation
of the finances of the Unification Church by the Internal Revenue Department.
No explanation or statement on how the money is spent is given to the
members of the Unification Church. He questions their "tax free status".

2. There are apparently many illegal aliens in the group.... Germans,
French, Japanese, etc. At one time when my son was in the California
mountain camp there was a rumor that the Immigration authorities were on
their way up to the camp. Every last foreign member of the camp "took
off" for a long walk in the mountains and told my son to "handle the
matter". They didn't explain to him what they wanted him to say or do,
and at that point he really began to ask himself what he was doing in a
situation like that. He couldn't see himself lying in order to "handle
the matter". All the foreign members of the cult should be thoroughly
checked out by the Immigration authorities.

3. Just before he left the cult, my son was at the Huntington Drive
house of the cult in Los Angeles. While there, a young woman with a baby
came into the group and wanted to stay and join them. She was told that
she could stay, but only if she got rid of the baby and gave it up for
adoption. My son even tried arguing with the Japanese leader of the group
about the matter, but they insisted that the young woman had to give up
the baby if she wanted to stay. For a cult that preaches "family" this
does not make any sense, and my son viewed it as the final unanswered
question to make him leave the cult. If such a thing is not illegal, it
certainly does not fall within any kind of Christian morality.

My son left the cult without telling them that he wouldn't return, although
he knew that he would not go back. He told them he was going home on a
"visit" and they even gave him money to buy a ticket back, which he returned
to them once he arrived home. In other words, he really didn't feel that
he could leave of his own free will. It was a bad experience for him and
we hope something can be done to prevent others from having such an experience.

NAME WITHHELD

Our son is in his fourth year as an unpaid, **obedient, anti-Satanic**
member of the Moon Unification "Church." After finishing his third year
of honors study at college, our son came home to work and study over the
summer at the local university. It was on the local campus that he was
approached by a Unification "Church" member. After long hours of persistent
efforts, the cultist convinced our son to leave his home and to enter a
local commune of the Unification "Church". Our son has never returned to
live with us, except for several very short periods (days) at very long
intervals.

After spending less than a year in the local commune, our son was
moved to a Philadelphia commune where he continued to sell peanuts,
flowers, etc. for the Unification "Church." We know of no tangible good
use by the cult of these collections. All of this time, and in the years
following, our son has received no pay, no health care insurance, no
medical care. He gave his savings of $1,100 to the cult early in his
membership.

During his membership in the Unification "Church" our son showed a
complete reversal in his religious, social and political views. Although,
for example, he had once scoffed at right wing organizations such as the
John Birch Society, he himself now moved even further right as a Unification cult member. He sees a Communist in any person who opposes the views
and practices of the Unification "Church." He is unable to evaluate realistically critical reports on the Unification "Church." His first duty and
"commitment" is to his new "true" parents, Mr. and Mrs. Moon. He speaks
about the possible need for the cult to "go underground". He devotes his
entire life to the will and demands of Mr. Moon. He has relinquished
normal relationships with friends, family and members of the opposite sex.
He has lost all goals which would enable him to make a living on his own,
but instead remains a staunch anti-Communist for Mr. Moon.

Although he appears superficially to be quite rational concerning his
reasons for remaining in the cult, he becomes quite agitated and emotional
when placed in a difficult position in defending Mr. Moon. At this point
he will shout and cry.

We do not wish to (nor have we attempted) to set a path for our son.
The theology of the Unification "Church" is not an issue with us; but we hope,
pray and suffer that our son will once more return to the capability of
thinking for himself - where his thoughts will no longer be controlled by
a man who is devoid of human compassion.

The following was excerpted from a testimonial submitted by a parent:

Our 21-year old son loudly ~~proclaimed~~ his intention to die in Korea for the Messiah (Sun Myung Moon) in August, 1974. ~~This was the first conflict with his family.~~ He is the oldest of   children. He had been an amiable, respected, industrious, successful 4th year college student.

He met the Moonies on the U. of Minnesota campus while waiting for his sister, with whom he shared a car. He told us he was going to a Christian retreat for the weekend in Spirit Lake, Iowa. His emotions exploded there. By his actions we knew that this was not a Christian group. We investigated and found the kind of deception our Bible warns against. He couldn't - or wouldn't - hear us.

He was promptly moved to a commune 80 miles away and allowed only short contacts with us. He tried to convince us of the movement's value, but the platitudes only thinly veiled Moon's obvious mission for power and money. They followed the con-man pattern of telling the victim lies he wanted to hear to get his money, then making him feel good about it. After months of grueling days fund-raising, not enough sleep, and emotional pressure-cooker weekends, he turned over his bank account. He had saved $1,150.00 while living at home, working part-time as a janitor, for his final year at college.

In '75, they pumped him up into thinking he was getting a scholarship, then flew him to Barrytown for deeper indoctrination. He wrote of guarding Moon's Lincoln Continental and working nights on the telephone switchboard.

We drove him away from Barrytown for a holiday in July. Many young people who had left cults talked to him on the way back home. His values had changed. Money, personal freedom and comfort seemed unimportant. He had regressed to the level of early teen dependence. He wanted to marry, but it didn't matter to whom since all Moonie women think alike. He seemed to be in a bizarre world of science fiction, but after 30 days, he promised not to go back. If we had had immediate psychiatric help in a professional Rehab. Center at that time, with necessary security, we would have had a better chance for success.

The cult was calling. They demanded to talk to him or initiate a police investigation and lawsuit on an alleged kidnapping charge. Our local police called them and told them that our son was free, that we didn't have to tell them where he was, and to stop harrassing us. He went to stay in a foster home with a couple who had had over 500 disturbed children from public and private agencies. We contacted the County Mental Health Clinic and gave them the background; they arranged for testing and counseling. It took a few weeks to get into this and many more to get him ready for family involvement.

The cult found his foster home, called and threatened them and alluded menacingly to their ten-year-old daughter. The mother became physically ill and was hospitalized, anxiety attenuating her illness. The stress was too much for them and our son seemed to be slipping back.

After he came home to stay, he found a good job near our home. He was, at last, willing to have us involved in Family Therapy. His father was ill and hospitalized for surgery. His emotions were straining from holding it all in and he told the therapist and me, "When I think like you, I've wasted a year of my life." On New Year's Eve, he watched Billy Graham's telecast and became visibly upset. He quit his job and secretly had the cult pick him up outside his place of work. They returned him home at the usual time for a few days until I discovered them. He expected to stay in the cult and continue Family Counseling, but we could not agree to this. He agreed to continue individual therapy, but has not done so due to being so busy out of state on the fund-raising tours.

February 13, 1976   MP-S40-A

is the youngest of three children. She was born ~~July 30~~, 1957. She graduated from high school in June 1975 and three days later moved into the Unification Church Center at Southeast 39th & Hawthorne in Portland. She has since been ~~transferred~~ to the Center at

was a four year honor roll student with a G.P.A. for four years of 3.89. She was a member of the speech team, the honor math club, and was active in tennis, journalism, and track. During her senior year she dropped all activities and wanted to graduate early to join the MOON group. I refused to let her do this but after graduation she joined them.

The group travel around to different towns and are expected to be up sometimes twenty hours a day trying to get others to join them and to earn from $1.00 to $200 a day selling candy, flowers and homemade grenariums. They have no service to people and all funds above their most urgent needs are sent to the MOON Headquarters.

Since last June I have seen very little of her. At Thanksgiving she came home for one day. Her father and I tried to talk to her but she withdrew and practically said nothing more to us. At Christmas she was home two nights and one day. During this time she was picked up three times by the group for a couple of hours and spent very little time with us. Christmas night her older brother asked three friends to the house to talk to her. One, a close girl friend, and the other two are bible students from an eastern bible college. One of the boys had written a college paper on MOON'S DIVINE PRINCIPLE and could compare it to actual Bible Scriptures. They talked with her from 5:30 p.m. to 3:30 a.m. She left once and came back saying she did not wish to talk to them anymore. After family pressure they again talked to her. They were unable to penetrate the MOON brainwashing.

On January 27th, her older sister, father and I found she was in   and tried to take her out for breakfast and visit with her. She refused to leave the group and we could only see her inside the Center. After twenty minutes the group started singing "You Are My Sunshine" so loudly that we could no longer hear. She intends to spend the rest of her life there.

has all the signs described in the many articles about the group. The exhausted glassy eyed, fixed facial smile. These remarks have been made to me by people at our home on Christmas Eve who know her well. She is not the same person.

Please help us in our endeavors for a Congressional Investigation.

My son was recruited in Los Angeles in January, 1975. He was then 22 years old, and had just been admitted to the　　　　　　　　　, quite an achievement since these unions are very difficult to break into. He was,ironically, working on a script about revolutionary patriots and their fight for freedom. The Dean of the International Community College, which he attended in　　　　　wrote me that, although he had practiced psychiatry for twenty years, he had never known a more emotionally stable boy and that all the members of the faculty had difficulty remembering how young he was because he seemed so mature. When he was recruited he was not suffering a sense of failure nor was he the emotional cripple the Church would have us belive they are rehabilitating.

One week after he joined I went to California and visited the camp where he was being "trained". I went one day, a Saturday, and then returned on Monday and spent three days. In one week he had been totally transformed. He could not talk about anything but the lectures he had heard. I could not communicate with him at all, although until then we had had, I thought, a very special rapport. What had been a beautiful mind had been replaced by a tape recorder. I talked with many of the others at the camp and attended lectures, somtimes for 11 hours a day! All the recruits behaved like people who were on speed --- excited, happy, spaced out. They could not think or talk coherently.

Since he has been in the Movement I have received only to or three short, incoherent notes from him. Formerly he wrote long, interesting letters full of plans and ideas. I have managed to keep in touch by calling the camp or center where he is and having him call me. The calls are probably monitored because his answers are guarded and often unrelated to what I have said.

This January I went back to California to see him. Very strangely he called me, the first time he had originated a call, and asked me to come. This time I stayed at a motel and he was allowed to spend a good deal of time with me. I think he was being tested and that he feared that I might try to "kidnap" him. He was very nervous and uneasy. We went to a long meeting on New Year's Day at which I was introduced to the group. Tim said afterwards that the leader was warning everyone that a stranger was in their midst and to be careful what they said. Later we went to a celebration at a camp in the San Bernardino Mountains. There were about five or six new recruits,(easily recognized because they had long hair and wore blue jeans) I commented on their strange behavior. He said that they didn't even know what was happening to them.

He is now in Barrytown. I have talked to him twice on the phone, but he still sounds strained and nervous when I call. He is still inarticulate and uncommunicative and aloof. I have tried to keep some lines of communication open between us. For that reason I have let him believe that if this is what he wants to do it is all right with me. I have not, however, been able to bring myself to endorsing the Church. Like many parents, I am fearful of alienating him, but am certain that the organization is an evil and subversive political organization. Anyone who has spent as much time as I have in its midst, but retaining my faculties, would surely agree.

To All Concerned,   MP-542-A

   This letter is to inform you of our son's involvement
in the Unification Church and our efforts to get him released
through the organization of Citizens Engaged in Reunited
Families, Inc.

   Our son, ██████ age 19 - honor graduate from North High
School, June 1975 - recipient of two scholarships....Youngest of
our four children, member of the United Methodist Church, ex
Boy Scout, member of DeMolay,....

   Through the usual tactics, days at the ██████ Center, working
on their cars, weekends at "retreats", three week "training" in
Minneapolis ("to see if he really wanted to join") -   was
brainwashed and taken into the Unification Church. By using him
they succeeding in getting his girl friend out of college at
██████████████, in September. He then was sent off to Barrytown,
New York for 40 days training. He was sure, when he left for
Barrytown that he would be home for Christmas. He was not, the
last day we saw him was October 16, 1975. We thank God that he
does contact us occasionally. He says: "I want to come home, but
con't" -- "The happiest day of my life will be when I can see all
of you again" -- "I miss home and all of you more than you can
imagine" -- "I would come home if I could, but I can't". Needless
to say we will do anything to get him back .

   We fear not only for the mental and physical well being of
██████ but also for all the special youth who have been taken into
such organizations in the world. Also, we feel such organizations
are a great threat to our country and the world.

   We pray daily that something can be done and will help in any
way we can.

   More detailed information about our experiences with the
Unification Church and ██████ involvement in it will gladly be
given upon request.

                                   Sincerely,

                                   ████████████████

February 16, 1976

Our son,   , has been affiliated with one or another of
Sun Myung Moon's many "front " groups for the past 3+ years, during
which time we have had many personal experiences which convince us
that Moon is engaged in personal aggrandizement and the accumulation
of political power, rather than truly leading a religious movement.

Any questions we have put to responsible members of the groups, including our son, relative to the flow of cash, or group insurance, or
group health plans for the members, have been met with evasions, generalizations, half-truths or lies. We have seen at first hand, serious
exploitation of the rank and file group members selling flowers and
the like on the streets of our cities, producing enormous money for the
movement, but living at a below-subsistance level, jeopardizing
their physical well-being.

Although Moon and his followers profess to aid the people of the world,
we have seen no evidences of the usual charitable assistance or retrain-
ing functions. We have seen instead, the purchase of palatial estates
and specially-built limousines. Other vast sums have been spent on
high-cost media promotions and lecture tours nationwide by Mr. Moon.

We firmly believe Sun Moon represents a serious threat, not only to
the members and families of his groups, but potentially to our entire
democratic society and institutions.

We urge strongly that Moon's claim to religious tax status be thoroughly investigated by the proper government agencies and another
investigation be mounted in the area of fiscal probity and responsibility.

           and I are prepared at any time to support the above
through personal experiences at Booneville, Oakland and Berkeley
California and New York, New York properties of Moon.

MID-HUDSON LEISURE

Weekly Supplement to

SUNDAY NEWS

Phone: (914) 473-9055

EDITORIAL OFFICES:
136 PARKER AVENUE

P.O. BOX 773

POUGHKEEPSIE, NEW YORK 12601

October 27, 1975

Dear Denise,

As promised I made you a star! Enclosed are several copies of the magazine.

You might be interested to know that earlier this morning our office received a "death threat" on my life by some outraged Barrytowner. You certainly weren't joking when you said the Moonies play rough.

I would be most interested in your comments. I'll try to call you this week, probably around Friday. Hope this finds you well and enjoying school.

Sincerely,

Mark

Mark Levine
Associate Editor

ease Note:-
MARK LEVINE IS NO LONGER
on THE STAFF, PROBABLY FROM
PERSONAL FEAR.
TOM WYATT HAS REPLACED
HIM.

PARENTS, BROTHERS NAMED

Feb. 1976

Sect member files suit

By NANCY PAULU
Minneapolis Star Staff Writer

A 25-year-old convert to the Unification Church is suing her parents and two brothers, claiming she was imprisoned for 26 days while they tried to break her ties with the religious sect.

Dorothy Paula Percic is suing Andrew and Pauline Percic, her parents, and Andrew F. and Peter Percic, her brothers.

Other defendants are Malka L. Goodman, a psychiatrist whom Miss Percic saw during the alleged imprisonment; Janice Ruchie, Kevin Morgel, Linda Lamberger and Kathy Mills, four "deprogramers" who she said counseled her to break ties with the church; Veronic L. Morgel, Kevin and Ms. Mills mother, and "Jeff Doe and John Roe," still unidentified parties she said were involved in the deprograming process.

MISS PERCIC IS asking for $600,000. She's requesting $150,000 from Dr. Goodman for "medical malpractice," $150,000 from Andrew F. Percic and the remaining amount from the other defendants.

Miss Percic alleges she was locked in a room during much of the 26 days and was "subjected to physical and/or psychological restraints" during that time, according to George M. Stephenson and Richard W. Johnson, her attorneys.

Miss Percic was told she would be recaptured if she tried to return to the church, and would then be taken to a mental institution where "her memory would be erased with shock treatments," Stephenson said.

Ms. Mills denies the charges. "At no time did anyone physically touch her or say she couldn't leave," Ms. Mills said.

THE UNIFICATION CHURCH is a religious sect headed by the Rev. Sun Myung Moon, a Korean evangelist. The sect claims the support of about 30,000 recruits throughout the country.

The church, its critics say, brainwashes young people and carries them away from normal lives. Some former members claim they raised as much as $500 a day — all of which went to the church — by selling peanuts, flowers and mints.

Stephenson said Miss Percic contacted him Jan. 9,

PERCIC
Turn to Page 3A

PERCIC: 26-day captivity claimed

Continued from Page 1A

the day after leaving the house.

Miss Percic, who had been living with other Unification Church members in Minneapolis, told him she went to her parents home in Fridley Dec. 13 to celebrate her 25th birthday, Stephenson said.

From there, she was "enticed" to go to Morgel's home at 227 23rd Av. NE. by promises of a religious discussion, Stephenson said. When she arrived, she found about 30 people present, Stephenson said. Some told her she couldn't leave, and that "if it took 10 months to bring her around, they'd do it," he said.

Miss Percic was locked in a room at 227 23rd Av. NE. much of the 26 days, Stephenson said, and people were stationed outside her door to keep watch.

MISS PERCIC left the house Jan. 8 when "one of her attendants fell asleep," Stephenson said. She eventually called friends from the Unification Church, who came to get her.

In investigating Miss Percic's situation, Stephenson said she discovered that her brother Andrew filed a petition Jan. 13 to have his sister committed to a psychiatric hospital.

The commitment petition says that Dr. Goodman saw Miss Percic Jan. 4 and believes she is "in urgent need of psychiatric evaluation and treatment."

Ms. Mills said Miss Percic spent part of the 26 days at her house, part of the time with her own parents and part of the time at Mrs. Morgel's house.

During the 26 days, Ms. Mills said, Miss Percic slept, read, watched television and had friends over. She also went roller skating, out to dinner with acquaintances, to the Guthrie Theater, to a movie and bowling, Ms. Mills said.

Ms. Mills denied anyone told Miss Percic she'd be given electric shock treatments.

All of above statements by Unification "Church" attorney are absolute lies.

Peter Percic
(D. Paula's Brother)

KAY RAMBUR JOINS THE CHILDREN OF GOD -- ⁵¹ -- by Betty Rambur   CGP.8.A

In July of 1971, Kay was a registered nurse at Mercy Hospital in San Diego. On her vacation, she stopped for a few days in San Fransisco to meet her boy friend. She seemed happy and well adjusted.....certainly not anticipating making a drastic change in her life style.....and planned to meet us in North Dakota.

The 1st indication of trouble was a phone call from her boy friend. "Have you heard from Kay?" Then we received a letter stating she would be going to a Bible College at the COG address in Los Angeles and that she had to give up what she loved most in order to serve the Lord. None of this made any sense.

We rushed to the Los Angeles COG commune but received only frustrating results. Unknown to us, they changed her name so they knew nothing about Kay. They kept sending us   out to different areas in Hollywood to look for her on the street. The next morning we went to the police. They phoned the commune and were informed she was there. We rushed over there again only to hear how sorry they were that we had missed her. She left on a bus for Texas the night before.

The following Sunday, we saw Kay on a TV religious program of Fred Jordon, then a partner with David Berg. She was not her normal nature and told of being a dope addict before joing COG. (We knew this was not true.)

We received several letters from her and in August drove to Mingus, Texas. We were cleared at the sentry and allowed through the legged-chained gate and virtually held prisoners on this ranch for nine dreadful hours. About 11:30 that night, Kay was literally dragged from our car by the leaders and she ran into the darkness. The gates were then opened and we were free to leave.

Several months later, Bill met with concerned parents in Dallas. He was spokes-man on a TV news conference and ask for someone to investigate the COG. We were sued for $1.1 million for slander. We spent the following two years preparing for these ridiculous charges. Our lawyers subpeonaed their personnel and financial re-cords three weeks before the trial and all charges were withdrawn immediately.

Near Thanksgiving David Berg sent many of the COG members to visit their par-ents to discredit the statements made by FREECOG, an organization of parents. Kay spent 5 days in our home and we spent many long hours trying to reason with her. She kept quoting Bible verses instead of answers to our questions which made any meaningful conversation with her impossible. The 4th night about 4 a.m., she did break down and lovingly put her arms around her father and cried. She said that she didn't want to go back and that the COG could go to Hell. She wanted to help her husband get away, so we agreed that she should phone him and ask him to visit us. With only this one conversation with her husband, her mind flipped back under the control of the COG leaders. She tried to run away and later became a violent person. She did return to COG the following day.

Within a week, Kay phoned our home and said,"Hi, Mom this is Me," an expression she had always used when in college. She asked me to convince her father to drop the lawsuit, which was stupid because COG was suing us. Bill agreed to meet with her, her husband and a lawyer. He waited at the designated restaurant for hours but no one ever came to keep the appointment.

We spent the next three years in helping parents with rehabilitation. It was soon evident that all groups were using a similar pattern of mind control. Ex-members were very helpful to inform us of the inner workings of each group.

CFF was organized in August of 1974 in Denver, with Bill as President. We have little hope of ever rescuing our dear Kay; however deem it necessary to con-tinue to expose these groups which are destroying the lives of our future leaders.

C6P-S29-A

TO WHOM IT MAY CONCERN

As a concerned parent, I wish to report our experience with the religious cult,
The Childred of God. Our daughter, ▓▓▓▓▓▓▓▓, graduated from High School
here in ▓▓▓▓▓▓▓; and then attended ▓▓▓▓ Women's University in her freshman
year in its nursing school. She transferred to ▓▓▓▓ University in 1971-1972
and it was during the Christmas vacation when she was home from school that
she was approached by the local Children of God. She visited them at their local
dwelling and made up her mind that she did not wish to return to school, and
she was taken by the local members to the El Paso commune. The following Summer
I travelled to Canada attempting to see her and was told that she was not available (a lie)
as she called me long distance from Canada the day after I returned to the US.
She has been gone for four years and two months, and during that time she has
been home twice (both times at our expense). She married someone with
whom she had a short acquaintance of which we learned via a telephone call when
they were headed to Canada. She has definitely changed from a loving, popular,
very likeable charming girl to someone who has been alienated from society,
her parents, her education, her friends, and her former religious beliefs.

It has certainly been a terrifying and sad experience for her family. To have her
estranged from us--instead of getting better as time goes by--only seems to get
worse! We love her so dearly--and it tears our hearts out to think of not being
near her.

She has travelled with the Children of God to Canada, Columbia, Venezuela,
Puerto Rico; and lately her letters have become farther and farther apart.

She came home on a one month's visit in December of 1975 so that we might get to
see our grandchild who was born in one of the group's houses in Puerto Rico.
It was wonderful to see her--but oh so hard to see her go again.

I would definitely say that the Children of God alienates its members from family,
school, church, and former friends. I think that a thorough investigation should
be made of David Berg and the financial backing that the Children of God receives.
Also check on brainwashing, Thought altering techniques, etc.
We need to keep our youth in America--especially the ones who are headed toward
a worthwhile career in a field that so badly needs useful workers. If you
need any additional information, I shall be more than happy to provide it. I
feel as though I have not done my fair share in combatting this cult's influence,
but to date the efforts have been divided and I'm glad to see us united into one
organization trying to investigate all of the damaging religious cults.

You can't possibly imagine the tears, hardships, longing and sadness that this
cult has brought to us.

A Loving Parent

ps Our daughter (prior to joining the Children of God) was a good student and
a wonderful daughter--she was not inclined toward becoming a dropout!

It is hard to explain the heartache and grief caused by the
disappearance of our daughter, aged seventeen, working at an office
job at that time, into the radical Children of God group back on
August 1, 1971.

She had gone on a swimming outing with friends on a Sunday afternoon,
and after swimming they all listened to some rock music in a park,
where the group had a van and were soliciting members. Although we
found her through friends the next day we could not get her out and
within three days she was shipped somewhere.

The house where she was taken from the park was in a bad slum area
and evidently they had just moved there and much commotion was going
on and many kids seemed to live there. After making us wait a considerable
length of time they finally brought her to us but we could not talk to
her alone or hardly get her off the porch as she had a big sister at
her elbow constantly. Although she hugged and kissed me she was quoting
Bible verses constantly and hardly paid any attention to anything we
said. She had a Bible in her hands all the time.

We tried to get help from our minister but he wasn't too concerned,
said he would go see her in a day or two. We got a lawyer but he
didn't know really what to do either. By the third day she was gone,
leader said she had gone on a bus with other kids to Cincinnati. We
immediately went there, had police cooperation, only got the runaround
and about four different stories were told.

We came back and hired a private detective, spent a lot of money,
didn't do any good. We didn't hear from her until three months later
when she called from Florida. We went and got her but she ran away a
few days later and then we didn't hear for a really long time, the next
year sometime.

We got two letters mailed from England. We had a London newspaper check
it out and they found the letters were only carried to England to throw
us off the track and she really was in Boston, Mass., an address given.
When we went to Boston they had already gotten her passport and she was
gone to the Caribbean islands somewhere.

We didn't hear from her at all, didn't know where in the world she was
until an old girfriend happened to see her on the streets of
and she informed us. We contacted the Salvation Army and they found out
where she had been a few weeks earlier but she had gotten married and they
had left with another couple getting a ride on a banana boat to some other
island. By the time we found her through authorities she was pregnant and
as we knew only the boy's name (through police) it took another long time
to find out where his parents lived.

They got them to come home for a visit through a death in his family and
we did get to see her a few days out that was two years ago and was the
last time we have seen her. She has had two children since then, is still
living on an island somewhere. We have received only some holiday greeting
cards, but no letters, all with only a box number.

I have had to leave out many details due to the necessity of brevity,
could write much more, everything true, and could be verified.

                Sincerely,

To Whom It May Concern:

CGP-S43-A

  Our daughter was recruited into the Children of God from
the   campus in late 1973. She was 18, and a
second year student at

  We may never know just why she decided to drop our of college
and forsake the family and friends who meant so much to her; we do
know the decision was agonizing for her. Her room-mate reports that
for almost a week before she moved out of the dormitory she did nothing
but weep and read the Bible. A COG drop-out -- the boy was going
with before their recruitment -- told us he did not believe Sue would
stay in the organization for very long because it was so hard for her
to forsake her parents. This was over two years ago.

  She was part of a group of 20 or so recruited at at about
the same time. About half the group went together to hold a giant
rummage sale to convert all their belongings to cash. Sue sold
everything she had taken to college with her, including things which
were not hers to sell. She told us the sale raised over seventeen
hundred dollars. The money was turned over to the COG recruiting
team.

  One of our most disturbing experiences since Sue was recruited
into COG concerns her health. The cult believes in faith healing.
Several months after she joined, she became aware that an ovarian
cyst was forming; she had had a similar cyst three years before and
could recognize what was happening. She tried to cure herself through
prayer, and by July of 1974 the cyst has grown to such an enormous
size she looked pregnant and was advised by the cult leaders to see
a doctor because her faith was not strong enough to effect a cure.
The doctor urged an immediate operation.

  She telephoned us to ask if her hospital insurance was still
in force. It wasn't, and she was admitted as a charity patient.

  I went to Houston to be with her during the surgery and for
four days afterwards. The doctor told me the cyst weighed over
thirteen pounds and if it had been permitted to keep on growing
it might have killed her.

  I suggested she come home for two weeks after the operation to
recuperate. She seemed interested in the idea, but after a talk with
her colony leader she said she could not come because the Lord had
promised her leadership opportunity if she remained in Houston.

  We did not hear from her for over a month after the operation.
She has apparently recovered satisfactorily, however we know she is
not taking the hormones prescribed. We also know that she will
never be able to have a child.

  We get letters from her on the average of about once a month.
She does not communicate with her grandfather, her cousins, or any
of the friends who once were a part of her life.

  I have tried to urge her to leave COG and support herself by
working for a living, or to return to school. She becomes angry
when I make these suggestions, and sharply criticizes my lack of
faith in God's ability to take care of her.

55

Dr. and Mrs. Watt M. Casey
P. O. Box 458
Albany, Texas 76430

DLP-P-A

To Whom It May Concern:

We feel that a class our son Rodney took in meditation at Trinity University
was a stepping stone to getting involved with Divine Light Mission.

Rodney received "knowledge" July 1974. He moved into the City of Love and Light
at that time. He lived there doing meditation and "service" as they call it for
10 months. During this time he divested himself of most of his material goods.
He gave them his car, money from sales of his expensive camera equipment, type-
writer, cattle, stocks etc. He worked at different jobs which someone in authority over him secured for him. He gave all of his pay to them at "Coll" and in
turn received a $5.00 weekly allowance. He gave and worked willingly.

Rodney had always been on the slender side. We believe to save money at "Coll"
on the grocery bills they encouraged fasting. He used to fast at least one--
perhaps two days a week.

He cut himself off from his family, his Church of which he was a member, and his
friends. All of his thoughts were centered on Guru Majaraj Ji. Rodney considered him to be God on earth. He was so programmed that he could not see anything
wrong with his working like a slave and turning over everything he made to the
Guru. That the Guru lived in complete splendor did not matter to his devotees.

Rodney began to withdraw more and more. After he left Coll he lived with us for
a while and then went to Africa with some cattle for his father. He appeared to
be a little more with it and even began eating meat. However, when he returned
to the States he stopped eating meat again. By fall he had lost a great deal of
weight and we were seriously worried about his health, mental as well as physical.
He was living with a 69 year old woman and trying to help her with her paranoid
son and also selling candles. (Both were devotees of the Guru.) He had tried
to reenter school but it was too difficult. Meditating under a sheet with a
prayer board from 2-3 hours a day took a lot of time. He would also meditate
off and on during the day. His eyes had a spaced out look that a lot of people
noticed.

He left this household to return home----why we don't know. He had gone down
hill considerably and we were becoming more and more worried about him. It was
very difficult for him to concentrate on anything. He almost never picked up
the daily paper and virtually did no reading unless it pertained to the Guru.
He was constantly listening to the Guru's tapes. This was very important to him.

It was at this time that we decided to attempt to have him deprogrammed by Ted
Patrick. We did this approximately 5 weeks ago. He has since told us that he
appreciated our deprogramming him more than anything we have ever done for him
in his whole life.

At this point he is helping to get other children out of cults and is hopeful
of getting as many out as possible.

March 15, 1976.

To Whom it May Concern: 56   *DLP-P-A*

One of our four children is enslaved by a man who calls himself the master of the universe, the Guru Maharaj Ji, and his lucrative enterprise is the Divine Light Mission.

Our daughter, Kerstin, was an above-average student. The Rotary Club chose her for a one-year exchange program to the Far East. There, suddenly a strange change took place. She stated that she had met with God, found knowledge. She wanted to stay and, in her own words, sit at the lotus scented feet of the master of the universe. The Rotary Club was able to prevent this. She was brought back home. We hardly recognized her. She was pale and skinny, she could stare at the picture of a young pudgy man, the Guru. Like a Pavlov's dog, this started a strange trance which could last for hours.

Then the Guru himself abandoned his "millions" of followers in India and set up headquarters in the U.S.A. Our daughter at once entered his commune in Denver. She used most of her savings for the privilege to work for this commune. Then, because of her good knowledge of German, she was sent to Frankfurt. There she got a considerable sum of money from her over-eighty years old aunt for a "good cause and her studies," meaning for the Guru. Then she had to work for several enterprises to earn money which all had to be turned in. Now all this may or could be her free will, her way of fulfillment in life. But I have good reasons to doubt this, as follows:

1. In order not to judge her unjustly, I took part in their many satsangs, their word for there religious services. We were always watched and never left alone.
2. She herself stated that they needed only three or four hours sleep a nite.
3. For her work in a free market competitive printshop, her begging from house to house for old clothes and distributing leaflets she was never paid. No social security was withheld and no medical insurance was provided. All that was provided was a mat on the floor to sleep on and a meager diet consisting mostly of rice and soybeans.
4. My husband flew thousands of miles to see her in Germany after over one year of separation. She was allowed to meet him only in presence of another believer.

From all this I must conclude that the cultists are artificially tired out, deprived of necessary protein, are constantly under peer pressure and observation. I definitely know of two of my daughter's friends who were going astray, wanted to return to their old form of normal life. It did not turn out that way, they both committed suicide.

I further suspect that her cult practices strange tax manipulations. The money earned through printshops, outlet stores for the worn clothes, dry-cleaning businesses, etc. is used for tax exempt purposes. One example: After my daughter was considered trustworthy enough to travel alone, she got an airline ticket paid by the commune and the trip was declared as a necessary trip to the commune in the other town. The money sent by our family for just this trip was acknowledged as a donation to the cult.

I respectfully submit that our government should look into the various cults, their activities, their psychological practices, their tax manipulations, and their possibly unconstitutional activities.

s/ Margarete Moller

To Whom It May Concern: SCP-P-A

    We have just lived through an experience which seems more
science-fiction than real..Our very open, intelligent, and caring
son joined Scientology to improve his studies and his abilities.
It advertises heightened awareness and making a sane world.
The ideas seem fine. Instead, in four months he became irrational
and robot like. He was put in a trance-like state. He was convinced
that Scientology had all the answers and he became a slave to a
totalitarian system that went against all his previous beliefs.
It uses psuedo-psychiatric techniques and thru auditing and hypnotism
one confesses all fears and guilts plus hallucinates past lives.
If you want to get out they use your confessions as blackmail.
Also, you are threatened and told to disconnect with all people
trying to interfere with your Scientology training. They are
masters of mind manipulation or brainwashing.

    The cost of the training averages $5,000.00 to $20,000.00.
How this has church status is beyond belief! They are very political
and go under front names such as Citizens Commission on Human
Rights. They are at present fighting Interpol, because Interpol
is investigating them. Many Congressmen and Senators may be
working for them unknowingly.

    The government also funds a drug program called Narconon,
which is Scientology. Charles Manson learned his techniques from
this program. It is funded thru LEAA. Another front organization
is National Commission on Law Enforcement and Social Justice. They
have educational program called Applied Scholastics. It is important
for all government officals to look into the background of all
programs to be sure they are not front organizations for these
political-religious fraudulent cults.

    My son has been rescued and is back at college. He would be
a fine witness for any investigation by our government. Scientology
as in Unification Church, is also ambitious to take over our
government. We have evidence of how they plan to do this.

    The Australian report by the Chief Justice of Australia
diagrams the evil practice of this group. Australia did get them
out of Victoria and has contained them. We must do the same.
    Thank you,

    Sincerely,

    Elaine Lieberman

58 SC P-P-A

109 Eastview Dr.
Urbana, Ohio 43078
Feb. 11, 1976

National Committee
Citizens Engaged in Reuniting Families, Inc.
P. O. Box 112H
Scarsdale, N. Y. 10583

Gentlemen:

I am glad to see you have set a Day of Affirmation and Protest
against destructive cults. May God grant a congressional investigation
from this.

We lost a son to Scientology. We have spent approximately three years
in trying to find out what made him suddenly have a personality change
that made him renounce God, his parents, his wife and son, and made
him give up a newly secured securities license in the State of Texas,
let his car be repossessed, and give up his dreams of what his future
might be.

We have not entirely lost track of him for more than six months at a
time. At the present time, I do not know where he is.

Scientology is appealing to the youth because it gives them hours of
personal attention. But those hours cost a person dearly, and as
he becomes entangled, he owes money to the church. I do know that my
son Joe is on a contract with this church, working for $15.00 a week.
He moved up from $4 to $5. He is working with Narconon, an outfit
that supposedly takes young people off drugs. I believe that it only
takes them off drugs to put them into the Church of Scientology and its
principles.

My husband and I believe that Joe is brainwashed. All he can think or
talk about is Scientology. We cannot otherwise communicate with him.
He has had a complete personality change, and seems not to care what
happens to his son or those dear to him. I believe, too, that Joe is
giving the $15 back to the church of Scientology, and at that rate will
be exploited for his entire life. Joe has risen in the group called
Narconon, and is trying to obtain national funding for them. I wrote to
Congressman Clarence J. Brown concerning this on July 11, 1975.

I have much material on the Church of Scientology and what I believe
it has done to my son. I would be glad to share it if someone is
interested.

May the one true and living God bless this endeavor.

Sincerely,

Marilyn Johnson

Marilyn Johnson
(Mrs. Mark E. Johnson)

134

To Whom It May Concern,
Box 5084,
Arlington, Texas. 76011   Re Scientology SCP-S24-A

Dear Sirs:

One evening, 4 or 5 years ago, I received a frantic, collect phone call from
my daughter in a west coast city. With no explanation why she desperately
needed $3,000 in cash, she had problems which could be overcome by taking
some cources...and this amount may have to be increased. I compromised by
promising to send $1,000 that night, insinuating that the remainder would
come later. In a few days, I learned that the courges originated with Scientology; a trip to the library revealed that Scientology was a con game!

Later on, my daughter sent me a "letter of disconnect" wherein she stated she
never wanted to see me again, told me never to come to her house, that there
would be no more letters between us. Perhaps a year later, I received a
letter from my daughter saying she desired to be my daughter again. Hubbard,
the originator of Scientology, is always changing his format to include
things which will prove more beneficial to Scientology. In this case, it
didn't appear wise to cut off all future possible sources of money.

At the start, Hubbard did not want religion to be mixed up with Scientology,
but when he realized by claiming to be a religion he could avoid all payments
of taxes, he was all for religion.

My daughter had a fair amount of equity in a house in a west coast city but
she lost this when she signed a lifetime contract with Scientology. She
explained to me she was selling everything because she didn't want anything
monetary value, including all her sterling silver wedding presents...and was
dickering with a jeweler to sell her mother's combined engagement and wedding
rings. Upon learning of this, I paid her twice the amount offered by the
jeweler. She thinks she will eventually get possession of the rings...but
she is in for a surprise.

Obscenities. Cults seem to be adopting a new tact, although the purpose is
anything but clear. My daughter never used obscentities, but during a phone
conversation perhaps six months ago, she disgustedly said "Horse s---" on two
occasions. It took me so much by surprise that I ignored it. A similar
experience was reported in the "News" of the Citizens Freedom Foundation in
connection with the cult, the Children of God.

One philosophy of Scientology: Lying is permissable if that lie benefits Scientology. Over the phone, I remember asking one of my granddaughters what she
did the previous summer. She said, "I went to Europe," which immediately
brought a "Don't lie to me!" from her grandfather. My daughter then came on
the line wanting to know "What's going on?" After I explained the situation,
she said, If --- said she had been to Europe, that was the way it was." And
flew into a rage. In order to become a scientologist, a person is "audited"
and this includes brainwashing. From then on, he is completely controlled by
the Scientologists. My daughter works a full day 6 days a week, and each evening goes back to "audit" other suckers. She considers it an honor and a priv-
aledge to work like that.

I believe it is high time that our $50,000 a year whiz-bangs plus extras spend
less time and money investigating the Love-Life of the tsetse fly and like
subjects and more on Scientology and other cults which are a threat to the
very existence of our country.

To whom it may concern:

Our daughter, Kathleen, was a normal 19 year old girl until she joined the Love
Israel cult a/k/a Church of Armageddon in Seattle. Her letters prior to joining
the cult show this and her friends and teachers can testify to this also. She was
home Christmas 1972. Her Christmas message to us shows she was not alienated from
her family. "...You two sure have been the kind of parents that unconsciously set
the balance right for yourselves and your children. I guess that is why we have
parents. I love you both and that is my eternal Christmas present to you..."

Her first communication with us after the holidays was a letter post marked from
Seattle January 8. 1973, in which she said she was living with a family that "read
the Bible a lot". Her second letter post marked January 27 said she would not write
again.
Our letters to her went unanswered. Letters sent to her certified and deliver to
addressee only were returned. An envelope we stamped and self-addressed along with
paper and pen were smuggled into her by a friend. She did write a few lines and
draw a sketch which we received by mail. The cult had confiscated all her property
and would not give her a stamp to write to her parents.

When we visited her we could not see her alone. Her personality had undergone a
complete change. She had been outgoing and independent, now she is weak and submissive.
Kathy said she had died to her past and was in heaven. Her face was covered with
scabies which had been left untreated and had become infected. Although she agreed
to a physical examination she was not allowed to see a doctor.

After several months of trying to get psychiatric help for her unsuccessfully, we
heard about Ted Patrick and with his help took her from the commune. CBS covered
our activities. We permitted this because we wanted the public to be aware of these
dangerous cults. It is public knowledge that our daughter tried to have her mother
arrested for kidnapping. She said she was 85 years old, had been born in Israel and
that her mother was New Jerusalem, the Spirit of Peace. She was 19, her birthplace was
Torrance, California. She is not insane according to Washington and California law.
She came a long way toward rational thinking through the process Ted Patrick calls
"deprogramming". She admitted Love Israel, the cult leader, is not God nor His prophet
and that she was not a spirit but flesh and bone like the rest of us. However we did
not break the hold the cult had on her for she ran away from us and rejoined the cult.

Two members of the Love Family died under "unexplained" circumstances from breathing
fumes of Toluene. A cult member testified the solvent was used for purposes of cor-
rection. No charges were brought against Paul Erdman, a/k/a Love Israel. He has an
arrest record which includes drug abuse, contributing to the delinquency of a minor,
grand larceny and embezzlement.

Ted Patrick was tried in U/S. District Court, Seattle(CR74 3206) for kidnapping and
acquitted. The judge said parents who would have done less than we had done would
be less than responsible loving parents. The Ninth Circuit Court of Appeals (75-1127)
upheld the acquittal. Our actions therefore were deemed justified by two Federal
courts but no actions have been taken against the cult to our knowledge.

The address of the Church of Armageddon is 617 West Mc Graw, Seattle, Washington.
They own property in several locations in Washington, Hawaii and Alaska. We no longer
have contact with our daughter.

James C Crampton
Henrietta Crampton
April 9, 1976

My name is Danny Fox. I was hypnotized without my knowing it into joining a religious cult in April 1975. I gave the group my car and about $300 in cash. The group structure and beliefs were set up according to the Bible, but the scriptures were taken out of context and used for the benefit and profit of the Elder, who assumed complete control. I was influenced to hate society, government, family, and not to trust anyone outside the group because they were of Satan.

During the time I was in this group from April to September, 1975, I wrote three letters and called home once. We were encouraged not to write home because our parents could be used by the Devil to draw us out of the group. The group I was in had approximately 60 to 90 members. It did not have a name but we referred to it as "the church", and called ourselves Christians. We wore long dark robes and short hair with beards. The sisters wore long dresses and most had long hair. The brothers wear trench coats and rain coats now.

We traveled from city to city in groups of twos and threes by hitchhiking and hopping freight trains. We camped in parks usually near a large city and almost always near a college campus where we would "witness" (recruit new members to the group). A large number of the members of my group were college students.

On September 12, 1975, in Fayetteville, Arkansas, I was involved in an accident. Thirty-two of us were riding in a two and one-half ton flat-bed truck when a motorcycle pulled out in front of us, causing us to swerve off and turn over in a ditch. There were several injuries, including the death of a five-month old girl. As for myself I received minor cuts and injuries and fractured my left arm. Since we did not believe in doctors we refused to go to the hospital. I went back to our camp and let some of the brothers set my arm and put it in a cast.

My parents found out about the accident and that I was injured in the accident. They came to Fayetteville and convinced me to go home with them. I returned to Tampa and through my mother's insistence I went to the hospital to have my arm X-rayed. The X-ray showed the position of the bone in my upper arm looked like this ⎰⎱1¼". I was hospitalized for two weeks with my arm in skeletal traction.

After my release from the hospital I was deprogrammed by Joe Alexander. Deprogramming is simply counseling the people with the Bible and showing them where their doctrines are taken out of context and therefore going against the Word of God. Since I was deprogrammed I have been helping deprogram other kids.

I hope this information will help you to realize these people need help to get out of these cults. Very few can leave on their own because they are brainwashed into the doctrines of the group, therefore leaving them no free will of their own.

The people behind these groups are using them as a means of becoming powerful and wealthy. If nothing is done to stop them they will soon be strong enough to control the minds of a large part of this country. Now is the time for people to take notice of what these cults are doing and have already done to our society, if it's not too late. ...

s/ Danny Fox, Florida

130 P - P - A

Dear Sirs;

For the past two years I have had various experiences with cults.
Everything from being solicited to on the street cornors, to
having my life thraatened.

My brother was taken into a small group called "The Church"
headed by Jim Roberts, an x-marine, in June 1974. We were vary
fortunate that he was arrested in Merridan, Mississippi,on January
31, 1975 'for eating out of a garbage can. When I returned him
to Minneapolis he was in a zombie-like condition with fully
dilated eyes. He had given his leader $2200.00 and in return
was brainwashed. He traveled over 12,000 miles on foot, wearing
only a robe, sandles, and carrying a Bible He slept under
interstate bridges or state parks and ate out of garbage cans,
"in search of the Lord."

After spending 9 days at General Hospital and being told that
there was nothing wrong with him we flew him to Ohio for
deprogramming. There he stayed for two months, before he began
to resemble his former self. His group tried every means of
contacting him, from calling every relative to searching our
mailboxes.

Since this experience with my brother we have helped many parents
rescue their young adults. The word DEPROGRAMMING has been
blasted in all the newspapers. The Army uses the word DEBRIEFING
and psychiatrists use COUNCELING. We are rescuing these young
people from one of the most dangerous evils that has fallen
on the United States-------MIND CONTROL.

                                        Sincerely

                                        Kathy Mills
                                        3939 Hayes St. N.E.
                                        Mpls., Minn. 55421

To Whom It May Concern:

In view of the alarming increase in pseudo-religious organizations as exemplified by the Unification Church and The Children of God, and other lesser known cults, I should like to relate the detrimental effects these organizations are having on individuals, families and society as a whole, as demonstrated by experiences endured by my family through the loss of a son to one of these cults.

I say lost, because the young people, or anyone as a matter of fact, recruited into these organizations is lost to his family or to any normal association with non-sect members, or society as a whole.

My younger son, whose name I am reluctant to use at this time, was lured (a far more accurate term than recruited) into an organization in Connecticut headed by an apparent psychopath named Julius and his wife, Joanne.

The first indication my wife and I had of our son's involvement with this cult, was a series of letters from our son declaring Julius to be "the second coming of Christ", and that he, our son, would be "saved from this world" through the teachings of Julius, and, indeed, these teachings would save the world.

Our son's letters were couched in the rambling, almost incoherent terms of a religious fanatic, extolling Julius as Christ, warning us of impending world doom, quoting extensively from the book of Revelations, outlining Julius' prophesies of imminent social disaster and imploring us to save ourselves from the holocaust by moving immediately to Connecticut, and joining his group.

All of this was from a youth of eighteen years of age, who could easily be described as a "typical American Boy". A recent high school graduate reared in a typical middle-class, white, Christian American home. A young man popular among his peers, intelligent, well mannered, with a well developed and active sense of humor, athletic and emotionally well adjusted.

Our son's complete psychological, emotional and religious reversal indicated that he had been "brainwashed" or had undergone some sort of psychological indoctrination, and during subsequent communications with him (over a period of some forty months) it is apparent that he has become a complete mental and psychological prisoner of Julius and his cult, and unless we can take steps (which might border on the illegal) he will be lost to us, himself and society for ever.

Sincerely

A sorrowful Mother and Father

To Whom it may Concern;

My daughter, at the age of 18, joined the Brother Julius Cult in
Meriden, Conn. quite suddenly three years ago. At that time we were
friendly and she told me how she fell in a faint on first meeting him
and immediatly became a believer.

She gave him all her belongings, collections and some things of mine
for what she said was a " tag sale"-- the probable worth was $200.00.
Julius gave her a bible.

She left home, left the Catholic church. resigned from High School
(even tho she had only six more weeks to go).

She lived with other female followers, until in Dec. 1974, Julius
said they all should be married. The boys lined up on one side, the
girls on the other-- and they chose partners. In Dec. alone, there
were over thirty such marriages.

We are not friendly any more. Her only interest is Julius and the
Bible, according to his interpretation. They have no interest in the
Government, education, the news, her family.

They hired a lawyer to try to take a little bit of money and stocks
I held. My lawyer told him it was ridiculous.

They dropped in one time to tell me that they were " Angels in the
flesh" and could do no wrong. They said I (and my family and even
my neighbors were all going to Hell.

Altho she was never a superior student, she acts now like a robot
or a retarded person.

NTP-P-A

My daughter, Margarett Rogow, escaped from the leaders of the New Testament Missionary Fellowship in December, 1973.

The N. T. M. F. is a cult headquartered in New York City and Chia, Colombia, S. A. The leaders are Hannah Lowe and John McCandlish Phillips.

The cult operates on Ivy League College campuses (Harvard-Yale, etc) and recruits among the Freshman, gradually alienating and isolating the young people -- getting them to break with the past, drop out of college, turn over their possessions to the leaders and work for them.

After Margarett's escape, she was examined and diagnosed as a classic case of "Brainwashing" by Robert J. Lifton, Professor of Psychiatry, Yale University, and distinguished author. Dr. Lifton stated that the leaders of the N. T. M. F. were able to gain complete control over Margarett, a highly intelligent, prize-winning student, through this well defined psychological process, using isolation and fear.

While a member of this cult, Margarett would do anything the cult leader ordered, including falsifying passport's numbers, lying to authorities on official forms, and being willing to break into our house for the express purpose of removing property.

As Brainwashing is a reversible process, Margarett has made a complete recovery and has returned to college where she is excelling and leading an independent and responsible life.

My older daughter, Elizabeth, who joined the N. T. M. F. at the same time is missing in South America.

Since Brainwashing robs the victim of his right of self-determination, guaranteed by the Civil Rights Law, it is felt Margarett's rights were violated by having this process practiced on her person by sophisticated adults.

Margarett has asked her Congressman, Robert Giaimo of Connecticut to assist her in making an official complaint to the Justice Department.

ALP-S1-A

Our daughter was in graduate school at ▇▇▇▇ in California in
1973. She met a group of young people who seemed to be an
effective witness for their faith in Jesus Christ.

She was 23, a graduate of the Univ. of ▇▇▇▇▇▇▇ in Occupational
Therapy, and we assumed she was capable of making sound judge-
ments and decisions.   Immediately following the academic work
at the Univ. of ▇▇▇▇ she spent nine months in affiliations:
Physical Rehabilitation, in ▇▇▇▇; Psychiatric, Psych. Institute in ▇▇▇▇▇▇▇▇; and Pediatrics, Univ. of ▇▇▇▇▇

After one semester in graduate school, she joined the Tony and
Susan Alamo Christian Foundation of Saugus, Calif.

From outward appearances they appeared to be a well meaning
group, helping young people.

We finally visited the Foundation in Calif., the letters and
information we recieved from her raised questions, and she had
repeatedly said she would not visit home again -- that the
Foundation was her home. This was very unlike our daughter.

We visited several days, and as we asked questions in a
friendly interested way, we began to realize she was reporting
everything to overseers. Then the barriers were up, they were
all suspicious and hostile. She stopped seeing us.

We realize she is mind-controlled, and a willing slave of the
group. Our daughter has been completely alienated from us,
we never hear from her. We are afraid to visit again for fear
of bodily harm. Others have been beaten.

We have always had very good communication with our daughter,
a fine, open relationship. This has been totally reversed.

After she joined the group, she signed over her car, possessions
and funds. And she wrote of earning funds for the Foundation
through jobs they were sent to in groups.

They are not allowed any outside literature, or information of
what is going on in the world. There are levels of control,
leaders, overseers, etc. They are never alone, or permitted to
go anywhere without another member. Poor diet and lack of rest
are used as part of this control.

They have formed an additional group north of Alma, Arkansas.

We desire laws to be enacted to permit conerned parents to
remove their young people, and return them to family and society.

Exploitation of youth for personal gain by cult leaders should
be controlled.

The Cunneen Family
448 Morris Drive
No. Valley Stream, N. Y.

To Whom It May Concern: ALP-P-A

My son Mark Cunneen left home Nov. 1972 and went to see his friend
in Riverside. One night the boys went out on the town and were accosted
by members of the Tony and Susan Alamo Foundation. They were invited to
their so called church where my son has been ever since.

We went to see our son when he told us he had been hurt while
working on the Alamo ranch. What we found there appalled us, the
young people live under the most primative conditions, they would not
let us in the church until they cleaned it up. and all the time we were
there the Alamos nerer left our side. we could not say one word to our
son alone. My son changed from a goo loving son into a zombie he
is so afraid he will go to hell if he disobeys the Gods Alamo. He keeps
telling us the world is going to end. We are a catholic family and
Marks fater is a retired New York City Police Captian. Mark has 3
brothers and 3 sisters . Mark took out a student loan when he was
in college and did not pay it back when he dropped out of school to
join the T. S Foundation New York State sent investagators out to
the Foundation and they said it was run like a Gestopo Camp they
never saw Mark and still have not got their money back.   I wrote to
Susan Alamo and asked her to let Mark ans. our letters I heard nothing

        Please do something before it is too late. We love our son
and will do anything to get him back

                        Sincerely,

                        Mrs. F Cunneen

143

Our son, ██████, was a second-year student at the University of ██████ When he was 'kidnapped' into the Hare Krishna movement. He was then 21 years of age and has been a member of this group for the past five years.

He had always been a very good student, good athlete, and always had several close friends. He received a religious education, attending Sabbath services with regularity. We were extremely proud of him. He was loving and devoted to us, his parents, as well as his grandparents, aunts, uncles, and cousins. He had a close relationship with his two younger brothers who shared his avid interest in sports. As he grew older, he became very interested in politics and enjoyed campaigning during election year. He enjoyed watching television and, wherever and whenever possible, would appear on a quiz or talk show.

The radical change in our son's behavior and personality since he joined this group is hard to believe; he is a totally different person - dehumanized and zombie-like. He has abandoned his entire past life; has no interest in former friends, nor in any of his family. His calls and letters are very few and far-between, despite our numerous attempts to communicate wih him. When we do speak with him it can never be on a personal level; it is strictly a sermonizing type of conversation. There have been serious illnesses within our immediate family, but his responses have been negative, completely devoid of emotion.

Recently, several months had elapsed when we had not received any communications from our son. We were informed by the president of the temple where he had re-sided for a number of months that ██████ had shown a 'weakening' tendency and, when this occurs, the devotee is moved about from temple to temple throughout the country in order to mingle with other devotees. This process is employed for the purpose of reinforcing the weaker devotee's beliefs in Krishna. Despite our numerous calls and telegrams to temples throughout the country, we received no response from or about our son. Quite by chance did we 'track' him down at the ██████ temple several weeks ago. He was more distant and detached than ever. He has since left for India with the group for an indefinite period of time.

We have been further informed by 'reliable' sources that, because my son was observed by his superiors to have a relatively good relationship with his parents (most devotees have nothing or practically nothing to do with their families, so it was regarded as highly irregular for him to show the concern that he did in the past) they set about to detach him further from us. Un-fortunately, their indoctrination has been successful.

We must reiterate that our son's attitude and detachment is wholly unlike his normal self. He had always been more than just dutifully concerned about his family. He was very much involved in family get-togethers and enjoyed meeting with his relatives on every occasion.

We hope and pray that the Hare Krishna movement, along with the many other cults, will be eliminated before their many victims have been totally destroyed.

TO WHOM IT MAY CONCERN:

Our son   a senior at SDSU, entered the Hare Khrisna temple in Los Angeles to become a Devotee the week before Christmas, he told us by phone on December 23, 1975. We believe he was receptive to a cult because of his introduction to T M on the campus, that lead to an interest in Self-Realization Fellowship study material. During that time, he became friendly with two boys whom we believe were Khrisna members.

Direct personal visitation was attempted by us but we were told in the presence of   that, "Being with his parents was not a congenial atmosphere for him and he should leave us."   followed his "leader" back into the temple!

Communications by telephone has not been possible as Khrisna tells us that   cannot come to the phone as he is busy or cannot be found. We have been told, "It is Khrisna's obligation to not allow agitating situations, such as his parents, to disturb his program of learning." and "If parents are inimical to the movement, they must be kept apart from their parents." Also, the daily schedule does not permit free time for communication because, "We keep the new ones busy." Devotees arise at 3 a.m. for a full day of work, chanting, meditation and instruction on "scriptures"; during the month of January,   said he was busy because he was taking five classes a day in such instruction!

Health and sanitary conditions are deplorable and dangerous. One of our other sons visited   and found him ill and lying on the floor of a cold and drafty room.   was pale, his mouth and lips dry and he said he had a Cold and now the Flu so he didn't feel like moving.   was covered with only a blanket so he wore a T-shirt, wool shirt, sweat shirt, ski cap, skirt and socks. A bucket of juice with a common dipper was at the door for   and four others, also lying on the floor. The bathroom across from the "sick room" had only a urinal and the floor was wet with urine and stained with same. In another bathroom, the toilet had no seat or toilet paper;   explained that they "stand or sit", use their hands and wash or shower to cleanse themselves. Usually   shares sleeping quarters with seven in a room which measures approximately seven by nine feet.

Because of the filthy living conditions, limited diet and   health without our proper medical attention, our son and friends returned the next night to remove him bodily from the de-humanizing situation at the temple.   was pleased to see everyone and went out to the car with them. But, before they had a chance to leave the temple "exploded" with Khrisna members;   was taken back into the temple, the boys were beaten but managed to escape.

On March 5, 1976   was brought to our home by Khrisna; he wanted the jewelry he owns, worth $1,100, to finance a trip to India he is planning. He was happy to see us and brought gifts of cookies and the newest "Godhead" magazine. We forced him to remain with us at home. However, later that night, at another house, he jumped through a glass window to escape. Khrisna picked him up and returned him to the temple. The next morning   was brought to our local police station where he charged his parents and brother with kidnapping. The Officer said, "   was prompted by a Khrisna member on what he should say."   said he would like to visit with his parents alone. However, private visits are not possible because Khrisna must be ever present to guide the Devotees in their decisions. (Even our Birthday card to   was returned after it had been opened and our letter to him removed!)

While   was at home on March 5th conversing with him was difficult.   would pause and chant when he couldn't answer a question, nod his head up and down slightly while speaking or stare and say nothing. He did explain to us that it is not unhealthy to eat off of the floor because they eat spiritual food, and the floor is mopped afterwards. (At one of Khrisna's Sunday Festivals a large black cockroach was not killed, but rather it was scooped up and dropped out the window!)

Strange behavior for a boy who received a commendation in high school from head of the English Dept. in his senior year, "   has achieved a 95 average, one of the highest ever given in this school...I thank you, as   's parents, for providing the kind of home envoirment which has made this growth possible. I congratulate you on having a son with such a potential."   previous physical bearing was erect, alert and broad shouldered; he lettered in high school track and cross-country, had many interests including skiing, surfing and was a talented violinist.   was educated in the Lutheran Church and School system, 1-8 grades.

On March 27th we found   on Hollywood Blvd. in L.A. passing out Khrisna invitations to the public. Upon seeing us he started trembling, backed away and shouted at us in anger, "Stay away from me! Stay away from me!" Very sad, he acted like a frightened animal, cornered and growling a warning that he would or could fight to protect himself, if necessary.

MONDAY, APRIL 19,1976

Dear Mrs. Slaughter,   HKP-S35-A1

We have just returned from a'visit' with our son, who is a two-year member of HARE KRISHNA cult, is 28 years old and completely brain-washed. He receives no mail, is allowed no communication with family or friends, and only by arriving unannounced and actually trapping him at the "temple" did we get to see him. We were permitted to listen to him harangue us about his "religion" in the constant presence of two other KRI$HNAS,constant interuptions by still other KRI$HNAS beckoning him to come back inside the 'temple'. Finally, our son was summoned by the "leader" and left abruptly on the leader's orders saying he had been told he had been away from KRI$HNA too long owing to our presence.

In the course of our son's harangue we gleaned these facts:
1. HE TAKES IN, CONSISTENTLY, $150.00 per day selling INCENSE, MAGAZINES, BOOKS
2. THAT HE ONLY KNOWS THE MONEY IS SENT TO LOS ANGELES TO THE HEAD GURU WHOSE NAME IS PRABHUPADA AND IS PUT IN THE PRABHUPADA TRUST. HE DOES NOT KNOW OR EVEN ASK WHAT BECOMES OF THE MONEY.
3. OUR SON SAYS THEY ARE NEVER SATISFIED WITH HIS $150.00 per day THAT HE BRINGS IN. THEY CONSTANTLY BERATE HIM THAT OTHERS IN OTHER "TEMPLES" AROUND THE COUNTRY BRING IN THOUSANDS PER DAY AND HE MUST REDOUBLE HIS MONEY MAKING EFFORTS IF HE EVER HOPES TO FIND FAVOR WITH THE IMPLACABLE GOD KRI$HNA.
4. WE ASKED HOW HE WAS GETTING ALONG WITH HIS RECURRING DEPRESSIONS AND HE ANSWERED THAT HE IS TOLD BY THE LEADER THAT DEPRESSION IS HIS PUNISHMENT FOR FAILING LORD KRI$HNA, THAT HE MUST SELL MORE INCENSE,ETC TO AVOID THE PUNISHMENT OF DEPRESSION.
5. HE IS EXHORTED TO THINK CONSTANTLY OF DEATH IN ORDER TO BE "READY" WHEN IT COMES. HE EXPLAINED TO US THAT IF YOU ARE NOT THINKING ABOUT DEATH AND KRI$HNA WHEN DEATH GETS YOU, THAT YOU HAVE A WHOLE LIST OF DREAD THINGS THAT HAPPEN TO YOU AFTER DEATH. HE BELIEVES THAT IF HE WERE TO LEAVE THE CULT HIS PUNISHMENT WOULD BE SURE HERE AND NOW AND AFTER DEATH AS WELL.
6. HE SEEMS TO BE A SICK, SMALL COG IN A VERY LARGE MONEY MACHINE.
7. HE HAS BEEN PROGRAMMED TO ANSWER IN "KRI$HNA TALK" EVERY CONCEIVABLE QUESTION ON BELIEF, KRI$HNA REASONS WHY HE MUST BE CUT OFF FROM FAMILY AND FRIENDS. HIS LOYALTY IS ONLY TO THE CULT, HE MUST OBEY ORDERS WITHOUT QUESTION.
8. WE LEARNED FROM AN ATTORNEY THAT THE LOCAL LEADER, MATHEW ZACKHEIM, ATTEMPTED TO SELL PROPERTY BELONGING TO OUR SON IN HIS ABSENCE AND WITHOUT HAVING DEED TO THE PROPERTY. ZACKHEIM WAS CAUGHT BY AN ALERT REAL ESTATE AGENT. ZACKHEIM HAS ASSUMED A HINDU NAME AND GOES BY THAT. THE ADDRESS OF THE "TEMPLE" IS 4544 Laclede, St. Louis, Missouri, 63108. Area code 314-367-4105.
8. OUR SON SAID THEY USE ANY SALES GIMMICK THEY CAN THINK OF(WE ARE COLLECTING MONEY TO HELP PEOPLE IN THE DRUG SCENE,ETC.) THAT WILL WORK. THEY ASK FOR A "DONATION" FOR A BOOK, BUT HE SAID THEY SNATCH THE BOOK BACK IF NO DONATION IS FORTHCOMING. THEY JUST SELL OUTRIGHT THE INCENSE. THEY HIDE THE FACT THAT THEY MUST WEAR ROBES AND SHAVED HEADS BY THE USE OF"CIVILIAN" CLOTHES AND WIGS AND HATS. THEY "WORK" BUSY STREET INTERSECTION, SHOPPING CENTERS, AIRPORTS, ETC. HARASSING PEOPLE WITH ANYTHING THEY CAN THINK OF TO GET THEM TO GIVE MONEY. THEY HAVE HAD CONFRONTATIONS WITH "MOON PEOPLE" AND TRY TO DISSUADE PEOPLE FROM LISTENING TO THEM AND TRY TO TELL THE "MOON PEOPLE" HOW EVIL "MOON" IS!

THESE ARE JUST A FEW OF THE THINGS WE KNOW ABOUT HARE KRI$HNA.
SINCERELY,

A few portions of the letter below were deleted for lack of space.

Wichita Falls, Texas
February 16, 1976

To Whom it May Concern:

WIV-P-A

In Sept., 1974, I was invited by a classmate, also a nursing student, to attend fellowship. It appeared to be a normal Christian group with vibrant and cheerful young people. After attending fellowhip for a number of weeks, I enrolled in Dr. Victor Paul Wierwille's basic foundational course known as "The Power for Abundant Living" which cost $85. It was supposed to contain the keys to living a more abundant life. The course was taught by Wierwille on tapes which were returned after the thirty-two hour course. Several paperback books by Dr. Wierwille and a year's subscription to The Way Magazine also came with the course. This basic course is designed to program recruits. The organization encourages members to gain more spiritual knowledge by taking numerous taped seminars at a cost of $30 to $40.

Due to my participation in this cult, my personality changed completely. I lost my identity and was only what the cult wanted me to be—a smiling puppet. They taught me that God's work comes first, regardless of tests or school work. They made me feel guilty if I did not attend fellowship. My grades dropped from B's to failing marks, which was not representative of my previous academic achievement.

Constant pressure was placed on members to become more committee to The Way Ministry, making one feel that his commitment is to God, thus being a more binding agreement. Tremendous pressure was placed on members to keep them from questioning the ministry or dropping out of the group. One reaches the point that he believes in the integrity of the leader, Dr. Wierwille and is no longer able to question his teachings. He destroys the individual's confidence in his ability to interpret the Bible with the guidance of the Holy Spirit. He is such a dynamic and persuasive leader that he has convinced the members that he is the only one in 2,000 years who has correctly interpreted the Bible. The organization discourages associating or living with non-believers, including parents or friends that might cause one to develop negative thoughts or to doubt The Way Ministry.

Dr. Wierwille encouraged us to try reading only The Way literature and the Bible for three months and assured us that we would be a changed person by doing this. This is one of his mind control techniques. We were also discouraged from reading the newspapers or watching the news on TV or anything that would cause us to develop negative thoughts. Positive thinking was so ingrained in our minds that we thought that any doubt of The Way Ministry was wrong or evil. Through the methods of brainwashing and mind control, I lived in a controlled environment. I lost my power to reason and to think realistically.

As I review my experiences in The Way, I realize that I was definitely brainwashed by subtle indoctrination techniques. To someone who has not been through this experience, it is almost impossible to believe that this could happen in America. What is so frightening is that this could happen to anyone without their being aware of it. Some of our most brilliant young people's minds have been captured by these cults. Many of them are graduate students seeking higher degrees--our future leaders...

Cults are one of our greatest threats to our American way of life and freedom today.

Sincerely yours,
s/Suzanne Toler

WIP-S37-A-1

This story will sound unreal to the general public if they have never had a personal experience of a loved one ensnared in an insidious cult group. To families who have personally experience this, the story of anguishand heartbreak will be very real and understandable.

Our son was a student at one of our state universities and majoring in religion. He was loving, caring, honest, easy going and a real joy to his parents. We brought him up in a liberal Protestant Church, and his religious nor parental training could have been considered "controlled."

At the time he was recruited into the cult group, he had been attending services in different Churches and reading about various religions. He called us from college and told us he had met a wonderful, loving group of people and he was attending fellowships with them and learning about the Bible. We were happy to hear that since he was a new student at the university and had experienced a break with his band friends.

On his first weekend home after taking The Way's Power For Abundant Living Course for $85.00, we found that it was impossible to discuss in a rational and loving manner the things he was learning. One did not have to be a student of the Bible to see that the things he was spouting were anti-Christian. He said the "adversary" (devil) would work through his parents to try to turn him away from God and the truth. Ignorant in the hypnotic techniques used by the cults, we tried to show him the error in what he was saying, and tried with all our hearts to get him to talk to a religious expert and not of our own faith. This he refused to do.

Since cult victims tell their leaders all that parents say, because of the fact that we were not accepting of his new faith, and in fact was criticizing the fact that his leader, Victor Paul Wierwille, was a multi-millionaire, he was sent away from us for a year to a distant state. He was not allowed to come home to visit us except for 2 days at Christmas.

We set out to investigate The Way almost immediately after our son joined. We found shocking information of lies and fraud, of how whole families had been cheated out of a lifetime of savings and then been kicked out of the group. We found the group to be teaching a series of contradictions, everything they claim they are or teach, we found the opposite to be true. For instance they claim to bind families together. The only families who have not been torn apart by this group are the ones where the victims were able to convert the parents and the rest of the family to join. Abundantly sharing up to 50% of income in order to receive more blessings.

Weirwille lies about having a doctorate, about his age, about how he started the group, about his teachings being original, and refuses to make public his financial statement. His assets now are said to be about 5 million. He claims to be the most patriotic of Americans, however he rips off the government for countless tax dollars. He purchased Emporia College of Emporia, Kansas from the Presbyterian Church. Though formerly accredited, the state of Kansas will not accredit it now. He has a sign in the front "Way College of Emporia" founded in 1892 (?) and the Way opened last fall, he is using the dates of the Presbyterian Church"s opening of the college.

There is no question that some of our brightest, most talented and most dedicated young people are victims of the hypnotic techniques used by Wierwille's robots. We owe it to Christ's Church and to society to free them from this vicious cult.

My 19 year old grandson, a winsome, bright "A" student and athlete (Freshman) at a distinguished U.S. eastern college, is a missing person. He left college ████████, 1976, driving his own car for a spring vacation of skiing and Camping in ████████

Since the case is still unresolved, I am using fictitious names, but full facts may be verified by calling me or his parents, or through the Citizens Freedom Foundation, P.O. Box 256, Chula Vista, California, 92012, or affiliated branch in Arlington, Texas.

My grandson,   , was accompanied by a fellow student whom, for this report, we 'll call Leon. Apparently   has come under control of a cult widely publicized as THE TWO, (or "Bo" and "Peep," or U.F.O. recruiters, or HIM, Human Individual Metamorphosis.) The founders and leaders, "Bo" and "Peep," were jailed last year but are now out. The cult are said <u>not</u> to use drugs though considering the undetectable minimal nature of lysergic acid (LSD) there has been evidence of this as a hooker. Their principal method is hypnotism, and subsequent procedures of isolation that reduce members to infantile dependency. They communicate by Post Office General Delivery, and have been credited with network telepathic communications.

    with Leon, disembarked from   car precisely at the site of a poster advertising a U.F.O. meeting in Taos Community House March 22, 1976 -- whether by some sinister connection unknown to their college community back in the east, or predisposing needs of Bill's own. Cults flourish on seekers and searchers.

    attended the meeting, Leon did not. An off-duty Taos policeman in plain clothes with whom we have been in touch since, went to the meeting and described it as a rough looking group, half of whom boo-ed and cat-called the propaganda and left early. Some stayed, and the policeman said a youth answering the description of   -- clean shaven with collar length hair, went up to the speakers' table afterward and talked with the "recruiters," but the officer did not bother him because "he looked so happy."

Tuesday, ████████,   decided to go with the 3 cult recruiters. He gave Leon his car containing suit case, skiis, camera, suit case and all his possessions and told him to drive it back to college. Leon complied.
    retained only a change of clothing, sleeping bag and traveler's checks ($500.00) He does not carry credit cards.

Sunday, ████████   parents in ████████ received two letters from   expressing love, appreciation for a happy family and privileges, sorrow at having to hurt them but that while he 'did not understand it himself,' he felt 'compelled to go with these people.' There were vague confessions of past misdoing (LSD, marijuana, having "loved women" which, while understandable and forgivable in our times, were so uncharacteristic of Bi as to make us suspicious he may have been under duress that was shrewdly hedging a law suit. He mentioned search for meaning in life, dis-illusionment with this country and the world, the family pattern, etc., The second short letter wandered off into space, citing passages from Revelations, which he had gone to the Taos library (in company?) to read.

We hypothesize that other predisposing factors may be of a situational nature: desire for independence, loss of a girl love object, disappointment at not making varsity baseball squad training in ████████ (Few Freshmen do.) He was also much impressed with a course in Hindu-Buddhism religions he was taking in college. All this was fertile ground for cultism.

We have been a happy family, allowing for normal strains that occur among bright thinking people. We are making every effort through legal and private means to rescue Bill. We believe these cults (1500 of all kinds in America) are using insidious mean to corrupt the finest youth of our country, and <u>they are protected by the Constitution as the victims are not.</u>
<u>Something must be done, and quickly!</u> ████████

UFV – P – A

To Whom it May Concern:

I would like to submit witness to a cult called "the Two." The two, sometimes referred to as "Bo and Peep," claim to be the two prophets written in Revelations 11, and that they will die (be killed), resurrect, and travel to the next evolutionary kingdom in a U. F. O. (actually a mental construct). I became involved with this cult by attending two meetings in Chapel Hill, N. C. After hearing "the information" presented by two members of this cult, I told them I was interested in joining. When I gave them a definite yes two days later, I was told to tie up all loose ends, financial and otherwise, give away all possessions but one suitcase of clothes and possibly light camping gear, and if I felt I needed to, tell my parents what I was going to do. They would be back in touch in 5 days (I designated the time) after all this was done, and I was ready to "walk out the door of my life" to join the cult. Walking out the door of one's life is supposedly a sincere gesture to God and an affirmation of faith in that you are willing to forget the past, family, friends, material possessions and devote 100 per cent of your energy to "the process" of getting to know God and letting Him provide all things for your existence. Hours before I was to officially join the cult, my parents came to Raleigh, where I was attending N. C. S. U. and took me home. I was unwilling to go and begged them to let me stay in Raleigh to receive a phone call telling me where to meet the members of the cult the following morning. I was physically, mentally, and emotionally drained and had not slept or eaten for 5 or 6 days.

I have been at home now for two months and my life has gradually been pieced back together with the help of my family, friends, and a psychiatrist.. Most of all, I can attribute my recovery to Jesus Christ and the new life given me by His spirit. The effect of the cults in the U. S. is being felt by families all over this country and I, from experience, can advocate any action taken to stop them. These cults are not the answer to the spiritual void felt in many of us today, especially our youth. There is only one way and I thank you, Jesus.

UFP-P-A

The DAP Committee received a gift copy of Let Our Children Go!, Ted Patrick and Tom Dulack, Authors (Clarke, Irwin & Company, Limited, Publisher) from authoress Dell B. Wilson who sent the card below:

Mrs. T. Henry Wilson   600 Tate Street   Morganton, North Carolina 28655

This book is a personal gift from
Mrs. T. Henry Wilson, sr.
whose lovely, trusting (see page 182) and intelligent 19 year old grandson (my son's son,) has come under the sinister hypnotic influence os the so-called "U.F.O." or "H.I.M." (Human Individual Metamorphosis" group founded and influenced by two Texans, Herff Applewhite and Bonnie Lu Trusdale Nettles, notoriously known as "Bo" and "Peep."

No acknowledgment of this book is necessary, but it is sent in confidence that responsible citizens will finally wake up and achieve a fair law to stop misuse of mind control that is threatening our youth, the United States of America, and the world.

Reproduced herein with the express permission of Mrs. Wilson.

DAP COMMITTEE
May 3, 1976

To Whom it May Concern:

FFP-59-A

My two teen age daughters were brainwashed by a group leader while we lived in ███████, N.Y. They were cajoled on the streets to join the Forever Family alias The Church of Bible Understanding. The girls have been told by the group leader, Chuck Marburger of 166 Hobart St., Utica, N.Y. 13501, Phone: 315-724-5810, to hate their family and mother and to run away from home to serve the Forever Family and its group leaders. The head of this Cult is Stewart Traill, a former nuclear physicist whose wife ran away with another man. My daughters are: ██████████████ -- now at the Forever Family house in: ████████████████████████████████, Michigan 48236. She has been trained to walk the streets and bring in money for her leaders.
At the present time, I have the 17 year old girl with me; because the police found her for me in ██████████ Michigan, when she was 16. The leader of this Forever Family, named Stewart Traill advised my 16 year old girl ███████, to run away across the border to Canada to avoid the police, because he told her "your mother has the police looking for you". After getting ████████, who was 16 at the time, home, she told me this.
There is also a Forever Family house with a leader named Jerry at 396 Alexander Street, Rochester, N.Y. 14607, phone: 716-473-1917. This all began while we were living in ███████ N.Y. and first the phone calls began. Three and four times a day and three and four times at night, strange voices were calling asking for my daughters. It was the Forever Family members at 166 Hobart St., Utica, N.Y., and they made dates to meet my two girls, and to pick them up in a van and make them walk the streets to find more recruits. At the time, my girls were 16 and 17, and when my ███████████ son and I moved to ███████, the two girls, ██████ and ████████ ran away to the FF house and when I called to ask the leader to bring them home, he harassed me and insulted me over the phone.
These leaders have taught my daughters to mistrust me and have turned them against their former church and the pastor of the church. They were formerly members of the Trinity Lutheran Church, ██████████
I keep receiving letters from the former friends of ██████████ asking her to run away and come back, to the Forever Family. She is happy at home and seems to be coming out of her "mind reforming" but she has a long way to go. I am so worried about ████████ she has low blood sugar, allergies and braces on her teeth, and the Forever Family will not let her get the proper care. Her health is not good because of the Forever Family leaders telling her to walk the streets late at night.
I would like to have Stewart Traill arrested for "contributing to the delinquency of minors" and for interfereing with the health, education, and general well being of my two daughters, besides alcinating my daughters from their mother.

Sincerely,

EXPERIENCE LETTER

Prepared 17 March 1976

GGP-P-A

Case: Merrilee Chalenor   **Group:** Garden Grove Community Church (Calif)

Parent: R.E. Chalenor, 18182 Hutchings Drive, Yorba Linda, Ca. 92686

BACKGROUND

Except for being a product of a divorced home, Merri was a reasonably normal 17½ year old high school senior. She had progressed through the Girl Scout movement, YMCA, music lessons and was a member of the Episcopal Church. Her home life was reasonably stabe i.e. she had lived in the same home for 10 years.

THE BEGINNING

One spring day Merri asked to attend a week end church camp out with her long time neighbor girl friend. At this camp she met a young youth minister and his wife. They continued the contact and urged (in writing) Merri to leave home and live in a church sponsored "Christian Foster Home". The minister's wife persued Merri even on public school grounds, during school hours urging her to be "Born Again" and to attend church services every night often until 10 and 11 PM. Appeals by the parents to the church senior minister brought no change.

THE SEPARATION

As the conflict grew between child and parent over reasonable hours of involvement in "religious" activity, the youth minister and his wife continued to urge (in writing as well as by voice) that the child leave home and enter a "Christian Foster Home". The youth minister and his wife took Merri to the Juvenile Hall where she declared she did not like her parents and would not go home. She was taken in by the authorities and eventually made a ward of the court by a Hearing Officer later identified as a life long friend of the church senior minister.

THE RESULTS

Merri soon reached her 18th birthday and was released by the court to live in a County subsidized, Christian Foster Home. This home was operated by the female cook of the church. During the "adjustment period" Merri tried to commit suicide, tried to murder another girl in the group (a "non-believer"), was raped and received drugs on the church grounds. She wrote several letters stating that she had to choose between her father and Jesus. She was treated by a church paid psychologist who specialized in "self-hypnotism". All attempts at reconcilliation have been futile.

SUMMARY

A reasonably normal young person was totally changed in personality, moral standards, and relationships with family and friends in a very short period of time. She committed acts of violence against herself and others. This change was initiated and is still maintained by"religious" indoctorination techniques. Although the church has terminated its involvement in this cult-like youth activity, church officials are unable to effect a reconcilliation between Merri and her family.

Oxford, Mississippi
                                               March 18, 1976
To Whom it May Concern: WCP-P-A

     This letter is written as a part of my effort to obtain help in the ex-
posure of the dangerous mind-controlling cults...We have not been able to obtain any help whatsoever from any government agency. They merely shrug us
off with that trite excuse that any attempt to quell the activities of these
dangerous criminals would be a violation of the freedom of religion clause of
the Constitution. I appealed to the FBI on several occasions to investigate
the Armstrong cult, which once called itself the RADIO CHURCH OF GOD, now the
WORLDWIDE CHURCH OF GOD...I had correspondence with them for several months,
directing my observation (at the insistence of the agency) to the Criminal
Division of the Justice Department, but when I followed those instructions,
something happened which I do not understand. All of a sudden, Clarence
Kelley slammed the door in my face by telling me that the Armstrongs had not
done anyghint. They could not investigate them unless I gave them proof that
the World Wide Church of God had broken some Federal laws...Evidently the
Armstrong-Rader-Kuhn coalition has much clout with the Federal Government.

     I had told this agency that I could furnish the proof that little chil-
dren had been allowed to die because the cult denied them all medical aid.
I could furnish a letter from the one-time director of ministers to all
"field ministers" all over the world instructing them on the devious, lying
methods of evading the law when a child was allowed to die. I said that I
could give them the proof that the Armstrong cult denied all members the
privilege of serving their countries in any capacity since all governments
are "of the devil" and are not worth supporting; and I also revealed that
members on occasion have been instructed to pray for the "soon-coming destruction of the United States." But the agenceis of the U. S. Government
were not concerned.

     They have shown the same indifference, even disdain, toward the efforts
of parents to expose all the cults by investigation, especially Moon's Unification Church, which has even penetrated the office of the Speaker of the
House of Representatives! Not more than six weeks ago the "Moonies" descended
on this University town to sell their cheap wares under the false pretense of
being for the benefit of mental retardation, etc. I reported them to the
police in the city of Oxford, who in turn alerted the University police. And
those young slaves, high on Moon, shook the dust off the town from their feet
but not before they took at least one distrubed young man (a homosexual) with
them after he agreed to sell his car and give them all the money it would
bring and go to a foreign country to sell Moon's diabolical subversion.

     All of the cults are essentially the same in their ability to mesmerize
their victims, alienate them completely from their government, families,
friends, their entire past--complete destruction of the individual (exactly
the same tactics used in prisoner-of-war camps by the Nazis and the Communists).
All education, religion and everything is of the devil unless it is a part of
the doctrine of the cult. I know what I am talking about because our son has
been an absolute slave of the Armstrong hierarchy for more than ten years. It
is heartbreaking to witness the destruction of his personality...When will our
Government wake up to the malignancy that is threatening to consume us and the
whole world, actually protected by this Government as they operate tax-exempt
and without any surveillance from any agency of this government whatsoever?
What kind of "religious freedom" do they think they are protecting anyway! Unless we, the people who have been hurt by these fiends, can be heard now,
every freedom guaranteed to all Americans by the Constitution will be lost forever   Sincerely yours, Mrs. Ralph Williams
                                            (Signed)

Mrs. Robert R. Woodruff (Helen)
1035 La Mesa Drive
Fullerton, California 92633
March 21, 1975

TO WHOM IT MAY CONCERN:

As a parent who had a cult try to alienate my daughter and her family from her blood family that truly love her, I swear that the following summary is true concerning the brutality and devious business deals of the "mail-order minister, leaders" of Phoenix Light Temple, 6835 N. Central, Phoenix, Arizona. The leaders are Harold Bell, 38, his wife Dorothy, 54, and her four adult children born to a previous marriage. Dorothy is the head of the operation.

1. Dorothey Bell claims God works through her. She has a special annointing. She has visions and revelations. Through her and her loyal followers God is going to bring his vengeance down on the land and they will go through the cities killing Mothers and babies. She teaches that all females are "demon possessed". It was inherited from Eve.

2. The doctrine of Phoenix Light Temple is the same as the Children of God, and the Susan and Tony Alamo Christian Foundation. They know oneanother. All lived in Hollywood and the Bells were once associated with Fred Jordan who had a "falling out" with Moses Berg, leader of the Children of God.

3. In order to gain control of their converts minds the Bells use the following methods: mass hysteria in thier services, hypnosis, inadequate diets, forbidding the women to plan thie families, submission of the wife to the husband and the Bells, beatings with belts, mind control exercises, humilation if they have a talent, spying by members on each other if they question the Bell's doctrine, isolation from their previous home and families, hate for all organized churches, (they teach homosexuality is taught in organized seminaries),they marry young people without a marriage if parents will not sign, ignore the laws of this country concerning tax laws and child custody, (threaten to hide the children where they will never be found), coerced the parents to sign a "covenant" giving the children to the one remaining in the cult, babies and toddlers are whipped for so much as whimpering in their long services.

4. The Bells have been under invertigation since last May for their activities. They are being sued in civil court for imprisoning members in a pit without sanitary facilities, feed or water for as long as seven days. Dorothy Bell also had loyal members try to ressurect her father from the dead with her power for approximately forty day. They hid the body six months so the pension checks would keep coming. A hearing is to take place March 26th in Payson, Arizona.

5. They young people live in near poverty while the Bells have accumulated over a million dollars by using them to work for nothing and pay them high rents on their satelitte houses or trailers. As many as six sleep in one small room.

6. The private detective agency in Phoenix,(Arizona-Investigations by Dick Todd) has uncovered many facts. The Bells are as dishonest as it is possible to be. They have expanded from fifty or so young people to over 400 and have branches in Oregon, California, New Mexico and communes in Willow Springs and Mt. View, Missouri. They are dangerous. All these cults are.

They are against everything this country stands for. Our Constitution is going to hve to be amended so that people like this can not operate. Do something before these subversive elements take over our country, and there will be no United States for the "huddled masses" to take refuge in.

Sincerely yours, a concerned citizen

Helen Woodruff

*Joseph Erlichman. Attorney is
the attorney.*

80

February 9, 1976

As a concerned Mother who has had three children virtually kidnapped
into one of the hundred of cults that have arisen in our states, I am
writing to you begging for your help in the drive to stop this vicious
sickness that has and is engulfing over a million of our youth.

Please talk and listen and DO SOMETHING about this terrible nightmare
that is disrupting the homes and minds of our youth and their families.

When you see how the   leaders of these cults take our youths mind and
recycle and brain wash them into robots that can no longer think for
themselves, how terribly,terribly frightening.

PLEASE, PLEASE attend the hearing against the Rev. Moon and the Unification
Cult which has been granted by Senator Robet Dole of Kansas. The meeting
is to be held on WEDNESDAY, FEBRUARY 18, from 1:30 to 3:30 pm in the Caucus
Room 1202, dirkson Office Building, on the corner of First and Constitution
Avenue, N.E.

When you see our youth working as virtual slaves for these cult leaders
and going hungry, eating from trash cans and giving every dime they can
locate and giving to these leaders so they can live in luxury. They have
taught them to hate and reject all family and to even kill if necessary.
These youths minds are brainwashed on the same system that was used in
Korea.

Please help us to do something before its too late and before all of
this terrible communist infiltration has destroyed the minds of all our
youth.

Sincerely,

Murrel Renfroe
401 N. Hurst
Angleton, Texas   77515
713   849-6022

From this National Conference, we hope to give enough factual information
fully documented, to stimulate a Congressional investigation, as well as
an investigation by the I. R. S., the Immigration Bureau and the Justice
Department.

I can not think of a meeting that you should attend that holds so much
importance as this one does. THE LIVES OF OUR YOUTH AND OUR NATION ARE
BEING HELD IN YOUR HANDS ON THIS DAY.

Dear Mr. Slaughter: I will be unable to attend but I am enclosing
a contribution and God Bless you in this important meeting. I think
you have talked with my sister Fern and Wayne Edwards at Dumas concerning
the salvaging of my children's lives.. Thanks for all your help.

                                        Mrs. Murrel Renfroe

REV. SUN MYUNG MOON

Chong Sun Kim

UNIVERSITY
PRESS OF
AMERICA

LANHAM • NEW YORK • LONDON

Copyright © 1978 by

University Press of America,™ Inc.

4720 Boston Way
Lanham, MD 20706

3 Henrietta Street
London, WC2E 8LU England

ISBN (Perfect): 0-8191-0494-9
LCN: 78-53115

PREFACE

Numerous articles about Rev. Sun Myung Moon, the controversial Korean preacher, have recently appeared in periodicals and newspapers in the United States. These articles dealt mainly with the way in which Moon proselytized and recruited his followers, and paid less attention to his native cultural and religious background in assessing the dynamics of his movement. Therefore, this work incorporates discussions of shamanism, which is the indigenous Korean religion, as a key to the source of his religious tenets and cult activities. Because Moon found thousands of zealous American adherents, the political, social, and intellectual pressures extant in American society are also discussed as factors contributing to Moon's popularity on college campuses and his success as a religious figure. Although this work utilizes a great many journalistic accounts, its approach is anthropological and sociological as well as historical, in order to broaden the student's understanding of this most curious movement of our time.

In writing this book, my colleague Professor James Findlay strengthened me with his warm and penetrating criticisms. Two other friends, Professors Robert Weisb ord and Arthur Stein, each read portions of the manuscript and made valuable suggestions. My deepest gratitude goes to Miss Shelly Killen for her assistance with factual knowledge and intellectual advice throughout the entire manuscript. I would also like to thank Charles Gallerani for his excellent editorial work. He generously offered his time to help in the revision of the manuscript, which became eminently readable. Finally, my affection goes to my wife Duksoon who proof read and did calligraphic work on Chinese and Korean characters.

CHONG SUN KIM
Narragansett, R.I.
January 1978

TABLE OF CONTENTS

161

I. INTRODUCTION

Unlike the multitude of contemporary gurus and other purveyors of eastern religions, Sun Myung Moon, The Korean Messiah has adopted the stormy stance and rhetoric of American fundamentalists, which he combines with his own hybrid theology that points to "Korea as the final bastion of the 'free world' in Asia." Although Moon's Unification Church avidly denies its political involvements, Sun Myung Moon repeatedly states that his movement will overcome the dreaded evil of Communism. The Unification Church-controlled International Federation for Victory Over Communism (IFVC) in Korea is an anti-Communist indoctrination center for Korean military and government personnel. Moon's followers both in Korea and the United States have openly stated their willingness to take up arms against North Korea and follow their spiritual Father in a prophetic march on P'yŏngyang. Moon has predicted a Third World War (between his "army" of the <u>Divine Principle</u> and Communism), which he attempts to hasten through his lobbying in America for military aid to South Korea. Moon claims that only the Unification Church can save divided Korea and the world from Communism. From his religious point of view, Korea is the new "Israel" which must first fall under his rule before he can rule over nations.[1]

Across the United States and around the world Moon's Unification Church operates numerous front groups like the Freedom Leadership Foundation (FLF). (See Appendix I, Front Organization of the Unification Church, p. 94   ). In the summer of 1969 Moon ordered his right-hand man Neil Salonen to form the "International Federation for the Extermination of Communism" in the United States. Salonen complied, but he cleverly labelled the new organization with a lower key and less provocative name, the Freedom Leadership Foundation. According to its former president, Allen Tate Wood, "FLF is listed as a nonprofit, nonpartisan educational corporation whose stated objective is to educate American youth about the danger of communism . . . ."[2] He says, further, that "objection to (Moon's political activities was considered infidelity to the master, and was like being disobedient to God."[3] Moon admonishes his followers that it would be better for them either to "march into the sea" or to "commit suicide rather than fail in their responsibility to him."[4]

The Unification Church favors martial songs, such as "We are the youth, soldiers of truth. Called by our God on High."[5] Psychiatrist John Clark has compared the Moon followers to the Hitler Youth League,[6] and Moon's technique of deception and false promises can be likened to the tactics of other totalitarian leaders. Moreover, the great wealth accrued from his various

1

business operations has enabled him to influence congressmen and journalists, as well as academics, who have joined the ranks of his new theological seminary and liberal arts college.[7] The Kingdom of Heaven on earth that Moon has promised his disciples is brought by their virtual slave labor, combined with his armaments industry. The free Korea that Rev. Moon wishes to safeguard from communism is in fact the puppet government of Park Chung Hee, a despotic ruler who has imprisoned, tortured, and executed his critics, including liberal Christian leaders, and the noted poet Kim Chi-ha. Park's opponents are not revolutionary communists in any sense, but they are constitutional reformists who seek neither communism nor monopoly capitalism.[8] It is the responsibility of those of us who choose a less simplistic approach to peace to unmask the vision of global unity and pseudo-brotherhood that this brilliant and manipulative religious businessman is selling to the young.

While President Park Chung Hee has succeeded in obtaining full United States military and financial support for his government, Moon has armed the Unification Church with bands of zealous young American college students who are prepared to assist their leader in the establishment of a Global Unification Church Theocracy with Moon and his lieutenants at the helm. Using the sophisticated techniques of modern advertising and American public relations services, Moon has staged gala million dollar public appearances and organized a conglomerate that is patterned after the most modern corporate business structures. Beneath the baroque intricacies of his so-called theology and unification principles lies a very simple philosophy, which he stated himself: "What I wish is your wish."

Recent articles have appeared on the Unification Church's political affiliation and its close ties to South Korean CIA activities in the United States. Journalistic accounts of Unification Church indoctrination programs and their after effects have also appeared in major newspapers.[9] Little attention, however, has been given to the origins of Moon's movement and the meaning of his fascination for the young. This book is intended as a study of Sun Myung Moon's origins in Korea and Japan, and of his adaptation of the Unification Church to the United States.

Much of the sensationalism that accompanies Moon's public appearances and the activities of the Unification Church generally has been the result of Moon's own public relations efforts. However a fair share of the current notoriety has come from the responses of the parents of "Moonies", who believe that Moon has brainwashed their children.

Former Moonists have been required to undergo so-called "deprogramming" sessions to counter their original indoctrination

2

and restore them to what their families view as normal. Since all of Moon's followers have voluntarily submitted to his indoctrination programs, his practices cannot be directly compared with the techniques of psychological torture employed in prisons from the U.S.S.R. to Chile. On the basis of the evidence at hand, however, there is no doubt that Moon has employed subtle techniques for controlling behavior, and that as a result numberous members of his cult have suffered both physical and psychological injury.[10]

Since Moon's appearance in the United States, two counter organizations have been formed: the Citizens Awareness Group and CERF (Citizens Engaged in the Reuniting of Families). These groups are pressing for congressional investigation of Moon's activities, serve to provide necessary help for parents whose children have joined the Church, disseminate information on the inner workings of Moon's organization, and urge state legislatures to put pressure on the movement.[11] Within three years of its founding in 1975, CERF, in particular, has grown into a 900 family organization. Rabbi Maurice Davis of the White Plains Jewish Community Center wrote a series of articles for the National Jewish Post describing his experiences with CERF and with families from his congregation, which had become involved with the Unification Church. After his articles appeared, Rabbi Davis received threatening phone calls and letters. In a sermon delivered on May 24, 1974, Rabbi Davis stated: "I hold this movement to be evil and dangerous. I hold Reverend Sun Myung Moon to be charlatan and a manipulator of people. I hold his inner henchmen to be devious, unscrupulous and false . . . . This movement preys upon the young, the young of all religions. The Moon people are out to get them all, to convert the world by 1980 for Sun Myung Moon and his Messiahship."[12]

Some parents of members of the Unification Church view Moon as "a saintly man dedicated to love of God, the sanctity of the family, and the avoidance of alcohol, drugs, and illicit sexual activity."[13] On the other hand, the general popular response to Moon has varied from "Moon should be banned or deported," to "Moon is just a fad." More important, however, than calling Moon names or dismissing him as a passing fashion is the need to understand and to explain this new religious phenomenon and the reasons for susceptibility to cultists like Moon. As Peter Tipograph, a former social worker who was briefly a member of the Unification Church said:

> If people just concentrate on Moon and not on why Moon is supported and thriving, then they've missed the whole point. That's why I get upset when people concentrate on Moon but don't look into their own back-yard and say 'Moon's just taken advantage of something that developed prior to this.' It makes you think that,

3

if Moon weren't so bad, maybe his movement would
have some merit and a right to exist. I feel very
torn about telling a yound person not to be in Moon's
group becuase they won't say, 'I'm in Moon's group
becuase of Moon.' They'll say, 'Oh we're the only
ones who seem to care.' Although I may say, 'I think
there's a lot more to it, there's a lot of contradictions, you're not always so caring,' how can I tell
them not to hold on to those values? And then, who
am I to tell them not to hold on to those values?
And then, where am I telling them to turn? Go back
home, where their parents are screwed up like they
were before? It gets very confusing and frustrating
at times.[14]

Our alienated life, with its lack of human relationships,
loss of identity, impersonal technology, broken families and
lack of intellectual stimuli in middle-American provides fertile
soil for charlatans and their fillowers. "To lonely young people
drifting through cold, impersonal cities and schools," says
Berkeley Rice, "the Church offers instant friendship and communion,
a sense of belonging. To those troubled by drugs, sex or material-
ism, the Church offers a drugless, sexless world of ascetic
puritanism. To those hungering for truth and meaning in a complex
world, it offers purpose and direction."[15] Rev. Sun Myung Moon
is quite clever and has played on the climate of the time and the
inadequacy of our social institutions which do not provide a
milieu for cooperative relations with others. The ease with which
Moon has exploited the situation and has persuaded thousands of
college students to adhere to his doctrines, points to a condition
of profound disorder and crisis in our society.

We cannot look upon Rev. Moon as a Korean Charlie Chaplain
playing Adolph Hitler, or a deranged fanatic who likes to rant and
rave before mass audiences in time of crisis. The fact that
Moon has a large following, including 4,000 in the United States,
and the reality of his power to produce converts who will blindly
follow him in his schemes, points to the importance of understanding this man not only in his relationship to our intellectual and
cultural pressures but also in his links with the South Korean
government. South Korea is an arsenal for nuclear weapons,[15]
and the United States has poured millions of dollars into military
aid for this nation led by the tyrant Park Chung Hee. Sun Myung
Moon has been sanctioned to train confused young adults to be
militant supporters of Park, who holds unlimited power over the
people in South Korea.

We must constantly remind ourselves that Adolph Hitler first
appeared as a comic figure to many people. He became less than
amusing to those who bore the torture he imposed upon them, and a

4

monster to those whom he exterminated. On December 22, 1971, Mr.
Moon, who echoes some of Hitler's beliefs about the Jewish people,
gave a lecture on "How God is Pursuing his Restoration Providence":

> By killing one man, Jesus, the Jewish people had to
> suffer for 2,000 years. Countless numbers of people
> have been slaughtered. During the Second World War,
> six million were slaughtered to cleanse all the sins
> of the Jewish people from the time of Jesus.[17]

Although we don't know exactly what Moon has meant here,
those who directly or indirectly sanction the holocaust of Hitler's
death camps and the "purification" of the species by mass murder
are sick. When such a questionable man has a vast following,
enormous property and business holdings, and a close connection
with a government that is practicing Hitler's policies now we cannot afford to view him as a clown.

5

II. BACKGROUND OF SUN MYUNG MOON

Yong Myung Mun (later changed to Sun Myung Moon) was born in North Korea, the fifth of eight children in a peasant family that later converted to Christianity. In Chinese characters, Yong Myung means "shining dragon". The name that was later adopted, Sun Myung, is equivalent in meaning to "shining sun". He clearly preferred to be identified with an image of serenity, hence the words that translated into English, endow him with associations with the heavenly bodies.

With his stock build, extraordinary energy, and perse verance in pursuing his numerous industrial enterprises, Moon echoes some of the qualities of the early inhabitants of North Korea, the people of Koguryŏ.[1] Old Chinese documents refer to the people of Koguryŏ as tireless and perse vering, and ancient texts describe them as people who ran when they walked.[2] The harsh climate, rocky land, and nearly untillable soil of ancient Koguryŏ nurtured a hunter-warrior society that survived by virtue of its re-markable tenacity, toughness, and ingenuity in adapting to an ex-ceptionally difficult environment. For many years these hard, militant people staved off subjugation by the Chinese and main-tained their independence as a proud, fierce people. They are noted to this day for their bellicose and aggressive temperament. Bold and energetic, the Northern people retain the courageousness, short temper, and dynamic character of their hunting society an-cestors.

Sun Myung Moon exemplifies many of the traits of his fore-fathers, including an inordinate skill in lengthy harangues, and an indomitable will to succeed at all costs. Moon's public per-formances have been called a "kung fu tantrum," and he usually laces his speeches with an assortment of karate chops in the air along with a wide variety of dramatic gestures. The bravura and fanatical commitment that Moon has given to his messianic projects bespeak an iron will and power to persevere that are worthy of Genghis Khan.

Modern North Koreans have notable skill as businessmen and dynamic entrepreneurs. They display the same talents as their hunter ancestors, but in modern forms. Since the communist government does not provide outlets for the skills of many North Koreans, large numbers have migrated to South Korea and to North America, where the environments better suit their native abilities. Sun Myung Moon, like many other Koreans who escaped from North Korea, is a businessman - an industrialist who has built up a diversified empire in such fields as armaments, pharmaceutical products, publishing, ginseng tea, fishing, and, of course, his world-wide Unification Church. Moon has also established large

7

169

schools in which to train his followers, including a liberal arts college and a theological seminary.

The warriors from Koguryŏ were known for their boldness and penchant for showing off. Moon's manners are so presumptuous and his claims to omniscience are so preposterous that his public behavior often makes him appear to be a caricature of Park Chung Hee, much as Charlie Chaplain burlesqued Hitler. An example of Moon's need to be boss can be gleaned from the report of a former West-Coast disciple, who claimed that Moon kicked him in public and then asked the audience "if they would not be willing to receive the same treatment."[3]

It is hard to say whether Moon carries his ancestral hunter's temperament in his genes, or needs to reenact cruelties that, as we shall see, were once perpetrated on him, but in either case his arrognace is that of a weak man, who needs to appear strong by bragging and bullying those below him. Despite his many tirades about himself and his followers as crusading soldiers against communism, Moon was cited as a draft dodger in a Korean newspaper. In order to avoid the draft in South Korea, Moon forged papers stating that he was forty-three when he was actually of draft age.[4] Despite his fervent cries against communism he did not show any eagerness to do battle against the north during the Korean War.

An understanding of the excessiveness of Moon's posture as a brave man and the picture of his followers as soldiers can be gleaned from his 1976 speech, "God's Hope for America," in which he stated, "For the sake of God, we will never retreat, but will win, whatever the sacrifice may be."[5] Parents of Unification Church members were told that "their" dedicated sons and daughters are champions of God crusading for the victory of God's will. As God's front line, they are declaring war against evil. They are courageously fighting this noble battle. We must overcome evil." Moon's language is reminiscent of the shaman generals in ancient Korea, who were adamant as to their power to conquer evil opponents.

The word "I" is repeated so often in almost every one of Moon's talks that he elicits doubt as to whether there really is an "I." The Unification Church has printed an official biography of Sun Myung Moon in the form of a glossy brochure in which he equates his greatness with that of Confucius and Buddha.[6] The organizational tract on its glorious leader is scanty on facts and excessive in its tributes to Moon's sterling qualities as a saintly man who will save the world.

One of the persistent themes in Moon's life is his wish to be someone other than himself. He claims at the age of twelve to

8

170

have "prayed for extraordinary things" such as "wisdom greater than Solomon's," and "faith greater than the Apostle Paul's."[7] Moon asserts his yearning to be the possessor of three doctoral degrees.[8] Although he claims to have actually graduated from Waseta University, Tōkyō, Japan, there is no record to indicate that he ever obtained a degree.[9] The pomposity of Moon's pretense that he knows what "God" wants for the entire universe precludes the possibility of his having any respect for real knowledge, and it is quite likely that his grandiose fantasies prevented him from achieving distinction through normal channels. There is also no evidence that Moon was ever ordained by any Protestant Church in Korea,[10] and his role as an Evangelist is more akin to the medicine man's identity as one who has been chosen by the spirits. Moon's two attempts to recognition as a bona fide member of the New York Council of Churches, suggest that he still desires acceptance from the traditional religious associations which never chose to have him among them.

Those who feel worthless or unwanted often compensate for their emptiness by conjuring up imaginary voices that tell them of their greatness. By Moon's own account he possesses qualifications as the next Messiah: "From childhood I was clairvoyant... I can see through people's spirits." Sun Myung Moon insists that on Easter Sunday, 1936, Jesus appeared to him and said, "Carry out my unfinished task." Then another voice from heaven supposedly informed him: "You will be the completer of man's salvation by being the Second Coming of Christ." Moon's telephone-call-type revelation from Jesus sounds like the fabrication of an adolescent weaned on Cecil B. DeMille's religious epics. William Butler Yeats in his remarkable poem, The Second Coming predicted the onslaught of beastly men, who would unleash fascism and create an era of monstrous agony for mankind. Yeats wrote:

> Mere anarchy is loosed upon the world,
> The blood-dimmed tide is loosed, and everywhere
> The ceremony of innocence is drowned:
> The best lack all conviction, while the worst
> Are full of passionate intensity.

In Asia, the Japanese fascists who ruled Korea in the 1930's were full of passionate intensity and imposed their will on the Korean people just as Park Chung Hee has tyrannized his own people in the 1970's. Calling for "East Asia Coprosperity," the Japanese forced Shinto Emperor worship on the Korean people, and erected shinto shrines throughout the land. Christians who did not comply with official Japanese orders were persecuted and imprisoned,[11] as they are by the current regime in South Korea. Students who did not bow before the Shinto shrines were expelled from schools under the Japanese domination.[12]

9

171

Natives were not allowed the use of their own names or their own language in public.

There is considerable evidence that many of Moon's "facts" about himself actually are fictitious, but there is little doubt that he is an intensely ambitious person, who grew up in a period when there were few avenues for achievement for young Koreans. An official survey from the 1930's gives some idea of the appalling situation that prevailed among Korean farmers:

> "Approximately 80 per cent of these farmers are of the indigent class. Most of these are people of no means, generally without benefit of education. . . . They annually complain of lack of food. Most of them earn 50 to 200 yen a year. When confronted with necessity, they cannot afford to consider the consequences; they merely accumulate high interest debts. Their year's efforts in the crops is mostly for payment of borrowed food or interest; they do not have any surplus. In extreme cases, considerable numbers of them rely on wild plants and trees for food during the spring."

From 1938 until the end of the World War II, the Korean people were almost completely in bondage. As the war frenzy mounted, the Japanese established an armaments factory in Korea and conscripted the people to work in them under conditions that amounted to enslavement. Before the war ended two hundred churches were closed and over two thousand Christians were imprisoned.[13]

Sun Myung Moon's parents were farmers who converted to Christianity when he was 10 years old. Moon gives no indication that he was ever persecuted during this period, and it seems quite likely that he adapted to Emperor worship. Due to his upbringing under the Japanese Colonial rule, Moon's life was quite harsh, and his omission of any facts about this period in his biography suggests that he prefers not to remember the painful experiences of his early childhood. (Similarly, Park Chung Hee is also reputed to have had a cruel childhood, and is said to have suffered enormously in the household of the relatives who raised him. One of the stories that circulated about Park Chung Hee in Korea was of his desire to seek vengeance in the world for his own misery. Tyrants and demagogues seem rarely to emerge from peaceful nations or environments of warmth and love).

The end of World War II brought neither independence nor peace to the Korean peninsula. Shortly after the Japanese surrender, Korea was divided into two nations, and that artificial separation crystallized into a monstrous civil war.

10

172

The mood that pervaded Korea after 1945 can be discerned from the poem of Pak Tu Jin, which is a chant to the sun. Pak implored the sun to dispel the night of doubt and sorrow so that he might once again enjoy the fellowship of man and nature. As is often the case, in periods of chaos and social disorder, popular religions flourish and provided many people with an outlet for pent-up tensions.

Sun Myung Moon established a pentecostal church in his native city of P'yŏngyang in 1946. The church is referred to as "The Jerusalem of the East" in Moon's Unification biography, and "The Broad Sea" (Kwanghae) in other Korean accounts. Ceremonies at the Broad Sea Church included vigorous hymn singing, handclapping, shouting, and healing. Neighbors are said to have reported the church to the police authorities for Moon's strange religious activity and the excessive noise that came from it.[14]

Intense emotionalism is often characteristic of pentecostal churches in impoverished areas, where people require an outlet for their many frustrations, and the preacher usually assumes the role of faith-healer and father figure. Ecstatic experiences in Moon's church would have made his services more like the native's indigenous shamanism religion. At some point in 1946, Moon left his church in the North and went to Seoul. Numerous predictions were being made in 1946 that a Messiah would appear to rescue the Korean people from imminent disaster.[15] Sun Myung Moon renounced his serpent-dragon name and assumed the identity of a savior in South Korea along with other revivalist preachers, all of whom responded to a climate of fear and tension by playing at being Messiahs. It is important that Moon be viewed against the background of a divided Korea which suffered untold hardships and economic depression. Without a climate of enormous misery and many fears about the future, Moon could not have enacted his Messianic role. His self limiting subjectivism would not be possible in a more balanced society that revered human life. As an ambitious man with no other means to achieve distinciton, Moon exploited his talents as a somewhat charismatic personality, and preyed on the vulnerability of frightened men and women who sought escape from reality.

Some time in 1946, Moon met Kim Paek-mun, the founder of a community known as Israel Sudo-wŏn (The Israel Monastery). The two men appear to have spent six months together, and Moon's book, the Divine Principle, is said to based on Kim's Theology of the Holy Spirit. Both Moon and Kim practiced a ritual called "blood sharing," or blood-cleansing," and in some references the rite is referred to as "serpent blood-cleansing" or body-soul exchange."[15] Behind the spiritual-sounding titles, this rite consisted of sexual intercourse with their female parishioners. This ritual was derived from the concepts of two shamanistic Christian ministers, Yi Yong-do and Hwang Guk-ju, whose ersatz theology sanctioned official

11

copulation between ministers and members of their parish.
Kim Paek-mun's book is viewd as as summation of the theology of
Yi and Hwang which was established by them in 1923.[17] Both
Yi and Hwang were criticized and expelled from the orthodox
Christian church, and both men went underground because of re-
pressive activities of the Japanese police against Korean
Christians. With the liberation of Korea in 1945, they began a
congregation in P'yongyang, but soon after, split up, and Sun
Myung Moon emerged from their group.[18]

Blood sharing is based on the fantasy that a divine being
with pure blood can pass his sanctity on to another through an
act of fornication. The notion of a divinity copulating with a
mortal is common to ancient planting society mythology, and there
is a particular legend, "The Serpent and the Maiden," that relates
to the theories of Yi, Hwang, Kim and Moon. Arthur Kinsler says
that there is also a Korean shaman legend, Si Chung Kut, about a
supernatural male figure who impregnates the maid Tamgun and makes
her divine, and that at one time this rite was practiced on the
East Coast of Korea. Professor Kinsler, who apparently was not a-
ware of Sun Myung Moon's activities as a Messianic "blood-sharing,"
noted that there was no evidence that this old myth was enacted by
a contemporary cult.

Moon and his associates practiced their "blood sharing"
ceremonies in private homes in P'yongyang and later in Seoul.
The "blood sharing" provided a rationale for indiscriminate
pleasure seeking, and at the same time restored an old Korean
fertility ritual into the domain of their so-called Christian
practices.

Some time in 1948, complaints were made against Moon, and he
was charged with committing adultery. As a result, he was imprisoned for 100 days in Daedong detention house, North Korea.[19]
The Unification Church biographers claim that established Christian
churches reported Moon as a heretic to the communist controlled
government, and that the communists allegedly "arrested him,
tortured him, and finally left him for dead."[20] The depiction of
Sun Myung Moon as a religious martyr and a fervent opponent of
communism in the 1950's is a cover-up for Moon's actual prison
sentence as an adulterer. Korean scholarly accounts all indicate
that Moon was incarcerated many months for committing adultery,
which he described as "holy blood-sharing."

After leaving prison, Moon resumed his activities and left
his wife to marry his follower, Kim. He referred to this marriage
as "God's wish." On February 22, 1949, the North Korean police
again arrested him on the grounds of bigamy and "social disorder."[21]
He received a five-year jail sentence in Hŭngnam prison. Moon
had never legally divorced his first wife, and although legally a

12

174

bigamist, he viewed his "blood-sharing activities as responses to the holy spirit.

Church history has recorded other puritanical revivalists who seduced their female followers, and Sinclair Lewis dealt with this theme quite ingeniously in his book Elmer Gantry. An excess of lustfulness and pious platitudes about purity are two sides of the same coin, but what distinguishes the Korean preachers from their American counterparts is the intricate and fustian character of of their theological retionale for having sexual relations with women other than their wives. Moon's exuberant indulgence in "blood-sharing" could be viewed as compensation for the restrictive Confucian sexual mores of the Korean family structure.

Thus, the motive of blood-sharing cults in Korea can be understood as an impulse to break the adultery taboos by sanctioning the act with the mask of religious ritual. Certainly, in primitive societies and the ancient world, religious ceremonies included sexual activity, music, and dance, and Tibetan tantric enlightenment is based primarily on sexual union through identification with male and female dieties. Moon's dionysian mode of worship may well have appealed to many Orthodox Korean Christians who were frustrated and dissatisfied with their dry, rational church services which did not fulfill emotional needs. The harsh prison sentence that Moon received at the hands of the North Korean government suggests that he was actually the scapegoat of "respectable" Koreans.

Two years after Moon's imprisonment, on June 25, 1950, the Korean War broke out, and on October 14, 1950, the United Nations forces occupied the prison and released all of the prisoners, including Sun Myung Moon.[22] In his official Unification Church biography, accounts of Moon's experience in the North Korean prison are rendered as tales about a saint, who was persecuted for his opposition to the regime. There is a fairy tale anecdote which tells of Moon's display of supernatural strength, by carrying a crippled comrade on his bicycle for 600 miles from North Korea to Pusan.[23] Another story describes Moon as being miraculously covered by a cross when a bomber flew over Hŭngnam prison. The pilot was so stunned by the vision of the religious symbol that he neglected to drop a bomb.[24] Almost all of the episodes that are described by Moon or his followers in the organization's tracts are examples of the naive fantasy world of the Unification Church leader. There are many Christian legends about the miraculous powers of saints and their ability to transcend death. When such legends are interpreted symbolically, they are a source of stimulation to the imagination, but when they are understood in a literal manner, they reinforce infantile thinking.

13

175

The following year, 1951, Moon and his cohorts Kim Wŏn-p'il and Pak Chong-hyŏk held preliminary conferences in various parts of Pusan, South Korea, for the establishment of his church. In 1954 Moon moved to Seoul and established the Holy Spirit Association of the Unification of the World Christianity. In March of 1955, Moon had begun to publish the church magazine, Songwha. On May 11, 1955 five professors from Esha University, and seventeen students from Yonsei University were dismissed from school on the ground that they had suspicious "sexual connections" with the Unification Church.[25] Incorrigible in his taste for "blood-sharing", Moon was arrested in July 1955 by the Seoul police on the familiar charges of causing "social disorder" and indecent activities.[26] The Segae newspaper, dated July 6, 1955, reported that 80 students from Ewha women's University and women of the high official classes were also involved with Sun Myung Moon.[27] Moon's elaborate theological retionale for having sexual intercourse apparently had considerable appeal for numerous Korean women, who either shared his fantasies about "pure blood" or simply enjoyed the sexual favors of a latter day Korean shaman.

The summer of 1955 appears to have been on of frequent "body-soul" exchanges for Reverend Moon, and in August of the same year he was again arrested in Seoul and jailed for his usual crime. In October of 1953 he was released from prison due to illness.[28] The Unification Church claimed that he was released from prison because of the fact that he was innocent,[29] and the current official biography simply neglects to mention that torrid year in the life of Sun Myung Moon. His favorite disciple and most enthusiastic proponent of "blood-sharing" was the woman Chŏng Dŏk-Oh, who had actively engaged in sacred "blood-sharing" at her Mt. Samgak base in Seoul.[30] According to T'ak Myŏng-hwan, Sagae newspaper dated March 18, May 13 and 20, 1957, alleged Moon to have had orgies with 70 female students.[31]

Although adultery charges were brought against Moon on many occasions, the women with whom he had "shared blood" usually preferred not to appear in court. One of the women who had had intercourse with Moon informed the police that at the time of their sexual encounter, she believed Moon to be God. Since immunity from punishment for almost all crimes can be "brought" with money in South Korea, he could very well have bribed himself out of trouble; or it is likely that he had influential friends. It is a common practice in South korea to release a prisoner on the false ground of illness if he has money or political ties and influence.

In a certain sense, Moon was reviving an old initiation ritual for women, but the fears and repressions concerning irregular sexual acts were so intense in Korea that there exist no records of discussions of "blood-sharing" with reference to old fertility rites. One of the most notorious leaders of the

14

176

"blood-sharing" cults is Moon's associate, Pak T'ae-sŏn, who had
ceremonies with his mother-in-law and his brother's wife, insist-
ing that he had to share his sacred "blood" with his family members first.[32] By acting out the incest wish, Pak hoped to break
one of the most powerful of social taboos, and it is quite easy
to understand why the Korean authorities and ministers of the
orthodox Christian church looked upon "blood-sharing" as heresy.
Finally, Reverend Paek Ynon-gi's wife, Chan Ae-sam, was compelled
to confess, in an open letter on March 10, 1957, her involvement
in Pak-Moon's "blood-sharing" ring. This incident precipitated
a public scandal and Reverend Paek sued Pak for defamation.[33]
The open letter is quite specific about Moon's early sexual
activities with his female followers and subsequent imprisonment
by the North Korean regime, and Pak's indiscriminate, "blood-
sharing" ceremonies in South Korea.[34]

On the other hand, Tungus tribes in Northeast Asia are of
Korean ancestry and anthropological studies have described Tungus
shamans as promiscuous. Confucian mores strongly influence Korean
family structure in both North and South Korea, especially in the
matter of adultery. It is possible that Moon was singled out by
other offenders as the scapegoat in order to assuage their own
guilty consciences. It is also likely that Moon convinced himself through an elaborate rationale to justify his own strong
impulse to possess women at his whim. Anthropologist Weston
LaBarre views the shaman as an essentially pleasure-seeking person who abdicates his ego-controls in favor of pure libidinous
self-indulgence.[35] Thus, there has been in Korea tremendous
tension between the indigenous cultural practices and the rigid
Confucian family codes imposed from outside. In the Divine
Principle and in his public speeches, Moon cites adultery as the
most serious of man's sins, which indicates that he carries
enormous guilt for his own acts.

When released from jail Moon intensified his activities to an
extreme pitch, and by July of 1957 had established thirty churches
throughout South Korea. He has been as tenacious as his Koguryŏ
hunter ancestors, who rose again and again from defeats at the
hands of the Chinese. From 1950 until 1976, Moon launched extensive campaigns against communism, and in the 1970's he became the
most important religious spokeman for Park Chung Hee. The
terrorism and total repression of civil liberties in Park Chung
Hee's police state are paralleled by the anti-communist campaigns
of Sun Myung Moon, who, Like the South Korean dictator, has used
the shield of "God-denying Communism" to mask his own strivings
for material power at the price of the Korean peoples' suffering.

Moon launched his missionary campaign in Japan some time in
1958. Ch'ae Sang-uk, a twenty-one-year-old Korean bachelor who
spoke fluent Japanese and had studied in Japanese missionary

15

schools, was sent to Japan, where he was arrested as an illegal alien. After being confined in a detention house, he escaped and went into hiding. While living underground, Ch'ae Sang-uk changed his name to Nishigawa Katsu. In 1959, Nishigawa Katsu began his missionary activities in Ōsaka, and preached about Moon's Divine Principles. Meeting little success in Ōsaka, he went to Tōkyō and had his first prayer meeting there on December 2, 1959. When he came to Tōhokuzawa, Tōkyō, Nishigawa had contact with the Rishōkōsei Buddhist Association, where he found 40 followers and established training sessions.

Nishigawa appears to have been a devoted follower, who suffered hardship and danger to establish a following for Moon. Despite his disciple's success in gaining members for the Unification Church, Moon disowned Nishigawa and claimed that he had pretended to be the true Messiah.[36] According to Japanese accounts, Nishigawa redeemed himself by bowing before Moon and reciting a classical Samurai poem:

> Even in this world where the mountain cracks
> And the sea rises
> How can I have two minds towards master?

Apparently Moon forgave him, and Nishigawa was later sent to the United States where he was given a prestigious position in the San Francisco branch of the Unification Church.

Moon claims to have 45,000 members in Japan, and is reported as having the support of ultra right-wing industrialists. Apart from his numerous public rallies against communism and the use of student groups to promote fierce hatred of communism, Moon heavily stressed fund raising activities in Japan. Groups known as "The Fund to Rescue Cuban Refugees," "The Fund to Rescue Pakistani Refugees," or "The Fund for the Prevention of Juvenile Crime" were founded, but in no case is there any record of how the millions of dollars they collected were actually spent. In the United States, Moon used organizations that were ostensibly charities to siphon off funds to the Korean lobby, which operates as a pressure group in Washington, D.C. to promote increased military aid to South Korea.

While in Japan, Moon claimed that he was too sacred to shake hands with ordinary human beings,[37] and he predicted that the Messiah would appear in August of 1963. When his prediction failed to come true, he claimed that the Messiah would show up on April 5th between 1960 and 1967, which he designated as the New Era.[38] Moon seems to have shifted his identification as a Messiah figure to that of one who was representing a higher power. According to John Loflander he has told those within his organization that he really is the Messiah, but that they are to keep this

16

secret to themselves.[39] Moon strengthens his followers' fantasy
of belonging to an elite group by dwelling on the theme of a
special secret that is known only to the inner sanctum of the
Unification Church.

The Divine Principles of the Unification Church were published in August of 1957, and in 1958 he sent Ms. Young Oon Kim abroad
as a missionary. Dr. Kim (former associate professor of religion
at Ewha Women's University in Seoul), whose nephritis is said to
have been cured by Moon's faith healing,[40] established 26 Unification Churches in different parts of the world. Sometimes called
the "brains behind Moon," Kim, a graduate of the University of
Oregon, also lauched the Unification Church program in Seattle,
Washington, in 1959. To accelerate conversions, Moon initiated
forty-day spartan training programs for his followers and by 1959
had established 70 Unification Churches in Korea.

In 1960, he married his present wife, Han Hag-Cha, whom he
refers to as "The Divine Mother." According to Tak Myŏng-hwan, a
Korean authority on new religion in South Korea, the marriage is
Moon's fifth and if this is true,[41] Moon is an extraordinary man —
in a society where divorce is totally taboo and family codes are
strictly observed. Although Moon has worn the mask of a respectable married man subsequent to 1960, there have been many rumors
of his having sexual relations with young members of his church.
In his public speeches, Moon cites adultery as a cardinal sin, an
indication of the extent of his hypocrisy and his prodigious talent
for lying. Mrs. Moon now presides with Reverend Moon when they
perform simultaneous weddings, dressed in white robes and wearing
abbreviated versions of the ancient Silla shaman crowns. Moon
favors a Hollywood style musical comedy setting for his varied
performances complete with his nubile singing team, known as
The Korean Angels.

The T'ongil Church celebrates important dates of Moon's life;
His birthday, the day he came out of the North Korean prison, the
day he was released from Seoul District Court, and the day of his
marriage in 1960 to Han, the "Divine Mother". The rigid, hieratic
structure and business-like character of Moon's T'ongil church in
Korea is similar in some ways to Pak T'ae-sŏn's Olive Tree Sect[42]
which established so-called "Villages of Faith". These "Villages
of Faith" are actually cities, huge religio-political-industrial
complexes built in response to Pak's prediction that the world was
coming to an end in 1957. To provide a haven for his following
Pak established industrial cities in South Korea, which produce
a wide variety of industrial goods, including soy sauce and under-
wear for the armies of the Republic of Korea. The two colorful
North Korean shamans, Pak T'ae-sŏn and Sun Myung Moon combine twin
talents as religious leaders and bustling businessmen who have

17

179

acquired vast tracts of land and costly buildings. Both migrated
to South Korea, because the political and economic system of the
South supported their talents and enterprises. Both Pak and Moon
began to function in the early 1960's as spiritual leaders who
used religion as a means to receive government benefits. In so
doing, both exploit the labor of their followers who are emotionally and economically dependent on their respective organizations.

In 1965, Moon toured the world on a missionary pilgrimage,
travelling to 40 countries within ten months. His unification
principles were translated into Spanish, Dutch, and French. In
order to become a member of the Korean orthodox church, Moon
began to donate large sums of money to churches. He held numerous
conferences, seminars and symposiums in South Korea, and participants were paid travel expenses and entertained at dinner parties.[43] In 1969 alone Moon organized six such large conferences
in which altogether 600 Christian leaders and professores participated. By April of 1970, the Unification Church succeeded in
being accepted as being a bona fide religious order in South
Korea. Moon claims to have 400,000 followers in 900 churches
throughout South Korea, but a more realistic figure would be
about 30,000.

Moon's smooth spokesman in the United States is Neil Salonen,
who had managed a psychiatric hospital in Washington, D.C. before
his conversion to the Divine Principle. Neil is the president of
the Unification Church of America and he explains, articulates,
advertises, and helps organize activities of the Unification
Church to attract and accommodate American followers. He effectively manipulates the doomsday theory by emphasizing the imminent danger to the United States from crime, alcoholism, broken
families, pornography, drug abuse, suicide, and the threat of
communism from abroad. He tells followers that God has sent
Sun Myung Moon to save the United States from these problems.
Moon's church has made rapid financial growth using tax exemptions and the free labor of his faithful followers. Moon's organization enjoys an annual income of $10,000,000 from official fund
raising and other contributions. The Unification Church claims
to have 10,000 to 30,000 followers including a core of 2,000 to
10,000 full-time members. Reliable estimates put the figure at
somewhere between 2,000 and 4,000. Before newspaper exposure of
Unification Church involvement in the scandalous Korea lobby's
payoff activities in the United States, the Church claimed to
have established 120 centers in cities across the country, with
missionary activities at 150 colleges.[44]

Until the time of his release from Hŭng-nam prison in North
Korea in 1950, Moon seems to have had a relatively small group
of followers and no plans that were comparable to the megalo-

18

maniacal schemes that he advocates today. Both Adolph Hitler and Joseph Stalin spent time in prison, and in each case the experience of harsh punishment for an act that was objectionable to society only served to fan the flames of vengeance, bitterness and contempt for other people. Similarly, Moon's imprisonment seems to have cultivated his image of himself as an imposing figure who could dominate the world.

The leitmotif of Sun Myung Moon's speeches is the absolute necessity of declaring war against communism. To satisfy his own vengeful feelings towards those who actually treated him cruelly, Moon would have his followers take up arms against communist countries. Sun Myung Moon was not treated compassionately for his alleged crime of adultery in North Korea, which he may well have believed to be a sacred act. In turn, Moon's vengefulness continues the cycle of punishment equally injurious to others.

When the Korean poet, Kim Chi-ha, was imprisoned and tortured by the agents of Park Chung Hee, he suffered as terribly as Moon could possibly have done when he was in jail. During his internment in a hospital, a Japanese interviewer asked Kim Chi-ha how he felt about those who tortured him and his friends. The poet, who is a Catholic, answered: "I cannot forgive those who torture, but I must because tomorrow is my confession day."[45]

Kim Chi-ha's genius is expressed in his power to write poems that stir the hearts of the Korean people and give them the courage to resist the tyranny of Park Chung Hee. The poet is also a Christian who stands by his beliefs, even when they mean risking his life and bearing the burden of tremendous pain. While Moon rants about God, simultaneously piling up a fortune, Kim Chi-ha is in a solitary confinement cell in the West Gate Prison of Seoul, awaiting a possible death sentence.

When religion is practiced by individuals with self-knowledge who do not suffer chronic fear and malice towards others, it can flower, as it has in the life of Kim Chi-ha, as a marvelous source of creativity. For frightened men like Sun Myung Moon who do not know themselves and need to appear bigger than life, religion becomes a source of fanatical activity against the self and others.

Had Sun Myung Moon been diagnosed as a sick man who needed to enact an archaic ritual, rather than as a criminal, he might have been a person quite different from the one who emerged in the 1950's. Had those who imprisoned Sun Myung Moon understood their own tradition of fertility rituals, they might have known that Moon was acting out a myth that was not a crime in his mind. Those who imprison others rarely think or feel deeply about them as complex and vulnerable human beings.

19

181

Prisons throughout the world are filled with those who have broken the laws of their country. Some of the imprisoned resemble Kim Chi-ha and some are like Sun Myung Moon. There are within prisons strong men who feel loved and weak men who feel despised. Those who despise themselves have emerged from prisons as Hitlers, Stalins, and Moons, and they find followers who do not know themselves and want to "save" the world from suffering. Sun Myung Moon's followers are undoubtedly idealistic people in search of "good" things for themselves and others. Those who begin by believing themselves to be their brothers' keepers often end up as their jailkeepers.

20

182

III. INITIATION INTO THE UNIFICATION CHURCH

The Korean name for Moon's church in Seoul is T'ongil and it has been described by Ch'oi Syn-duk in his article entitled "Korea's T'ongil Movement" in the Transactions of the Royal Asiatic Society (1967). Ch'oi calls T'ongil a church that is so systematically organized that its members appear to be posing as "heavenly communists."[1]

In 1967, under the leadership of an executive named Yu Hyo-wŏn, the Unification Church was organized into a communist-type centralized structure comprising numerous Divine Principle indoctrination centers, executive committees, bureaus, sections and cell organizations. In Korea the most noteworthy of these subdivisions is the Unification Central Committee that oversees student affairs in such areas as education, finance, art, physical education, cultural development, international studies, and Divine Principle studies, with headquarters at Seoul National University and Ewha Women's University. Parallel structures were set up in both Japan and the United States. In all three countries, students formed the majority of the members of Moon's organizations. Generally, infiltration of a university was accomplished by cadres of experienced members who enlisted a few members and then established headquarters on the campuses of the schools. Moon's church usually recruited from among the more confused and inexperienced freshmen students, most of whom were disappointed, for one reason or another, by university lectures. Typical of the effects of these sessions is this tearful statement by a Japanese student convert to Moonism:

> After three days of the Divine Principle lecture,
> I began to know for the first time the meaning and
> purpose of man's existence.[2]

When prospects for membership are approached, the recruiter rarely mentions Moon's name. Usually he says that he belongs to a Christian group at a college campus. The first introduction is a dinner at which the brothers and sisters chat and show hearty friendship. The next step for potential converts is a weekend workshop. After the weekend seminar the recruits are encouraged to stay for training seminars that last 7, 21, 40, or 120 days. During the training periods, participants are drilled intensively on Moon's principles, and practice calisthenics while chanting prayers addressed to the "Father" Moon. There are regular intervals of hymn singing and chanting "Father, oh, Father, please help us." Reporters who have attended these Unification Church sessions describe the members as jerking spasmodically, or being in a state that resembles the ecstasy of voodoo sessions or primitive rituals. New recruits are never left alone, and are discouraged

21

183

from asking any questions. Former Unification Church members characterize the seminars as exhausting to the point that the individual is unable to think. William James explains in his study The Varieties of Religious Experience that religious conversion "occurs most often by those beset by a sense of incompleteness and imperfection, and frequently during states of temporary exhaustion." As told by one ex-Moonie, "They put you through seven days of fatiguing your body and mind and they stay on." Indeed, most former Moon followers consider themselves to have been brainwashed during the indoctrination period.

Isolated from their own communities and subjected to the rigorous repetition of Moon's ideas, it is quite likely that attendants at the Unification training bases actually do lose the power to make rational judgments. Those who have observed followers of Moon's cult closely have noted a glassy, far-away look in their eyes, which, combined with their fixed smiles, gives them the appearance of mesmerized robots.

Berkeley Rice's article "Messiah from Korea" contains a good account of several stages of formal training programs in the American branch of the Unification Church. He writes:

> "Those attracted to Moon's Family or his religion get invited . . . to a weekend workshop devoted to further study and friendship. The weekends follow an exhausting and rigidly structured pattern with little time for sleep and none for private reflection. Recruits get a daily dose of six to eight hours of mind-numbing theology based on Moon's Divine Principle. By the final lecture they learn that God has sent Sun Moon to save the world in general, and themselves in particular.
>
> After each lecture, recruits and Moonies join in small discussion groups to answer questions but also to explore any personal problems, and to offer comforting attention. The rest of the days are filled with group activities: Calisthenics, meals, sports, and lots of singing and praying. After dinner, and often lasting well past midnight, there's more group singing and praying, with testimony by Moonies of how they came to find peace, purpose, love and joy in the Family. Never left alone, the recruits are encouraged to pour out their hearts to their new brothers and sisters. Many do . . . .
>
> . . . . For most of those who sign up for the seven-day workshop, the next stop is the Church's training headquarters at Barrytown, N. Y., about 90 miles up the Hudson from New York City. Barrytown is big time.

22

Indoctrination there becomes more serious, the study more rigorous, and the life more spartan than that of the cadets just down the river at West Point. The program leaves neither time nor opportunity for contacting relatives or friends on the outside.

At the end of the week comes the pressure for commitment to full-time membership in the Family. The recruits reach this moment of decision worn out from lack of sleep, numbed by the endless lectures, cut off from the advice of family and friends, and softened up by the embracing warmth of the group. ."It was like being taken care of," one ex-Moonie recalled. "The people were very friendly, and you really thought they did love you . . . Also, I was kind of afraid of going out into the world."[3]

More than half of the Moonists stay on after the week long seminar. The Church is a safe refuge to those who are afraid of the outside world, or who are unwilling and unable to cope with the frustration of living on their own. The new members then become fund raisers under the guise of a drug abuse program or some other Christian youth work. Those who do not meet their individual fund raising quotas often spend the evening in prayer, asking God to help them in their next day's work.

Campaigns to attract converts, as well as the publications of the Unification Church, are adapted to suit the particular trends in each nation. In Korea, the T'ongil church has spread to college campuses and rural areas. Generally speaking, naive and emotionally disturbed individuals are attracted to the paradise of Sun Myung Moon, who plays on their superstitions and the shamanistic fear of evil spirits. In lectures to Korean audiences, Moon claims that it will be necessary for the whole world to learn Korean, and he stresses the role of Korea as the Chosen Land. In the Divine Principle, Moon states that "the nation of the.East where Christ will come again will be none other than Korea"[6] and "the Second Jesus definitely uses Korean, and it will be then the mother tongue. Accordingly, all the people in the world will have to use this language of the motherland of the Second Jesus. Then, mankind will unite into one people using one language."[7]

Historically, millennialism often gains prominence against a background of wars, droughts, plagues and other disasters. Moon therefore compares the suffering of the Korean people during and after the Korean War to the situation of Israel in the first century A.D., Moon asserts that Korea is the center of the world and the successor of Abraham's faith because the Israelites relinquished their role as the chosen people through the crucifixion of Jesus. To further heighten patriotic fervor among Koreans, Moon plays on the theme of Korea as Adam and Japan as Eve.[8]

23

In Japan, the Unification Church emphasizes the suffering of the Korean people during the 36 years of Japanese colonial administration, and further to bolster guilt feelings among Japanese followers Moon points out their history as exploiters and persecuters of the Korean people. Japanese student members are required to chant "Heavenly Father! Please forgive us the crimes committed by the Japanese."9 By inducing guilt feelings among his disciples for crimes committed by their ancestors, Moon increases their own self-loathing and dependency upon his good will for forgiveness.

In the United States Moon's followers come from suburban areas and small towns, and are usually college students who have left school after one year. Articles by former members of the Unification Church have appeared in publications directed toward college-age readers. "I was a Robot for Sun" by Janice Harayda was printed in April 1976 issue of Glamour, and "A Couple of Summers" by Eric Rofes was in the September 1975 issue of The Harvard Crimson. Paul Engel of Binghamton, New York has also written a statement called, The World of the Cult, which was included in the Union of American Hebrew Congregations Information Kit on the activities of Sun Myung Moon. These writings present a similarity of experience that includes: seduction by friendly Moon disciples, entry into an entertaining world of songs and talks, isolation from the community and indoctrination at a Unification Church training center, and subsequent exhaustion and suffering as an active member of the cult. Harayda and Rofes echo the comments made by most former disciples of Sun Myung Moon in that they believe that the organization exercised mind control and prevented them from thinking clearly. Initial attraction to the Unification Church has been attributed by members to their sense of aimlessness, disillusionment with life, loneliness, and a desire to be engaged in meaningful activity with their peers. Since A Couple of Summers and The World of the Cult sum up the essential views presented by other members of the cult, we include them here to give the reader American college students' perception of their own experience in the Unification Church.

1. A Couple of Summers by Eric E. Rofes.

Last January I decided I would spend my summer vacation on the Pacific coast pursuing the California Dream . . . . I made my way to San Francisco, checked into the Youth Hostel and went looking for work. . . . Money was getting low, jobs were scarce, and I was lonely. . . . I went to the Berkeley Student Union to ponder my predicament. I sat there, confused, a little depressed, considering my options. A smiling, humming, attractive Jewish-looking woman walked in. . . . She came over, friendly, talkative, from Long Island originally. Small talk, poetry, politics, time passes. Then I received an invitation to dinner--"I live with

24

this big family and we always have lots of people over to dinner
. . how about it?"

Her house was the old Hearst Mansion--huge, beautiful and
filled with smiling young people. What kind of family is this?
I said to myself. Everyone was friendly, talkative, young and
beautiful. We ate a great meal, sang some folk songs, and then
someone announced that there would be a "lecture" to explain
the principles that bind the family together. Again my mind was
speeding--could this be a political group? Religious? Drug
commune? No, no, I told myself stop being so doubtful, keep
an open mind.

The lecture was given by "Doctor D," a professor of English
Literature at a nearby college. He explained that the family
was unified by a common goal; to help and care for all people.
His lecture was not as straight-forward: he filled it with
psychology and sociology and threw in some Wordsworth and Eliot
quotes that I remembered from English 10. He seemed to be a nice
guy and since I had read a little psych, it seemed sound to me.
Yeah, these were the people I'd been looking for--intelligent,
personable, and liberal.

I could not have been more mistaken.

Next there was a slide show of their scenic farm up north
in Mendocino. It looked exciting, full of young people
communing with nature: my middle-class paradise. We were all
invited up for the weekend and, keeping an open mind, I jumped
at the opportunity.

Two busloads of young people headed up to Mendocino that
night, including seventy new "brothers and sisters." I stayed
on the farm for almost two weeks and I came up against the
greatest challenge to my life and my value that I have ever faced.
I was confronted with a lifestyle and a system of beliefs that
robbed me of my rationale and free will. I had walked head on
into Reverend Sun Myung Moon's indoctrination center.

I don't believe myself to be unusually susceptible to
political or spiritual causes but the propaganda system set-up
at this center was infallible. Each day was organized with two
things in mind: everyone has a good, fun time, and no one has
a free minute to think. The entire day is programmed, everyone wakes up at the same time in the morning, washes, goes to
exercise, eats breakfast, cleans up, and off to morning lecture.
At these lectures new members are slowly instructed on the
beliefs of the family. Gradually, carefully, one is indoctrin-
ated into the religion. Through Moon's interpretation of the
Bible, we were made to understand that there is a God, an after-
life, and a spirit world. The religion is primarily Christian,

25

187

stressing the power of Christ and the imminent second coming of
the messiah. Moon's followers believe, through their understanding of Revelation and the cycles of human history, that the
messiah has arrived and, though he is never mentioned in lectures,
that Reverend Sun Muyng Moon is that new messiah.

The cause for the fall of man, according to Moon's interpretation of the Bible, was Eve's fornication with Satan (the
snake and the fruit are seen as symbols). We are, therefore,
the children of Satan, rather than the children of God, we
require purification and repentance to bring us back to our
intended state. Moon people use no drugs or alcohol, and sex is
not permitted until forty days after marriage. After that time
the woman becomes a baby machine; there is no concern for over-
population in the heavenly kingdom.

In retrospect, I wonder why so many people would give up
their wild times for these beliefs. Moon requires his followers
to sacrifice everything for the cause. All possessions and monies
are given to the church and one's family, friends and future plans
are all forsaken. In exchange for these sacrifices Moon provides
a strong, supportive community, a powerful father figure, the
basic necessities of life, and eternal salvation. With these
assets, the movement is growing at a tremendous rate.

My experience on the farm cannot be sufficiently captured in
writing. After a week there I thought I was ready to join the
family. I was believing all the lectures, singing my heart out and
having a great, happy time. I was ready to give up my complexities of Harvard, my thesis and my Gen. Ed. requirements and live
this life of righteousness, direction and meaning. Of the seventy
people who went up to the farm with me, two weeks later I was the
only one to leave. Many are still there and will become part of
Reverend Moon's family, walking through Berkeley or Boston or
Paris, bringing in new blood or selling flowers on the street.
I left while others couldn't and only through an understanding
of my own motivation to leave have I begun to understand the
power of this movement.

. . . . I had to talk to all the lecturers, all the leaders,
explain why I was leaving and where I was going (which I did not
know). I was told that the devil was in me and I was forsaking
Jesus and damning myself and my ancestors. It all sounds crazy
to me now, but while they were telling me this, I believed it and
felt ashamed. Still, my gut said to go, and after a great display
of determination I was driven down to Berkeley.

Such is the story of Rofes who tells us about how subtle the
Church's indoctrination method is and how they use communal living

26

as "brothers" and "sisters" for proselytization of Moon's doctrine. What is more appalling is that once the initiates enter the dormitory they lose their free wills. Rofes was the only one out of those 70 who was able to leave the church, and this only with great determination. The Unification Church apparently satisfies the emotional needs of many of its adherents, and their successful emotional manipulation is such that even "intelligent" students of many prestigious universities in the nation, including Ph.D.'s, have been involved in Moon's cult. Next is the story of The World of Cult by Paul Engel who presents a more detailed account of his initiation in and encounters with the Unification Church.

2. The World of the Cult by Paul Engel.

While hitching through the Oakland-Berkeley area, I was approached on the street by a smiling, clean cut guy. He invited me to dinner with "entertainment" and a lecture with discussion on educational principles. He informed me that this was just a group of people looking for a better way of life and this was called a Unification Center. When I mentioned that I was approached in Los Angeles by a couple of Unification Church members and asked if there was any connection, he quickly denied this and told me that this was in no way religious.

When I arrived at the house, I met all these young people who were forever smiling. There was singing, a short meditation, dinner, and more singing. The lecture was given and the concept of God was introduced in a scientific manner. I thought nothing of it as I was so involved with these energetic and seemingly happy people.

I was then persuaded to go on a weekend seminar. The weekend with its many lectures and group activities seemed to rush forward. I felt as though I were being pushed forward against my will. But the activity was so intense and incessant, I had no time to think about it. The only time I had for myself was during sleep. Every minute was accounted for.

There was no real time for discussion or thinking about the lectures. Doubt and disagreement were implicitly frowned upon while "revelations" from established members dominated the short discussion. Most questions were left unanswered with the promise of explanations in later lectures.

At the end of the weekend it was revealed that this was in fact part of the Unification Church. My "sponsor's" denial of any connection with the Church was only the first in a series of lies I was told, but I was made to overlook the lies, the unanswered questions, and the unwillingness to allow discussions,

27

189

by the overwhelming and mesmerizing enthusiasm of the people. It certainly felt wonderful to be served, given such attention, and made to feel important. In a matter of days, virtual strange by pleading and persistence, and proclamations of love, had succeeded in eliciting my love and trust in return, and I was persuaded to go on a long seminar up on their farm in Northern California.

Lectures started rather low-keyed but as the week progressed they became more emotional. The "fall of man" lecture was design ed to give you a sense of guilt about not being perfect and to instill the fear that Satan could come and influence you to do wrong. If you became sleepy or tired during the lecture, you would be kept awake by being asked to stand or by having your bac hit or rubbed.

These lectures which became progressively more emotional, finally culminated in the announcement that the Second Coming of Christ, the Messiah, had to come from Korea and may already be here, therefore you had to be ready to accept him. I was able to deduce that the Messiah they spoke about was "Reverend" Moon, because of my contact with the members in Los Anglees. At this point, in spite of the battering our emotions had taken, one othe newcomer and myself were detached enough to see how cleverly the had prepared us to accept "Reverend" Moon as the Messiah. You couldn't help but appreciate their artful manipulation of people

Later that day about fifty of us climbed a mountain in silence. After about an hour of climbing and struggling, we reached the highest point of the land and looked out over the valley. In this carefully staged setting, it was "revealed" to us that "Reverend" Moon was in fact the Messiah and the Second Coming of Christ.[10] His supposed sufferings and the miracles he performed were read. Moon's "sufferings" made Jesus' crucifixion look like child's play. Even knowing beforehand about the "revelation," I found myself getting emotionally involved in the reading and the subsequent deep personal prayer. It was hard not to feel guilty with my small struggle compared with the stories ("Reverend" Moon and the crying out in prayer all around me.

Then we were threatened. We were told that if you did not (what the Unification Church ("Reverend" Moon) told you, you would live in everlasting hell. By this time we had been worked on so intensely and been so psychologically swung from joy to fear and back again that it was hard not to believe it.

But what kept me after this first week was my trust in the leader of the farm. He promised me that I would learn more and be able to ask him personally many questions.

28

190

For the next two weeks I was bombarded with the same lectures day in and day out, sometimes four and five lectures a day, and further subjected to alternating intense emotional levels of grief and joy through the lectures, group singing, and group prayer.

For three weeks I lived in total isolation from the world. We were prevented from having any news of the outside world. There was no radio, TV, or newspapers. (After I had managed to get a newspaper, it was confiscated out of my backpack.) There was only talk about the Church and its "Divine Principle," the "Bible" of the Church. It had taken over my life.

At this point I was sent out onto the street to sell flowers in homes, bars, and shops. Being out in the world again was a shock; a cultural shock in which I was unable to deal with reality. My isolation by the Church had been so successful that everyday sights such as hamburger stands and TV's, even the people, looked foreign, of another world. I had been reduced to a dependent being! The Church had seen to it that my three weeks with them made me so vulnerable and so unable to cope with the real world, that I was compelled to stay with them.

Up until this time it had not occurred to me that there would be any conflict between my life in the Church and the world of family and friends that I had left behind. But one day I received a message that my father had called and wanted to speak to me because my mother was ill. Before I was able to call back, my group leader "programmed" me.

She told me that my mother was ill because Satan had possessed her. Satan was working through my family to try to take me away from the Church. She further explained that this was a test of my faith, that I must not give in to any desire to see my family, because I would not be strong enough to combat their Satanic influence if I left the Church. (I had also been taught that my parents were only my physical parents and not my true parents. My true "spiritual" parents were supposed to be "Reverend" Moon and his wife. Naturally, under normal conditions I would never accept such an outrageous idea. It was a measure of the control the Church had over my mind that I believed her.)

On the phone, my father said that my mother was ill because she believed I would never come home. I was torn by the idea of causing my family such suffering. But not knowing what my family knew about the practice of this cult, I could not understand why they were so concerned. To make sure that I did not waiver, my group leader stood by and cued me while I talked with my father. I felt as if I was not really doing the talking, but was somehow forced to say what she wanted me to. (I learned that all telephone calls from the farm were always made in the presence of a

29

member in authority.   They took no chances.)

The next day, after rejecting my family's plea to come home, I "graduated" from the farm and became a member of the work force in Berkeley. Here I experienced more blatant lies coming from the people I had come to trust and to love. Previously, during the latter two weeks on the farm, I was instructed to deceive new-comers by withholding knowledge, just as the older members initial-ly deceived me. When I asked for time off to attend to my personal needs and affairs, time to think about all that I had gone through the past three weeks, they promised I would have it. I never had it. Three times I asked, and three times they promised I would have it. I never had the time off and I know now they never in-tended to give it to me.

Instead the church gave me less time to myself and started to drive me hard. They decreased my sleeping hours overnight from the normal eight hours to four hours a night. They also disrupted any semblance of regular meals by arranging it so I would miss dinner, the only real meal of the day. There were only liquids at breakfast and perhaps a sandwich at lunch. There was very little protein in the diet and the food was almost totally carbohydrates (cookies, ice cream, cake and peanut butter and jelly sandwiches).

I worked most of the time for ten hours a day or more, with-out pay. With the lack of sleep and food and with the work conditions the way they were, I regularly felt tired; too tired to think. This, of course, was their purpose in driving us so hard. Freedom to think for oneself worked against the Church. Fatigue was their ally. I have since read enough about mind control to recognize these tactics as typical of brainwashing techniques.

So we were put to work for a long period of time selling flowers, cleaning carpets (the carpet cleaning company belonged to the Church), and witnessing. Witnessing consisted of going out onto the street or campus, striking up conversations with young people and by one means or another getting them into a Church center. I was told to lie to those people we were trying to en-list or those from whom we tried to raise funds. I was told that I shouldn't ever say that we were the Unification Church or connected with "Reverend" Moon because all those Satanic influences in the outside world had given the Church and "Reverend" Moon a bad name.

They justified denying connection to the Unification Church and "Reverend" Moon because they were supposedly incorporated under the name N.E.D. (Soon after that, though, because of a television program about Moon on NBC, they discarded that name for a new one, "Creative Community Project." I also learned that in this area alone they had used four or five such ambiguous names in the past).

30

192

Any possible means for getting money or people was justified on the grounds that the whole world outside was evil and Satanic. Any communication with the outside world except for selling or witnessing was usually suppressed or at the very least made difficult. As I've said newspapers were confiscated. There was no cooperation in receiving mail. I was lucky to find mail addressed to me in a back room. My time was almost so completely taken up by the demands of the Church that I often had to use even my few hours of sleeping time to write letters or to try to think.

The last section of Mr. Engel's paper describes his leaving the Unification Church on the basis of an appeal made by his father, from which he came to realize that he had become more attached to the Church than to family or friends. Engel titles his presentation on exiting from the Unification Church "My Escape From a Hell." As with other statement made by ex-followers of Moon, for himself or his duplicity in joining an organization that he perceived as artfully manipulating people.

Engle perceives himself as a passive being, who could be given "a sense of guilt about not being perfect." It is most unlikely that any individual could suddenly become guilt ridden about his imperfections, if he had not carried within him for many years a model of goodness based on being "perfect". Thus, we see that rather than actually controlling minds or instilling guilt, the Unification Church preys on already existent tendencies, which are vulnerable to manipulation, and reinforces false beliefs about the self that have been nurtured in young people by their families and their own culture, without much effort at reprogramming.

Although Mr. Engel has definite doubts about the authenticity of Sun Myung as a Messiah, he notes that what kept him in the organization was his "trust in the leader of the farm." The alacrity whith which members of Moon's groups give up their own thoughts and capitulate to the platitudes that are presented to them indicates their predisposition to accept falsehoods when they are accompanied by approval from peers. Other-directed behavior is a characteristic tendency of our society, in which being liked has priority over being true to oneself. Had the students who became followers of Moon acquired a sense of self-esteem they would be less prone to forsake their own awareness for tokens of friendship.

Three weeks is an extremely short period of time for a person to feel so isolated from the world that he suffers a "cultural shock" by coming into contact with those outside the church. Mr. Engel believes that the church had made him unable to cope with the real world and so vulnerable that he was "compelled to stay with them." It seems far likelier that vulnerability and

31

193

difficulties in coping with those who have different views
existed prior to indoctrination in the church, and the cult
exacerbated an already present tendency to be with people who are
like the self.

Biologist George Lockland has made an analogy between the
behavior of a developing organism and fanatical, cult groups in
American society. Mr. Lockland notes that if a group of cells
were put in a position in their environment in which they were
deprived of either proper nutrition or feedback, they would regress
to earlier and lower forms of behavior. Lockland further notes
that cult-like groups are "driven to grow by making everyone like
themselves; their own perception screening apparatus limits incom-
ing psychological nutrition to that which is like themselves.
They do not, and cannot mutualize with other segments of society
because that would weaken their attempt to control self-
extension."[11]

Often there is a tendency for students from small towns
to be undernourished in terms of their potential for contact with
a wide variety of people who have cultural backgrounds and modes
of life unlike their own. Conformity is the common denying force
of man. Affluent students from suburbs and small towns in the
United States are conformists because they lack active mutual
relationships with others and stimulation from individuals who
think differently from themselves and their families. They are
therefore good candidates for mavericks, renegades, and eccentrics
are difficult candidates for brainwashing because they have already
established an inner identity based on their awareness of themselves as distinctive individuals. What William Sargant says in
his Battle for the Mind is highly relevant to the so-called
"normal" or "ordinary" character of most Moon clientele:

> "It is not surprising that the ordinary person, in
> general, is much more easily indoctrinated than the
> abnormal . . . . A person is considered "ordinary"
> or "normal" by the community simply because he accepts
> most of its social standards and behavior patterns;
> which means, in fact, that he is susceptible to
> suggestion and has been persuaded to go with the
> majority on most ordinary or extraordinary
> occasions."[12]

Although reports on humiliations, "brainwashing," and suffering experienced while in Moon's church are common in the United
States, there is only a little information available from Japan.
However, Arai Arao's book, Nihon no Kyōki (Japan's Frenzy)
which deals with the Unification Church in Japan, contains similar
but more rigorous Japanese warrior type training imposed on the
Japanese followers for proselytization into Moonism. The book
contains a most harrowing account of initiation into Moon's

32

194

organization which appeared in the July 16, 1967 issue of the
Sankei newspaper in Japan.[13]

A young man, Yamada Tats...), who had been a student at Kansai
Univeristy joined the Unification Church, and shortly after
became extremely disturbed. Yamada jumped from a second story
window in the church, and was later bound and beaten by Moon's
disciples, who left him to starve, bleed, and die in a "sacred
hall" of their building. When Yamada was finally taken to the
hospital he was declared dead from weakness and wounds, and an
"empty stomach." The Tsugigi Police investigated the death, and
suspected the church of committing the crime of negligence. When
questioned by the police, Daguchi Tamiya, the dormitory director
of the church, said that there were "spiritual powers" during
dormitory activities that would have cured Yamada, and in any case,
the boy would be reborn. Although the police reported that they
were planning to send records of Yamada's death and charges against
the Unification Church to the District Prosecutor's office, the
case appears to have been dropped.

According to his friends and family, Yamada was a healthy,
pleasant boy who had planned to be a lawyer, and belonged to a
research society for legal studies at his university. When he
entered the Unification Church, Yamada had in his possession ten
tapes and a tape-recorder, and only five tapes were found in the
dormitory. From the account on one tape, Yamada appeared to have
been involved in an argument with a member of the church, and
there were sounds of angry voices, which were suddenly cut off.

It is quite possible that Yamada became deranged by the
obsessive character of the Unification church indoctrination
sessions, and it is also likely that his disagreement on doctrine
might have elicited fear and rage among other members of the
organization. The brutal treatment that Yamada received speaks
for the callousness and insensitivity to life that is bred by
adherence to Moon's doctrines, and the ultimate inhumanity of
young religious fanatics who consider "spiritual powers"
of higher value than a man's life.

Many Moonies, in escaping from the reality of their own lives,
have found a haven in a secure womb-like world that protects them
from the difficulties of a complex, contradictory world. The
price they pay for their false emotional security is alienation
from their own identity. Moon has cited his church as the
solution to the problems of drugs, alcohol, etc., but in
actuality he has created another form of flight from pain. Sun
Myung Moon's Unification Church differs from other sects by
virtue of its political affiliations, exceptionally severe methods
of "indoctrination," and harassment of individuals who leave the
organization.

33

195

There have been reports of several other suicides within the Unification Church, and some of the young people who have left the organization require hospitalization and extensive psychiatric treatment.[14]   In the United States, some parents hire a "deprogramming expert" like Ted Patrick, and they pay as much as a $15,000 fee plus expenses for the "recovery" of their children.

Currently the move to legalize "deprogramming" has been started by Michael Trauscht, a former deputy county attorney in Tucson, Ariz., who set up the tax-exempt Freedom of Thought Foundation. Trauscht and parents of "Moonies" argue that the cult followers are the helpless victims of Moon's mind control. They use this argument in applying for court injunctions to get temporary custody of the young believers, they use "conservatorship" laws originally designed to protect the mentally incompetent. The parents of youngsters who go through the 30 day rehabilitation program at the Freedom of Thought Foundation are charged as much as $10,000 by Trauscht for his legal work, travel and living expenses. Although Trauscht claims to have rehabilitated 80 cultists, the American Civil Liberties Union seriously questions the legality of Trauscht's program and ACLU executive director, Aryeh Neier, stated that "deprogramming" was "a dangerous trend which could be used against political as well as religious dissidents."[15]   Despite this escalating controversy, Trauscht's new tactics have gained much support across the country. However, neither the ACLU nor the "conservatorship" laws touch upon the climate of our alienated life or the root cause of our impersonal social organization, which abet false prophets like Moon.

34

IV. MOON'S DIVINE PRINCIPLE

The tenets of the Reverend Moon have been published in a book entitled The Divine Principle. What Sun Myung Moon presents as theology is actually a composite of excerpts from the Old and the New Testaments, liberally sprinkled with the inventions of Moon himself and the theories of two Korean revivalists of the 1920's. Like other false prophets, Moon tears a scrap out of scriptures and sews it into a motley patchwork quilt of notions bereft of any meaning. Ted Patrick, who has "deprogrammed" many American Moon followers, describes the Divine Principle as a tract that was deliberately written to be incomprehensible.[1] The obtuse and confused text provides the Moon spokesmen with an excellent alibi when novices are unable to understand it. A standard retort to the bewildered reader of Moon's bible is "Don't worry, if you don't understand it . . . you'll get it later . . ." or, "Satan must be confusing you."[2] Many college students, who are accustomed to accepting "American democracy" on faith from university pundits and a multitude of media experts rarely question the inanities that the Unification Church has passed off as respectable theology.   A former Moon follower, Shelly Turner of Warwick, Rhode Island, sums up the American students' gullibility in her comments from Ted Patrick's book, Let Our Children Go: "They'll put two plus two equals five on a blackboard and if they can prove it on two other blackboards, most college kids are going to believe them. All their life they've been taught that what goes up on the blackboard goes down in their notebooks as the truth."[3]

The opening sentence of the Divine Principle reveals the assumption that is the foundation of Moon's crude, but eminently successful, snow job. "Everyone without exception is struggling to gain happiness."[4] How Moon has succeeded in discerning what "everyone" in the universe is doing remains a mystery that can only be fathomed by attributing omniscience and divine powers to the self-ordained representative of God on earth.

Sigmund Freud never depicted the pleasure principle as a theological one, but claimed that it was derived from the general tendency of organic life to return to the peace of the inorganic. The impulse of the organism to reduce tensions within the psyche can be related to the state of Nirvana, in which all unpleasurable sensations have been quelled, but these phenomena have little bearing on our subjective and moral lives. There is nothing that commands us to identify ourselves with this tendency, and we could equally assert that our moral task is to oppose the rule of such forces with all our strength. Pleasure, as such, is not the goal of our aspirations, but the consequence of attaining them. Contemporary existential psychologists and theologians have

35

197

pointed out that the pleasure principle overlooks the intentional quality of all psychic activity. Psychiatrist Victor Frankl wrote in <u>The Doctor and the Soul</u>: "In reality, life is little concerned with pleasure or unpleasure. For the spectator in the theater it does not matter so much that he sees a comedy or a tragedy; what allures him is the content, the intrinsic value of the play. When we set up pleasure as the whole meaning of life, we insure that in the final analysis life shall inevitably seem meaningless. Life teaches most people that we are not here to enjoy ourselves. Those who have not learned this lesson might be edified by the statistics of a Russian experimental psychologist who showed that in an average day the normal man experiences incomparably more unpleasant sensations than pleasurable ones."[5]

The pleasure principle as gospel was spawned by one-sided 18th century rationalism and adopted by the advertising industry as a device for manipulating the true-believing public into consuming unnecessary goods and services. Sun Myung Moon's promise of a heavenly kingdom on earth is offered as a panacea that will magically cure unhappiness, crime, drug addiction, and alcoholism if one blindly conforms to the teachings of the Korean Messiah. Moon's <u>Divine Principle</u> text inundates the reader with a torrent of rhetoric culled from a variety of sources and consistent only in the vacuity of the generalizations. The evangelist who promises global salvation studiously avoids particulars, and relies heavily on the "everyone," "everything" generalities as used in the selling of detergents. Moon has a distinctive talent, common to many politicians, for saying nothing in grandiose terms. His edge over other hardsell revivalists is his taste for the word "global": "From small individual affairs to history-making global events, everything is an expression of human lives, which are constantly striving to become happier."[6]

"Good" in Moon's book is equated with what Moon says, and evil can be transposed into "communism" or contradiction. Invariably all-knowing, Moon writes "Everyone is now living in circumstances which can drive desire in the direction of evil rather than the direction of goodness."[7] To exacerbate the reader's anxiety, Moon employs the brinksmanship gambit of former U. S. Secretary of State, John Foster Dulles: "Due to his fall, man is always near the point of destruction."[8] The complex, paradoxical nature of reality is anathema to Moon, who also identifies "evil" with contradiction, stating that, "All life, all matter is doomed to destruction as long as it contains such a contradiction."[9]

It is difficult to understand how Moon's followers can accept his preposterous theology without concluding that home, school, and church training have squelched their ability to think critically. Yet, although most ex-Moonies lay claim to having

36

been brainwashed, there are individuals who have not been subjected to Moon's indoctrination programs but who also subscribe
to his ravings. Professor Robert Ellwood, Jr., of the University
of Southern California, characterizes the Moon philosophy as a
"new paradise of total restitution."[10]

Uncritical acceptance of the Divine Principle concepts by a
California academic suggests that thought itself has become so
blurred through habitual lying that it is no longer concerned
with the difference between fact and opinion. Hannah Arendt in
her book Between Past and Future cogently points out that "The
result of a consistent and total substitution of lies for factual
truth is not that lies will now be accepted as truth, and the
truth be defamed as lies, but that the sense by which we take
our bearings in the real world and the category of truth vs.
falsehood is among the mental means to this end--is being destroyed."[11] The confusions of the present generation and their
attraction to cult religions such as the Unification Church can
be understood as a response to growing up in an environment
where few distinctions were ever made between "truth" and "falsehood" on either an emotional or an intellectual level.

The most picturesque and fanciful aspect of the Divine
Principle is Moon's exposition on Original Sin, which he intro-
duces with a prolegomena on adultery: "There is one social vice
which is beyond the control of many men and women today. That
is adultery. Christian doctrine holds this sin to be the
greatest of all sins. What a tragedy that today's Christian
society cannot halt this degradation into which so many people
today are rushing blindly."[12] Moon, as we have seen was himself
convicted on numerous occasions of committing adultery. Like
the character of Antonio in "The Tempest," Moon had to make a
"sinner his memory, to credit his own lie."

The Divine Principle interprets the story of eating forbidden
fruit from the Tree of Knowledge as an allegory representing Adam
and Eve's immoral and unlawful sexual relations. According to
Moon, the fallen Archangel in the body of the serpent tempted
Eve to adultery, and she in turn, tempted Adam. From this union
of Adam and Eve, Moon pronounces their descendants (mankind) the
children of Satan and the bearers of bad serpent blood.

The next step in this clever syllogism is the notion that
all people have been subjected to Satan's dominion and have
become Satan-centered and Satan-entered parents of Satan-centered
children. Since that era of 6000 years ago, God has been working
to restore innocence. His will, however, has been delayed and is
not yet fulfilled because of man's rebellion against him. To save
mankind and restore innocence, the Lord of the Second Advent will
come in the status of the True Parent of man. In the Divine
Principle, Moon states that "Man fell both spiritually

37

199

and physically; so he must liquidate even the original sin through
'physical rebirth.' Therefore, Christ must come again to accomplish man's physical salvation by being born on earth."13 Moon
elaborates this point by stating as follows:

> . . .however devout a Christian may be, since he has
> not been able to liquidate original sin coming down
> through the flesh, no difference is found between him
> and the saints of the Old Testament Age in light of
> their both not having been able to remove themselves
> from the lineage of Satan. . . . Therefore, the Lord
> of the Second Advent must come to restore the whole
> of mankind to be children of God's direct lineage.
> Consequently, he must be born on earth, in flesh, as
> Jesus was.14

The Second Advent, therefore, will be of "pure blood" and
able to overcome Satan and will thereby establish the Kingdom
of Heaven on earth. Sun Myung Moon testifies to having received
a revelation from God at the age of 16, and that with his "pure
blood" he will now save the world as the True Father of man.
Moon practiced "blood-sharing," defining himself as the pure
Messiah figure who can rescue people from their false parents.
The concept of passing on qualities through the blood would
have meaning in Korea, where the caste system was based on the
notion of "royal blood." It is not too difficult to see how a
man who wished to be a divine power might emulate the actual
tradition of the ancient Korean kings and aristocrats. Most of
the Korean "blood-sharer" Messiahs came from humble origins and
suffered considerable personal hardships in early life.15 The
notion of being a sinless man who can pass his purity on to
others and thereby save the world must surely have appealed to
Sun Myung Moon in his twenties.

Apart from providing themselves with a religious alibi for
illicit fornication, Moon and his associates, as mentioned
earlier, had actually resurrected an old fertility ritual in the
guise of a Christian ceremony. The popularity of "blood sharing"
among Moon's cult in the late nineteen-forties suggests that
traditional patterns do persist, though deeply imbedded in the
minds of people, especially when a new religion that does not
provide outlets for old customs is adopted. Korea's Protestant
churches were originally formed in the 19th century by missionaries from the western evangelical Protestant tradition, who are
world-famous for their intense puritanism and rigidity concerning
sexual affairs, and they surely disapproved of the traditional
fertility rites that accompanied shamanistic beliefs. Although
Catholicism does offer fertility figures, such as St. Priapus,
that can provide a symbol to link believers with their pagan
past, Protestant services are notably lacking in modes of expression for the sensual aspect of experience. In an agrarian culture

38

like Korea, sex would normally be associated with fertility, and Christian puritanism would be a unyielding strait-jacket for robust followers with hardy sexual appetites.

Publicly, however, Moon asserts that "adultery was the cause of the downfall of numerous nations, national heroes and patriots." Only Moon the Messiah can prevent mankind from committing adultery. What Moon is actually saying is that only Moon, masked as the Second Advent is able to practice adultery and call it something else. Although Korean males are in no way averse to using giseng (equivalent to Japanese geisha) girls as sex partners, sex acts with respectable women or married women are frowned upon. As a non-conformist shaman type, Moon appears not to have been able to control his promiscuity. When he became a Messiah figure, he made a religion out of his own impulses and incurred the disapproval of the community. Moon's blood-sharing ceremonies were performed with well-to-do married women and college girls.[16]

Based on the public lecture given by Professor Sin Sa-hun of the Department of Religious Studies at Seoul University, Moon seems to have indulged in a shaman-flavored sexual ritual with one of his young women. According to Sin, Moon confined and starved a woman for three days, while reciting prayers over her. The fasting aspect of the rite is reminiscent of fertility legends in which the male-god is identified as nourishing food. Moon dressed himself and his companion in white clothes and then flashed on bright lights.[17] The white clothes symbolize the savior's purity, and the lights symbolize the inner light of the Jesus figure.

The Divine Principle is a curious mixture of the Holy Bible and the Chinese yin yang school of thought. Although the Divine Principle is compounded of quotations from both the Old and the New Testaments and Eastern mysticism to give it a profound flavor, a close investigation would reveal that Moon's understanding of both Christian thought and Chinese philosophy is superficial. The Divine Principle is a bizarre theory of a Christian God based on a Chinese concept of reciprocal interaction between yin and yang. In the Divine Principle, Moon states that "God, being the First Cause of all creation. . . exists because of a reciprocal relationship between the dual characteristics of positivity and negativity."[18] Moon then concludes that God is "a neutrality which is caused when the positive and negative elements neutralize each other."[19] For Moon all things revolve around polarity: moon (yin) and sun (yang), female and male, narrow and wide, rear and front, inward and outward, and weak and strong. Within these interactions of yin and yang is the confusing hierarchical Four Position Foundation. God is the head of this hierarchy, male and female are in the middle, and the child on the bottom as New

39

201

Four Position Foundation

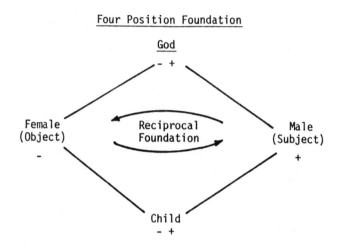

Life. In short, propagation of children without sin is possible
only when male and female form a home based on the Divine
Principle God. However, according to Moon the Four Position
Foundation has been negated for centuries because of Satan's
sexual relations with Eve in the Garden of Eden. Moon, therefore, believes that the mission of his United Family is to
restore the right order to the Four Position Foundation.

The concept of God in the Divine Principle is significantly
different from that of God generally accepted by many Christian
theologists, who believe in strictly one transcendent God,
creator and rule of the universe. The Christian God is not the
force of nature, but He exists independently and separately from
the world, not bound by laws or principles of the universe. In
the Divine Principle, Moon not only discusses the yin yang
relationship, but also mentions the Five Elements (Metal, Wood,
Water, Fire, and Earth) which form the Chinese concept of
rotation, that things succeed one another as the elements take
their turns. A pair of opposites and their alternation and
interaction, and the cyclical rotation of the Five Elements in
the Chinese classics, unlike Christian theology, are understood by the Chinese as the forces of nature. These laws of
nature were called the Ultimate, and Moon curiously equates this
Ultimate with the Christian God.

Another point which sharply differs from the accepted
Christian belief is Rev. Moon's explanation of the concept of
redemption. The concept of redemption, like that of sin, is a
central issue of Christian theology, and Moon presents a rather
simplistic explanation of the circumstances leading to the

40

crucifixion. Although in the Divine Principle there appears the term "redemption," Moon does not seem to understand the orthodox Christian interpretation that Jesus died on the cross for His love of mankind and as a preparation for man's higher destiny, his union with God. Moon rather interprets the crucifixion as Jesus' defeat and failure.[20] At a meeting in 1973, when a question was asked of Rev. Moon by a disciple about the extent of Jesus' accomplishment, he replied that "nothing was accomplished, nobody, no disciples at all, nothing. Just death. Christianity started after his death anyway."[21] In the Divine Principle, Moon writes, "What does the reality of the life in faith of the Christian teach us? It tells us straightforwardly that redemption through the cross cannot completely liquidate our original sins, and that it leaves man's original nature not yet perfectly restored. Jesus promised the Lord would come, because Jesus knew he could not fulfill the purpose of his advent as the Messiah through redemption by the cross."[22] Under the long heading "The Limit of Salvation through Redemption by the Cross, and the Purpose of the Lord's Second Advent," Moon explains that Jesus' crucifixion was not the teaching of God and, "If Jesus had not been crucified. . . . He would have accomplished the providence of salvation both spiritually and physically."[23] Contrary to accepted Christian belief, Moon shows his belief that Jesus was a human like us when he states that "Jesus, on earth, was a man no different from us except for the fact that he was without original sin. Even in the spirit world after his resurrection, he lives as a spirit man with his disciples. . . . If Jesus is God himself, how could he intercede for us before himself? Moreover, we see that Jesus also called upon 'God' or 'Father' for help, which is good evidence that he is not God Himself. . . . If Jesus was God Himself, how could God have been tempted by Satan, and finally crucified by the evil force?"[24]

The Divine Principle argues that "Man was created to have both spirit and body. . . . Naturally, salvation must include both. . . ,"[25] and Jesus could not meet this criterion. Moon now claims to be superior to Jesus, since Jesus died at an early age on the cross and was unable to have an ideal family through the blessed marriage, which God first intended for Adam and Eve. To round off his version of holiness, Moon calls his own last marriage (at the numerologically significant age of forty) the Feast of the Lamb, and his attractive teen-aged wife has been dubbed the "Divine Mother" or "Mother of the Universe." Since original sin was sexual, Moon's marriage symbolically restores fallen mankind and fulfills Revelation 19:7-8:

> Alleluia! The Lord our God, sovereign over
> all, has entered on His reign! Exalt and
> shout for joy and do Him homage, for the

41

> wedding day of the Lamb has come! His bride
> has made herself ready.

Moon is now the True Advent. His "holy" marriage in 1960 ushers
in the new age in which sinful tribal, national and international
systems are purified. To be a true member of the new order, one
is required to marry under the guidance of the True Parents of
the universe, Rev. Moon and his "Heavenly Wife." They conducted
joint weddings of their followers in Korea, the chosen land of
the new Messiah, involving 36 couples in 1961, 74 in 1963, 124
in 1965 and 430 in 1968. In 1970, 777 couples, including 231
couples from Japan, joined the simultaneous ceremony. Moon, who
is a believer in numerology,[26] was eager to give some mystical
meaning to the number 7, but it is said that there were actually
780 pairs in the wedding.[27] In 1975, 1,800 member couples from
24 countries, including 70 couples from the United States, held
mass matrimony. Moon makes the final decision on the selection
of the spouse, including church guidelines on matrimony and the
proper relationship between man and woman. The aim of the joint
marriage presided over by the "True Parents" is ostensibly to
cleanse all "impure blood" from the world through "holy matrimony" which is said to propagate children without sin.[28] But
the real aim of the ritual is to reaffirm the married couples'
faith in the Divine Principle and their loyalty to the "True
Parents" of the United Family.

When Arai Arao, the author of the Divine Principle movement
in Japan, asked a Moonist if he really believed that the joint
marriage could purify Satanic blood in the world, he stated that
"it is difficult in one generation, but it will do a complete job
within three generations."[29] There are many couples in the
church in Japan who had been married before they became followers
of Moon. One such couple are Kuboki Osami, the President of the
Unification Church in Japan, and his wife, who had been married
before they became followers of Moon. Although they were legally
married, they were "Satanic" in terms of the Divine Principle.
When 430 couples married in Seoul in 1968, the Kubokis officially
joined the "holy" ceremony, after which they were recognized as
true husband and wife by the "Messiah." Moon hailed this as the
turning point in the history of Japan, because, according to him,
this heralded Japan's opportunity to receive pure blood through
the Kubokis. However, the Kubokis' son, born during their
secular marriage, was still Satanic according to the Divine
Principle. For this reason, the Kubokis had to give him away
to a relative.[30]

In recent months, Moon's Divine Principle has caused furor
and indignation among Jewish leaders who have identified Rev.
Moon as an anti-Semite.[31] Rabbi Marc H. Tanenbaum, the American
Jewish Committee's director of interreligious affairs, has urged

42

"both Christian and Jewish leadership to combat any effort by Rev. Moon to bring the horrendous baggage of bigotry into the mainstream of American religion and culture."[32] According to Rabbi A. James Rudin, Moon's book is not only "replete with hostile and vicious anti-Jewish stereotypes,"[33] but also it is a "feculent breeding-ground for fostering anti-Semitism."[34] His contention that Moon is an anti-Semite is derived mainly from the following accounts, which appear in the <u>Divine Principle</u>, about Jews who are directly in league with Satan in causing Jesus' death:

> . . . due to the Jewish people's rebellion
> against him, the physical body of Jesus was
> delivered into the hands of Satan as the
> condition of ransom for the restoration of
> the Jews and the whole of mankind back to
> God's bosom; his body was invaded by Satan.[35]

Whether or not Rev. Moon is an anti-Semite has been the subject of much conjecture. In the Unification Church, Jews occupy somewhere between 15 to 20 per cent of the membership, and some of them hold relatively important posts in Moon's hierarchy.[36] Why should Jewish youth be more suspectible to a religious organization such as the Unification Church? According to Earl Rabb, "Jews . . . [are] generally more alienated than others, and therefore more susceptible to movements of alienation. Jews remain that much more marginal in the American society, with its emotional intellectual consequences. They feel that much more lonely, they feel that much more unsettled, they feel that much more questioning of the way things are. Or they just may want to escape the special pressure of being Jewish."[37] Many Jewish followers can see no contradiction in being Jews and Moonists at the same time. According to David Silverberg, Jewish Moonists "believed they were doing worthy work, compatible with the aims and ideals of Judaism."[38] Silverberg interviewed Dan Fefferman, a church member since 1968 after dropping out of the University of California at Berkeley, who said that there was no anti-Semitism in Moon's organization, but admitted that "it believes the 6,000,000 Jews who perished in the Holocaust were paying indemnity for the crucifixion of Christ."[39] Trize Shiligi, a former member of a kibbutz who joined the Church from Israel, declared that Judaism and the <u>Divine Principle</u> are the same in essence, though in the beginning it was difficult for her to accept the idea that the Jewish people were responsible for Jesus' death.[40] "Though some aspects of <u>Divine Principle</u> might be considered anti-Jewish in tone," says Silverberg, "it cannot be considered anti-Semitic. In the actual workings of the Church, there is no sign of discrimination against or hatred of Jews." What the <u>Divine Principle</u> says is, according to her, "'The Jews had their chance to restore Eden and they failed, the Christians had their chance and they failed--now

43

it's our turn and we're going to succeed!' For Rev. Moon, the Jews are no longer the Chosen People--his followers are."41

In the last three chapters of the Divine Principle, Moon claims that historians have written inaccurate histories, and he now sets out to rewrite an entire history of mankind, from the fall of man to the present. Like St. Augustine, Moon reduces human history as the unfoldment of the will of God, believing that historical events have followed or will follow according to the divine plan. Moon's historical themes are as diverse and the subjects as varied as Toynbee's, but none of these topics contain any substantial discourse which can be called historical in today's sense of the term. His brief but confusing discussions on primitive communalism, clan society, Jewish people, the Renaissance, and the Industrial Revolution lack coherent historical links, and they are at best a view of history based on continuous divine intervention in human action. Furthermore, the two world wars are reduced to simplistic struggles between the righteous force of God and the force of Satan, and Moon predicts the inevitability of World War III, in which his army of the Kingdom of God will ultimately triumph. Moon is an anachronistic figure who is unable to make a distinction between history and divination. The Divine Principle also contains discussions of various ideologies and institutions such as monarchy, feudalism, democracy, socialism, and imperialism. His treatment of these subjects is full of sweeping statements, half-truths, and generally conveys his lack of understanding of these complex systems and ideologies.

The mishmash of the Divine Principle was purportedly revealed to Mr. Moon over a period of twenty years, with Moon communicating frequently with God, Jesus Christ, and a variety of Saints in Paradise. A companion piece to Divine Principle and a more sophisticated exercise in erudite gibberish is Young Oon Kim's Unification Theology and Christian Thought. She borrows bits and pieces from the works of Kant, Freud, Fromm, Toynbee, Einstein, Neibuhr, and any fashionable writer on theology, philosophy, or psychology that was available to her. Ms. Kim's work is at best an incoherent patchwork or collection of numerous quotations from these writings which are distorted to support Moon's Divine Principle. It has no meaningful themes except that on several occasions Ms. Kim abruptly interjects statements blaming the growth of communism in the world on the failure of Christian practice. Both of the Moon bibles are sufficiently pretentious to convince naive college students of their weightiness. Beneath the superficial weightiness, there is a very simple message: "Man's separation from God brought spiritual death to man and has caused all the sorrow, misery, tragedy and evil within himself and in the world."42 Thus the Unification Church claims that if one believes in the Divine

44

Principle, all such problems of man--poverty, ignorance, and disease (both physical and spiritual), will disappear. Sun Myung Moon's ostensibly spiritual teachings most closely resemble edicts of a self-proclaimed Divine King who demands that his people follow his arbitrary rule, no matter how his law denies reason or the well-being of the individual.

The quest for Salvation may well be an authentic human need. In his great novel, The Brothers Karamazov, Dostoevsky gave voice to this impulse with the following advice:

> And what must I do to gain Salvation?
> Above all, never lie to yourself.

Sun Myung Moon's Divine Principle is a paradigm of self-deception and mottled semi-truths. As a reflection of the workings of a sick, manipulative individual, they can provide insight into the personal psychopathology of Mr. Moon. A purported guide to the perplexed followers of the Unification Church, the Divine Principle serves only to heighten their confusion. All of Sun Myung Moon's writings serve the purpose of creating for his disciples a new reality which strengthens their dependence upon Moon and weakens their ties to the outside world.

Rhetoric and monologue have always been the preferred mode of communication for demagogues. Within the Unification Church there is no occasion for dialogue, skepticism, or criticism of Moon's doctrines. Like all dictators, Moon identifies his word with law. Moon's secular counterpart, Park Chung Hee, meanwhile, imposes his law upon the Korean people by imprisoning and torturing those who do not subscribe to his arbitrary rule. In ancient Korea, the despotic kings employed shamans who assisted them in manipulating the people through demonstrations of magical power and divination in the service of the king's interests. Sun Myung Moon and Park Chung Hee are modern variations on the early teams of rulers and sorcerers who kept the Koreans in bondage by playing on fear and superstition with military power, word magic, and shamanistic displays of miraculous strength.

45

V. MOON AND KOREAN SHAMANISM

Korea's legendary founder was called Tan'gun. He was known
in folklore as an extraordinary shaman, endowed with miraculous
powers, and a bringer of many benefits to his people. Tan'gun
means the "King of Sandalwood" because his father, who married
the mythical "bear-woman", descended from heaven through a sandalwood tree on Mt. T'aebaek. This tree is a familiar symbol for
the "world tree" or "cosmic pillar" which can be found in many
ancient shaman cultures. Tan'gun set up his royal residence in
P'yŏngyan (Sun Myung Moon's birthplace) and bestowed the name
Chosŏn (the Land of the Morning Calm, or Korea) upon his kingdom.
Tan'gun was said to have ruled for 1,500 years and then returned
at the age of 1,908 to Asadal on Mt. T'aebaek, where he became a
mountain god. The legend is interesting in that it reveals the
old tradition that Korean kings were also shamans. From
antiquity to the present, the shaman has been a key figure in
Korean life, and any study of Korean history warrants a close
investigation of shamanism. In Korea the links between evangelical
religions and shamanism are particularly strong because shamanistic beliefs have persisted down to contemporary times.

Shamans are said to have contact with the animal world, the
realm of sky, the realm beneath the earth, and the realm of the
dead. The shaman masters the spirits through incantation and
ritualized chanting and dancing to induce ecstasy or invoke curses.
The Oxford Universal Dictionary defines shamanism as "the primitive
religion of the Ural-Altaic peoples of Siberia, in which all the
good or evil of life are thought to be brought about by spirits
which can be influenced only by Shamans." As descendants of the
Tungus tribes from Siberia, the Koreans have been practitioners of
animistic shamanism for many centuries. Within the Korean home,
individual members of a family have presided as shamans, and the
occupational shaman is sought out as a healer, a fortune-teller,
and an emissary who can contact the realm of the spirits. Words,
songs, music, and art are the shaman's tools, which can be used
either to heighten or deaden awareness.

Considered to be the oldest religion practiced by mankind,
shamanism was particularly strong in Northeast Asia, but it is
a phenomenon that has been endemic to all hunting societies.
Shamanism, moreover, persists as a technique for manipulating
human behavior in countries throughout the world. Among the
Tungusians, who lived in a hunting society and depended upon the
reindeer for survival, the shaman healer wore a headdress that
incorporated the reindeer's antlers. The most impressive artifact
that gives evidence of a relation between the Siberian shamans and
the Korean rulers is the gold crown excavated from Kyŏngju, the
ancient capital of the Silla Kingdom,[1] that bears a mark of

47

resemblance to both antler and "tree-of-life" patterned headgear worn by the Tungus. Soviet anthropologist S. Shirokogoroff's work, entitled Psychomental Complex of the Tungusian People, includes numerous interviews with Siberian shamans. The tree motif is of major significance to the sahman, and Shirokogoroff quotes the comments made by Semyonov Semyon from the Tungus tribes about the relation between shamans and trees: "Up above there is a certain tree where the souls of the shamans are reared, before they attain their powers. And on the bough of this tree are nests in which the souls lie and are attended. The higher the nest in this tree, the stronger will the shaman be who is raised in it, the more he will know, and the farther he will see."[2]

Several of the official brochures for Moon's Unification Church have glossy cover photographs of water, mountains and trees, an echo of his own shamanistic belief that the spirit resides in the elements. The snake is also a familiar symbol of the shamans and in 1946 Moon dispensed with his given name Yong, which means dragon or snake, and adopted his Savior identity as Sun, the Chinese character for bright, vivid, clear and new. Moon has presided at official Unification Church ceremonies in white robes and miniature versions of the Silla shaman headdress. He also favors red, white, and blue flag covers for his American booklets, as emblems of his theocratic state. Christian symbols never appear in the pamphlets distributed by Sun Myung Moon's followers, for they are not appropriate to Moon's religion, and the crucifixion is rarely referred to in any of Moon's theological discourses or in his speeches. The main prayer that is chanted by members of the Unification Church is an invocation to Sun Myung Moon as the Second Advent who was sent by the Father to "destroy Satan and restore the myriad things."[3]

The singing group that accompanies Moon when he shamanizes in public is known as "The Little Angels of Korea," and his dancers are called the "Little Angel Korean Folk Ballet." The angel is the Christian modification of the bird, which is known as the protector of the Siberian shaman. Moon uses his "birds" to charm audiences and dignitaries like Richard Nixon and enchant them with light songs that are usually bereft of any meaning. Buddhist monks from the Silla period used dancing girls, singers and glamorous displays to impress and dazzle the public with their external opulence. Moon is also known to have employed his pretty young female disciples to entertain American congressmen and seduce young men into joining his church.

Shirokogoroff coined the term "arctic hysteria" to describe the outbursts of violence, weeping, cursing, and incessant repetition of words that were common among the Tungus people. The Soviet anthropologist interpreted their hysteria as a

48

210

harsh environment and the concomitant unpredictable possibilities for success in their hunt.[4] Arctic hysteria can manifest itself in a single individual or among a whole group as a form of mass hysteria. The person or group possessed by this condition is believed to be overwhelmed by the spirits, and the disorder is expressed by fits of screaming and the breaking of social taboos. The frequency with which Moon has changed wives, indentities and residences, echoes the instability which is a main characteristic of the Siberian shaman.

Cultural anthropologist Weston La Barre adapted a Freudian model to explain shamanism as a religion that allows for a temporary abdication of the ego, a disenthronement of the super-ego for the purpose of hearing the pure voice of the id. He accounted for the outburst of arctic hysteria among the Tungusians as a compensation for frustration and deprivation, and noted that it was most common in adolescent males who were not able to possess reindeer or women, two symbols of status in Tungusian society.[6] To focus attention on themselves and release their tensions, the young Tungusians might begin to curse, take women, and break social taboos. The state of hysterical frenzy would be interpreted as shamanistic possession, and with the guidance of an older, established shaman, the adolescent Tungusians could acquire social recognition as shamans rather than be labelled as juvenile delinquents. There are close parallels between the Tungusian pattern of shamans who commit adultery in the guise of shamanistic rites and the adulterous episodes of Sun Myung Moon which he purports to be inspirations from the Holy Spirit. Both violations of customs are ways of breaking taboos without being censured.

Within the earliest hunting tribes, the shaman was probably the individual who was infirm in such a way that he could not participate in the hunt. To compensate for their weakness, certain individuals developed skills as weapon-makers, diviners, cultivators of herbs, singers, dancers, and story-tellers. Shamans are characteristically individuals who have suffered from personal misfortune or psychological crisis, which they cure through fasting, arduous ordeals, and entrance into a trance-like state.

Female shamans were also common among the Tungusians. Moon himself has employed a woman assistant, Miss Young Oon Kim, to launch his American campaign for converts. When she was very young, Ms. Kim is reported to have had hallucinations in which voices informed her of a future as a highly revered spiritual leader.[7] Sun Myung Moon has also claimed to hear voices. To play the role of the prophet it is necessary to be clairvoyant, and both Sun Myung Moon and his assistant, Young Oon Kim, have laid claim to knowledge of the future. Moon has told his

49

211

followers that the time will come when it is no longer necessary
to plant, to sow, or to harvest; one will simply pray and everything will magically grow.[8] These presumptions to miraculous
powers and magical modes of thinking are common among Korean
shamans. There is a Korean woman shaman, Yi Ch'ang-Kyu, who
leads a sect named Tan'gun, after Korea's legendary shaman founder. She actually performs archaic rituals and avers that she has
supernatural skills. In 1964, Miss Yi warned her followers that
the world was coming to an end and led them to a southern coastal
city in Chǒlla province, where she reportedly gave lessons in
how to fly over the globe, make clouds, move mountains and
perform other such miracles to prepare her followers for the
predicted end of the world.[9]

Weston La Barre has identified shamanism as a defensive
compensatory response to external threats, but shamans like Moon
and Yi manufactured hysteria by projecting their own inner fears
and rages onto the external world. Crucial to shamanistic thinking is the belief that death, illness, and personal misfortune
result from the action of evil spirits. It is a religion that
nurtures a paranoid society, inclined to magical thinking and
flight from reality through ecstatic rituals. Weston La Barre
cites the American Plains Indians as an example of a shamanistic
culture that became increasingly dependent upon incantation and
group ecstasy when threatened with extermination by the white
man.[10] La Barre views the Plains Indians as having attempted to
escape from life through a form of self-hypnosis, when reality
became difficult and painful. Thus, shamanism is a religion
that is practiced most intensely at a time of crisis, as a means
of escape from seemingly impossible difficulties.

Many young American college students have been attracted to
Moon because they seek a way to escape from the complexities and
dehumanization of modern life. Modern man labels symptoms of
flight from reality such as drug addiction, suicide, crime, and
alcoholism as problems that must be "solved." Our obsession
for labeling is itself a magic technique for not confronting
real questions. Our institutions insure the perpetuation of this
obsession by educating our young people in the use of habitual
labels. This serves to add to their problems and make them
likely prospects for shamans like Moon, who offer them instant
"salvation."

Shamanistic thinking also invariabley fosters fantasies of
immunity to realities such as sickness and death. Modern
"merchant" shamans sell products that are purported to insure
their users against aging. Sun Myung Moon distributes an
herb known as ginseng, which is advertised as guaranteeing
youthfulness and protection from illness. Siberian shamans
fantasized that they were impervious to old age, and when

50

recruited into the Russian army, even believed themselves immune to bullets.

Sun Myung Moon's associate of the late 1940's, Pak T'ae-sŏn, is the contemporary Korean shaman who most closely resembles the ancient shamans of Korea in his claims to supernatural powers. Founder of the Olive Tree Sect, Pak T'ae-sŏn is a faith healer who employs the traditional shaman treatment of massage. He has reportedly killed a few clients through excessive application of his cure.[11] Pak's followers drink his bath water to heal their ailments and use water that he prayed and breathed on to cleanse sin. In some cases he dispenses his urine as a curative. His believers are told that they will become immortal by eating candy and bread that is mixed with water, over which he has prayed, and Pak has made a large profit from selling his followers "life candy" or "life bread."[12] Pak has a larger following in South Korea than has Sun Myung Moon, but remains essentially a native-style shaman rather than a global theocrat.

To impress his followers with his ability to transcend death, Pak T'ae-sŏn announced that should anyone kill him, he would arise after three days and fly into the sky. The grandiose statement of this modern shaman is close to that of the ancient shamanistic minister Yangmin, who swore to his emperor, "When I die, I shall be reborn in Koguryŏ, where I shall become prime minister and ruin the kingdom to avenge my wounded Emperor."[13] Pak T'ae-sŏn has assured his followers that to show his vengence toward those who may kill him, he will destroy two-thirds of mankind, and become greater than Daniel in the Old Testament.[14]

Fear is at the root of Moon's religion. Sun Myung Moon has made many threats against those who do not obey his wishes, and ex-members of the Moon organization are warned that they will belong to Satan if they leave the group.[15] When he was in Korea, Moon's church was supposedly guarded by two disciples every night, and "each of the three districts takes the responsibility of watching the church around the clock for ten days . . ."[16] Guards are told that they are defending the church from Satan, "who already controls the rest of the world, and who, liking darkness, is more likely to come at night."[17] To demonstrate to his followers how powerful they will become by adhering to their master, Moon once told them that they will eventually be "united into one with (themselves) and with that as a bullet we can smash the world."[18] It is unclear exactly what Rev. Moon has in mind.

Moon like many shamans has identified himself as a healer. In his speech "God's Plan for America," Moon told his audience the kind of medicine man he is:

51

213

> God has sent me to America, in the role of a
> doctor, in the role of a firefighter.
> That is why I have come to America. Good
> medicine may taste bitter, and an operation
> may involve some pain, but the treatment
> must be at once. Should the patient complain
> and push away the doctor's hand when he touches
> the infected part?[19]

The instant cure that Sun Myung Moon has recommended to his
followers can be more harmful than the illness or unhappiness they
actually suffer. As a shaman who has not healed himself, Moon
prescribes hatred and delusions of grandeur to his patients.

Although shamanism has become a fashionable subject and the
shaman is currently viewed as a mystical figure, the political
aspect of the shaman has been curiously neglected in most anthropological studies. A primary attribute of shamanism is the
projection of all evil and bad impulses onto the outer world. As
the ancient shaman exorcised evil spirits from the individual, so
a modern shaman, Sun Myung Moon, blames all our problems on
"evil communists," and his political counterpart, Park Chung Hee,
declares war on long hair and tortures his opposition as if they
were evil spirits. The Tungus shamans, ancestors of Koreans like
Moon and Park, were of an exceptionally bellicose nature, frequently engaged in battle, and laid great importance upon revenge. Out
of fear of the bad spirits of the dead the Tungus and Korean
shamans would dismember and mutilate their enemies to be sure they
did not return to avenge themselves the one who had injured them.

In 1973, Sun Myung Moon echoed the vengeance motif and taste
for exaggerated threats common to the shaman when he stated:

> Those who judge me will be judged . . . by me in the
> future. They will fall into misery. The present
> U. N. must be annihilated by our power. The whole
> world is in my hand, and I will conquer and subjugate
> the world.[20]

On February 14th, 1974, Moon told his followers, "And even on
earth whoever goes against you, that man must be subjugated
and he will be subjugated," and "Now no one will oppose the
Unification Church, except perhaps communism. When all the
communists die, then we and we alone will remain."[21]

Shamans employ cursing, hysterical frenzy, endless repetition
of words, music, dancing, and incantation to drive out the "bad
spirits." The early Christians used exorcism as a technique for
purifying the world of "devils" in their numerous missions, which
is an indication of how shamanistic practices were incorporated
into other religions. Some aspects of modern revivalist

52

Christianity are similar to primitive shamanism, and Sun Myung
Moon's popularity is a reflection of modern man's unconscious
attraction to an archaic religion predicated on good and evil
spirits outside of the self. Moon's theology is removed from
evolved forms of Christianity, Buddhism, and Taoism which have
attempted to look inward for the source of our human problems.

In the Divine Principle, Moon states that " . . . at the
consummation of human history, both the heavenly side and the
Satanic must come to dominate the world in their respective
ways . . . . For the final separation and unification of these
two worlds, there should come world wars."[22] According to him,
there are two ways for World War III to be fought; one is to
subjugate the Satanic communist world through his Divine
Principle, and the second is to conquer the Satanic side by the
sword.[23] Although Moon describes himself as the best Christian,
his view of evil as an external that must be destroyed is anti-
thetical to the injunction of the New Testament which centers evil
within the self: "and why beholdest thou the mote that is in
thy brother's eye." Moon's position of fighting communism and
triumphing over the "enemy" is characteristic of the Korean
shamans who were notorious for their vendettas and passion for
battle. Though it is difficult to determine the degree of
shamanism incorporated in the New Testament, its view of "resist
no evil" plays no part in Sun Myung Moon's theology.

Crucial to the effectiveness of the shamans are their
charismatic personalities. They are colorful dramatic speakers who
can induce their audience to yield attention to them. The shaman
employs incantation, not unlike the revivalist who uses hymn
singing, weeping, and handclapping to bring his devotees into a
similar trance-like state. Shaman sorcerers who used effective,
exaggerated phrases and bombastic warnings were employed by
ancient Korean kings to support them in warfare and to stir up
the people against opponents, so that the kings could live in
luxury while turning the populace against a common outer "enemy."
Kings themselves had shamanistic powers in many instances, and
a team of king and sorcerers combined their talents to enhance
their wealth while exploiting the people.

Shamanism has demonstrated a pervasive pattern throughout
Korean history. During the Silla period, when Buddhism was
adopted as the state religion, it was a distinctly shamanistic form
of Buddhism, which reinforced the Sillan theocracy, just as Moon's
Unification Church is united with the Seoul dictatorship. Buddhist
monks, who incorporated shaman chanting with Buddhist prayers, were
said to be miracle workers, immortal, and immune to disease
Sillan kings employed the monks as shamans who would make
predictions that were favorable to the tyrannical state, and
rewarded them handsomely for their assistance in maintaining
social control through fear and ignorance. Silla Buddhists were

53

215

notoriously patriotic, militaristic and wealthy. The increased
power of the Buddhists as organization men in the service of the
King was reflected in their acquisition of huge tracts of land,
numerous temples, and pagodas. Moon, like the Sillans, has
acquired various estates: The New Yorker Hotel, The Columbia Club,
and five-story town houses. Reverend Moon has also purchased
Tarrytown, New York, for $625,000, and furnishings for the house
for an additional $50,000. In addition, he acquired a 234-acre
estate in the same area for $5,000,000, and a 1.5 million dollar
seminary. He also owns his own yacht and a limousine. Moon,
the Messianic master, also owns a large cruiser from which he is
said to fish with $300 worth of bait a day.[24] According to one
Unification Church official, he gives $200 coats as gifts to his
section chiefs as incentives for them to set a good example.

Although the Unification Church keeps no financial records,
Moon is known to amass at least 10 million dollars a year through
the soliciting activities of his followers. To justify his vast
wealth (purported to range from 24-60 million dollars) accrued
through his many industries, Moon has told his audiences: "I
know that God sent me here to America. I did not come here for
the luxurious life in America. Not at all!" In his God's
Hope for America, Moon declares, "Am I pursuing my own honor?
Is money my goal, or power? No! Never!"[25]

It is difficult to believe Moon's disavowal of desire for
the bills and coins inscribed with the adage he cited as
beautiful in one of his speeches: - "In God We Trust."[26] Like
many fortune-tellers and professional soothsayers, Moon tells
people what they want to hear and then has his palm crossed with
silver. The extravagances, wealth, and opulence of Moon's life
can be paralleled with an ancient Korean poem called "In Praise
of the Two Ragged Monks."

> The feasting monks call their rich friends
> to feed their gilded images
> And to admire their newly made pictures of
> silver Buddhas
> The living Buddha in the human mind is often
> lost sight of,
> Just as the faint moon over Harper's Rock
> is overcast with clouds,
> And its somber shadow is reflected in the
> pool with dim and broken ways.[27]

The Sillan Kings and their lackey monks accrued enormous
wealth to themselves while the multitude of the Korean people
starved. There is an account in the ancient chronicle, the
Samguk Yusa, of an abbot who gave his temple slave two chestnuts
for his supper. The indignant slave brought suit against the
abbot because of his meager rations, and the magistrate ruled
against the slave.[28]

54

216

While Moon lives in luxurious quarters, many of his disciples are sustained for 72-cents-a-day on high starch diets and use sleeping bags for beds.[29] Moon's 15 million dollar a year conglomerate (titanium, heavy machinery, pharmaceuticals and M-1 rifles) industries in Korea employ volunteers from the Unification Church who work at sub-standard wages, for the glory of serving their great master. The average Moonist in the United States collects about $50 to $200 a day from street fund-raising, and the more successful can solicit up to $500. Every penny is turned in to the team leader, who in turn hands it over to the Unification Church. A former member of the Church said, "I would sell peanuts, tea, candy, and flowers at inflated prices to 'recapture money from a Satanic world'."[30] The most profitable fund-raising activities are conducted under false pretenses by knocking on doors and saying: "We are here to raise money for a drug program in Iowa and we like Americans. We think that democracy is great."[31] Since 1965 Moon has raised millions of dollars through emotional solicitation, ostensibly to save starving children of the world under the Childrens Relief Fund. The money, however, was used to influence U. S. congressmen and officials to support the Park regime. Of the 1.3 million dollars solicited in 1973 only eight per cent went towards food for the starving children. A portion went to promote the Little Angels of the Korean Folk Ballet and for political lobbying. Most of the solicited money was invested in Moon's 25-million-dollar real estate ventures.

Moon brought 500 to 1,000 aliens into the United States on tourist visas; aliens whose sole occupation consisted of fund-raising to subsidize Moon's religious, political and financial ventures. Allen Tate Wood, former president of the Freedom Leadership Foundation, testified before the congressional hearings that in September of 1972 about 400 Japanese who had come to the U.S. on tourist or visitor visas were mobilized by the Unification Church to raise money for Moon. At that time, Wood reported, the Church turned out 2,000 to 3,000 candles a day. Members of the Church sold door-to-door for 400 or 500 per cent profit. Wood stated that 200 to 300 of these Japanese youths went out every single day in Belvedere, Maryland, from dawn to dusk to sell these candles. They made $10,000 to $15,000 a day to "set the example of how dedicated followers should raise money" for Moon.[33]

The Moonists also perform most of the repair, renovation and maintenance work of the Church without pay. Allen Tate Wood also testified that in 1972 everything within the Church was collectivized, and Moonists were ready to sacrifice and contribute large amounts of money out of their own pockets. For example, Wood's wife, a member of the Unification Church who earned about $12,000 a year as the director of the Columbia Heights Day Care Center, gave every cent of her income to the Church.[34]

55

217

According to a recent NBC television broadcast (February, 1977), the Moon organization owns a carpet cleaning company which has contracts to clean the federal office buildings and the FBI building in San Francisco. Two U.S. congressmen are now under investigation for being involved in this bizarre affair.

Moon also added to his wealth through contributions from wealthy individuals and firms. For instance, in the early 1960's a wealthy Britisher contributed a large sum to the Unification Church. And very recently DeWitt and Lila Acheson Wallace, owners of the Reader's Digest, gave Rev. Sun Myung Moon's Korean Cultural and Freedom Foundation (KCFF) more than half a million dollars before they realized that it was what their lawyer calls "a bum outfit."

As a shaman master laying claim to worldly possessions, other men's wives, and powers of omnipotence, Sun Myung Moon is a convincing figure in the tradition of Sillan Korean sorcerers who called themselves Buddhists and coolly asserted to visiting "spirits," "Thanks to your gracious protection, all my wishes have been fulfilled."[35] Love of one's fellowmen, forgiveness, voluntary poverty, and a treasuring of inner light are qualities that are as foreign to Sun Myung Moon as they were to the Sillan shamans. The posture of omnipotence and the desire to mold other creatures to one's wishes are the antithesis of the teachings of Christ, Buddha, and Confucius. Conscientious Christians and Buddhists from both the ancient worlds have kept the spiritual qualities of Jesus and Buddha alive in their daily existence.

Rev. Moon emulates the American Fundamentalist Billy Graham who says, "I am selling the greatest product in the world; why shouldn't it be promoted as well as soap?"[36] Moon is also akin to the ancient Korean Buddhist shaman Jajang in his equating of God's (or, in Jajang's case Buddha's) will with that of the ruling class. Jajang, the Sillan monk wrote: "Silla is Buddhist soil and in the past, many Buddhas enlightened the people, if the people returned to the Buddhist faith, Silla would be protected by Buddha and the more Silla Believes in Buddhism, the more prosperity she would gain."[37] Moon, in his Bicentennial God Bless America Festival on June 1, 1976 at Yankee Stadium, employed the standard device of flattery known as sadae, a Korean term for "serving the larger," to impress Americans. The sadae policy of bowing before the strong and bullying the weak is a common practice among the Korean people, who have long been ruled by a colonial power and forbidden to directly oppose those above them. As a result, they have often transferred their frustration against their own people. Moon, who has demonstrated his need to be obeyed by his inferiors (followers) and his willingness to be humble before his superiors (America), gives us a glimpse of his sadae leanings in the following quote:

56

218

America is a microcosm of the world. Transcending
nationality and race, America has created a model
for the ideal world. God Himself had purposely
hidden this land of America from civilization
until His time was full, and then upon her God
raised up this model nation. In His Providence
God anointed America with oil; He poured out
abundant blessing upon this land. In a short 200
years, God raised this nation to be the mightiest
nation on earth.[38]

This speech was addressed to the United States Congress on
December 18, 1975, under the erstwhile subject heading of "God's
Plan for America." On this occasion, Reverend Moon introduced
himself as a man who had become an increasingly controversial
figure, and acknowledged his gratitude to the mass media for dis-
playing photographs of him that enhanced his good looks. After
identifying himself in a jovial and cocksure manner, the Korean
preacher brought up the subject of complaints that he had been
brainwashing members of the Unification Church. His remarks were
characteristically a _sadae_ technique of bowing to the larger power:

Are Americans really that foolish? Can they
really be brainwashed by Reverend Moon, a
Korean? I know your answer is no. My answer
is no, too. No American is so foolish.[39]

Sun Myung Moon himself speaks little English. His speech to
the Congress was delivered by his translator Colonel Pak Bo Hi
(former Assistant Defense Attaché at the Korean Embassy in
Washington, and a person known to be an operative in the Korean
Central Intelligence Agency). Moon's interpreter Pak Bo Hi is
also his notorious link with Park Chung Hee, whose insecurity,
like Moon's, motivates his flattery of those above him. As a token
of his submission, and demonstrating the mentality of the _sadae_,
Park presented a 17-ton "Friendship Bell," the largest ever cast
in Asia, costing $400,000, as a Bicentennial thank-you gift to
America.

As an advocate of theocracy and a flag-waver, Sun Myung Moon
resembles the zealous, propagandizing ancient Korean monk when
he proclaims: "America must be willing to sacrifice for God's
purpose. She must rush forward as God's flag bearer. When
America does this, her prosperity will be eternal."[40] Empty
promises and assurances of good fortune are the standard fare of
many shamans who prefer pleasant illusions to unpleasant realities.
Moon goes on to state that "On the other side of the world, the
God-denying ideology of communism has risen up and is ready to
undertake an all out offensive against the free world."[41]

57

219

In his paranoid shamanistic vision Moon asserts that "Destroying
America is the communists' final and ultimate goal . . . . America
cannot win this battle alone. She needs God" and " . . . . once
God becomes real in our lives, soon there will be no trace of
Communism. When the sun rises, the darkness automatically passes
away. With God everything is possible: no problem is too big.
Without God, however, our problem is beyond our reach."[43]

A trait that both Shirokogoroff and Weston La Barre noted in
the Tungus shamans was their alternation between states of extreme
passivity and of marked aggressiveness. This oscillation between
subservience and meglomaniacal dominance has been nurtured
through her sadae (serve the larger) policy in dealing with foreign
powers. When T'ang China held sway in the Silla period the Korean
rulers and religious officials aped Chinese mores and bowed before
the foreigners. Koreans made themselves small before Chinese
officials, and compensated by bullying and exploiting their own
people.

Park Chung Hee, the political shaman, bows to his superior
(America), and bullies his inferior (the Korean nation). During
World War II he betrayed his own people by volunteering to serve
as an officer in the Japanese Imperial Army, and when he assumed
the presidency by force in Korea he sold his country out to
Japanese business interests. The louder President Park shouts
"self-sufficiency" and "unification" for Korea, the more dependent
he makes the nation upon Japan and the more unlikely the actual
prospects for unification with the North.

Sun Myung Moon apes American advertising techniques, the
style of American dress, T.V. appearances and Billy Graham-type
gala spectacles in his public campaigns. After Richard Nixon was
forced out of office Moon begged for clemency in his behalf. It
is, therefore, no great feat of the imagination to surmise how
humble he is in the presence of military and corporate magnates
who find him useful for their interests.

Moon, in his official hagiography, describes his own proverty-
stricken childhood in a manner similar to that of many autobiograph-
ies of evangelists which describe childhood suffering or feelings
as social outcasts. Shamanism flourishes in poor, deprived
societies where there are few outlets for ambitious young people
who cannot conform to strict mores. Korea, with its long history
of acute economic inequity, rigid social control and colonialism,
has been the breeding ground for shamanism, just as the overly
bureaucratized western technologies have produced the mania for
rock music, narcotics, the occult, and the new wave of cult
religions. Much attention and sensational media coverage has
been given to imbalanced individuals like Charles Manson and his
family of followers who were ready to murder for him. Less focus

58

has been placed on the pathological mass murder committed by whole nations under the leadership of supposedly sane men. Similarly, shamanism, when imposed by the state, is far more destructive than the singular shamanism of individuals. The kind of shamanism practiced by the ancient Korean kings and their religious cohorts exemplifies the deceptions and manipulations that are currently being employed by Sung Myung Moon and President Park Chung Hee.

Both Sun Myung Moon and Park Chung Hee play on the power wishes of the Korean people by banging the shaman drum of fanatic patriotism. Moon declares that the "Second Advent" will be born in Korea and that He will bring glory to the "virtuous and loyal" Koreans who suffered in the past.[44] Park's government proclaims that its accomplishments in the economic field are "miraculous." In a nation whose peasantry is often near to starving, the President allocates vast sums of money to the military and to the upkeep of the "patriots" monuments. In shamanistic fashion, Park concerns himself with the spirits of ancestors and conducts public memorial services for the dead in the Seven Hundred Patriots Tomb, while living patriots languish in the West Gate Prison.

Moon's mask as a "champion of God" thinly veils a narcissistic shaman whose fantasies of power are parallel with those of fanatic fascists like Kita Ikki of the 1930's whose goal of the establishment of the "supremacy of sacred Japan" appealed to the unconscious wishes of the Japanese people. Hitler hypnotized the Germans with public speeches, martial music, chanting youth, and with promises that Germany would wipe out communism and rule the world. Moon stages his rallies in Yankee Stadium, dresses his followers in red, white, and blue, waves flags, sings hymns, and preaches anti-communism and a global theocracy for the solution of the "drug, crime, alienation" problems. As in Hitler's time, the play of offering, a seemingly reasonable patriotism at the outset could eventually lead to greater demands later on.

The shamans still dazzle us with their glittering promises of false utopias. Rev. Moon's "sacred" chantings and prayers are neither a panacea for alienation nor a harmless retreat from difficult reality. If Moon were a performer of rock music, he would be an amusing shamanistic entertainer, but as a cult leader, he is dangerous and is capable of injuring the minds and bodies of young followers. Conditions of political and social stresses within a society can best be dealt with by individuals who are able to think and make critical judgments for themselves. When Moon shouts "I am thinker, I am your brain,"[45] he perpetuates the atavistic rites of deranged shamans.

59

221

VI. THE PREACHER WHO DANCES TO THE GOVERNMENT'S TUNE

For most Americans the dictatorship and torture in South Korea are matters of little concern. Yet to some Americans the South Korean government has become a reality through their personal involvement with the self-proclaimed Korean Messiah.

On December 13, 1973, several young members of the Korean Youth Council for Protecting Democracy, including Lee Jae Oh, Kim Chong Tae, Choi Il Jon, and Kim Dal Su, were arrested and imprisoned.[1] While the Korean Central Intelligence Agency was torturing these four men into confessing that they were North Korean spies, a tree-lighting Christmas ceremony was taking place at the White House in Washington, D.C., with Sun Myung Moon and twelve hundred of his misty-eyed disciples in attendance. Christmas is not a true holiday for Moon, since the Unification Church celebrates his birthday, January 6, as the savior's birthday. He and his devoted flock had not, however, come to the nation's capital as celebrants of Christmas, but instead were demonstrating their support of the then President of the United States, Richard Nixon.[2] Even though Nixon already appeared to have met his Waterloo at Watergate, Reverend Moon's entourage came forth with well scrubbed faces and beaming smiles, carrying placards that read "God loves Nixon," "Support the President," or simply "God."

When President Nixon came to greet them, they knelt down as he drew near, offering the homage usually associated with divine kings or deities.[3] This Unification Church ritual recalled to mind the ancient Roman rite honoring the God of Agriculture, Saturn. Saturn's temple was on Capitoline Hill, and his worshippers bowed before his statue with uncovered head. Sun Myung Moon brought his own Saturnalian festival to the White House.

Moon's group of singers and dancers entertained the president with standard patriotic songs. The Korean preacher prayed fervently for Mr. Nixon and asked the American people to forgive him his wrong doings. Even though the entertainment briefly cheered the troubled president, Moon's prayers were not answered, and Richard Nixon was forced out of office.

During the summer of 1974 Moon began advertising his New York City rally with billboards reading, "Christianity in Crisis, New Hope, Reverend Sun Myung Moon." When he arrived in Manhattan full page ads appeared in major newspapers, showing a center page photograph of a smiling Korean man in his middle years, posed against the capitol dome. Mr. Moon appeared at Carnegie Hall on October 1, 1974. Through his translator, Lieutenant Colonel Pak Bo Hi, he delivered a message about Adam, Eve, the Holy Spirit,

61

and satanic communism to the American audience. At the time, the press viewed Moon as a slightly odd evangelist. His followers, who solicited money in exchange for flowers or candy, were seen as harmless innocents.

A month before his appearance at Carnegie Hall, Sun Myung Moon received a request from Park Chung Hee to appear in Seoul at a government rally that was called EXPLO.[4] Park Chung Hee also believes himself to be a deity, and to prove this, he wrote the Yushin Constitution that empowered him to hold office for the rest of his life. Mr. Moon and his followers flew to South Korea's capital city from one of his many bases in Japan. Millions of people were said to have participated in the event, and some receiving travel subsidies from the government so that they could behold Sun Myung Moon. To ennoble the rally with religious significance, the Republic of Korea's government issued a special stamp commemorating the internationally famous native preacher.[5]

The purpose of the Seoul rally was reportedly to show that the Park Chung Hee regime, far from oppressing Christianity, was a generous supporter and protector of religious groups. American promoters at the rally praised the great accomplishments of the Park government, despite the fact that Christian leaders had been arrested and jailed for criticizing their frenzied leader. Some Korean people were said to have exclaimed, "whatever the government situation, what's wrong with gathering to listen and pray?"[6] Other Koreans, who were acquainted with the machinations of Sun Myung Moon, said, "the preachers simply danced to the government's tune."[7]

For the people who were not impressed by pomp and circumstance , the government rally in 1974 brought to mind the bloodstained declarations of Christian pastors who have been imprisoned by Park Chung Hee for criticizing his phony constitution and the emergency laws that deprived the people of civil liberties. Others at the rally thought of the poet Kim Chi-ha who had been tortured and imprisoned for writing brilliant poems that lampooned the corrupt regime of Park Chung Hee. Some attending the Seoul rally remembered that on the eighth of August, 26 people were given three-to fifteen-year prison sentences for violating the "anti-communist" law designed by the government to silence critics.

The avalanche of imprisonments was heavy in the summer of 1974 in South Korea, and a large number of the jailed were distinguished members of the church. On July 16, the Catholic Bishop of the City of Seoul, Tji Hak Sun, was arrested, as were numerous preachers who weren't dancing to the music of Park Chung Hee and the Korean Central Intelligence Agency. Sun Myung Moon

62

sang the same songs as the South Korean President, and so did Moon's chief interpreter, Pak Bo Hi, who is personally close to Park Chung Hee.

Park Chung Hee and Sun Myung Moon have numerous traits in common, and both are notable as boastful egomaniacs who fancy themselves bigger than life and worthy of adoration. The religion that President Park enforces is worship of himself. His close associate, Kim Hyong Uk (former chief of the KCIA), who was a believer "in the religion of Park Chung Hee and ready to serve him at all times," left the country because he was not safe and was fearful that the President might turn upon him, accusing him (Kim Hyong Uk) of a crime against his person.[8] As an object lesson to the Korean people, Park had eight innocent citizens tortured until they admitted to belonging to a non-existent "People's Revolutionary Party." These men were all executed and their bodies were so brutalized by torture that the government refused to return them to their families. Some people who had seen the remains at the cremation site testified to viewing the marks of chains and dotted whipmarks, as well as dismembered bodies and torn flesh.[9] As did Hitler, Park hides behind anti-communism as a mask for murderous acts that enhance his own power.

As we have seen, Park had a harsh early childhood. Betraying his people to the nation that had subjugated Korea, Park enlisted as an officer in the Japanese Army during World War II and was promoted to company commander. One source spoke of his fervent dedication to the Japanese Emperor.[10] After the defeat of Japan in 1945, Park became a colonel in the Korean Army and was reported to have been either an anti-communist spy within the army or a turncoat communist who betrayed his comrades.[11]

Rarely a day goes by but there is a major article about President Park in the Korean newspapers. His portrait decorates the walls of meeting halls throughout Korea. Official statements about Park are similar to those of North Korea about their "heroic" leader, Kim Il Sung. September 1976 issues of the Korea Herald contained the following commentaries on South Korea's ruthless ruler:

> His every thought and his tireless energy are wholly dedicated to the future of our people. By his unbounded kindness and complete sincerity we are led forward continuously in progress towards a better future. . . .
>
> He sets new faith aflame in our hearts, and from our labors brings forth a national harvest without equal.

63

. . . . . .
> . . . The pulse of the President's will beats
> throughout this land to every shore, awakening us
> from a 5000 year slumber to go forward to ever
> greater achievements in the future. . . . Let us
> take up our shovels and follow President Park.[12]

The Korea Herald's stories about Park Chung Hee describe him
as a Divine Emperor and a national father figure, who inspires
his people to labor voluntarily for the future of the nation.
Textile workers who are not sufficiently fired up to enjoy
eighteen hour work days on Sunday are branded "communists" and
silenced in the government's prisons.[13]

Like many tyrants, Park Chung Hee insists that children love
him, and in the South Korean schools, the young people are forced
to sing songs that praise the president. Even the movies in Seoul
are said to have daily news reviews of Park's wondrous accomplishments.[14] Although Park Chung Hee has enacted all of his special
edicts to protect his country from Communism, the only thing that
seems certain about the Korean President, and he said it himself is, "Only when I die will I vacate this presidential seat."[15]

To rally around Park, Moon organized 7,000 core members of
his International Federation of Victory over Communism (IFVC).
Since 1965 they have held 2,000 public lectures every year for
some six million Koreans to drum up their anti-communist frenzies
in support of Park's policy. For these ambitious nationwide,
pro-government drives, Moonists are known to have received over
850 letters of high commendation from ministers, governors,
mayors, and police chiefs.[16] With close ties to the KCIA and
with the support of the Korean government and industrialists, in
addition to the large membership and financial resources of the
Unification Church, Moon's IFVC grew rapidly as a world-wide
network. Its tactics were altogether different from previous
Korean anti-communist propaganda and activities which had been
mainly handled by a small group of North Korean defectors.
Moon's pro-government campaigns under the slogan of "Victory Over
Communism" culminated in the government's militarization of
college campuses and some Buddhist monasteries where students and
monks were organized into combat-ready units. Moon has estab-
lished his international anti-communist bases in the Philippines,
Taiwan, Southeast Asia, Europe and the United States, and Japan's
IFVC, under the leadership of Kuboki Osami, president of the
Unification Church of Japan, is the most active outside Korea.
Moon sponsored the IFVC conferences many times in the past. A
prominent American delegate to IFVC conferences was Senator Strom
Thurmond of South Carolina.[17] The honorary chairman of these
conferences is a prominent Japanese industrialist named Ryōichi
Sasakawa. Sasakawa, who was a fascist youth leader in the 1930's

64

and who was convicted as a Class 'A' war criminal at the end of World War II, is known to have proudly told the members of the Korean Unification Church that he was "Mr. Moon's dog."[18] In 1974, Sasakawa formed the World Karate Federation and became its first president, with Jhoon Rhee from Korea as one of his officers. Rhee is a Moon devotee, and as a karate master has successfully proselytized on Capitol Hill over the past years by influencing, financing and recruiting legislators for the Moon cause. In addition to Sasakawa, Yoshio Kodama and many other prominent Japanese figures, including former Japanese Prime Minister Kishi, are supporters of Moon's IFVC. Kodama, who is a staunch supporter of Park Chung Hee, is currently under indictment in the Japanese Lockheed case.

The extent of Moon's political ties to Park can be easily surmised from the American Congressional hearings on the KCIA activities in the United States which were held in March, 1976. These hearings were published by the U.S. Government Printing Office. There appear in this document mysterious "security deletions" in the dialogue between the Committee Chairman, Donald M. Fraser and Donald L. Ranard, former Director of the Office of Korean Affairs in the State Department. In the following, one can only conjecture about the so-called "security deletions."

> Mr. Fraser. Do you have any knowledge of any relationship between the Unification Church that is headed by Reverend Moon and the Korean Government or the Korean CIA?

> Mr. Ranard. Well, I would start first with a large area of some suspicion about the Unification Church and then I would try to document that by one particular instance that I recall. My first suspicion would be that given the nature of the Korean Government and what I considered to be a near totalitarian system, given the nature also of their repression of religious organizations in Korea--at least western religious organizations--I would find it hard to understand how the Unification Church would seem to exist completely beyond the control of the Korean Government. That would therefore raise with me some doubts to begin with, but specifically I recall on one instance [security deletion].

> Mr. Fraser. [Security deletion.]

> Mr. Ranard. Yes

65

[Security Deletion]. You may recall, Mr.
Chairman, that beginning sometime in 1974 the
Unification Church became closely identified with
defense of President Nixon as the episode of
Watergate was beginning to close in. There were two
or three occasions when the youngsters from the
Unification Church held demonstrations in support of
President Nixon, one in Lafayette Park at which the
President's daughter went over and was photographed
shaking hands with them.

I think the connection was that the Unification
Church, beyond whatever is its fuzzy religious philosophy, is anti-Communist. [Security Deletion.]][19]

From the above dialogue it is not difficult to see the ties between the two leaders, Park and Moon, who justify any of their
activities in the name of a "holy" crusade against communism.
Moon, of course, denies any connection with the Park regime, but
Donald Fraser has stated that "We have received information
which strongly suggests that persons and associations close to Sun
Myung Moon have had a cooperative relationship with the Korean
Government."[20] Fraser also noted that "Our information shows a
pattern of activity that raises serious questions as to the
nature and purpose of Moon's various organizations."[21] Robert
Roland, a former acquaintance of Pak Bo Hi, testified before the
Fraser Congressional Hearings that in 1974 he knew a man by the
name of Jo Dong Suk in Seoul, a member of Moon's cult, who acted
as liaison between Moon and Park's Blue House for a period of ten
years.[22] Allen Tate Wood also testified that in 1970 he had
several sessions in Korea with Moon, who outlined his plan to use
front organizations of the Unification Church to "dictate policy
on major issues, to influence legislation and move into electoral
politics" in the United States. "Of paramount importance," says
Wood, "was the issue of guaranteeing unlimited American military
assistance to South Korea. . . ."[23] While in Korea Wood was given
a tour of the Korean CIA as an important official of the
Unification Church whose friendship and trust were indispensable
to the South Korean government. Thus, Wood confessed that Moon's
and Park Chung Hee's political goals in Korea "overlap[ed] so
thoroughly as to display no difference at all."[24] Several of
Moon's organizations even signed a large contract in 1971 with a
Washington, D.C. printing firm called Colortone Creative Graphics,
Inc., running into thousands of dollars, to publish Park Chung
Hee's book To Build a Nation.[25]

American members of the Unification Church are taught to
regard Korea as the real "fatherland," and Moon has outlined the
following basic formula to lobby the U.S. Congressmen for the
purpose of upholding the South Korean Government.

66

What you do is you go to a Senator's office, or a
Congressman's office, and you tell him that you live
in his state. You live in his district. You are
eager to help, and you want to know what the problems
are, and how you can be responsive and a responsible
citizen.

Then he has your name and he runs into trouble.
He needs some help, and he calls you up. You work
for him. Later you go back and you get some flowers,
and you get him a gift of flowers. You go back and
you bring two beautiful girls with you. They give
him flowers.

When it comes time for re-election, you take 10 or
15 people to work just doing the hardcore canvassing,
or whatever it takes. If he runs into trouble, you
try to bail him out.[26]

Since 1969, the Unification Church in Washington, D.C. and
its local groups in the United States have engaged in all-out
campaigns to support Congressmen and Senators for a hardline
stand in Asia. For example, Chris Elkins, a former member of the
Freedom Leadership Foundation, a political front of the Unification
Church, testified before the congressional hearings that he sat up
at night working on typing letters to members of Congress concerning military aid to South Korea and Southeast Asia.[27] In
October 1974, the FLF actively participated for Charles Stephens
in his election contest against Richard Ottinger. During this
same period members of the New Hampshire Unification Church
actively campaigned for Louis Wyman's bid for the junior Senate
seat. In return for the campaign work Wyman offered staff
positions to members of the Unification Church if he were elected.[28]

Moon's own public statements give a clear picture of his
vision of a theocracy in which Park and the Unification Church
will hold sway. In May of 1975 Moon stated: "We must have an
automatic theocracy to rule the world. The separation between
religion and politics is what Satan likes the most."[29] Although
Moon flatters Americans by calling America "God's country," he can
hardly approve of the fundamental American principle of the separation of church and state. Neither does Moon like the American
electoral system, since that would give those who do not agree
with him an opportunity to register their disapproval. On March
24, 1974 the Korean preacher spoke to a large audience on the
subject of the Unification Church and the United States. Mr. Moon
presented a rather colorful plan for turning the world around to
suit himself.

67

If we can turn three states of the United States
around, or if we can turn seven states of the United
States to our side, then the whole United States
will turn. Let's say there are five hundred sons
and daughters like you in each state. Then we could
control the government. You could determine who
could become senators and who the congressmen could
be. From the physical point of view, you can gain
no faster success than in this way.[30]

Moon has also promised his followers that "If the U.S. continues
its corruption and we find among the senators and congressmen no
one really usable for our purposes, we can make senators and
congressmen out of our members."[31]

In some ways, Park Chung Hee seems relatively modest, compared to Sun Myung Moon, when he addresses his disciples. The
Korean evangelist's following statements reveal the breadth of
his fantasies:

Out of all the saints sent by God, I think I am
the most successful one already. Don't you think so?
If and when we have a nation of our own restored to
God's side, how fast will our mission be realized?
By that time we can stir up the whole world. Won't
that be true?[32]

On June 7, 1974, Reverend Moon publicly announced that members of
the Unification Church were to organize an army to defend their
religious fatherland, South Korea. He stated:

It is the world members of the Unification
Church who believe Korea is their religious fatherland and their holy land. . . .This means that the
world members of the Unification Church love Korea
as their own physical bodies. . . . They believe it
is God's will to protect their religious fatherland to
the last, to organize the Unification Crusade Army and
to take part in the world as a supporting force to
defend Korea and the free world.[33]

Sun Myung Moon, who identifies Korea as the birthplace of
the new Messiah (himself), says that America is the nation chosen
to receive the Messiah for "ultimate world salvation in our
century."[34] A pious proponent of indemnity, Moon believes that
"America's 200 year history has served as indemnity to pay for
the 2,000 years of history since the crucifixion of Christ."[35]
Calling the United States "the second Israel," Sun Myung Moon has
stated that the time is ripe for America to "spearhead a movement
of Victory over Communism."[36] In his Bicentennial address

68

"America in God's Providence," Sun Myung Moon informed his audience that "Unless this nation, unless the leadership of this nation, lives up to the mission ordained by God, many troubles will plague you. God is beginning to leave America. This is God's warning."[37] Moon's prediction that God was planning to pack his bags and leave the Americans with plagues is reminiscent of a speech made by a Korean "god-man" in 1092 on Mt. Maryong (Horse Peak) in ancient Korea. That "god-man" said "Your country has been forsaken by Buddha. It will fall into ruin very soon."[38]

While the Unification Church was still under congressional investigation, Sun Myung Moon launched a multi-million dollar tuna fish industry in the United States. Last summer, Moon's Tong Il Fishing Company of New York City bought about five per cent of the entire East Coast tuna catch on wharves in Gloucester, Massachusetts, and from boats on the high seas. This enterprise exists to exploit the lucrative Japanese sashimi (raw fish) market, which pays a premium price for the meat of the giant bluefin tuna. Two and a quarter million dollars of Moon's seemingly unlimited finances have also gone towards the acquisition of the seven-story Tiffany building to use as headquarters for his newspaper the News World. On the basis of Moon's actions, it would seem that God's Plan for America was the sponsorship of the Korean evangelist who uses religion as a mask for his own pecuniary enterprises. Moon's Unification Church is a vast political, religious, industrial network. Whether Moon obtained his numerous industries and vast wealth entirely on his own or with assistance from the governments of South Korea and the U.S. is a point that is open to speculation. Knowledge of the fact that Dow Chemical Corporation is prepared to spend 150 million dollars on petrochemical complexes in Korea[39] suggests that American entrepreneurs have a vested interest in supporting a fanatic anti-communist leader like Sun Myung Moon.

The President of South Korea sends all his military personnel and civilian officials to Moon's training school outside of Seoul to study anti-communism, and Moon manufactures air rifles for the South Korean Army. One could fairly say that Mr. Park and Mr. Moon have a close political and business relationship. Allen Tate Wood, former president of FLF, testified that in 1970 he visited Moon's training center, where he saw about 200 civil servants and peasants being instructed in anti-Communist ideology by members of the Unification Church. Wood further stated that Korean military officers and government officials, ranking from the provincial level up, were required to go through this indoctrination, and that this is one of the ways in which Moon has made himself indispensable to the Park government.[40] "By the KCIA's unpublicized charter," says Lee Pai Hyon, "this area of 'anti-Communist indoctrination and internal propaganda' is explicitly under the control of the KCIA's Second Bureau, which also controls the press,

69

231

with censors and supervising agents in each newspaper and broad-casting station."[41]

Moon's subsidiary political organizations include groups with lofty-sounding titles, such as: Project Unity, One World Crusade, Center for Ethical Management and Planning, World Freedom Institute, International Cultural Foundation, Inter-national Ideal City Project, Professors Academy for World Peace, and Committee for Responsible Dialogue. Moon engages in his political activities through these satellite organizations that are directly linked to his church by interlocking boards of directors, personnel, and advisory committees. These organiza-tions, which masquerade as charities and cultural foundations, collect funds for the Korean lobby to pressure congressmen into requesting aid for the Park regime. Similarly, another Moon front organization, American Youth for a Just Peace, lobbied to support the invasion of Cambodia.[42] Under the cloak of freedom, peace, unity, love and dialogue, Mr. Moon's followers spent $50,000 to $60,000 a year on lobbying. In 1973, they spent $73,000 on newspaper ads defending Richard Nixon and his Watergate accomplices.[43]

It is said that the KCIA requested Pak Bo Hi, a chief aid and translator for Moon, to arrange massive demonstrations in 1973 and 1974 against the impeachment of Richard Nixon.[44]

According to a report from the New York Times written by Ann Crittenden on May 25, 1976, the Unification Church has access to Park Chung Hee through South Korea's diplomatic pouch and communi-cations system. This report was corroborated by a statement of Professor Lee Pai Hyon, a former official in the Korean Embassy in Washington, D.C. He stated that no private person was allowed access to the diplomatic cable channel. Yet, one day in 1970 he was present in the Ambassador's office when one of the Embassy's communications officers came in and told the Ambassador that he had received a message from Pak Bo Hi which was to be sent to Seoul.[45] The Unification Church as a "religious" organization is protected from investigation under the First Amendment and it enjoys a freedom of action and security not even available to the Korean Embassy or the KCIA fronts.[46] Pak Bo Hi, who used the Korean Embassy's cable channel to Park Chung Hee, is the president of an ultra right-wing organization in Washington, C.C., called the Korean Cultural and Freedom Foundation (KCFF). The purpose of the KCFF is to raise money for Moon and to gain influence with wealthy people and government officials.[47]

Robert Roland was told by Pak that the latter knew President Park Chung Hee personally and had met him on a number of occasions. Roland was also told that Moon's activities in the United States were looked upon with enthusiasm by the South Korean government.

70

Pak further confided to Roland that "his primary aim was to
establish influencial contacts with the government and social
elite" in Washington.[48]

Lee Pai Hyon testified that "in 1970 or 1971 Park Chung Hee
sent out on government stationery, over his signature as president,
a personal letter soliciting contributions for . . . [Pak Bo Hi's]
Korean Cultural and Freedom Foundation." This letter was mailed
to at least 60,000 prominent Americans, including many senators,
congressmen, bankers, and businessmen.[49] Pak used contributions to
Radio Free Asia (a subsidiary of the Foundation) to finance the
Korean lobby's multi-million dollar bribery activities in the
United States.[50]

The KCFF was formed in 1964 with Admiral Arleigh Burke as
its first head. The 1974 report of the foundation lists 140,000
contributors, and its income is reported as well in excess of $1 mil-
lion annually.[51] Pak's Radio Free Asia, a broadcasting networth
patterned after Radio Free Europe, was formed in 1966. In
October 1970, Radio Free Asia, which is a subsidiary of KCFF,
mailed 60,000 letters bearing Park Chung Hee's endorsement to
prospective contributors. Park stated: "From the inception of
Radio Free Asia in 1966, I have given my hearty support for this
project. The Korean government was then, as it is today,
privileged to lease our broadcast facilities to Radio Free Asia."[52]
During the Vietnam War, Radio Free Asia used the Government-owned
and Government-operated Korean Broadcasting System's transmission
facility and its broadcasting time free of charge to beam programs
to Vietnam.[53] The Unification Church has an organization called
the National Prayer and Fast Committee whose members work on
Capitol Hill to befriend politicians. Chris Elkins, a former
member of FLF stated that the committee had an office in the
Washington Hilton and its 12 to 15 members were all young women.
According to him there was a similar staff in New York who worked
at the United Nations. The committee later grew to about 25,
including some men.[54] In the past the Unification Church had
placed a Korean lady church member, Sue Park Thompson, in the
office of the Speaker of the House.[55] Sun Myung Moon once told
his followers that:

> The master needs much money. Also, Master needs
> many good looking girls--300. He will assign
> three girls to one senator; that means we need
> 300. Let them have a good relationship with them.
> One is for the election, one is to be the diplomat,
> one is for the party. If our girls are superior
> to the senators in many ways, then the senators
> will just be taken by our members.[56]

71

233

Sue Park Thompson, who associates with Yung Hwan Kim, the KCIA
station chief in the Republic of Korea Embassy, grequents the
Moon center at 1611 Upshur Street in Washington, D.C.59 Sue
specializes in expensive annual birthday parties for congressmen and their wives, and charms them with Oriental delicacies.
An article by Maxine Cheshire in the Washington Post, dated
February 19, 1976, provides detailed accounts of Miss Thompson's
association with Carl Albert and her travels with Congressional
delegations to South Korea.

According to Frank Baldwin, the Korean lobby is "a loose
coalition of individuals, groups and institutions that promote
the Park government's interests. It presently centers on
Ambassador Hahm Pyung Choon and Yung Hwan Kim . . . . ., and
includes key individuals in the U.S. national security bureaucracy
the Congress, the Council on Foreign Relations, a few universities
and the media."58 The purpose of the Korean lobby's activities is
to petition, bribe, seduce, and influence American congressmen,
government officials, and journalists so that they will support
the South Korean regime and continue military aid. Park received
billions of American dollars in the past and 754 million more for
the fiscal years 1976 and 1977. The annual cost of U.S. troops
stationed in South Korea is approximately $600 million.

Recent newspaper and journalistic accounts frequently
mention Tongsun Park, who like Pak Bo Hi, is a prime figure
in the Korean lobby. According to Governor David Proyor,
"Tongsun was a mystery. All of a sudden he had popped up out
of newhere and started giving big parties, inviting society and
press people. He had many associates, a beautiful home,
limousines and spent money like water."59 Tongsun Park, Pak Bo
Hi, and Sun Myung Moon control nearly half of the stock in the
Diplomatic National Bank of Washington of which syndicated
columnist Jack Anderson was once chairman of the executive
committee.60 Tongsun Park gave many lavish parties in Washington
in the late 1960's and early 1970's and as many as 300 members
of Congress attended these affairs.61 The list of political
officials involved in Korea's lobby bribery is growing, and
already five politicians have acknowledged accepting money and
expensive gifts. When he ran for re-election in 1974, for
instance, House Majority Whip John J. McFall received $3,000 in
hundred-dollar bills from Park. Rep. Richard Hanna of
California is known to have accepted $22,000 in gifts from Park
over a period of months. Two of the recipients of gifts were the
fourth-ranking Democrat in the House of Representatives, Chief
Deputy Whip, John Brademas of Indiana ($4,900), and the wife of
former Rep. Edwin W. Edwards (D) of Louisiana, now the state's
governor ($10,000).62 Of the 241 congressmen who voted for
continued military aid to South Korea, 60 are known to have
received one favor or another from the South Korean lobbyists.63

72

234

Morton Kondracke of the Chicago Sun-Times reported on June 6, 1976 that Park Chung Hee's officials extended to Congressman Don L. Bonker offers of a $200 digital watch and "an attractive woman who would be pleased to meet with the Congressman on matters of mutual interest." Bonker, a member of the House International Relations Committee weighing at that time potential troop cut-backs in South Korea, rejected the offers, and he never saw the woman. He sent back the watch left on his desk by the Korean Embassy's KCIA agent, Col. Choi Yae Heun, and National Assembly-man Ohm Young Dal. Bill Keller reported in the Oregonian on June 10, 1976 that in an interview he was told by Ohm that the watch which Bonker mailed back cost $23 and thus was under the $50 limit on gifts federal employees can legally accept from foreign emissaries. Congressman Bonker also emphasized later that "he did not construe the offers as 'bribes,' though he believes it is improper for members of Congress to accept any gratuities from foreign emissaries."64 The defensive posture of Congressional leaders toward their indefensible ally and its notorious KCIA operation in the United States is manifested in the words of Edward J. Derwinsky, a member of the Fraser Congressional Committee investigating the KCIA activities, who is consistently critical of Professor Lee Pai Hyon for "making charges before a congressional committee about the foreign policy conduct of an ally."65 Derwinsky then scornfully suggests, "if you are so devoted to your position. . . . I think that you should go directly to the FBI, and see that they follow through . . . If you feel that your letter66 proves that our laws have been broken turn it over to the proper authorities. A Congressional committee is not an investigative arm of the Government."67

Seoul, the capital of Korea, is known as a fun city for the rich and for government officials. A few American congressmen who have visited Seoul at the South Korean government's expense were lavishly entertained, and before leaving for home they received honorary doctoral degrees from Korean universities.68 Clement J. Zablocki (D-Wis.), for example, who is on the Advisory Council of Rev. Moon's front organization, Korean Cultural Freedom Foundation, was entertained by the Korean government and received an honorary degree at a Korean university. When Pryor asked Tongsun Park, a graduate of Georgetown University, about his source of money, the latter vaguely replied that "his family has owned gold mines in North Korea that had been confiscated, and that a brother was the owner of a chain of gasoline stations in South Korea."69

A large portion of the multi-million dollar Korean lobbying funds is said to have derived from rice delivery to South Korea by the U.S. government under the Food for Peace program. In 1965 Tongsun Park made a deal with the KCIA whereby he would influence members of Congress in return for the KCIA's support

73

235

to have him as a middleman between U.S. rice dealers and the
South Korean government.[70]   According to Mrs. Mun Myung-ja,
formerly U.S. correspondent for the Munhwa Broadcasting Corporation in South Korea, Tongsun Park did badly as a businessman
before General Park Chung Hee came to power in South Korea through
the coup of May, 1961.[71]   However, with Park Chung Hee in control.
Tongsun Park (not related) prospered very quickly, and from the
commissions received from the rice deals, he made millions of
dollars. In addition, Tongsun Park earned more than five million
dollars through real estate investments and an Indonesian-
Japanese shipping deal. The magnitude of Park's financial
holdings was revealed recently when the Internal Revenue Service
announced that he owed $4.5 million in taxes for the years 1972
through 1975. Meanwhile, the IRS has imposed liens on his
property in the United States. Famous for sumptuous party giving.
Park, in the past, became known as a sort of male Perle Mesta and
according to The Christian Science Monitor (Oct. 29, 1976), his
"fashionable supper club, the Georgetown Club, included among its
members and customers President Ford."

The KCIA, a political arm of Park Chung Hee, is behind the
Korea lobby's operations in the United States. Park Chung Hee
himself directs the Washington political payments.[72] The KCIA
even uses intimidation and threats against American correspondents who criticize the South Korean government.[73] In early June,
1974, Ambassador Hahm Pyong Choon told John Hughes, editor of
The Christian Science Monitor, that Elizabeth Pond, a Monitor
correspondent, might be "received discourteously" if she visited
South Korea again. Asked whether the statement implied physical
violence, Hahm hinted that his government might not be able to
control an "incident manufactured by North Korean subversives
posing as South Korean thugs."[74] Professor Lee Pai-Hyon stated that
"ambassadors, diplomats and consular officers are in actuality
nothing other than a slightly more respectable facade of the
KCIA."[75]

There are as many as 50,000 persons who work for the KCIA and
its network in Korea, either as direct employees or as agents.
More than 30 KCIA agents and hundreds of their informers operate
out of the Washington embassy, and they infiltrate the businesses,
churches, and political organizations in Korean neighborhoods in
the United States. In Korea, it is virtually impossible to
conduct profitable business and gain lucrative government contracts without contributing money to the KCIA in order to obtain
their behind-the-scenes approval. The notorious KCIA is known
to have kidnapped intellectuals from West Germany and a leading
political opponent of Park (Kim Dae Jung), from a Tokyo hotel.
They intimidate and threaten to kill those Korean residents and
Korean-Americans who oppose Park Chung Hee.[76] KCIA agents even
operate within U.S. academia. Under the cover of the Korean

74

236

Traders Association they have contributed one million dollars to Harvard University to "promote" Korean studies there. The KCIA also checks theses and newspaper articles written by dissident Korean intellectuals. For instance, Kim Woon-ha, editor of a Korean language paper New Korea in Los Angeles, was given three alternatives by the KCIA concerning the articles he published in his paper about the Park regime. They were: (1) stop criticizing the Korean government in exchange for a newspaper fund or a government position, (2) sell the paper or close it down, (3) face retaliation, which meant that the KCIA would isolate him from the Korean community through slander and discredit him as a communist spy. Mr. Kim chose to ignore this ultimatum, and the KCIA proceeded to threaten or bribe his advertisers into withdrawing their ads from his newspaper. Gregory Henderson of the Fletcher School of Law and Diplomacy stated in the Congressional subcommittee hearings that the KCIA "is devoted to dirty tricks, sabotage and assassination," and "to this day, Koreans in this country are intimidated from expressing their opinions because they fear that at any time they might be kidnapped by Korean CIA agents here, falsely grabbed, and tortured to death if and when they visit their homeland. . . ."[79]

Just as KCIA members were trained by the American CIA, so South Korean lobbyists in the United States were said to have been given guidance by the Nixon administration in preparing a list of congressmen vulnerable to bribery and instructed how to manipulate members of Congress considered to be "problems" for the South Korean regime.[78] The American CIA has been known to bribe foreign politicians, assassinate constitutionally-elected presidents abroad and terrorize the people of the world by installing dictators, and the Korean protege' has followed suit and simply "danced to Uncle Sam's tune."

Through the alliance of President Park Chung Hee and Rev. Sun Myung Moon, the Unification Church's satellite organizations have been an important factor in the Korean lobby's attempt to influence U.S. congressmen and government officials. Moon and Park, these two impassioned spokesmen for anti-communism, are Tweedle-dum and Tweedle-dee cohorts in ultra right-wing political movements similar to those of Nazi Germany and Fascist Japan in the 1930's. Robert W. Roland states in his letter to the Fraser Committee that Moon's relationship with the government of South Korea cannot be divorced from his related political activities in the United States," and ". . . I do not suggest that we can make policy, or interfere in the internal affairs of another nation; but we do not have to aid and abet the tyrant in his continuing oppression of basic human rights. In this, our Bicentennial year, when the word 'freedom' is ringing loud throughout this land, let us not stand silent nor finance the slavery of others.[79]

75

237

Korea's secular ruler, Park Chung Hee and Reverend Sun Myung Moon, the industrialist-evangelist-savior, bear an uncanny resemblance to the kings and shamanistic Buddhists from the ancient Silla period. Like many of the later Sillan kings, Park Chung Hee took power by force and made his country beholden to foreign powers by floating an external debt of $6 billion and relying on U.S. military support. Today a large segment of Korean industry is controlled by Japanese and American interests. In order to make exports competitive, the government imposes low wages and prohibits labor strikes, forcing laborers to work under crushing conditions. Just as the Sillian kings formed an alliance with T'ang China to achieve phony unification, Park Chung Hee has gained "stability" in South Korea through U.S. military backing based on the Korean lobby, which has close links with Sun Myung Moon. The price of Silla's royal alliance with T'ang China was a regular payment of expensive tribute, kowtowing before the Chinese Emperor, and ignoring the starving populace. Similarly, Park Chung Hee's government pays off American congressmen by inviting them to Seoul where they are feted like princes. When, on separate occasions, Lyndon B. Johnson and Gerald Ford were invited to Korea, the Park administration mobilized vast crowds to greet the leaders of the "Free World." Richard Nixon was worshipped by Moon through a Washington, D.C. mass rally.

Many American leaders including former Secretary of State Kissinger, say that Korea is too strategic an area from which to withdraw American troops, because it would leave that country vulnerable to Communist attack. However, it is poorer strategy to support a fascist dictator like Park Chung Hee who is not truly approved by the people. South Koreans are profoundly suspicious of Kim Il-sung's iron rule, and Communism is not a threat within South Korea. It is an undeniable fact, however, that South Koreans are losing their will to defend themselves against Park's regime, where people are harassed and tortured, and academicians and church leaders are imprisoned in droves.[80] E.F. Carey wrote in The Christian Century with regard to the Korean situation:

> For me, the problem is not that of assembling more and more facts in order to get all sides of the picture. . . . It is what we do with them that is crucial. . . .

> One can decide to remain neutral, for whatever reason. Those who engage in a never-ending search for "more facts" are usually in this category. In actual fact, taking this position means acquiescence in the government's policies;

> . . . . . .

76

238

We do not need to be educated further on "the
other side of the picture." We cannot afford to
straddle the fence, especially when so many in
Korea have made their choice at a great cost to themselves. I remember too much about the Hitler regime
to be convinced by those who would have us look at
the Park regime more benignly.[81]

On September 15, 1976, Senator George McGovern, in a speech to
the United States Senate, expressed our need for the removal of
all tactical nuclear weapons and a phased withdrawal of our
forces from South Korea. "We must deal with nations and with
human beings," said McGovern, "rather than with power blocs or
ideological camps. Our postwar world design had the virtue of
simplicity. It was them or us; iron curtain or free. Now the
world must be understood as more complex. . . . Some of our so-
called "free world" allies are more dangerous to the peace and
to our values than some of the countries loosely aligned with
Moscow or Peking."[82]

77

239

VII. MOON AND ALIENATION IN THE UNITED STATES

Anthropologists label shamanism as the religion of primitive and acutely impoverished people. Shaman rituals have provided villagers with an occasion for ecstasy and escape from their wretched reality and at the same time kept believers in a dependent state. As mentioned earlier, in Korea, centuries of an extremely rigid system of social control, coupled with an exploitative ruling class and equally oppressive foreing powers nurtured an environment enabling shaman bluffers to prey on the fears and misfortunes of the people.

Shamans are noted for their special talent for persuading others to accept their beliefs in times of crisis. A paradigm example of this is the modern revivalist, who is generally a dramatic orator and who can induce his audience to his millenarianism and into entering a stage open to mass suggestion through the use of hymn singing, hand clapping, and repetition of powerful phrases. Some American fundamentalists play heavily on the theme of imminent doom, salvation through instant conversion, or blind faith in the charismatic personality of the minister.

As a technician of ecstasy, Moon leads his followers in prayer meetings that involve sobbing and chanting. One person who attended a Unification Church meeting noted that participants cried spasmodically, moved jerkily, and exhibited trance-like behavior. The loss of reason and the induction of an intense emotional state, are common to both shamanistic ritual and revivalism. The success of religious leaders is contingent on the susceptibility of thier clients. Without an unconscious wish to cooperate on the part of the audience, neither the shaman nor the revivalist can wield his "magic" power. Alienation, fear, loneliness and repressed emotions are influencial negative factors leading to shaman success in captivating large masses of willing believers.

Despite modern man's technological miracles and prowess, his psychic structure is closely akin to that of his primitive ancestors. In the face of frustration he often reverts to dependency on shamanistic charmers, who offer instant magical solutions to pain and suffering. The push-button world of modern technological society, characterized by a callous lack of spiritual meaning in life, has provided grounds for escape into occultism. Technology has relegated man to a rigid, artificial and monotonous life. "The depressing monotony of megatechnic society," Lewis Mumford in his book entitled The Myth of Machine, says "With its standardized environment, its standardized foods, its standardized invitations to commercialized amusement, its standardized daily routines, produces a counter-drive in

79

241

over-stimulation and over excitement in order to achieve a
stimulation of life . . . . with . . . . its . . . . supersonic
flights from nowhere to nowhere, modern technology has helped to
create a counter-culture whose very disorder serves admirably to
stabilize the power system."[1]

Technology has also raped the environment, ruthlessly
destroying the delicate balance between people and nature and man.
Our oceans are slowly dying, our land is being contaminated in a
number of ways, and our air is becoming increasingly unbreathe-
able. Beneath sophisticated technology, ours is perhaps one of
the most barbaric periods in history. Some historians have
designated the medieval period in European history as the "Dark
Age". No period in history, however, can parallel the darkness
of the 20th century, with the hideous deforming and tormenting of
masses of human bodies through the use of weapons like atomic bombs,
the neutron bomb. Among the faces of the 20th century are those
of women and children repulsively burned by napalm, and the tortured faces and hands disfigured by the Minamate (mercury poisoning)
disease in Japan.

These disfigurements are reflected in modern art in which the
use of distorted and grotesque forms is at its peak. Broken
mufflers reassembled, parts of pipes welded together, cut-up
newspapers and metal sheets conjoined, wires suspended from the
ceilings, wrinkled papers glued to blank canvases, and paint
sprayed haphazardly on paper represent much of contemporary art.
Artists like Picasso foresaw the grotesqueries and distortions
of the human body that became horrible realities in World War II
and Vietnam. Cubism presented an image of mechanistic, robotized
mankind that became reality in the schizophrenic world of the last
five decades.

Violence and crime ravage our cities. The proliferation of
such T.V. programs as Have Gun Will Travel, Policewoman, Kojak,
Hawaii Five-O, and The 6 Million Dollar Man one-sidedly emphasize
physical force and celebrate aggressiveness. The "smile face" or
"happy button" appeared at the peak of the Vietnam War, when the
United States was depressed internally and destructive externally.
Rage and alienation were masked with superficial smile buttons,
and the taste for extremely bright, day-glo-colored rainbow
patterns prevailed at the time. Long hair, gaudy clothes for men,
rock music and microbiotic diets were another expression of the
movement toward the yin as a counter response to the yang power of
the Pentagon and the increasingly destructive mega-technological
state.

At no time in history has man acquired so much power at the
expense of wisdom. Man's existence becomes increasingly determined
by depersonalized technology and invisible institutions and organizations. Many sophisticated traps and artificial values are so

80

242

skillfully imposed by the mass media and advertising agencies that it is exceedingly difficult to maintain a sense of oneself. The counter-culture of the 60's, the interest in drugs, communal living and radical politics all indicate how young Americans, turned off by the spiritual malaise of modern times, sought answers from different sources.

The Vietnam War tended to change the texture of the American society. Criticism of that war turned into criticism not only of the government, but also of the life style in the United States. Many joined the anti-war movement, while many others adhered to counter-cultural movements as a means of self-examination and soul searching. After the war, however, the energies that participated in opposing the war seemed to fade on college campuses, while cult religions began to flourish, following a usual pattern of transforming facuses of interest. A recent survey indicates that 6 million people are involved in Transcendental Meditation, 5 million in yoga, 3 million in the Charismatic Renewal, 3 million in mysticism, 2 million in Eastern religions, and many more millions in Jesus and other revivalist movements.[2] The end of the war left many of America's internal problems unsolved. Using the climate of spiritual uneasiness, Sun Myung Moon persuaded his followers that theirs is the task of assembling 144,000 converts to constitute a "foundation" for the New World. He has promised those who believe him vast significance as saviors of the troubled world.

The cults which developed hand in hand with counter-cultural movements in the United States are complex phenomena ranging from the negative cultists like Charles Manson to some positive aspects of "hippie" culture, however limited. Regardless of the various manifestations of these cults and counter-cultural movements, one cannot doubt that they sprang from an overly materialistic and competitive society, a society that was characterized in many ways by insensitivity and willingness on the part of individuals to step on others in order to advance.

The late Vince Lombardi, ex-Green Bay football coach, who symbolizes the American concept of success and whose hard-driving philosophy is shared by many, stated the following:

> Winning is not a sometime thing; it's an all-the-
> time thing. You don't win once in a while, you
> don't do things right once in a while, you do them
> right all the time. Winning is a habit. Unfortunately,
> so is losing.

> There is not room for second place. There is only
> one place in my game and that is first place.

81

. . . .

> Running a football team is no different than
> running any other kind of organization--an army,
> a political party, a business. The principles are
> the same. The object is to win--to beat the other
> guy. Maybe that sounds hard or cruel. I don't
> think it is.

Our obsession with power, colored by the perverted concept
of winning at any cost, is not limited to football fields, but
has permeated many segments of our society. Parallel with this
development as a response to these social demands, is the rise of
the mechanical personality. In order to compete and be victorious,
one must be cold and "rational." It is imperative above all, to
suppress the emotions to maintain poise and overcome difficulties.
One of America's most celebrated heroes is the pointed-eared Mr.
Spock of T.V.'s science fiction series, "Startrek," who never
shows his spontaneous human feelings. For both the individual and
the nation, what should be most dreaded, says Norman Cousins, "is
not the loss of power but the loss of feeling. What is happening
today is that the entire society is undergoing a decline in
sensitivity--sensitivity to brutality, sensitivity to beauty,
sensitivity to the possibilities of deeper living." Paul Simon
expressed the emptiness and lack of feeling in our society in his
song, The Sound of Silence:

> And in the naked land I saw
> Ten thousand people, maybe more
> People talking without speaking
> People hearing without listening
> People writing songs that voices never shared
> And the people bowed and prayed
> To the Neon God they made.

Today man is without roots, his work is often meaningless,
and he has no sense of direction as he is caught up in the rush
of society. Friendship is superficial, fragile and shortlived,
and personal relations are shallow and motive oriented. Man has
lost the deep need to share and to feel as a member of a group.
There is a great deal of distrust, cynicism and indifference, and
everybody is to everybody more or less an object. As people
specialize in only a portion of the manufacturing process, they
no longer gain the feeling of satisfaction and accomplishment in
the end product. We are what sociologists call alienated; lonely
and fragmented individuals who have lost our identities.

According to the U.S. National Institute of Mental Health,
about 125,000 Americans suffering from depression enter hospitals
every year, 200,000 undergo treatment in outpatient clinics, and
four to eight million need psychiatric assistance. Of the 50,000

82

244

Americans who commit suicide every year, half are known to have suffered from depression.[3] The situation is similar in other "developed" countries. American homicide and alcoholism rates were the highest with 8.5 murders and 3,952 alcoholics for every 100,000 members of the adult population.[4] Two thousand children are murdered every year by their parents. Few can deny that homicide and alcoholism are symptoms of underlying unhappiness. The American people have led the medical statistics of the world in heart attacks, nervous breakdowns, and acute depression for a prolonged period of time.

The music and lyrics of the 1960's not only express the tension, pressure, loneliness, and mental breakdown created by the competitive system, but also the profound longing for a return to a simpler life. These songs relentlessly protested against the hypocrisy of the establishment and invariably opposed the middle class American dream of success at any price. The following Beatles' song summed up how desperate young people were and why they were in need of spiritual warmth and vision to lift themselves from the sad state of human affairs in modern time.

> Love, love, love, love, love, love love, love
> There's nothing you can do that can't be done,
> Nothing you can sing that can't be sung
> Nothing you can say but you can learn how to play the game
> It's easy.
> There's nothing you can make that can't be made,
> No one you can save that can't be saved.
> Nothing you can do but you can lean how to be you in time
> It's easy.
> All you need is love, all you need is love,
> All you need is love, love, love is all you need
> Love, love, love, love, love, love, love love, love
> All you need is love, all you need is love,
> All you need is love, love, love is all you need . . . .

In these lyrics the Beatles express their genuine and sincere concern for the callous lack of human feeling in modern time. However, "love," like justice or unity, is a two-edged sword which can either enrich or deceive humanity. The wielder of the sword, not the sword itself, determines its use. throughout history, many political and religious leaders without concrete social programs for the wretched and the underprivileged, often have used such catch words as "love" and "unity" to acquire power. Hitler rose to power during a period of economic and political crisis via his promises to bring "unity" and "dignity" to the German people. The sixteen-year old Guru Maharaji of the "Divine Light Mission" amassed wealth and promised to bestow power upon the young Americans when he declared that he would establish "peace" and "love" in the world by 1980. Reverend Sun Myung Moon is this type, and he effectively manipulates lack of love in our alienated society to his own gain.

83

Tom Gariepy of the Providence Journal noted that "The
initial approach by a Unification member is always on the
basis of idealistic general principles--love, brotherhood and
peace. Then, newcomers are shown a little of the communal way
of life, maybe over dinner, and are flattered to be the center
of attention."[5]   Those newcomers to the organization who are
disturbed or confused by the complexities of society are eager to
be befriended by a group that offers them immediate warmth and
fellowship. Moon uses "mind control" over young people who
are seeking acceptance, love, protection, and a sense of
commitment to a "higher cause." In return for the "friendship,"
he asks his followers for total submission to his wishes, and
complete abandonment of previous thought. As a religious
leader and friend of the families of ex-converts to the Moon
cult, Rabbi Maurice Davis has compared Moon's organization to
a "boy scout's paradise"[6] where everyone is clean, smiling,
in agreement, and proud that they are God's children. Moon has
adopted the traditional shaman's role as an all powerful healer
of alienation and loneliness in modern times.   John Loflander
in The Doomsday Cult noted that friendship bonding was the major
technique used by the Moon proselytizers in obtaining new members."[7]
Between 1962 and 1963, the Unification Church experimented with a
wide variety of soliciting forms for attracting potential converts.
Many of the public relations campaigns were failures, and it was
largely the friendly missionary activities of passionate converts
that brought new disciples into the organization.

Within the Church, the loneliness and fear of individuals is
sublimated, and they feel a sense of belonging and protection
because a peer group suddenly listens to them. Moon's Unification
Church offers his followers a sense of importance, imbues them
with "divine" purpose, and assures them of a secure world in
which all spiritual and economic needs are cared for by the
organization. Members of Moon's church understand that they will
play important roles in the forthcoming global theocracy.
Knowledge of the acquisition of costly properties and lavish headquarters give them a notion that they are members of an "important"
establishment. Not only are converts to Moon's cult assured of
being "demi-gods for eternity," but they are given tangible
signs of their Master's significance by his mass public rallies,
and his offering of status and daily activities that are widely
covered in the mass media.

The followers of the Unification Church are neither delinquents
nor ex-junkies. They are known to be "idealistic" and "innocent"
young people;"[8] but this "innocence" can hardly be a fruitful
trait in grownup individuals who are faced with life in a highly
complex, technological society. Genuinely idealistic organizations such as anti-armament and international amnesty groups are
not attracted as many young followers as has Moon. Rabbi Davis

84

says that when he points out the absurdity of Moon's Divine
Principle to members of the Church, the most typical answer
he gets is; "What I believe may be nonsense, but at least I
believe in something. My parents don't believe in anything."9
This indicates how idealism and innocence can easily degenerate
into blind faith. The Rabbi feels that Moon's movement "preys
upon . . . . the disturbed, upon the frightened, upon the
idealistic, upon those who hunger for acceptance . . . . upon
those who are unhappy at home, unhappy with themselves, unhappy
with their parents, unhappy with the doubts and the struggles of
life itself."10

    Sun Myung Moon's followers in the United States, come mostly
from middle-class suburbia, and they are, by and large, affluent
college students between the ages of 18 and 25 who have not known
real economic hardship. Suburbia despite its affluence is a
depersonalized atmosphere because of its isolation from cultural
centers and lack of both intellectual stimulus and human interaction. Suburbia is an anaesthetized environment which does not
provide for aesthetic needs. This cultural limitation is one of
the reasons for joining the Unification Church, and it is expressed by a Moonist who said, "I was interested in truth, in meaningful life, and getting together with different nationalities
transcending my own cultural background to become a more universal
person."11 An ex-Moonist, Eric Rofes, in his article "A couple
of Summers," describes more succinctly some bases for the
success of the Unification Church in the United States:

        The people in the family are not the hallelujah
        holy-rollers I would imagine them to be. They are
        all young, middle-class, well-educated people. Many
        are Ivy-leaguers, many M.A.'s and Ph.D.'s were
        among the family. Despite their education, however,
        these people were drawn together by factors quite
        common in young people--dissatisfaction with their
        lives and a search for truth and direction. The
        movement fulfills these needs; it tells you what you
        want to hear, and "proves" that there is a God, there
        is meaning in this crazy life, there is heaven, there
        is love. All that's required of you is the belief,
        simple faith.12

    Berkeley Rice, who has written several articles on Rev. Moon,
states that a typical explanation for taking refuge in Moon's
commune was, "I didn't like the world the way it was. I wanted
to change it. I had tried several Christian groups, and the
Maharishi. This was the first movement I tried that offered real
answers."13 Wendy Helander, whose story has been much publicized

85

247

throughout the United States because of legal controversies between her parents and the Unification Church, said that she joined the Church because the members "radiated so much love, so much warmth."[14]   Wendy later described herself as being attracted to Moon's movement because she was troubled by the lack of "meaning-ful life" in the world. Although Ted Patrick tried to deprogram her, it didn't work and she left home again."[15]   Like Wendy, thousands of young Americans joined Moon's "world family," leaving their homes, school, and jobs, and hundreds of parents fought the Church privately or through a national organization to get their children back.

One may wonder how some of the Moonists maintain their own involvement in the face of disapproving parents and society. An answer can be gleaned from a letter by a Moon convert:

> I wrote my family a very long detailed, but very plain
> letter about our movement and exactly what I received
> in spiritual ways, plus the fact that Jesus had come to
> me himself. The week passed and I heard nothing, but
> I waited with deep trust in God. This morning I
> received a letter from my mother . . . .
>
> She called me a fanatic, and went on to say 'My constant
> fervent prayer is that time will show you the fruitless-
> ness of the way you have chosen before it consumes you
> entirely. A real true religion is deep in the heart
> and shines through your countenance for all to see.
> One need not shout it at the house tops either.'
>
> At first it was the deepest hurt I had ever
> experienced but I remember what others in our
> [Unification Church] family have given up and
> how they too experienced a similar rejection. But
> so truly, I can now know a little of the rejection
> that our beloved Master experienced.

Through the continual support of their peers and faith in Reverend Moon, it is not difficult for converts to tolerate disapproval from their parents.

Many Moonists of Catholic or Protestant background were not only disenchanted by the unfriendly and boring small towns and suburbs they came from, but they also were quite disillusioned by dried-up and, in some ways, out-moded Christian churches, which provided merely routine business-like services, devoid of imaginative and creative responses to our serious moral crises. Some Moonists even believe that "most of the church people were hypocritical in their everyday life," and that they emphasized "physical appearance in order to impress others."[16] Martha, a

86

follower of Moon, and a former nursing student, said her
disappointment with the traditional church was as follows:

> I have a strong religious background, as my father
> is a Lutheran minister and I attended the church
> every Sunday. But I felt extremely disappointed
> with my church life, mostly because there was no
> true Christian love being practiced among members
> of my father's church. From my childhood, I always
> wanted to be a missionary nurse and I found the
> Divine Principle guiding me to fulfill my dream, that
> is, to sacrifice myself to love others. I experienced
> true Christian love in the Unified Family.[17]

American universities, like the churches, have become
bureaucratic, routine and monotonous, and fail to provide
stimulating environments. To the idealistic college daydreamer,
Moon's organization can appear glamorous and exciting. Human
beings have a need to feel exalted. If this need is not satisfied
in their daily lives, and if their energy cannot be channelled
into meaningful activity, they are bound to be attracted to movements such as the Unification Church, The Divine Light Mission,
Jews for Jesus, The Children of God, and the most recent sect to
ornament the streets of major American cities, OM Lovers.[18] The
number of college drop-outs who joined these cult movements
reached a peak in the late 1960's and the early 1970's as a
response to the one-sided rationalism and vocational character of
the American universities. Professor Holmes Welch observed the
moral decay of university education as follows:

> . . . . instead of teaching [a student] to unlearn
> all the vicious competitive ways he has acquired
> from childhood, it reinforces them. Instead of
> turning his mind inwards, it fills him with
> ambition. Instead of making him quiet and
> opening his ears to intuitive understanding, it
> disturbs him and stifles his inner powers. The
> factual subject matter of college courses is
> harmless enough, but the perversion of character by
> college life is terrible indeed![19]

Because of the business-oriented character of American education
and because of the non-contemplative and non-aesthetic character
of higher institutions in the United States due to her particular
historical developments and social demands, American universities
have failed in many ways to perform critical social functions.
Those students who are attracted to milleniarism are usually those
who are politically passive and inexperienced, and who are unable
to understand the serious political and economic ramifications of
Moon's movement.

87

249

The apparent philosophical poverty and limited political consciousness of those who joined the Unification Church is also attributable in part to the daily influence of the mass media. Social scientists have already pointed out the serious harm television has wrought on the students' ability to think, write and express thoughts on paper. Much of the entertainment in popular films, literature, and television plays on the theme of a simplistic universe of "good guys" versus "bad guys." The basic notion underlying the Unification Church's ideology was the ascription of all natural events to two opposing forces that were locked in a life-or-death struggle. These forces were viewed as being in "a continuously hostile encounter," and the convert as playing a major role as a crusader for the "good." The convert to Moon's church is much like the comic book character of Batman or Superman, far from the reality of men and women who struggle against injustice in a most imperfect world.

To Wendy Helander, a Messiah appears instantly to save the troubled world, just as the heroes of Dragnet, 6 Million Dollar Man and Kojak simplistically and miraculously emerge to wipe out all crimes in the cities. Wendy attended a Unification weekend session in Maine where she suddenly discovered the "truth," and her quest in life had been fulfilled. She called her mother jubilantly to ask if she had heard the "good news." "What good news?" asked Mrs. Helander. "That theere is a new Messiah on this earth," said Wendy.[20]

The notion of instant salvation takes root in a spiritually impoverished society. This notion stems in part from material affluence which makes easily available an ample variety of food and toys, electric toothbrushes, ten-speed bikes, stereos and musical instruments, and where children who know no starvation feel that everything can be obtained without effort.

If one compares the option of attending a community college and sitting at home watching TV in the evening with being the member of an organization that sponsors conference in plush Washington, D. C. hotels, or the Waldorf Astoria in New York City, one can see how appealing the Unification Church can become to the average eighteen year old resident of suburbia. The Unification Church spent $500,000 for its three-day "Conference on the Unity of Sciences" held in Washington, D. C., and Nobel prize winner, Sir John Eccles, was a leading participant at the conference. When Eccles was asked by a New York Post reporter how he "reconciled this search for truth with the unanswered questions about the conference sponsor that have been raised by the Justice Dept. investigation?" he answered: "Journalists must have victims. You had Watergate and now you need something new. You are doing a grave disservice because this conference is the only one of its kind. Top thinkers from the fields of

88

religion and philosophy, social sciences, life sciences, and physical sciences are asked to set aside their individual disciples to seek overriding absolute values."[21]   Nobel prize winners like Sir John Eccles and Eugene P. Wigner and other educators, theologians, and Ph.D.'s who have participated in the Unification Church's projects, help lend legitimacy to Moon's enterprise.

Moon rose to fame during the era of the "happy smile button." The glassy-eyed followers of Moon are all wearers of happy smiles. Cheerfulness is the unofficial emblem of the Unification Church, and Mr. Moon himself wears a fixed smile in public. One of the parents who approves of the Moon Church said, "I watched them and was impressed. There was something special in their faces."[22]   Mrs. Carter of Virginia, the wife of a medical doctor, is the mother of 7 children whose two sons joined the Church. She had this to say:

> The changes in our son all seemed to be positive:
> he smiled, he ate "regular" food, he wore more
> conservative clothing . . . . In addition, the
> church finds the spread of Communism so alarming
> as to see its defeat as a major goal for themselves.
> No thinking person can argue with that![23]

It is the attitude of the fixed smile that irritates many individuals into speaking harshly to a solicitor for Moon's church. The fly in the ointment, according to Rabbi Davis, is the fact that Moon's children are not allowed to think.[24] In speaking to Moon's disciples, one can readily sense their buried anxieties and uneasiness as soon as there is a point of disagreement. Beneath the mask of contentment the Moonists are frightened children who believe in demons, satanic forces and a phantom world of spectral powers that can punish them for disobeying their father figure.

In his interviews with converts, John Lofland noted that the majority of them believed in "an active supernatural realm from which spirits of some variety could intervene in the material world."[25]   Lofland characterized the true believers in Moon's cult as frustrated, ambitious individuals who were subject to hallucinatory episodes." The spokesmen for the Unification Church interpreted individuals' hallucinations and all events as revelations of hidden meanings that took on coherency and purpose when seen from the perspective of Moon's Divine Principle ideology. Whatever voices or images an individual had experienced prior to conversion were interpreted as preparations for acceptance of the truth as known by Sun Myung Moon.

89

It is the policy of the Unification Church for members not
to spend more than three consecutive days in their parents'
homes once they have become active participants.[26]   Any member
of Moon's church who spends extra time with friends or family,
is shipped out of the area and sent on some kind of special
mission far from familiar surroundings. Mr. Arthur Turner from
Warwick, Rhode Island, reported that his daughter, Shelley, was
shipped out of Rhode Island the day after he publicly denounced Moon
as a fraud during the Reverend's New Hope Tour in Boston.
Shelley Turner was the first Moon convert to be "deprogrammed,"
and it took her fourteen months before she was able to function
in a moderately "normal" manner.[27]   Shelley accepted the Moon
doctrine that anyone who was not a member of the church belonged
to Satan. Soliciting funds in bars or on the street, she
believed at the time that those who refused offerings would be
damned for eternity. If she didn't procure funds or new converts
to Moon's cult, Miss Turner was sure that not only she but her
ancestors would be damned for an offense to the Master.[28]
Brought up as a Catholic, Shelley was attracted to the friendliness that she found in the Unification Church and the sense of
high purpose and altruistic goals, which she was led to
believe the Moon group embodied. After discovering that the
warmth was superficial, and that she was used to collect funds
for Moon, Miss Turner was too frightened and threatened by her
peers to leave the organization.[29]   Doubts are dangerous for
members of the Unification Church, for the indoctrination
methods are quite stringent and despite their instinctive fears,
the newly learned messages of damnation and punishment keep
young people from following their impulses and exiting from
the commune.

The Latin word persona is derived from the actor's masks
worn in Greek dramas to identify the role that was being
played. Our social personalities are usually a multiplicity of
masks, but to the degree that we become identified with a
single false mask we become alienated from the complex reality
of our inner selves. Alienation has been given as an explanation
for young people's attraction to a "masked" cult leader such
as Sun Myung Moon, who supplies his followers with instant
identity as members of an elite organization that will save the
world from satanic communism. In actuality, Moon alienates his
disciples even further from themselves, and assists them in
sacrificing their personalities on the altar of conformity to
his beliefs.

Sun Myung Moon is a Messiah for children in an alienated
world, children who spend a good part of their day watching
television shows (created by adults) seeing "good" defeat "evil,"
miraculous detergents triumph over dirt, and the "free world"
combat "communist aggression." If children are taught to hate

90

252

"evil" or "communism," they are then likely candidates for a
demagogue like Moon who states the following:

> . . when America retreated from commitments to
> safeguard free nations such as Vietnam and allowed
> them to be victimized, America's credibility fell
> to an all-time low. The cries of accusation are
> getting louder and louder. The United Nations has
> lost its original function and it has unfortunately
> become an arena for Communist propaganda. Israel,
> the United States, and Korea are being pushed further
> and further into the corner. We increasingly reap
> only shameful embarrassment.

> But, this is not all. America has been plagued by
> domestic problems which are becoming more serious
> every day. The racial problem is one, the drug
> problem another, juvenile delinquency,   dissociation
> of the family, ever-increasing crime, and not one
> of them is easy to solve. The most vicious of all,
> however, is the problem of Communism . . . .[30]

The projection of all that is undesirable onto other individuals,
groups, nations, or religions is a standard device that lessens
one's capacity for facing the undesirable side of the self.
Analytical psychologists have called these projections the
shadows of self, or in the case of a cultural projection, the
collective shadow.

Carl Jung cited the collective shadow as the dark other
side of the collective ideal. The general European ideal of
the 19th century was a mixture of Christianity and liberalism;
love, progress, purity, friendliness, sobriety, and chastity.
The collective shadow of that epoch contained hatred,
imperialism, Dionysian ecstasy, and orgiastic tendencies.
It expressed itself most vividly in the blossoming of pornograph-
ic literature. Adolph Guggenbuhl-Craig, a medical psychotherap-
ist, noted that the collective shadow of 19th century England
could be studied from the point of view of the history of famine
in Ireland or the expulsion of the Scottish Highlanders. By
looking at the dark side of the official ideals of the British
ruling class, we see their brutality, power, and greed.[31]

In Twentieth Century America, the official ideal is that of
a strong, democratic, fair nation that is a peacemaker for the
world. In reality, the United States is internally weak,
alienated from its own rapidly changing values, ineffectively
bureaucratized, and serves as the armament supplier for
military dictatorships all over the globe. Sun Myung Moon's
Unification Church gives lip service to the United States and
assists in denial of the American shadow. Moon tells his

91

253

American audiences that "America has created a model for the ideal world. God Himself had purposely hidden this land of America from civilization until His time was full, and then upon her God raised up this model nation."[32]

Members of the Unification Church live communally, but they give up all of their earnings to the Master, and they hero-worship Sun Myung Moon in much the same manner that the North Koreans worship their leader, Kim Il Sung. By a simple dictionary definition of communism, converts to the Moon cult are living a communist existence, in that they share property in common. However, Moon himself is an eminently successful capitalist who opposes communism, and supports the most inequitable Park regime, and moreover, he owns the means of production in his various industries, and members of the Unification Church work hard for his empire without pay, except for the leaders in the highest apparatus in the Church. Although Moon claims to be saving the satanical world from sins, he has neither tangible social programs at the national level nor concrete movements for non-members for doing this. Most of his energies are geared toward acquiring more money, more profitable investments, and more membership for his own power. He calls this system in his <u>Divine Principle</u> "coexistence, co-prosperity and common cause."

If young people are able to accept fear, anxiety, errors and failures, they can find the means to live with their conflicts and establish personal ways of integrating their destructive impulses into their lives. Both Freud and Jung recognized a "murderer and suicide" in all of us, who takes on the figure of the devil in fairy tales, legends and myths. Unless individuals have the opportunity of entering into a relationship with their "devils," they will project them onto others, the environment, or social structures. Everything negative that happens is understood as being caused by the wicked outside world, which must bear the blame for a younster's own frustration and rage.

Until evil is seen as an inner problem, it creates new misery and suffering for those who become identified as "Satan." Moon spoke of America's declining by being "subjugated by satanic hands." Refusal to face the reality that satan is not within is a genuine danger that can be withstood by a frank confrontation with inner impulses, and a tolerance of other people's bearing of the same painful reality. Although Moon warns his listeners that "Satan is becoming the master," there are many young Americans who have chosen the difficult path of non-conformity to the power drives of the state. Veterans of the Vietnamese War have protested from wheelchairs against militarism. Young Americans have walked across country to peacefully oppose armaments and the building of nuclear weapons. There is a small

92

but steady manifestation of individualism in the United States that is wed to an awareness that we are but one nation in a larger world and not entitled to our gluttonous consumption of goods and services. There are many young Americans who risk failure, uncertainty, anxiety, and the disapproval of their peers in a search to become themselves.

There are active young Americans who express their creativity through symbols and social action. There are inward-looking, young Americans who are painting, sculpting, dancing, writing plays, and engaging in a wide variety of activities that are beneficial to themselves and others; and these people are not attracted to new cults such as Moon's. The antidote to the questionable cults can be found in the sponsoring of meaningful arts and labors, and raising the political consciousness that is of value to both the individual and the group.

Sun Myung Moon has cited New York City as a "jungle of immorality and depravity."33   The preacher whose simple theology is based on the premise that mankind is evil and who is in love with his predictions of "God's punishment" is not acquainted with the millions of people who struggle daily to be fully human amidst an inhuman landscape. He has nothing in common with those who actively resist dehumanization through creativity, compassion, and a show of kindness towards their fellow creatures. The likely friends of Moon in Washington, D. C., who cut off funds for health, education, and welfare in major American cities, are actually responsible for the "jungle of immorality." As the co-founder of the Catholic Worker, Peter Maurin, said, "we have to work towards building a world in which it is easier for people to be good."

93

VIII. CONCLUSION

Things change so rapidly in our world that we tend to forget
how emotionally similar we are to our primitive ancestors. Along
with our ability to travel in space, invent computers and build
supersonic planes, we carry with us the capacity to conform, rage,
laugh, and worship, just as our forefathers did. Descendants of
the planters, we must conform ourselves to nature, which is realized in the dispositon of those who like to administer, regulate
activities, and adapt themselves to the mores of the group.

Agrarian societies produced God-kings who embodied the power
of the divinity on earth. Priests assisted the God-kings in regu-
lating affairs and presiding over society by the performance of
regular rituals. There was no sacrifice that was considered too
great for the people, if it entailed pleasure and long life for
the "divine" ruler.

The planter's way of life, according to Gotthard Booth, was
"characterized by subordination of its members to ritualistic
observance of the seasons, and to depersonalized, hierarchical
forms of religion....Their modern descendants are living in accord
with analogous principles: anxious preoccupation with time
schedules, and subordination to the socio-economic exigencies of
the machine age."[1]

Descendants of hunters, we express their temperament through
bold individuals who like to take risks, follow their own initiative, and live independently. Booth pointed out that "the hunt of
free-ranging animals of vastly superior physical power demanded
not only the capacity for differentiated action, but also individualistic initiative and spontaneous cooperation of the members of the tribe. Their religious systems were characterized by
dependence on the individual inspiration and leadership of shamans.
Their modern descendants are those who pursue individualistic ways
of life even when they have to defy the conformistic majority of
contemporary society."[2] Hunting societies produced spiritual
leaders known as shamans. Although the shaman was a gifted
hunter and was believed to be capable of controlling the spirits
of the animals, the early shamans in paleolithic hunting societies
were probably the sick or weak hunters who did not have enough
strength for the chase. To balance their inability to provide food, the paleothic shamans, wearing the skins and horns of
reindeer, would chant, dance, and go into trance-like states
that enabled them to contact the spirit world. They received
visions that were of value to the tribe, and became painters,
story-tellers, and healers. The shaman was thus an artist, a
medicine man, a divinator, a learned man who knew the lore of
the tribe at great length, and who was often the political leader
of his group.

95

The divinity of rulers and the magical power of shamans are myths with which mankind has had to live for many centuries. Some people still believe that they are deities, and they often become tyrannical heads of state. In infancy most of us experience the divinity of having our every wish met by a large and loving figure. Through the magic of our cries, we command great beings to move about and do our will. Giving up this special role and magical power is a difficult task, and until recent centuries, there were rituals that celebrated and helped adolescents become men and women.

There are, however, several types of shaman leaders; one weakens his people by giving them a vision that robs them of self-reliance and increases their dependency upon him. Another can stregthen his people by giving them a vision that enables them to increase consciousness and to face reality with added courage. The former loves only himslf, and uses his talents to enslave other beings. The latter employs his talents to heal mental illness, increase confidence and release energy to face life. Rare people like Lao Tzu or Christ or Kim Chi-ha did not care too much whether people approved or disapproved of them, but instead followed the voice of their conscience. They believed that crime was not transgression of external laws but that it originated in the minds and conduct of human beings.

Still other shaministic figures have been obsessed with purifying the species of alien elements, and to this group Sun Myung Moon belongs. These shamans express their shamanistic thinking when they create labels for people of whom they are frightened. In large complex societies that support shamanistic thinking about the "bad spirit" are other people who are somehow different from the group. Words can be powerful. Dubbing individuals as "niggers," commies," or "gooks," symbolically kills the person, and transforms him into an abstract thing. Moon, as did many demagogues in the past, represents the kind of shaman who appeals to frustrated people during extremely difficult periods in history. Reverend Sun Myung Moon offers his followers easy answers to difficult realities, and diverts serious anxieties onto "alien elements" or "satanical blood." The Japanese fascists chose the Koreans as Japan's national scapegoat and massacred Koreans after the Great Tōkyō Earthquake in 1923.[3] Moon has chosen those who do not follow him as the "evil spirits" who can be held responsible for all man's misfortunes.

In order to drive out "evil spirits," Moon and his shaman accomplices employ gala spectacles, public performances, subtle indoctrination techniques, and the use of his vast wealth. Capitalizing on greed and unemployment, Moon offers high salaries to academics whom he hires to teach at his Unification Church theological seminary. Money is the magical wand that Moon has waved to obtain all of his instant shamanistic wishes.

96

Behind the luxuries, the brass bands, balloons, American flags
and fire crackers of Sun Myung Moon's Bicentennial fire and brim-
stone speeches, there is a Korea in chains. While Moon's followers
were singing "God Bless America," the KCIA were decimating the
staff of the Seoul Metropolitan Community Organzation, and imprisoning a courageous worker-priest, the Reverend Park Hyung Gyu.
As Moon shouted "we must protect freedom," the Seoul court sentenced 18 democratic Christian patriots to two to eight years in
prison for the crime of requesting President Park's resignation.
As Moon ranted and raved about anti-communism and Satan, Kim Dae
Jung, the former South Korean presidential candidate, was refused gravely needed medical attention in the Seoul prison.
Reverend Moon is a fanatic supporter of Park Chung Hee and his
henchmen. Behind the miraculous "economic progress" that the
latter pronounces in the Korean newspapers, there are pollution,
dehumanization, foreign debts, rampant corruption, and a hungry
peasantry. Beneath the miraculous "growth and stability" that
Park Chung Hee has brought to Korea there are torture chambers,
mutilated bodies, silenced men and women, and a people living in
a state of terror.

The shaman who loves his fellow creatures uses his power to
enhance their well being. The poet, Kim Chi-ha, has been in
solitary confinement since March 1975 for violation of the
Republic of Korea's anti-communist law. When he was first imprisoned, he was tortured for a week without food or sleep, and
forced to confess in a state of semi-consciousness. Later, Kim
Chi-ha recanted in an essay entitled A Declaration of Conscience,
which he smuggled out of prison through his friends. Kim Chi-ha
is both a shaman and a Saint of the 20th century, who can conjure
up spirits with his words. His lampoons on government corruption and his ballads were so magical and powerful that Park Chung
Hee had him first arrested for the miraculous wonder of his
words, that spoke to the hearts of the Korean people. Kim Chi-ha
does not fancy himself a Korean Messiah, but in his play, The
Gold Crowned Jesus, he gives us a vision of the Christ who can
bring freedom to Korea. This Jesus figure is imprisoned in a
concrete statue and a leper speaks to him:

Leper: Who put you in prison? Tell me who they are.

Jesus: You know them well. They are like the Pharisees....They
        pray using my name in such a manner as to prevent my
        reaching out to poor people like yourself. In my own
        name, they nailed me down to the cross again.
        They boast about being my disciples, but are egotistical,
        cannot trust each other, do not suffer loneliness, and
        are without wisdom, as were those who initially
        crucified me....

97

Leper: Jesus, what could liberate you? Resurrect you again? What would make you live again and come to us?

Jesus: I cannot do it by my power alone. You have to liberate me. Those who want to be close to comfort, wealth, honor, and power cannot give me life again. Those who try to enter the Heavenly Kingdom all by themselves and turn away from the wretched misfortunates in front of their eyes cannot give me life again. Those who are not lonely cannot give me life again. Those who see injustice and do not protest, but instead submit to it, cannot give me life again. Those unable to resist and struggle in spite of the evil gangs in power who torment, exploit, deceive, and oppress innocent people cannot give me life again. With prayer one has to act. Those who act for the poor and the oppressed and only those who are generous like yourself despite poverty, wretchedness, and being driven against the wall, can give me life again. You opened my mouth. You will liberate me.

Leper: Jesus, as you can see, I am helpless. (Points to his crippled body) I cannot even take care of myself. How then can I help you?

Jesus: It is for that exact reason you <u>can</u> help me.[4]

The Jesus that Kim Chi-ha evokes in his brilliant play is the man who is nailed to the cross in his own name by the Sun Myung Moons who believe that they are deities. Moon, who worships The Gold Crowned Jesus, brings hypocrisy and inequity into the world. The compassionate shaman like Kim Chi-ha has no idol, only an inner voice that gives him infinite power to treasure complicated truth beyond his own life.

98

260

Appendix I

Front Organizations of the Unification Church

The Unification Church
Project Unity
One World Crusade
International Cultural Foundation
International Federation for Victory Over Communism
Collegiate Association for the Research of Principles
Freedom Leadership Foundation
The Rising Tide - publication of the Freedom Leadership
Foundation
Rising Tide Bookstore
World Freedom Institute
Little Angels of Korea
Little Angels Korean Folk Ballet
Professors Academy for World Peace
Unification Church of New York, Inc.
Unification Church, International
National Prayer and Fast for the Watergate Crisis
Unfied Family
International Re-Education Foundation
The Weekly Religion
The Way of the World
Tongil Seigei Monthly
Tong I (or Tongil) Industry Company
I Wha (or Il Hwa) Pharmaceutical Co.
I Shin (or Il Shin) Stoneworks Company
Tong Wha Titanium Comapny
Tae Han Rutile Company
American Youth for a Just Peace
Sun Myung Moon Christian Crusade
Korean Folk Ballet
New Hope Singers International
Committee for Responsible Dialogue
Day of Hope Tour
Unification Church of America
Unification Thought Institute
International Conference on Unified Science
Council for Unified Research and Education
D. C. Striders Track Club
International Pioneer Academy (San Francisco)
International Ideal City Project (San Francisco)
Korean Cultural Freedom Foundation
New Education Development Corporation
Center for Ethical Management and Planning

99

261

APPENDIX II

THE AMERICAN JEWISH COMMITTEE

165 East 56 Street

New York, New York   10022

JEWS AND JUDAISM IN   REV. MOON'S <u>DIVINE PRINCIPLE</u>

A REPORT

by

A. James Rudin, Assistant Director

Interreligious Affairs Department

December, 1976

101

THE PERIL OF REV. MOON

There are several levels of significance implied for the American people, and, especially for the Jewish community, in this study of the basic text of the Rev. Sun Myung Moon's movement -- the first systematic study, to our knowledge, that has been published of the "sacred scriptures" of Moonism.

The first is that Rev. Moon is contributing to a theologically reactionary mentality whose traditional fixations on anti-Semitism have been repudiated in recent decades by virtually every major Catholic, Protestant, Greek Orthodox, and Evangelical group and leader -- from Vatican Council II, the World and National Council of the majority of enlightened Christian leadership throughout the world is laboring to uproot the sources of the pathology of anti-Jewish hatred which culminated in the Nazi holocaust, Rev. Moon appears to be embarked on a contrary course of seeking to reinfect the spiritual bloodstream of mankind with his cancerous version of contempt for Jews and Judaism. On this level, therefore, this document is published as a clinical diagnosis intended to expose the Moon infection in order that both Christian and Jewish leadership will be vigilant to the need for combatting any effort of Rev. Moon and his followers to enter the mainstream of American religion and culture with his horrendous baggage of bigotry.

A second consideration is that we are now dealing not only with an ersatz spiritual phenomenon but one that has potentially serious political implications as well. The recent revelations that Rev. Moon and his Unification Church are allegedly involved as a front group for the South Korean Intelligence Forces in this country who are charged with illegal lobbying and bribery raise the serious issue of whether Moon's anti-Semitism is intended to be used for the ideological objectives of his political backers. If that is the case, then the American people must be alert to the emergence in the Moon phenomenon of an ideological campaign whose antecedents trace back to the Nazis and to Stalinist Communism. Those totalitarian movements consciously and cynically employed anti-Jewish hatred as a major vehicle for realizing their apocalyptic goal of undermining the Biblical and democratic values of Western civilization. The troubling question cannot be evaded: why are Rev. Moon and his political backers resorting to the Nazi model of exploiting anti-Semitism for ideological purposes? Every American Congressman, Senator and public official who is approached by the Moon movement ought to be alert to this ideological land-mine of fanatic hatred when courted for support by Rev. Moon and his backers.

102

264

And finally, this document is intended for the consciences of Jewish young people who, most incredibly, have been enticed or seduced to become a "Moonie." It has been estimated that nearly thirty percent of the Moonies today are Jewish young men and women who have been subjected to this latest form of totalitarian brainwashing. During the Korean War, 1951-53, the Communists captured 3,778 American soldiers and subjected them to psychological coercion which involved, first, a "mind-conditioning" phase in which the American prisoners were intensively persuaded to hate their own country, and, second, a so-called "suction" phase in which they were taught that life was superior under Communism and they should spread the gospel of Communism. Whatever the psychological or sociological reasons for their attraction to Rev. Moon's movement, at some time in their search for personal meaning Jewish youth must confront the evidence of this document whose central message is that they are being asked to find salvation in a "third Messiah" whose gospel is the hatred for and destruction of their own people, their religion and culture, their very families. In the face of this understanding of what Rev. Moon is really teaching about Jews, a continued involvement in his movement can be nothing other than an exercise in self-hatred and self-debasement. Surely, young Jews and Christians have other, more humane alternatives for finding meaning for their existence and self-fulfillment.

RABBI MARC H. TANENBAUM

National Interreligious Affairs Director

American Jewish Committee

December 1976

rpr

The Rev. Sun Myung Moon is a Korean-born (1920) religious
leader who moved to the United States in 1973. Since then, his
teachings and beliefs have received extraordinary attention in
the Western World as he embarked upon a widespread and highly
visible campaign to gain new members for his Unification Church.
It has been a campaign filled with bitter controversy, including a Congressional investigation of Rev. Moon's tax-exempt
status and an acrimonius court case that was instituted by the
parents of a new convert to his church. In the past three
years nearly 30,000 Americans, most of them under thirty years
of age, have flocked to Rev. Moon's banner and have become
active and committed members of the Unification Church. Rev.
Moon claims a worldwide membership of over 600,000.

While public attention has been focused on many aspects of
his movement, very little has been said about his -- and the
Unification Church's -- attitudes and beliefs regarding Judaism
and the Jewish people as reflected in Divine Principle, the
basic text of Rev. Moon's movement.

A systematic analysis of this 536 page document* reveals an
orientation of almost unrelieved hostility toward the Jewish
people, exemplified in pejorative language, stereotyped imagery
and sweeping accusations of collective sin and guilt.

Whether he is discussing the "Israelites" of the Hebrew
Bible or the "Jews" as referred to in writings of the New
Testament period, Rev. Moon portrays their behavior as reprobate,
their intentions as evil (often diabolical), and their religious
mission as eclipsed.

There are over 36 specific references in Divine Principle
to the Israelites of the Hebrew Bible (Old Testament) -- every
one of them pejorative. The "faithlessness" of the Israelites
is mentioned four times on a single page (p. 330).

-----

*The work has gone through several revisions and enlargements
since it was first published in Korean nearly 20 years ago.
This study is based on the 1974 English edition, published by
the Holy Spirit Association for the Unification of World
Christianity, 1611 Upshur St., N.W., Washington, D.C.

104

Moreover, the accusation is leveled collectively: "The Israel-
ites all fell into faithlessness" (p. 315). "All the
Israelites centering on Moses fell into faithlessness" (p. 320).
"The Israelites repeatedly fell into faithlessness" (p. 343).
(Emphasis added.)

In similar fashion, Divine Principle records some 65 specific
references to the attitudes and behavior of the Jewish people
towards Jesus and their role in his crucifixion--again, every one
hostile and anti-Jewish. Thus, not only were the Jewish people
of Jesus' day "filled with ignorance" (p. 162), "rebellion"
(against God) (p. 359), and "disbelief" (p. 146 et passim), but
they "betrayed" (p. 453), "persecuted" (p. 155), and "derided"
Jesus (p. 135), finally "delivering him to be crucified"
(p. 200). Rev. Moon goes even beyond the infamous deicide--
"Christ killer" charge against the Jewish people. In two
separate instances in Divine Principle (pp. 357 and 510), the
founder of the Unification Church specifically links the Jews with
Satan in bringing about the death of Jesus:

> As a matter of fact, Satan confronted Jesus, working
> through the Jewish people, centering on the chief
> priests and scribes who had fallen faithless, and
> especially through Judas Iscariot, the disciple who
> had betrayed Jesus.
>
> Nevertheless, due to the Jewish people's rebellion
> against him, the physical body of Jesus was delivered
> into the hand of Satan as the condition of ransom for
> the restoration of the Jews and the whole of mankind
> back to God's bosom; his body was invaded by Satan.

The anti-Jewish thrust of Rev. Moon's writings about the
ancient Israelites and the Jews of Jesus' time carries forward
into his interpretation of Jewish history and of the current
status of Jews and Judaism in our own time. There are some
26 pertinent references in Divine Principle   Once again, in
tone and in substance, they are viciously anti-Jewish, reflecting
the worst aspect of traditional Christian displacement theology,
and viewing the persecution of Jews across the ages as punishment for their sins. Thus, "The Jewish Nation was destroyed"
(p. 431); due to "the Israelites   faithlessness, God's heritage
(has been) taken away from the Jewish people" (P. 519), and
"the chosen nation of Israel has been punished for the sin of
rejecting Jesus and crucifying Him" (p. 226). Rev Moon brings his
teachings up to modern times.

> Jesus came as the Messiah; but due to the disbelief
> of and persecution by the people he was crucified.
> Since then the Jews have lost their qualification

105

267

as the chosen people and have been scatterd,
suffering persecution through the present
day. (p. 147).

The sole mention of the Nazi Holocaust is found on page 485.

Hilter imposed the strict primitive Germanic religious
ideology by concluding a pact with the Pope of Rome,
thus founding a national religion, and then tried to
control all Protestantism under the supervision of
bishops throughout the country. Therefore, the
Catholics as well as the Protestants were strongly
opposed to Hitler. Furthermore, Hitler massacred
six million Jews.

It is true that many of Rev. Moon's most virulent teachings
about Jews and Judaism have their parallels (if not their sources)
in a tradition of Christian anti-Jewish polemic which stretches
from the early Church Fathers to the Oberammergau Passion Play.
St. John Chrysostom (d. 407 C.E.) wrote of the Jewish people:
"Of their rapine, their cupidity, their deception of the poor . .
. . they are inveterate murderers, destroyers, men possessed by
the devil . . . . they are impure and impious . . . ."
Tertullian (d. 222), another Church Father, attempted to refute
Judaism, especially the permanent validity of the Mosaic covenant. St. Justin (d. 165), one of the first Christian leaders
to link the Jewish people with the crucifixion of Jesus, wrote:
"The tribulations were justly imposed upon you, for you have
murdered the Just One." St. Hippolytus (d. 235 or 236) taught
that Jews will always be slaves because "they killed the Son
of their Benefactor." Origen (d. 254), echoed the deicide
and punishment theme: "We say with confidence that they will
never be restored to their former condition. For they committed
a crime of the most unhallowed kind, in conspiring against the
Saviour of the human race . . . ." Chrysostom believed the
rejection and dispersion of the Jews was the work of God, not
history: "It was done by the wrath of God and His absolute
abandon of you." A fourth century Christian historian,
Sulpicius Severus, wrote: "Jews are beheld scattered through the
whole world that they have been punished on no other account than
for the impious hands which they laid on Christ."

All of these themes--the "faithlessness" of Israel, the
abrogation of the Covenant, collective quilt and punishment--come
together in the Oberammergau Passion Play, which is presented
every ten years in Germany. Thus, Jesus is represented as
renouncing Judaism: "The Old Covenant which my Father made with
Abraham, Isaac, and Jacob has reached its end." (1970 version,
pp 41 f.) In the Bavarian pageant, the Jewish crowd cries,
"Drive him with violence that we get on to Calvary . . . .

106

268

On, drive him with blows . . . . He deserves crucifixion . . . ."
(1970 version, pp. 106 and 109.) The so-called "blood curse" is
clearly directed at the entire Jewish people:

> "Chorus: Jerusalem! Jerusalem!
> The blood of His Son will yet avenge on you
> the Lord.
>
> People: His blood be on us, and our children!
>
> Chorus: Be it then upon you, and your children"
> (1970 version p. 99)

These and many other examples attest to the anti-Jewsih
sources in Christian tradition from which Rev. Moon has obviously
drawn. But in recent years, Christian church leaders have
made vast efforts to come to grips with this anti-Jewish legacy,
to repudiate its most negative and hostile elements, and to
affirm the ongoing validity of God's covenant with the Jewish
people.

Thus, the Roman Catholic Church in its Declaration on non-
Christian Religions (1965), affirmed that responsibility for
Jesus' death could not be laid to the Jews of his time or to
the Jews of today, and asserted: " . . . . the Jews should not
be presented as rejected or accursed by God, as if this followed
from Holy Scriptures." The Lutheran Council in the USA,
representing three Lutheran bodies, advised in 1971: "Christians
should make it clear that there is no Biblical or theological
basis for anti-Semitism. Supposed theological or Biblical
bases for anti-Semitism are to be examined and repudiated." The
twelve-million member Southern Baptist Convention resolved in
1972 " . . . . to work positively to replace all anti-Semitic
bias with the Christian attitude and practice of love for Jews,
who along with all other men, are equally beloved of God."
The newly-revised Book of Confession of the Presbyterian Church
in the United States affirms:

> We can never lay exclusive claim to being God's people
> as though we have replaced those to whom the covenant,
> the law and the promises belong. We affirm that God has
> not rejected His people, the Jews. The Lord does not
> take back His promises.

The Archdiocese of Cincinnati, in 1971 guidelines, declared:
"The Jewish people is not collectively guilty of the passion and
death of Jesus Christ, nor of the rejection of Jesus as Messiah.
The Jewish people is not damned, nor bereft of its election.
Their suffering, dispersion, and persecution are not punishments
for the crucifixion or the rejection of Jesus . . . ."

107

These are among the many indications of a growing sense of
responsibility among Christian leaders to teach positively and
fairly about Jews and Judaism. It is profoundly unfortunate
that these developments find no echo and no acknowledgement
in Rev. Moon's teachings. Having drawn upon the most anti-Jewish
elements in Christian tradition, Rev. Moon has totally ignored the
conscientious efforts of Christians to correct them.

Moreover, the Holocaust, when one-third of the Jewish people
was murdered by the Nazis, is gratuitously mentioned by Rev. Moon,
and nowhere in Divine Principle do we find any calls for repentance
or for self-examination in the face of six million dead. The
United Mehodist Church, in a 1972 statement, expressed "clear
repentance and a resolve to repudiate past injustice and to seek
its elimination in the present." But not Rev. Moon.

Two leading Christian bodies, the National Council of Churches
and the Roman Catholic Archdiocese of New York are sharply
critical of Rev. Moon's teachings.

A working paper prepared by the Faith and Order Commission
of the NCC asserts that many principles of the Unification
Church differ substantially from accepted Christian theology and
the Commission finds serious fault with Rev. Moon's major beliefs:

> Divine Principle contains a legalistic theology of
> indemnity in which grace and forgiveness play little
> part. The central figures of providence fail even
> when they are not believed--a vicarious failure is
> certainly not central to Christian affirmation. That
> is, Christ failed because the Jews did not believe
> in Him and put Him to death. That is double indemnity
> indeed, and its penalties are continuing anti-Semitism
> and the requirement that another savior come to
> complete the salvation of Jesus Christ.

Dr. Jorge Lara-Braud, a member of the Presbyterian Church in the
U.S. and the Faith and Order Commission's Executive Director,
and Dr. William L. Hendricks of the Southwestern Baptist
Theological Seminary in Fort Worth were the principal authors of
the working paper.

The Roman Catholic Archdiocese of New York has warned its
priests about "acute dangers" that the Unification Church
presents for believing Christians. "It is important to bear
in mind that several points of Rev. Moon's teaching are in direct
conflict with Catholic theology, and therefore render his movement suspect for Catholic participation," Father James L. LaBar,
an official of the Archdiocesan Communications office, said in a
letter to pastors.

108

270

When referring to Jews and Judaism, we are confronted with over 125 examples of an unremitting litany of anti-Jewish teachings. Nowhere in Divine Principle does Rev. Moon acknowledge the authenticity and integrity of Jews or Judaism, either ancient or modern. From Abraham until the present day, Jews are seen only as people, devoid and emptied of any genuine faith and spiritual qualities. "The inner contents are corrupt" (p. 532.) The Jewish people are depicted as collectively responsible for the crucifixion of Jesus as allies of Satan. They have been replaced by a "second Israel" (who interestingly enough, must soon be replaced by the "third Israel": the followers of Rev. Moon.) Further, the Jews have lost God's "heritage" and are still being "punished" for their many, many sins.

Rev. Moon's Divine Principle is a feculent breeding-ground anti-Semitism. Because of his unrelieved hostility towards Jews and Judaism, a demonic picture emerges from the pages of his major work. One can only speculate on what negative and anti-Jewish impact Divine Principle may have upon a follower of Rev. Moon.

Rabbi A. James Rudin

76-700-89

RPR

109

271

APPENDIX III

Raab, Earl, "Reverend Moon & the Jews - The San Francisco
Experience, "Congress Monthly," December 1976.

The perverse affinity between Reverend Sun Myung Moon's
movement and the Jews was recently dramatized by the sudden
appearance of "Judaism: In Service to the World" in the San
Francisco Bay Area when several pairs of pleasant young women
engaged in a whirlwind solicitation of Jewish organizations and
leaders.

They were not soliciting for money; indeed, they offerred to
give some of that away. They wanted mainly moral support for
their organization, and for a program it was about to present.
Their printed brochures read: "Judaism: In Service to the World
presents the Tel Aviv Quartet." On an inside page, the brochure
explained the purposes of the organization, all of which were
explicitly Jewish. The first listed purpose was "to promote the
Jewish religious, artistic and cultural heritage and its value
to the world." The others were similar: to sponsor speakers on
Judaism and the Jewish heritage, to promote understanding about
Jewish ideals, to publish monographs on Jewish thought, to
combat anti-Semitism, to preserve Jewish historical landmarks.

Many of the prominent Jews approached by the young ladies
were understandably captivated. It was as though a genie had
asked them: what kind of Jewish young person would you like to
see appear before you? Here they were: carefully groomed,
modestly dressed, smiling, soft-speaking, respectful, and stiff
with a dedication "to promote the Jewish religious, artistic and
cultural heritage."

Rochelle explained that her grandparents were Orthodox Jews,
but her mother never went to synagogue, her father went only when
he felt guilty, and neither understood God. After years of aim-
less disillusionment, Rochelle had become anxious to intensify
her Judaism and her relationship to Jewish living.

Sylvia had also been disillusioned by the paucity of the
religious life led by her rich Jewish parents in the East, and by
their suburban synagogue. She had gone to spend a year in an
Israeli Kibbutz--and had been struck, on seeing Jerusalem,
that there was God and there was a Bible. She began to look for
a new spiritual experience in the context of her Jewish tradition.

The general aspect of their youthful enterprise was inspiring,
especially to the battered residents of the San Francisco-Berkeley

110

272

area. Tickets were taken, and other names given to the young
women.

But a couple of people recognized the name on the back
page of the brochure: "Dr. Mose Durst, president, Judaism:
In Service to the World." Dr. Durst is closely identified with
the labyrinthine world of the Sun Myung Moon movement. (One
fascinated Moon-watcher has listed almost five dozen different
"front" organizations in the world.) Durst's relationship
begins with two organizations entitled Creative Community Project
and New Education Development Systems, Inc. He indicates that
the former is merely the popular name for the latter.

David Stoller, the vice president of Creative Community Project, met last December with campus press in California to
"explain what we are and clear up a lot of confusion." What he
cleared up was that in 1972, when he first became involved, "the
name of the group (Creative Community Project nee New Education
Development Systems, Inc.) was the International Re-Education
Foundation."

In its 1972-73 tax statement, the International Re-Education
Foundation had flatly stated that it was "a religious organization
of the Unification Church, International, which had contributed
most of its San Francisco members to the national missionary work
of the Church . . . .   Preparations are now being made (by the
International Re-Education Foundation) for the second national
tour of the Reverend Sun Myung Moon." Furthermore, the International Re-Education Foundation had owned some land in Booneville,
California, sometimes known as Ideal City Ranch, which it turned
over in a simple transfer of title in 1974 to the Unification
Church, and is also advertised in the literature of Creative
Community Project as its major retreat.

The Creative Community Project invites people to come to
nightly dinners and discussions at a San Francisco address which
the San Francisco telephone directory and at least one Unification
Church directory list as the San Francisco headquarters of the
Unification Church.

Dr. Mose Durst is the president of the Creative Community
Project and the New Education Development Systems, Inc. He
lectures regularly at Booneville. A recent account by one
reporter who attended his lectures indicated that "Moon's ideas,
his 'divine principles' about unification were at the center of
every lecture . . . . Durst indicated a new Messiah would appear
soon. He didn't say who it would be, but he went through a
long talk about Jesus and suggested that the world was ready for
a new Jesus-like figure." Dr. Durst, who teaches English
literature at an Oakland community college, is also a member of

111

the board of directors of the Unification Church theological seminary at Tarrytown, New York. This is the same Dr. Durst who is the president of Judaism: In Service to the World.

The question was put to Rochelle and Sylvia: "How can a man who is so closely associated with a basically Christological church also be president of an organization whose aim is to promote the Jewish religious heritage?" "He has many different interests " explained Rochelle.

Is there any connection between Judaism: In Service to the World and Reverend Moon or his church? No, of course no, said Rochelle and Sylvia. They answered all questions matter-of-factly, without rancor or stress. It turned out that both young women spent most of their time working for Creative Community Project. Rochelle's residential address was the same as that of the Creative Community Project in Berkeley.

They were asked whether there was any connection between the Creative Community Project and Judaism: In Service to the World. No, they replied, there is no connection; some of us happen to be heavily involved in the work of the Creative Community Project, but there is no connection between the two organizations.

They were asked whether there was any connection between the Creative Community Project and Reverend Moon or the Unification Church. No, they replied, there is no connection. "I know that the Unification church people meet at Booneville, and I sometimes run across them there," said Rochelle quietly. "I don't really know much about them or what they stand for. I have read about them in the newspapers which, of course, often distort the facts."

In desperation, the ultimate question was put to Rochelle and Sylvia: "Are either of you members of, or interested in, Reverend Moon's church or movement?" They both said firmly that they were not, and had never been. "I am a Jew," said Rochelle simply. "That is all I want to be. Why should I be interested in the Unification Church?"

About an hour later, the questioner talked to a young man who had recently left the Moon organization. He knew Rochelle as well as one of the movement's hard workers who had joined him many times in the daily "Moonie pledge," a pledge of fealty to "our Father (who) has preserved for 6,000 years the sacrificial way of the cross." A Moon-watcher explained that there was an operating phase used in the Moon movement: "celestial deception."

By concert time, a sufficient load of bricks had fallen on the Jewish community. The Tel Aviv quartet, on a strictly

112

274

commercial tour and hired through a talent agent, was shaken and
bewildered by the information brought to it, but fulfilled the
contract to which it was legally committed. However, only
about a hundred people showed up at the concert, most of them
from the circles of Judaism: In Service to the World, Creative
Community Project, or whatever. Judaism: In Service to the
World persisted in offering a thousand dollar check to the
Welfare Federation, which rejected it, and then to the Jewish
National Fund, which returned it.

But a couple of puzzling questions remained. What exactly
was the game? And why such a concentration on Jews? The general
game seemed clear enough: evangelizing the Jews. But all that
heavenly deception threw everyone off. Jews are used to frankly
evangelical groups, such as Christian Missions to the Hebrews.
This was more like a Communist Party front operation. And the
air of innocence with which it was done was startling.

After the affair of the Tel Aviv String Quartet, Durst
wrote to members of the Jewish community:

> It appears that a new process of scape-goating,
> misinformation and religious persecution is now being
> centered upon Reverend Moon or anyone who associates
> with the Unification Church. I would think that the
> Jewish people would be well familiar with this process
> . . . . and I hope that we can all diminish fear,
> hatred and prejudice.

He then stated that Judaism: In Service to the World is
"unaffiliated with any organization." That, of course, may be a
piece of celestial interpretation. After clearly pointing out
the direct genetic relationship between the Unification Church,
the International Re-Education Foundation, the New Education
Development Systems, Inc. and the Creative Community Project,
David Stoller had then denied that there was a real relationship
in these words:

> The charges that Reverend Moon is secretly
> behind everything that we do, funding us and
> sponsoring our activities, is absolutely false.
> He does not know that the Creative Community
> Project exists. The connection that we have
> is that part of the course of study that we
> teach and participate in is derived from principles
> that he teaches.

In the same vein, Dr. Durst redefines the term, "Jew," to
justify his presidency of Judaism: In Service to the World, which
he still insists, exists "to promote Jewish ideals." Asked

113

275

whether he thinks that a person can be a Jew and a Christian at
the same time, he replied: "The answer is 'no' where the
definition of each of these is incompatible." But he then points
out that

> Christian and Jew have a common witness to bear:
> at all times, even contrary to appearance, God
> remains King over the whole earth. I value then
> all religious heritage which promotes the witness
> to this ideal, and that is why I am president of
> Judaism: In Service to the World.

Thus, Durst does believe that a person can be a Jew and a
Christian at the same time, as, indeed, he is a Jew and a
Christian at the same time. He further submits and subscribes
to a document which clearly enunciates the standard evangelical
principle:

> God especially cares for the Jewish people . . . .
> The very fact that the Jews have suffered so much
> can only imply that God expects more from them
> than from other people . . . .
> The failure of the Jewish people to embody God's
> standards, as represented in the words and life of
> Jesus, brought about suffering for the Jews.

There is a straight line between that and the words of the
Reverend Moon:

> The Jews thought they were devout believers of God.
> But they didn't think about God's words more than
> their own individual things, their own family things,
> their own tribal things, and their own national things.
> That's the reason why they came to kill Jesus. So,
> by the Crucifixion of Jesus, the Chosen People were
> lost. To take the place of the chosen people, Jesus
> established Christianity and now the Christians are
> in the position of Jesus.

> By killing one man, Jesus, the Jewish people had to
> suffer for 2,000 years. . . . During the second World
> War, 6 million people were slaughtered to cleanse all
> the sins of the Jewish people from the time of Jesus.

> To make a nation, the tribe of Jesus and Jesus
> should have become one, and made all of Judaism one
> with them. We are restoring this at the present time.
> This is the crossing-over peak. So this year we called
> more than 1,000 ministers to our church to give them

114

Divine Principle training. The Jews who crucified
Jesus still remain on the earth and still deny Jesus.
But during this 20-year course we have to indemnify
that.

So, when all the hocus pocus is cleared away, what is the difference between this effort and the standard evangelisms-to-the-Jew
with which we've long lived and been bored? And how is it that
so many Jewish youths are attracted to such a standard evangelism?
It is estimated that about a third or more of the young people
in this movement are Jewish (perhaps 1,500-2,000 in number). But
the conventional experience has been that disenchanted Jewish
youth may gravitate to anything from atheistic Marxism to Zen
Buddhism, but less often to basic Christianity, the ultimate
taboo.

Many theories have been proposed for the affinity between
Jews and the Moon movement. There may be a degree of truth in
most of them. But most of them do not apply to the Moon movement itself, but only to movements "like" Moon's. For example,
one social scientist suggests that the Jews are particularly
susceptible because they tend to be raised in authoritarian
family settings thereby developing a dependency need which can be
met only by authoritarian settings in the larger world. This
would apply, he says, to Leninist political movements or to
movements like Moon's. In both cases, there is a higher authority,
and all questions are answered. One reporter quotes a Moonie as
saying: "I've been looking for something like this for years.
It answers all the questions I was asking."

The premise about the Jewish family's authoritarian nature
is problematic enough, but in any case the same syndrome can
be explored by other Jewish "character" tendencies. Out of history,
culture and religion, there is a Jewish leaning toward a
systematization of the world. Indeed the "unity" impulse in
Jewish thought has some superficial parallel to the "Unification"
theme in the Church of Reverend Moon. This drive to systematize
towards certainty would also apply to Leninist movements as well
as to movements like Moon's.

A progression of that theme is the relative susceptibility
of Jews to millenarianism. Basically, millenarianism movements
propose that there is a great and dangerous chaos in the world,
primarily created by a conflict between immiscible forces of
good and evil. Usually we think of millenarian movements as
religious in nature; the Moon church is certainly millenarian.
But certain antireligious political movements also have a
millenarian quality, with their emphasis on good and evil forces,
and their reliance on natural and immutable laws of history.

115

277

All of these explanations have a kind of pathological taint. Indeed, it might be proposed that the most susceptible people are those with such special psychological needs. One study of the Jesus People found that they scored significantly lower than average on self-confidence and personal adjustment. It is not startling to find that these movements attract a disproportionate number of young people with special anxiety problems.

Nor would it be surprising to find that these movements attract a disproportionate number of people with nonclinical problems of loneliness. It is a self-defining situation. These movements--both political and religious--provide special warm beds of instant fellowship and "community." Indeed, the term in the Moon movement as in the commune movement, is "family." There are much-noted reasons related to mass society, loss of extended family, weakened centrality of family, for these times to throw off increasing numbers of "lonely-feeling" young people.

It is difficult to find any new reasons why Jewish youth should be disproportionately susceptible to these various anxiety-producing, lonely-producing factors. But there are, of course, still all the old reasons for Jews to be generally more alienated than others, and therefore more susceptible to movements of alienation. Jews remain that much more marginal in the American society, with its emotional intellectual consequences. They feel that much more lonely, they feel that much more unsettled, they feel that much more questioning of the way things are. Or they just may want to escape the special pressure of being Jewish.

In that connection, another simple factor probably operates: association. The Moon movement obviously has a special theological investment in interesting Jews, along with all Christian evangelical movements. But the very fact that the Moon movement, or Hare Krishna, has a disproportionate number of Jews in it at any given time, serves in itself to draw more Jews. The same kind of natural pattern can be found in the occupational world.

One also suspects that the extensive Jewish leadership in the American Moon movement must have a special compulsion to draw in other Jews. Dr. Mose Durst was raised in a Jewish family, spoke Yiddish before he spoke English, had a good Jewish education, taught in Jewish religious schools, served as cultural director at campus Hillels. His stake in attracting Jews to his project must be complex indeed.

But none of these explanations explain enough, finally. The nagging question still is: pathological fringe aside, what is the pull? What does the Moon complex provide that institutionalized

116

Judaism does not? There is the matter of intimate communal life,
of course; as evidenced by the Havurah movement's attempt to meet
that need in Jewish life. But to rely on that as a total
explanation is somehow to demean the religious needs which some
young Jews feel are not met in Judaism. In some ways, this may
be a more serious and durable problem.

When Rochelle and Sylvia were asked what Judaism: In Service
to the World could provide which no other Jewish institution could
provide, they answered vaguely enough but in terms of a "more
universal approach." That was strikingly reminiscent of another
response, from members of another movement in California called
Creative Initiative, which has attracted rather spectacular
numbers of middle class young married, disproportionately Jewish.

Two young Jewish women from that organization recently appeared before a rabbinical group to urge oppositon to the building of
nuclear plants, the first public issue in which Creative
Initiative has become involved. The rabbis were more interested
in the organization itself which reputedly built a distance
between members who were Jewish and their Jewish commitment.
The women said that there was no conflict between being Jewish and
being members of Creative Initiative--but then went on to say that
Creative Initiative "added something" to their lives which,
Judaism did not, "a more universalistic outlook."

Some of the listeners were annoyed and bewildered. "Don't
these people know about the Jewish prophets? Don't they know
about the Judaic principles of universalism, of social justice?"
But they missed the point. It is not the universalism of social
justice which is attractive to the followers of Creative Initiative or the Creative Community Project.

The women from Creative Initiative, an awareness group, and
those from Judaism: In Service to the World were using the
word in a different context, in an esoteric rather than exoteric
sense. Their "universalism" was related not to the social universe,
but to the natural universe, not to social conscience but to
cosmic consciousness. They were posing their universalism not
against the particularism of Jewish tribalism; but against the
particularities of the Jewish religion. The primary objective is
not social ethics but what Hinduism calls Sat-Cha-Ananda, Being-
Consciousness-Born. The thrust among the young of the "consciousness movement," from ancient Eastern religions to transcendental meditation, has perhaps not yet been fully comprehended.

The consciousness movements do not require clinical analysis.
When Mario Savio pulled the string on all campus rebellion in the
1960's, his cry was: "Stop the machines." That struck the nerve.
It was a revolt against the Age of Reason, as it applied to

117

279

technology and to politics. Even the New Politics was anti-
politics. And with the end of Vietnam, even that collapsed
for most young people. There can be many analyses of why the
revolt took place--it had begun to take place in the 1920's
among affluent youth, and was interrupted by the Depression
and the war--but something obviously did begin to take place,
with the flower children, and the drugs and the burgeoning of
the "consciousness" movements.

     Political disillusionment certainly had a hand, but the
action started long before Watergate. Undoubtedly more
critical was what Jacob Needleman, an astute analyst of the
consciousness movements, called "the despair of people relentlessly getting what they want." There was a spiritual hunger,
played against the background of what was perceived as a failure
of the ascendancy of Reason, which had produced only material
abundance. The religions associated with and tied to that Reason
were not found to be freeing enough. Needleman, commenting on
the prodigious growth of the Eastern consciousness movements
in California, said that it was "not reality which Californians
have left behind; it is Europe . . . . I begin to see that my
idea of intelligence was a modern European idea: the mind,
unfettered by emotion, disembodied, aristocratically articulate,
gathering all before it in the sweep of its categories."

     If a disproportionate number of Jewish youth, for some of
the reasons suggested above, were thrown to this pole of dis-
affection--as a disproportionate number were undoubtedly thrown
to the other, diminished pole of political millenariansism--
then they would feel disaffected indeed from Jewish life as
they perceived it. The description of the "modern European
idea" was a description of the "Jewish idea," as most people
experienced it. That Jewish idea is God-man-society centered,
freighted with individual obligations. For the consciousness
movements, there is not that division between God and man,
Divinity is Being itself, the self is not freighted with that
kind of importance. This seems to provide a dramatic sense
of spirituality, of sharp separation from the earthly, material,
reason limited boundaries associated with modern Judeo-
Christian experience. The Jewish youth who were looking for
that sharp break, could not find it in modern Jewish life, any
more than Christian youth could find it in modern Christian
life.

     But the attraction of so many young Jews to the Moon
complex--probably more than to Hare Krishna or Maharishi--then
seems to be an anomaly. The Unification Church is finally very
much in the Judeo-Christian tradition, with Moon himself as the
emerging Messiah. But here may be the key to the significance
of the elaborately articulated structure of Moon "front"
groups, and to the importance of celestial deception--which

118

280

distinguishes it from most other evangelical groups--and which may explain its special attractiveness to certain Jewish youth. In short, the Moon complex accommodates to the kind of "consciousness trip" which engages so many American youth. To begin with, the particular divinity of Jesus is underplayed. Durst was asked whether he subscribed to the Christological elements of the Reverend Moon's teaching. His reply:

> Historically, the Jews believe that God is without form, and so they could never accept the traditional Christology that Jesus was the Son of God. The Divine Principle of Reverend Moon emphasizes that Jesus was a human being sent by God "to achieve God's purpose of salvation . . . . the purpose of the restoration of man to a state of oneness with God."

[Divine Principle Study Guide]

This statement is, again, not completely candid. Moon does refer to Jesus as the Messiah, and as the "true son of God." But it is true that the working emphasis is not so much on the divinity of Jesus as on the non-universality of Judaism. The appeal is not so much to the particularity of Christ as to the universality of some post-Judaic religion. The Jews were too preoccupied with "their own tribal things, their own national things." This is the same appeal which has carried many Jewish youth into the arms of the Maharishi and Hare Krishna.

But, most significantly, the "disconnected" outposts and inlets of the Moon complex remain exclusively in the "consciousness" mode, or at least a parody of it. Creative Community Project, for example, does not in its literature come close to mentioning Jesus or any sectarian religion. The first issue of its paper, The Bridge Builder, starts with two quotes, one from Socrates ("Let him who would move the world first move himself") and one from Dr. Mose Durst ("Let us look at the Universe and think not of how small we are, but how large we can be.") Its statement proclaims:

> The principal aim is to strive towards a comprehensive strategy for managing the future by sponsoring, organizing and coordinating programs designed to clarify important social relations and interrelationships, and precipitate a collective and realistic commitment to action. It is our thesis that ecological principles govern all Natural and Social Systems. Each system interlocks with others to form more extensive organizations. Awareness of

119

281

these relationships is essential for comprehensive and realistic management and planning. It is our Hope and Anticipation that we can not only increase our awareness, but lay the ground work for a new strategy, a strategy of Hope and Positive Action.

The program is nowhere made more precise than that. The projects of the Creative Community Project have to do with ecological conferences (the natural universe) and school programs to "educate the conscience of the child, thus establishing a foundation of universal character and value for intellectual and emotional growth." This rhetoric is, of course, "consciousness" talk, higher-awareness talk, more mantra than meaning. The outposts of the Moon territory offer no more than that--and good fellowship, and good food.

But when one attends the "home-grown dinner, music, discussion" of the nightly dinners of the Creative Community Project, one also sees a slide presentation "about our Booneville farm," and one is invited to "participate in our weekend seminars on the farm in Booneville." Certainly a weekend gathering in Booneville would have been on the schedule of Judaism: In Service to the World. If one stays for the weekend--a pressure cooker of song, food, consciousness-raising and, above all, compulsory collectivity--then, one is importuned to stay for the "week-long program," and so on, literally ad infinitum.

It is during this longer period that Creative Community Project provides "a series of lectures concerning the integrated philosophical, religious, and scientific principles upon which Creative Community Project is based." Dr. Durst, the main lecturer, says that "we teach some of Reverend Moon's ideas as well as the ideas of Moses, Buddha and Jesus." But, in fact, this training period does not serve as a bridge builder to either Judaism or Buddhism. Reverend Moon's name does not even arise in the early stages--but somehow there are those who come to savor Creative Community Project who phase into the Unification Church.

In short, the Moon complex does not attract Jewish adherents by calling them to Christ. Rather, it attracts novitiates by adopting the "consciousness movement" style. Within that style, it builds a systematic and rigid ideological structure. It is, in that sense, a devious approach, whose vulnerability would lie in the exposure of its outposts for what they are. But its success, shorn of celestial deception and psychological coercion, might hold some clue for embattled traditional Jewish institutions.

120

282

FOOTNOTES

Chapter I

[1]Moon's aim is then the establishment of his own theocracy throughout the entire Korean peninsula where he would reign as "divine" king. "Once we become indispensable to the (South Korean) government," says Moon, "then the government will realize it can no longer operate without us. Then we will begin to dictate policy." Colonel Pak Bo Hi, Moon's translator and constant travelling companion in public rallies in the United States, once "spoke of the eventual reunification of the Korean peninsula, under Moon's domination, as a foregone conclusion."

In a certain sense, according to Allen Tate Wood, Sun Myung Moon became President Park Chung Hee's competitor for power. Wood, a former Unification Church official, testified before the Fraser Congressional Hearings that "In (1970)...there was some danger that Mr. Moon might be assassinated by agents of the South Korean government. To prevent this from happening, the Unification Church in Korea and Japan was engaging in an all-out effort to convince President Park that he had nothing to fear from Moon, and that, in fact, in Moon he would find his strongest ally and supporter. So far, Moon's staunch anti-communism has won him at least the unspoken blessings of the Park regime. Today in Korea, a land in which the free expression of religious conscience is often met by the government with charges of treason and sedition Moon and his lieutenants enjoy a kind of diplomatic immunity." U. S., Congress, House, Committee on International Relations, Activities of the Korean Central Intelligence Agency in the United States, Part II, 94th Cong., 2nd Sess. (June 22, Sept. 27 and 30, 1976), pp. 13, 16, and 34.

[2]Ibid., p. 36.

[3]Ibid, p. 21.

[4]Ibid.

[5]The New York Times, 11/18/76.

[6]Ibid.

[7]The Seminary located in Tarrytown, New York, on a 258 acre site, and which cost Moon $1,500,000, is the training center where serious converts undergo a three-month indoctrination program.

[8]During Syngman Rhee's time and the Korean War, most communists in the south were virtually eradicated. In actuality,

121

283

there were no communists left to whom the anti-communist laws could apply. Park used the laws against students, liberal intellectuals, and Christians who verbalized dissent.

[9]For example, an ex-Moonist, Ms. Denise Peksin said: "I just did whatever I was told. I had never really believed in God, but within one week they had me believing that Moon was the Messiah, that I was saving the world, that my parents were Satan, and that no one else would be able to understand what I was doing, so it was pointless to try to explain." While in the Unification Church, Denise also had to read a manual which says, "I have no joy for myself because Moon's joy is my joy." See Janice Harayda, "I was a Robot for Sun," Glamour, April 1976, p. 256.

[10]See pp. 43-45 and note 9, Chapter II.

[11]The New York Times (February 19, 1976, p. 10) stated under the heading "300 Parents of Reverend Moon's Followers Meet in Washington to Seek Federal Investigation of Group":

> At a meeting arranged by Senator Robert Dole, Republican of Kansas, the parents and some 300 spectators jammed a Senate caucus room while spokesmen presentd their case to representatives of the Internal Revenue Service, Department of Labor, and other agencies. Rabbi Maurice Davis of White Plains addressed the audience: "The last time I have ever witnessed a movement that had these characteristics - with a single authoritarian head, fanatical followers, absolutely unlimited funds, hatred for everyone on the outside, suspicious against their parents - was the Nazi Youth Movement, and I tell you I am scared." Speakers at the meeting included a psychiatric social worker, Jean Merritt, who asserted that "she had seen more than 150 young people who had left the movement and that 50% were schizophrenic or had borderline psychosis, presumably as a result of their indoctrination."

[12]Maurice Davis, "The Moon People and Our Children," Jewish Community Center Bulletin, vol. 20, no. 18 (July 10, 1974), p. 3.

[13]Mrs. Grace Raucci of Brooklyn, a Catholic whose 26 year old son affiliated with the Church, also said: "It all seems pretty good to me. Reverend Moon is bringing God to a brainwashed world. I'm grateful that I have a son who is dedicating his life to missionary work," The New York Times (9/6/76).

[14]David Silverberg, "'Heavenly Deception,' Rev. Moon's Hard Sell," Present Tense (Autumn 1976), pp. 55-56.

[15]Berkeley Rice, "Messiah from Korea," Psychology Today, (January 1976), p. 47.

16According to CDI estimates, there are as many as 686 nuclear weapons on the 38th parallel.

17"How God is Pursuing his Restoration Providence," Master Speaks, 12/22/71.

123

Chapter II

[1] There were three contending kingdoms in the Korean peninsula between the fourth and seventh centuries. Koguryŏ was in the north, Paekche in the southwest, and Silla in the southeast. Koguryŏ Kingdom was the most powerful but it was conquered in 668 by the combined forces of China and the Silla Kingdom.

[2] San Kuo Chih, Ch'in-ting ed., 30/5b.

[3] Sun Myung Moon, Messiah or Madman?, ECLIPSE (San Francisco, 1976), p. 11.

[4] Tonga Ilbo, 6/28/58.

[5] Sun Myung Moon, God's Hope for America, Bicentennial God Bless America Committee (New York, 1976), p. 10.

[6] Sun Myung Moon, Unification Church of America (New York, 1976), p. 25.

[7] Ibid.

[8] Ibid.

[9] T'ak Myong-hwan, Hanguk ŭi Sinhung Chongkyo (Seoul, 1972), Vol. 1, p. 73. According to T'ak, Japan's Mainichi Newspaper Co. investigated this matter and it could not find Moon's name on the university graduation list.

[10] Sin Sa-hun, "T'ongilkyo ŭi Chŏngch'ae wa kŭ Bip'an," (Lecture held in Seoul, May 4, 1975), p. 1.

[11] Yun Kuk Kim, "The Korean Church Yesterday and Today," Korea Affairs, Vol. 1 (March/April 1962), pp. 92-94.

[12] Ibid.

[13] Yun Kuk Kim, p. 93.

[14] T'ak Myong-hwan, p. 74.

[15] At Seoul, in October, 1968, Moon proclaimed officially that he was the Messiah. See Arai Arao, Nihon no Kyōki (Tōkyō, 1971), p. 85.

[16] On "blood-sharing," see T'ak Myŏng-hwan, pp. 74-78, Arai Arao, pp. 94-112, Kim Kyŏng-rae, Sahoeak kwa Sakyo Undong (Seoul, 1957), pp. 25-42 and pp. 71-79, and Sin Sa-hun, pp. 1-7.

125

287

[17]Arai, Arao, p. 99.

[18]Ibid.

[19]T'ak Myŏng-hwan, p. 74.

[20]Sun Myung Moon, p. 27.

[21]T'ak Myŏng-hwan, p. 74, Arai Arao, pp. 96-97, and Sin Sa-hun, p. 4. Arai thinks that Moon received 5-year and 10-month jail sentences. Kim, whom he married, received a 10-month term.

[22]Ibid.

[23]Sun Myung Moon, p. 29.

[24]Arai Arao, p. 74.

[25]T'ak Myŏng-hwan, p. 75.

[26]Ibid.

[27]T'ak Myŏng-hwan, p. 75.

[28]Ibid.

[29]Ibid.

[30]Arai Arao, p. 100.

[31]T'ak Myŏng-hwan, p. 78.

[32]Kim Kyŏng-rae, p. 29.

[33]For detailed account of this event, see ibid., pp. 25-34.

[34]Ibid.

[35]Weston LaBarre, The Ghost Dance, the Origin of Religion (New York, 1970), pp. 99-100.

[36]For a detailed story on Nishigawa, see Arai Arao, pp. 113-125.

[37]Ibid., p. 20.

[38]Arai Arao, p. 85.

[39]John Lofland, Doomsday Cult (New Jersey, 1966) p.

126

[40]Ibid., pp. 35 and 50-51.

[41]T'ak Myŏng-hwan, p. 77.

[42]Pak T'ae-sŏn calls himself Olive Tree because the term appears in Zechariah 4:11 in the Old Testament and Revelation 11:4 in the New Testament.

[43]T'ak Myŏng-hwan, p. 77.

[44]The study, conducted by the B'nai B'rith Hillel Foundations, found that Moonist activities on college campuses made no headway. "Only a few campuses in the New York, Washington, Philadelphia and Berkeley and San Francisco areas, 'where the Moon people have expended enormous amounts of money and energy and resources,' have experienced some intensive missionary efforts by adherents of the Unification Church," but these had been "'marginal' in terms of gaining converts." See the New York Times, 1/14/77.

[45]David Silverberg, p.56.

127

289

Chapter III

[1]Ch'oi Syn Duk, "Korea's Tong-il Movement," Royal Asiatic Society, vol. XLIII (1967), p. 172.

[2]Arai Arao, Nihon no Kyōki (Tōkyō,. 1971), p. 131.

[3]Berkeley Rice, "Messiah from Korea," Psychology Today, (January 1976), p. 40.

[4]Arai Arao, pp. 21 and 152-153.

[5]Chōi Syn Duk, p. 172.

[6]Divine Principle, The Holy Spirit Association for the Unification of World Christianity (Washington, D.C., 1973) p. 520.

[7]Wŏlli Kangron, Segae Kidkkyo T'ongil Sinyŏng Hyŏphoe (Seoul, 1966), p. 556. This statement appears to be so embarssing that the English version of the Divine Principle has omitted it.

[8]Arai Arao, p. 162.

[9]Ibid., p. 175.

[10]Janice Harayda in her article, "I Was a Robot for Sun," in Glamour magazine (April, 1976, p. 256) describes a similar incident. "One event, however, looms especially vividly in Denise's (Denise Peskin - see note 3, Ch. I) mind. After she had been at the ranch a week, she and the other new recruits were forced to run up to the top of the mountain. Some, who collapsed, were taken down in trucks. ('It was the most sickening thing you ever saw,' admits Denise, in a rare expression of the emotion she may have felt while in the movement. But she quickly adds that she forced herself not to think about those who fell, but to continue chanting and praying to herself as instructed.) At the top of the mountain, it was announced that Moon was the new Messiah who had come 'to save the world'."

[11]George Lockland, Grow or Die (New York, 1973), p. 222.

[12]William Sargant, Battle for the Mind (New York, 1957), p. 80.

[13]Arai Arao, pp. 148-151.

[14]See ibid., pp. 21 and 134-148.

129

[15]The Providence Journal, 5/25/77.

130

Chapter IV

[1]Ted Patrick, <u>Let Our Children Go!</u> (New York, 1976),
pp. 28-29.

[2]<u>Ibid</u>., p. 31.

[3]<u>Ibid</u>., p. 241.

[4]<u>Divine Principle</u>, The Holy Spirit Association for the
Unification of World Christianity (Washington, D.C., 1973), p. 1.

[5]Victor Frankl, <u>The Doctor and the Soul</u> (New York, 1970),
p. 15.

[6]<u>Divine Principle</u>, p. 1.

[7]<u>Ibid</u>.

[8]<u>Ibid</u>., p. 3.

[9]<u>Ibid</u>., p. 2.

[10]Robet S. Ellwood, Jr., <u>Religious and Spiritual Groups in
Modern America</u> (New Jersey, 1973), p. 293.

[11]Hannah Arendt, <u>Between Past and Future</u> (London, 1961), p. 45.

[12]<u>Divine Principle</u>, p. 7.

[13]<u>Ibid</u>., p. 216.

[14]<u>Ibid</u>., pp. 368-369.

[15]See personal history of Pak T'ae-sǒn, T'ak Myǒng-hwan,
<u>Hanguk ǔi Sinhǔng Chongkyo</u>, vol. 1 (Seoul, 1972), p. 108.

[16]Arai Arao, <u>Nihon no Kyōki</u> (Tōkyō, 1971), pp. 94-112.

[17]Sin Sa-hun, "T'ongilkyo ǔi Chǒngch'ae wa kǔ Bip'an,"
5/4/75 (lecture in Seoul), p. 2.

[18]<u>Divine Principle</u>, p.24.

[19]<u>Ibid</u>., p. 20.

[20]"Fourth Director's Conference," <u>Master Speaks</u>, 7/14/73.

[21]<u>Ibid</u>.

131

293

[22]David Silverberg, "'Heavenly Deception', XX, Rev. Moon's Hard Sell," Present Tense (Autumn 1976), pp. 141-142.

[23]Divine Principle, p. 147.

[24]Ibid., p. 212.

[25]Ibid., p. 147.

[26]Moon told his followers that 1981 is the deadline for achieving his goal of ruling the Korean Peninsula. If he fails in this, he said he has to wait 21 more years, or three 7-year periods. U. S., Congress, House, Committee on International Relations, Activities of the Korean Central Intelligence Agency in the United States, Part II, 94th Cong., 2nd Sess. (June 22, Sept. 27 and 30, 1976), p. 40.

[27]T'ak Myŏng-hwan, p. 3 (Hwabop'yŏn).

[28]Arai Arao, p. 165.

[29]Ibid., p. 166.

[30]Ibid., p. 168.

[31]The Community Voice, 12/16/76.

[32]New York Post, 12/3/76, p. 37.

[33]Ibid.

[34]A. James Rudin, Jews and Judaism in Rev. Moon's Divine Principle, The American Jewish Committee (Dec. 1976), p. 7.

[35]Earl Rabb, "Reverend Moon and the Jews--The San Francisco Experience," Congress Monthly (Dec., 1976), p. 10.

[36]Divine Principle, p. 510.

[37]Ibid.

[38]David Silverberg, p. 52.

[39]Ibid.

[40]Ibid., pp. 52-53.

[41]Ibid., p. 55.

132

[42]Kim, Young Oon, _Unification Theology and Christian Thought_ (New York, 1975), p. 39.

133

Chapter V

[1]The Silla Kingdom conquered both the Paekche and Koguryŏ Kingdoms with the aid of T'ang China, and unified the Korean peninsula in 676. This kingdom ruled Korea until it was succeeded by the Koryŏ Dynasty in 935.

[2]S. M. Sirokogoroff, Psychomental Complex of the Tungus (London and Shanghai, 1935), p. 48. Semyonov's identification of the tree as a repository of the shaman's soul may serve to shed light on the 1976 conflict between North Korean soldiers and American soldiers at the demilitarized border zone in P'anmunjŏm, in which two American officers were axed to death. The North Koreans claimed that the United States military had cut down the trees in order to see further into Korea, thus provoking the attack. Although frequent conflicts and tension in the border zone are political, one cannot overlook the ancient belief in a "cosmic tree," a belief which does not miraculously disappear simply because modern man likes to think himself rational. North Koreans call themselves communists, but they are also descendants of the Tungus shamans, and, furthermore, the capital of North Korea, P'yŏngyang, was the legendary home of T'angun. Perhaps the souls of shaman ancestors still do reside in trees. To wantonly cut down a tree had been a serious crime to the Tungusians, and only "rational" modern man is capable of disregarding the life within all natural forms.

[3]Arai Arao, Nihon no Kyōki (Tōkyō, 1971), pp. 66-70.

[4]S.M. Shirokogoroff, pp. 255, 264.

[5]Ibid.

[6]Weston La Barre, The Ghost Dance, the Origin of Religion (New York, 1970), pp. 171-172.

[7]John Lofland, Doomsday Cult (New Jersey, 1966), p.35.

[8]Ibid., p. 28.

[9]Yi Chong-sŏk, "Sinhŭng Chongkyo," Sintonga, no. 72, (Seoul, 1970), pp. 226-227.

[10]Weston LaBarre, p. 41.

[11]Kim Kyŏng-rae, Sahoeak kwa Sakyoundong (Seoul, 1957), p.7, and Yi Chong-sŏk, p. 240.

[12]Ibid., pp. 64-65 and 81-84.

135

297

[13]Ilyŏn, _Samguk Yusa_ (Translated by Tae-hung Ha and Grafton K. Mintz), Seoul, 1972, p. 195.

[14]T'ak Myŏng-hwan, _Hanguk ŭi Sinhŭng Chongkyo_ (Seoul, 1972), p. 117.

[15]Interview with Shelley Turner, Warwick, Rhode Island, 10/5/76.

[16]Ch'oi Syn Duk, "Korea's Tong-il Movement, _Royal Asiatic Society_, Vol. XLIII (1967), p. 4.

[17]_Ibid_.

[18]Parent's Day, _Master Speaks_, 3/24/74.

[19]Sun Myung Moon, _God's Hope for America_, Bicentennial God Bless America Committee (New York, 1976), p.9.

[20]"3rd Director's Conference," _Master Speaks_, 5/17/73.

[21]"Indemnity and Unification," _Master Speaks_, 2/14/74.

[22]_Divine Principle_, The Holy Spirit Association for the Unification of World Christianity (Washington, D.C., 1973), p. 491.

[23]_Ibid_.

[24]Interview with Shelley Turner, 10/5/76.

[25]Sun Myung Moon, _God's Hope for America_, p. 10.

[26]Sun Myung Moon, _America in God's Providence_, Bicentennial God Bless America Committee (New York, 1976), p. 6. Moon states: "In this respect America is a unique nation. Even your bills and coins are impressed with the beautiful inscription, 'In God We Trust.' No other nation does such a thing. Really, then is this your money? Is it American money? No, it is God's money."

[27]Ilyŏn, p. 351.

[28]_Ibid_., p. 305.

[29]Interview with Shelley Turner, 10/5/76.

[30]"Sun Myung Moon, Messiah or Madman?," ECLIPSE (San Francisco, 1976), p. 1.

136

[31]U.S., Congress, House, Committee on International Relations, Activities of the Central Intelligence Agency in the United States, part II 94th Cong., 2nd Sess. (June 22, Sept. 27 and 30, 1976), p. 25.

[32]Ibid., p.21.

[33]Ibid., p.24.

[34]Ibid., p. 38.

[35]Lives of Eminent Korean Monks, The Haedong Kosŭng Chŏn, Translated with an Introduction by Peter H. Lee (Cambridge, 1969), p. 76.

[36]Cited by Erich Fromm, The Sane Society (A Fawcett Premier Book, 1955), p. 109.

[37]Ilyŏn, p. 352.

[38]Sun Myung Moon, God's Hope for America, p. 6.

[39]Sun Myung Moon, America in God's Providence, p. 26.

[40]Ibid.

[41]Sun Myung Moon, God's Hope for America, p. 11

[42]Ibid.

[43]Sun Myung Moon, America in God's Providence, p. 24.

[44]Divine Principle, pp. 526-527.

[45]"3rd Director's Conference, "Master Speaks, 5/17/73, p. 12.

137

CHAPTER VI

[1]T. K. (anonymous), Letters from Korea, Translated by David L. Swain (New York, 1976), p. 81.

[2]There was a medical doctor named Kennedy in Atlanta when Nixon was running into trouble. In the early fall of 1973, Kennedy, who knew Neil Salonen, approached the latter suggesting to him that the Unification Church take up the banner to defend Nixon. Allen Wood testified before the Fraser Congressional Committee that "Salonen approached Moon and suggested this plan as a public relations ploy to get in close with the Government and with the power structure. Moon did not like the idea. Moon was in the middle of his speaking tour through 21 cities, and he had to go back to Japan for a conference. . . . When he came back, he said God had told him while he was in deep meditation in Korea, 'forgive,' 'love,' and 'unite.' Then the full-page ads appeared, and Mr. Moon issued the order that all Unification Church members in America should send telegrams of support to President Nixon, and that was carried out." U.S., Congress, House, Committee on International Relations, Activities of the Korean Central Intelligence Agency in the United States, Part II, 94th Cong., 2d Sess. (June 22, Sept. 27 and 30, 1976), p. 39.

[3]Reverend Moon offered the following prayer for Richard Nixon. "I have been praying specifically for President Richard Nixon. I asked God, 'What shall we do with the person of Richard Nixon?" The answer was . . . 'Love. It is your duty to love him. . . .' Do you criticize him? . . . Of course not. You comfort him. You love him unconditionally . . . This nation is God's nation. The Office of the President of the United States is sacred. God inspires a man and then confirms him as President . . . God has chosen Richard Nixon to be President. . . . Our duty, and this alone, is that we . . . support the office itself." Moon's demonstrations in support of Nixon lasted from December of 1973 until the time of Nixon's resignation in August of 1974. See Maurice Davis, "The Moon People and Our Children," Jewish Community Center Bulletin, vol. 20, no. 18, 7/10/74, p. 2.

[4]T. K., pp. 223-224.

[5]T. K., p. 223.

[6]Ibid., p. 224.

[7]Ibid.

[8]Ibid., p. 14.

139

301

[9]Mun Ch'ŏl-ho, "Komun," Hanyang (Feb./Mar., 1976), no. 129, p. 28.

[10]Chŏng Kyŏng-mo, "Han Minzokchuŭicha ŭi Sengae," Hanyang, no. 129, (Feb./Mar., 1976), p. 42. Professor Gregory Henderson reviewed President Park's history as a person "well acquainted with the baser vocabulary of repression. As a Japanese officer whom Japanese sources allege to have been a 'special action'--in other words, political assassination and repression--officer of the Japanese forces in Manchuria in World War II, he knew first hand the instruments by which Japan repressed colonial Korea--the thought control police, the Kempeitai or ruthless military police, censorship, ubiquitous agents, secret subsidization of front organizations, torture, kidnaping, debauching, and defamation of character." See U.S., Congress, House, Committee on International Relations (Part I), p. 3.

[11]See note 23 to Chapter V and Guardian, 4/24/71, p. 16, and Chong Kyŏng-mo, "Yŏksa ŭi Kyohun," Hanyang, no. 132 (Aug./Sept., 1976), pp. 23-24.

[12]T. K., pp. 26-27.

[13]Ibid., pp. 5-6.

[14]Ibid., p. 27.

[15]Ibid., p. 29.

[16]Yi Chong-sŏk, "Sinhŭng Chongkyo," Sintonga, no. 72 (Seoul, p. 247.

[17]Sun Myung Moon: Messiah or Madman?, ECLIPSE, San Francisco, p. 11.

[18]Ibid.

[19]The New York Times, 5/25/76.

[20]Ibid.

[21]U.S., Congress, House, Committee on International Relations (Part II), p. 35.

[22]Ibid., p. 21.

[23]Ibid.

140

[24] Ibid., p. 17.

[25] Ibid., pp. 37-38.

[26] Ibid., p. 53.

[27] Ibid., p. 46.

[28] "3rd Director's Conference," Master Speaks, 5/17/73, p. 12.

[29] Parent's Day, Master Speaks, 3/24/74.

[30] Ibid.

[31] Ibid.

[32] Washington Post, 8/24/75, p. 1.

[33] Sun Myung Moon, America in God's Providence, p. 21.

[34] Ibid.

[35] Ibid., p. 23.

[36] Ibid., p. 7.

[37] Ilyŏn, Samguk Yusa, Translated by Tae-hung Ha and Grafton K. Mintz (Seoul, 1972), p. 197.

[38] According to the New York Times (11/13/76), the Dow Chemical Company had broken ground for an $862 million petro-chemical complex in South Korea in which the American company is investing $150 million. Other plants in the Dow complex would include a naphtha cracking plant to be built by a unit of the government-run Korea General Chemical Corporation and a joint venture derivatives plant.

[39] U.S., Congress, House, Committee on International Relations (Part II), p.

[40] Ibid., pp. 8-9.

[41] Ibid., p. 37.

[42] Maurice Davis, pp. 1-2.

[43] New York Post, 11/18/76 and the Providence Journal (The Evening Bulletin), 11/8/76.

141

[44]U.S., Congress, House, Committee on International Relations (Part II), p. 23.

[45]A Unification Church leaflet printed in Washington, D.C. in 1971 stated as follows: "Since a church is the safest and most recognized form of social organization, Mr. Moon founded the church in 1954 in order to have the greatest freedom of action." Ibid., p. 36.

[46]Ibid., p. 33.

[47]Ibid., p. 51.

[48]Ibid., p. 15.

[49]Ibid., p. 9.

[50]New York Post, 11/13/76.

[51]U.S., Congress, House, Committee on International Relations (Part II), p. 16.

[52]Ibid.

[53]Ibid., p. 9.

[54]Ibid., p. 54.

[55]Frank Baldwin, "The Korea Lobby," Christianity and Crisis, vol. 36, no. 12 (July 19, 1976), p. 165.

[56]"Day Training Session," Master Speaks.

[57]Robert W. Roland, Statement to Fraser Committee, p. 10.

[58]Frank Baldwin, p. 162.

[59]The Providence Journal, 11/11/76.

[60]Ibid., 11/14/76.

[61]The Providence Journal, 11/11/76.

[62]The Washington Post, 11/5/76 and The Christian Science Monitor, 10/29/76.

[63]The Providence Journal, 12/6/76.

[64]U.S., Congress, House, Committee on International Relations (Part II), p. 30.

142

304

65Ibid., p. 31

66This is a letter Lee received from a person in Cook County, Ill. He stated that the nature of this letter was confidential to insure the safety of the sender, who was an insider. Ibid., p. 22.

67Ibid., p. 30.

68Ibid., 11/6/76.

69Ibid., 11/11/76.

70The New York Times, 11/17/76.

71The Christian Science Monitor, 11/1/76.

72Washington Post, 5/23/76.

73Newsweek, 11/22/76, pp. 38-43. Professor Gregory Henderson stated before the Congressional hearings: ". . . [the present Korean laws and criminal code] have specific reference not only to Koreans but to foreign critics and correspondents. American correspondents have been warned by the South Korean Minister of Public Information that they might fall under this law when they were in Korea reporting for the benefit of the American public in English for American newspapers, and we also must remember that the law provides for as much as 7 years' imprisonment for anyone damaging the security, national interest, or prestige of Korea at home or abroad." See U.S., Congress, House, Committee on International Relations (Part I), p. 62.

74U.S., Congress, House, Committee on International Relations (Part II), p. 5.

75Ibid., p. 4.

76The Providence Journal, 11/30/76. "Under the new organization in the United States, new KCIA officers assigned here will report to Han Pyung Ki, the deputy ambassador in the South Korean Observer Mission at the United Nations in New York. . . . the new KCIA chief in the U.S., Ambassador Han, is married to the daughter of Park and his first wife, whom he divorced many years ago. . . . Han reportedly supervised a Korean gift of $1 million to Harvard University. . . . The Korean source said that the Korean Traders Association, under instructions from the KCIA, had collected the funds from Korean businesses for the gift." Also see U.S., Congress, House, Committee on International Relations (Part I), pp. 108-110.

143

[77]Ibid., p. 6. For example, a total of 17 persons were kidnaped from West Germany, France and the United States. Along with other dissidents, these intellectuals were placed on trial in South Korea, and on October 9, 1967, all received prison terms but two; they were executed.

[78]The Providence Journal, 11/21/76.

[79]Robert W. Roland, p. 11.

[80]Henderson described the terrorist activities of the eight bureaus of the KCIA, including the third bureau, which "appears to manufacture more spies than it apprehends. The current trend toward arresting the anti-communist name conservative and respectable patriots with far better anti-communist records than President Park is more likely to weaken the anti-communism of Koreans either in South Korea, or, to some extent, here than almost any other means." U.S., Congress, House, Committee on International Relations (Part 2), p. 7.

[81]The Christian Century, 11/3/76.

[82]"Time to Reconsider Korea," Address by Senator George McGovern in the United States Senate (Sept. 15, 1976), p. 2.

144

Chapter VII

[1]Lewis Mumford, The Myth of Machine (New York, 1969),
p. 31.

[2]The Providence Journal, 12/30/76.

[3]Ibid., 5/30/74.

[4]Erich Fromm, The Sane Society (New York, 1955), pp. 17-18.

[5]The Providence Journal, 5/18/76.

[6]Maurice Davis, The Moon People and Our Children,
Jewish Community Center, Bulletin, Vol. 20. No. 18, (July 10,
1974), p. 2.

[7]John Lofland, Doomday Cult (New Jersey, 1966), p. 175.

[8]Interview with Rabbi Maurice David, 11/3/76.

[9]Ibid.

[10]Maurice Davis, p. 3.

[11]Byong-suh Kim, Ideology, Conversion and Faith Maintenance
in a Korean Sect: The Case of the Unified Family of Rev. Sun
Myung Moon, A Paper Presented at the University Seminar on
Korea of Columbia University on May 21, 1976, p. 17.

[12]Eric Rofes, "A Couple of Summers," The Harvard Crimson
(September 30, 1975), p. 3.

[13]Berkeley Rice, "Messiah from Korea," Psychology Today,
(January 1976), p. 42.

[14]Berkeley Rice, "The Pull of sun Moon," The New Times
Magazine (May 30, 1976), p. 8. Also see Lindsay Miller, "All
They Wanted Was a Glimpse of Wendy, "New York Post, 11/20/76.
Miller says: "Wendy dropped out of her freshman year at the
University of New Hampshire two years ago to follow Moon. Twice
her parents have snatched her from the group and tried to have
her "deprogrammed." Twice she has gone back. The Helanders
sued, charging Moon with mind control. A federal district judge
ruled there was insufficient evidence."

[15]Ibid.

[16]John Lofland, pp. 55-56.

145

307

[17]Byong-suh Kim, p. 10.

[18]Ibid., pp. 9-10. OM Lovers has a bible called "Reality
Versus Illusion in Sacramental Life." The main tenet of the OM-
people is expressed in their song, "OM is the basis of sacred
fucking..." "There are no transient senses, no bodies that must
die - Such is but illusion seen with the outward eye." OM lovers
promote what they call "Fucking in Accord with Sacred Injunction -
Viewed as perfect." See Reality Versus Illusion in Sacramental
Life, OM United World Publishing Country)New York, 1976), p. 1.

[19]Holmes Welch, Taoism: The Parting of the Way (Boston,
1957), p. 167.

[20]Berkeley Rice, "The Pull of Sun Moon," p. 8.

[21]New York Post, 11/27/76.

[22]The New York Times, 9/16/76. Denise Peskin, an ex-
Moonist who is now an anti-Moonist crusader, stated that the
Unification Church had classes in which Moonists were taught to
smile. See David Silverberg, "Heavenly Deception,' Rev. Moon's
Hard Sell," Present Tense (Autumn 1976), p. 50.

[23]Judith Harris Carter, A Personal Observation (June, 1975),
pp. 2-3.

[24]Interview with Rabbi Maurice Davis, 11/3/76.

[25]John Lofland, p. 46. "According to a recent Gallup survey
based on personal interviews with 1,553 American Protestants -
and a third of all Americans - say that they have been "born
again." That figure comes to nearly 50 million adult Americans
who claim to have experienced a turning point in their lives by
making a personal commitment to Jesus Christ as their savior.
Even more surprising is Gallup's report that 46 per cent of
Protestants - and 31 per cent of Catholics believe that the Bible
is "to be taken literally, word for word," a doctrine held only
by the most conservative Christians." See Newsweek, October 25,
1976, p. 68. The interpretation of symbolic religious images as
literal concrete facts is characteristic of the new evangelical
organizations and Sun Myung Moon's group, which mistake personal
or parochial convictions for universal and absolute truths.
Psychologist Carl Jung emphasized the importance of religious
symbols as psychic facts, which make no sense whatever when
interpreted as physical realities.

[26]Herbert Engel, the father of Paul Engel (a former Moonist
who wrote an article on "The World of the Cult"), said: "You

146

are concerned that you may never see your child again. All the
relationships built up over twenty years are gone. You're
talking to a stranger and there is no way to get through. The
feeling is as though someone died." David Silverberg, p. 55.

[27]Interview with Shelley Turner, 10/5/76.

[28]Ibid.

[29]Ibid.

[30]Sun Myung Moon, America in God's Providence, Bicentennial
God Bless America Committee (New York, 1976), p. 23.

[31]Adolf Guggenbuhl, Power in the Helping Professions (New
York, 1971), p. 113.

[32]Sun Myung Moon, "God's Hope for America," Bicentennial
Speech at Yankee Stadium, June 1, 1976.

[33]Sun Myung Moon, God's Hope for America, Bicentennial God
Bless America Committee (New York, 1976), p. 9.

147

Chapter VIII

[1]Gotthard Booth, Jung's and Rorschach's Contribution toward a Psychobiological Typology (Reprinted from Toward a Discovery of the Person, Oct. 1974), p. 63.

[2]Ibid.

[3]In September 1923, shortly after the great earthquakes in Tōkyō and Yokohama, the Japanese military and police forces summarily massacred Korean children, women and men under the pretext that the Koreans might revolt amidst social and economic dislocations created by earthquakes.

[4]Kim Chi-ha Chŏnjip, compiled by Hayang-sa (Tōkyō, 1975), pp. 388-389.

BIBLIOGRAPHY

American Banker, 6/14/76.

Arai Aroa 荒井荒雄, Nihon no Kyōki 日本の 狂氣 (Tōkyō, 1971).

Arendt, Hannah, Between Past and Future (London, 1961).

Baldwin, Frank, "The Korea Lobby," Christianity and Crisis, Vol. 36, no. 12 (July 19, 1976), pp. 162-168.

Bicentennial God Bless America Committee, God's Hope for American (New York, 1976).

Black, David, "The Secrets of the Innocents: Why Kids Join Cults," Woman's Day (January 1977), pp. 91, 166, 168, 170, 172, and pp. 174-175.

Carter, Judith Harris, A Personal Observation (June 1975) Chicago Sun-Times, 6/6/76.

Chŏi Syn Duk, "Korea's Tong-il Movement," Transactions of the Royal Asiatic Society, Korea Branch, Vol XLIII (Seoul, 1967), pp. 167-180.

Chŏng Kyŏng-mo, 鄭 敬謨, "Han Minzokchuŭi-cha ŭi Sengae," 北民族主義者의 生涯 Hanyang, No. 129 (Feb./March 1976), pp. 33-49.
          "Yŏksa ŭi Kyohun," 歷史의 敎訓 Hanyang, No. 132 (Aug./Sept., 1976), pp. 17-24.

Chosŏn Ilbo 朝鮮 日報 , 10/30/70, 11/2/70, 11/6/70, and 11/10/70.

The Community Voice, 12/16/76.

Chukan Chungwang, 週刊中央 , 11/10/68, 2/20/72, and 10/18/70.

Chukan Han'guk, 週刊韓國, 5/11/69, 11/16/68, 10/25/70.

The Christian Century, 11/3/76.

Christian Science Monitor, 10/29/76, 11/1/76, 11/2/76, 11/19/76, 1/19/77.

Dallas Morning News, 9/4/75.

Eliade, Mircea, Shamanism-Archaic Technique of Ecstasy (New York, 1964).

Ellwood, Robert S. Jr., Religious and Spiritual Groups in Modern America (New Jersey, 1973).

Engel, Paul, "The World of the Cult," Information Kit on the Activities of Sun Myung Moon, Union of American Hebrew Congregations (August 1976).

Far Eastern Economic Review, 4/16/76, 6/18/76, 6/25/76.

Frank, Victor Emil, The Doctor and the Soul (New York, 1966).

Fromm, Eric, The Sane Society (New York, 1955).

Graaf, de John, "Perils of Counterculture," North County Anvil, No. 17 (March/April 1976).

Guardian, 4/24/71 and 6/2/76.

Guggenbühl, Adolf, Power in the Helping Professions (New York, 1971).

Han Ch'ŏl-ha 韓哲河, "T'ongilkyo ŭi Saeksŏ Mot'ibu," 統一敎의 세스모티프 Wŏlkan Chungwang, No. 35 (Seoul, 1971), pp. 136-145.

Harayda, Janice, "I was a Robot for Sun," Glamour (April 1976), pp. 216, 256 and pp. 261-262.

The Holy Spirit Association for the Unification of World Christianity, Divine Principle (Washington, D.C., 1973).

Jewish Community Center Bulletin, Vol 20, no. 18 (7/10/74).

Kim, Byong-suh, Ideology, Conversion and Faith Maintenance in a Korean Sect: The Case of the Unification Family of Rev. Sun Myung Moon, A Paper presented at University Seminar on Korea at Columbia University on May 21, 1976.

Hanyang-sa 漢陽社, Kim Chi-ha Chŏnjip 金笑河全集 (Tōkyō, 1975).

Kim Kyŏng-rae, 金景來, Sahoeak kwa Sakyoundong 社會惡과 邪敎運動 (Seoul, 1975).

152

Kim Paek-mun 金白文 , Sinhang Inkkyŏkron 信仰人格論(Seoul, 1970).

—————————— , Sŏngsin Sinhak 聖神神學 (Seoul, 1954).

Kim, Young Oon, Unification Theology and Christian Thought (New York, 1975).

Kim, Yun Kuk, "The Korean Church Yesterday and Today," Korean Affairs, Vol. 1 (March/April 1962), pp. 81-105.

Korea Herald, 9/21/76.

La Barre, Weston, The Ghost Dance, the Origin of Religion (New York, 1970).

Lee, Peter H. (Translated with an Introduction), Lives of Eminent Korean Monks, The Haodong Kosŭng Chŏn (Cambridge, 1969).

Lifton, Robert J., Thought Reform and the Psychology of Totalism (London, 1960).

Lockland, George, Grow or Die (New York, 1973).

Lofland, John, Doomsday Cult - Study of Conversion, Proselytiza- tion, and Maintenance of Faith (New Jersey, 1966).

Los Angeles Times, 11/21/76.

Master Speaks, 12/22/71, 5/17/73, 2/14/74, and 3/24/74.

McGovern, George, "Time to Reconsider Korea," Address by Senator George McGovern in the United States Senate, September 15, 1976.

Meerloo, Joost A. M., The Rape of the Mind (New York, 1956).

Militant, 12/3/76.

Mook, Jane Day, "The Unification Church," A.D., (May 1974), pp. 30-36.

Moos Felix, "Leadership and Organization in the Olive Tree Movement," Transactions of the Royal Asiatic Society, Korea Branch, Vol XLIII (Seoul, 1967), pp. 11-27.

Mun Ch' ŏl-ho, 文哲鎬 , "Komun," 拷問 Hanyang, No. 120 (Feb./ March 1976), pp. 22-29.

153

New Hope Herald, Vol. 1, No. 1, q/4/76.

New York Post, 9/20/76, 11/13/76, 11/20/76, 11/27/76, and
    12/3/76.

New York Times, 9/16/74, 9/17/74, 9/19/74, 9/20/74, 9/22/74,
    12/18/75, 1/11/76, 2/11/76, 2/19/76, 5/25/76, 8/29/76,
    9/16/76, 9/20/76, 10/2/76, 10/25/76, 10/28/76, 10/29/76,
    10/30/76, 11/2/76, 11/5/76, 11/8/76, 11/9/76, 11/10/76,
    11/11/76, 11/13/76, 11/14/76, 11/15/76, 11/16/76, 11/17/76,
    11/21/76, 12/9/76, 12/23/76, 1/8/77, 1/9/77, 1/11/77,
    1/14/77.

New York Post, 9/20/76, 11/13/76, 11/20/76, 11/27/76, and
    12/3/76.

Newsweek, 10/15/73, 6/14/76, 11/22/76 and 2/21/77.

Oregonian, 6/9/76.

Patrick, Ted, with Tom Dulack, Let Our Children Go! (New York,
    1976).

Providence Journal-Bulletin, 10/8/75, 5/16/76, 5/17/76, 5/18/76,
    9/24/76, 10/29/76, 11/8/76, 11/11/76, 11/13/76, 11/14/76,
    11/21/76, 11/30/76, 12/1/76, 12/2/76, 12/5/76, 12/6/76,
    12/15/76, 12/29/76, 12/30/76, 1/1/77, 1/22/77, 2/10/77 and
    2/16/77.

Raab, Earl, "Reverend Moon and the Jews - The San Francisco
    Experience," Congress Monthly (December 1976), pp. 8-12.

Rasmussen, Mark, "How Sun Myung Moon Lures America's Children,"
    McCall's (Sept. 1976), pp. 102-115 and p. 175.

The Reporter Dispatch (White Plains, N.Y.), 5/28/76

Rice, Berkeley, "Messiah from Korea," Psychology Today (January
    1976), pp. 36-47.

_____ ,   "The Pull of Sun Moon," The New York Times
    Magazine, 5/30/76.

Rofes, Eric, "A Couple of Summers," The Harvard Crimson
    (Sept. 30, 1975), pp. 3-4.

Roland, Robert W., Statement to Fraser Committee (1976)

Rudin, James A., Jews and Judaism in Rev. Moon's Divine Principle,
    The American Jewish Committee (Dec. 1976).

Samguk Sagi 三國史記, Koten Kankōkai ed.

The San Antonio Light, 8/31/75 and 9/7/75.

San Kuo Chih, 三國誌, Ch'in-ting ed.

Sargant, William, Battle for the Mind (New York, 1957).

Schmit, Joy, "Three Days at the Capitol," The Way of the World,
    VI: 7 (August, 1975), pp. 110-137.

Segae Kidokkyo T'ongil Sinyŏng Hyŏphoe, 世界基督敎 Wŏlli
    Kangron 原理講論 (Seoul, 1966). 統一神靈協會

Sekai Kirisutokyō Dōitsu Sinrei Kyōkai,
    Atarashii Kyōsanshugi Hihan 新しい共産主義批判 (Tōkyō,

Shirokogorov, S. M., Psychomental Complex of the Tungus (London
    and Shanghai, 1935).

Silverberg, " 'Heavenly Deception,' Rev. Moon's Hard Sell,"
    Present Tense (Autumn 1976), pp. 49-56.

Sin Sa-hun 신사훈, "T'ongilkyo ŭi Chŏngch'ae wa kŭ Bip'an,"
    통일교의 정체와 그 비판 (Lecture held in Seoul,
    May 4, 1975).

Stentzel, James, "Rev. Moon and His Bicentennial Blitz,"
    Christianity and Crisis, Vol. 36, No. 12 (July 19, 1976),
    pp. 173-175.

_____, "South Korean Exposure Bad News for President
    Park,". The Nation (January 22, 1977), pp. 77-80.

Sun Myung Moon, America in God's Providence, Bicentennial God
    Bless America Committee (New York, 1976).

_____, God's Hope for America, Bicentennial God Bless
    American Committee (New York, 1976).

T. K. (Anonymous), Letters from Korea, Translated by David L.
    Swain (New York, 1976).

T'ak Myong-hwan, 卓明煥, Hanguk ŭi Sinhŭng Chongkyo
    韓國의 新興宗敎 (Seoul, 1972).

Time, 11/2/70 and 11/10/75.

155

317

U.S., Congress, House, Committee on International Relations,
    Activities of the Korean Central Intelligence Agency in
    the United States, Part 1, 94th Cong., 2nd Sess., March
    17 and 25, 1976, Stock No. 052-070-03527-7.

Unification Church of America, Sun Myung Moon (New York, 1976).

Union of American Hebrew Congregations, Information Kit on the
    Activities of Sun Myung Moon (August 1976.

Washington Post, 6/29/75, 8/20/75, 8/24/75, 2/15/76, 2/19/76,
    2/29/76, 5/23/76, 5/17/76, 6/7/76, 6/19/76, 6/31/76,
    8/23/76, 10/15/76, 10/17/76, 10/24/76, 10/26/76, 10/27/76,
    10/28/76, 10/29/76, 10/30/76, 11/1/76, 11/2/76, 11/5/76
    11/7/76, 11/12/76, 11/13/76, 11/14/76, 11/15/76, 11/16/76,
    11/22/76, 12/29/76.

Washington Newsworks, September 9-15, 1976.

Washington Star, 11/4/76.

Welch, Holmes, Taoism: The Parting of the Way (Boston, 1957).
Yi Chong-sŏk,   李鍾駟 "Sinhŭng Chonggyo,"   新興宗敎
    Sintonga, No. 72 (Seoul, 1970), pp. 226-249.

Ideology, Conversion and Faith Maintenance in a Korean Sect:
The Case of the Unified Family of Rev. Sun Myung Moon
by Byong-suh Kim

Introduction: Problem and Method

    Ever since the counter-culture youth movement
of the sixties turned into the Woodstock syndrome
of hallucinogenic drugs and rock music, there appeared new interests which expressed themselves in
a variety of Eastern sectarian movements--the Hare
Krishna, Zen Buddhism, the Meher Baba, Soka Gakkai,
and Guru Maharaji Ji. While some of these movements showed significant decline in membership,
organizational strength and religious impact upon
the youths, the Unification Church of Rev. Sun
Myung Moon recently attracted thousands of American
youths and has rapidly developed into a major religious youth movement in American society in a
relatively short period of time. According to Neil
A. Salonen, the President of the Unification Church
of America, there are about 30,000 American

8

followers, including 7,000 core membership of full-time workers in the United States and more than two million followers in over 120 nations in the world (The New Hope Herald, 2/4/76). It is certainly a remarkable growth considering that an active proselytization by Moon in the United States started since 1972.[1]

The primary concern of this paper is to explore some significant structural and psychological sources which may explain such an unusually rapid growth of the Korean Christian sect called the Holy Spirit Association for the Unification of World Christianity which was founded by Sun Myung Moon on May 1, 1954, in Korea.[2]

What accounts for the total commitment of American youths to such a new and relatively unknown Korean sect? What makes them maintain their faith in Sun Myung Moon and his ideology? What makes them leave their homes and live in the Unified Family[3] in the face of denunciations and accusations by some parents and the press? In recent years, numerous articles and columns and documentaries have appeared in major newspapers, journals and on T.V. networks. Most of them have been extremely critical and even cynical of the movement, and many religious groups and individuals rejected the doctrine of the Moon sect as "heretic" and "false."[4]

Rev. Moon's movement, however, should be considered sociologically in terms of a religious group with a particular set of beliefs, values, and practices. One of the best attempts to seek universal elements common to all conventional religions was made by Emile Durkheim as follows:

> *A religion is a unified system of beliefs and practices relative to*

9

> sacred things set apart and forbidden--
> beliefs and practices which unite into
> one single moral community called a
> church all those who adhere to them
> (1965:62).

The Unification Church to its adherents is a system of beliefs, symbols, values and practices which would provide answers to questions about man's nature, purpose, origin, destiny or future. One Moonist[5] stated:

> I found answers and solutions to the
> problems I had by studying the Divine
> Principle. I now understand what true
> love means and I learned how to love
> others as Rev. Moon has shown to us
> (Interview:7/3/75).

One of the top executives of the Church I interviewed recently put it more succinctly this way: "The rapid growth of the Church was due to the fact that God helped us through Rev. Sun Myung Moon. There are two things which made our Church so successful. The first is the Divine Principle, the ideology of our movement, and the second is the leadership of Rev. Moon, who has a special quality to unite us into one family of God" (2/9/76).

Such is the claim, but from a sociological point of view the Unification Church has other significant dimensions which should be investigated and explained in order to understand fully the conversion and faith-maintenance of the Moonists. The unique process of bond-formation of the members of the Unified Family, tactics of proselytization, organized activities such as "street peddling" or "fund-raising" and formal training, interpersonal association in the Unified Family, and rituals for

10

communal solidarity are all important factors for the growth of the Unification Church.

I would also argue that on the structural level, the rise of Moonism is partly the function of the youth's social relations to the larger society. As pointed out by Robert Bellah (1965, 1970, 1974), religion in America once served as a dominant force for societal value-integration but has now turned into a "broken and empty shell." To the youths who are growing up in the relative absence of the spiritual and metaphysical grounding and a highly fragmented society, the Unified Family gives a sense of direction; ability to work with and for others selflessly; and a disciplined, positive life affirmation. I will further argue that their maintenance of faith and loyalty to the Divine Principle and Rev. Moon is mostly the result of the communal solidarity which is formed by communal living as "brothers" and "sisters" banded together with the True Parents[6] in the Unified Family. Their sharing of "secrets" of the Master[7] and participation in street proselytization and fund-raising make them reaffirm their loyalty to the Family. The ritual symbolism of praying in the name of the Father, endless singing of liturgical songs calling for unity with the Father,[8] and being "blessed" in holy matrimony by the True Parents all contribute to the communal solidarity of the Unified Family.

This exploratory case study utilizes the methods of qualitative analysis with an emphasis on participant observation as a major technique of data collection. I believe the best way to learn about a relatively closed sectarian group such as the Unified Family is to get the seat of one's pants dirty in the real world of research, as Robert Park used to say, and to "submit oneself in

11

the company of the members to the daily round of petty contingencies to which they are subject" (Goffman, 1961, ix-x).

I have been closely following the major events of the Unified Family for the past three years. I have had many interviews with staff members, many rank-and-file members, ex-Moonists, as well as the critics of the movement. I have attended numerous formal and informal meetings, lectures, seminars, banquets, and crusades of the Unification Church during the years 1974 to 1976.

All the data collected were sorted on the basis of four basic analytical units: meaning systems, socio-historical settings, activities for proselytization and conversion, and ritual symbolism for communal solidarity.

Phase analysis was employed as a major method for delineating structural and psychological sources in order to make sequential explanations on the three inquiries set forth above (why joined, how became converted, and why remain). It should also be noted that there has been a temporal overlapping of data collection in participant observations, interviews, and analytical work and hence a reconstruction, since I had to reflect back to earlier observational experiences in my later stage of analysis.[9]

The Ideology of Divine Principle and Sun Myung Moon (文鮮明)

The Unified Family movement is based on a belief system called "Divine Principle" (原理講論) which is claimed to be God's truth revealed by Sun Myung Moon. Divine Principle, for the Moonists, is a book of God's new truth, the Completed Testament, about the world, the destiny of man, and the

12

role that the new Messiah is to play. In the General Introduction, the Divine Principle says:

> *With the fullness of time, God sent his messenger to resolve the fundamental questions of life and universe. His name is Sun Myung Moon. . . . The Divine Principle revealed in this book is only part of the new truth. We have recorded here what Sun Myung Moon's disciples have hitherto heard and witnessed. We believe with happy expectation that, as time goes on, deeper parts of the truth will be continually revealed (Divine Principle:16).*

While some scholars like Sin Sa Hoon (申四勳) dismissed the doctrine of Divine Principle as "a sort of socerer's story" (1957:121), So Nam Dong (徐南同), a noted theologian in Korea said, "Divine Principle is the best theological work which has ever been produced in Korea in its imagination, originality and organizational quality" (1970:58). Since this paper does not concern itself with an advocacy or criticism of any doctrine or religious ideology, my discussion will focus on the essence of the Unification Church doctrine as the Moonists believe and how such a belief serves for effective proselytization, conversion, and faith maintenance.[10]

The doctrine of Divine Principle is divided into three parts: the Principle of Creation, the Fall of Man, and the History of Restoration. Young Oon Kim in her recent work, Unification Theology and Christian Thought (1974), an official interpretation of Divine Principle, described the three parts, which may be summarized as follows:

13

Creation

*God created Adam in the image of God and Eve for
Adam to have a happy and perfect life. God bestowed three blessings on Adam and Eve: to be
fruitful (unite with God); multiply (unite with
each other); and have dominion (unite with creation). These three blessings would be completed
on the basis of four positions--God, man, creation
and Kingdom of God on earth. Man was created to
have "spiritual body" and "physical body," and
they both grow together. God also created the
universe to bring joy to men.*

Fall

*Eve was seduced by the Archangel, Lucifer, who en-
vied Adam as His child, yet loved the Archangel as
servant. Gradually, Lucifer drew Eve away from
Adam and "seduced her" and Eve "responded." The
result was the spiritual fall of the Archangel and
Eve by an act of fornication forbidden by God's
design. Eve desired to recover her previous position in God's favor. Feeling that she might re-
verse conditions by making love with Adam--cancel-
ling the act of love with the Archangel--Eve
tempted Adam to behave as her husband. Adam responded and had sexual relations with her prema-
turely, as they were in the period of growth as
brother and sister, not as husband and wife. By
this action, Adam and Eve were cut off from God.
Since that time, all mankind as decendant of Adam
and Eve were also cut off from God.*

Restoration

*God has worked to restore man from the fallen state
since the Fall. In fact, history of man is the
history of restoration. The history of restoration
is divided into three parts: the Old Testament*

14

326

*Age, the New Testament Age, and the Age of Second
Advent--the Completed Testament. From the prehis-
toric age to the time of Abraham through Moses until the time of Milachi, it was a continuous
"prunning" process of indemnity (蕩減) and
restoration (復歸).*

*Finally, God sent Jesus, the Second Adam, the Mes-
siah, to establish the Kingdom on earth. Jesus
was to fulfill the divine mandate given to his
original ancestor; that is, to establish a God-
centered domination. The Second Adam, Jesus,
should have united with a woman in the position of
Eve, married with divine blessing and reared
children who would provide the nucleus for a true
family of God. Man could have been restored to
his original perfection by being "grafted" both
spiritually and bodily into Jesus. But by his
physical death on the Cross, Jesus could not accomplish the mission of restoration both spiritually and physically. He accomplished only the
spiritual side. Jesus is no longer the Son of God
as He failed to accomplish his mission. He does
not have the character of divinity as the doctrine
of Trinity indicates.*

*For the complete restoration both in body and
spirit, there had to be the Second Coming of the
Messiah, the Third Adam. This is the age of the
Second Advent to establish the Kingdom of God on
earth. The new Christ of the Second Advent will
subjugate Satan completely and restore the entire
universe.*

Who is the New Messiah, the Third Adam who
can "subjugate Satan completely and restore the
entire universe"? Divine Principle does not explain who the new Messiah is, though it suggests
the time and the place of the Coming of the Second
Messiah. According to Divine Principle, the

15

entire period of human history, that is, from the
time of Adam to the Second Advent should be calcu-
lated by 6000 years: 2000 years from Adam to
Abraham, 2000 years from Abraham to Jesus, and 2000
years from Jesus to the Second Advent. The end of
World War I was significant, as it marked the beginning of the Age of the Completed Testament. Divine
Principle describes three stages through which the
Second Advent takes place:

> *The first stage was the arrival of the*
> *Lord of the New Age to the world. This*
> *was preceded by the counter-acting force*
> *of Wilhelm I who caused World War I.*
> *The second stage was the start of his*
> *ministry, which was preceded by the*
> *counter-acting force of Hitler who*
> *caused World War II. The third stage*
> *is the initial fulfillment of his mis-*
> *sion, the role of Jacob in the Cosmic*
> *Restoration, which was marked by an*
> *event in 1960. This was preceded by the*
> *counter-acting force of the Communist*
> *regime of the Soviet Union (Divine Prin-*
> *ciple:207).*

The "event in 1960" above refers to the marriage of
Sun Myung Moon to his second wife, Han Hak Cha
(韓鶴子), then only 18 years old and a high
school girl. It is also noteworthy that the end
of World War I, 1918, approximately coincides with
the year Sun Myung Moon was born, 1920.

As to the birthplace of the Second Messiah,
Divine Principle concludes that "the nation of the
East where Christ will come again would be none
other than Korea" (D.P.:520). In order to prove
that Korea is the birthplace of the Second Messiah,
Moon cites the following reasons:

16

*(1) the significance of Korean people's
suffering in preparation to receive the
New Christ during the 40 years of Japanese colonial domination.
(2) the division of Korea by the North
and the South as the providence of God's
restoration, making the land as the
front line facing the power of Satan in
the Communist North Korea.
(3) the Korean national character which
highly values loyalty, filial piety and
virtue, and
(4) the Korean's belief since the 500-
year reign of the Yi Dynasty in the
prophecy that the King of Righteousness
would appear in Korea, according to
"Chong Gam Nock"* (鄭 鑑 錄) *(D.P.:
520-528).*

Is Sun Myung Moon, then, the Second Messiah,
the Third Adam, the Lord of the Second Advent?
Every Moonist I interviewed identified Rev. Moon
as a "prophet." An official statement of the
Church also identified him as a "prophet," saying:

*Sun Myung Moon was born in Korea in
1920. . . . Even as a child he prayed
desperately not just to find a way to
help himself or his family, but to
help his nation and his God. The
answer came on Easter when he was 16
years old. While he was praying on a
mountainside, Jesus Christ appeared to
him and told him that he was called to
be a* Prophet *(NYT:1/1/76).*

Whenever I persisted in asking if Moon were indeed
the Second Messiah, the Moonists would not answer
directly, neither denying nor admitting with a
curious smile. Some other sources, however, show

17

329

that Moon himself has clearly implied that he is "the true olive tree--the New Messiah."[11]

In short, the ideology of Divine Principle is, then, a combination of Biblical millenarianism, which asserts the Unified Family as the fundamental structure of the New Age of the Completed Testament; the Messianic authority of the Third Adam, Rev. Sun Myung Moon (based on Revelation 7:2-4); Korean ethnocentricism (stressing Korea as the promised land and Korean language as the universal language in the New Age[12]); and some Oriental mysticism, such as Chong Gam Nok. Yet, the Divine Principle and the Messianic authority of Sun Myung Moon serve as an ideological corpus of the Unified Family with the potency to regulate, interpret, and create a world view to which several thousand American youths become completely committed. Here, I will discuss how such an ideology functions to attract and convert youths in this society.

Receptivity to the Divine Principle

How one becomes completely committed to a sectarian world view such as the ideology of Divine Principle may be best discussed in terms of various factors which have been successively accumulated, leading to the point of conversion. Some sociologists (G. Swanson, 1964, 1967; Lantenari, 1963; Lofland, 1966; Anthony and Robbins, 1975) focused on an analysis of total societies as related to individuals' involvement with religious movements, emphasizing religious beliefs as a source of social solidarity. Guy E. Swanson, for instance, proposed that the existence of belief in the supernatural will vary in accordance with the contact, or lack of it, with "the society's primodal or constitutional structures" and attachment or alienation from these structures of a larger society (1964: 188-189). Others (Lantenari, 1963; Cohn, 1961) also

18

suggested that millenarian religious movements can
be seen as reactions to oppression and to perceived
threats to cultural systems by forces extrinsic to
society.

In the case of the young Moonists, the involvement in the Unified Family can also be understood, in part, as reflections of their social relations to the larger society.

Most of those whom I interviewed[13] stated
that prior to joining with the Unified Family, they
had felt a keen sense of disappointment and frustration with established institutional arrangements
and processes. Such disappointment and frustration
were consistently expressed, as illustrated in the
following cases:[14]

> *Martha: age 16 when joined, a former
> nursing student, said, "I have a strong
> religious background, as my father is a
> Lutheran minister, and I attended church
> every Sunday. But I felt extremely dis-
> appointed with my church life, mostly
> because there was no true Christian love
> being practiced among members of my
> father's church. From my childhood, I
> always wanted to be a missionary nurse,
> and I found the Divine Principle guid-
> ing me to fulfill my dream, that is, to
> sacrifice myself to love others. I ex-
> perience true Christian love in the Uni-
> fied Family" (Interview, 10/6/75).*

Martha, thus, dropped out of her nursing school and
joined the Church four years ago. She is now 21
years old and working full-time for the Unification
movement, mostly witnessing and fund raising.

19

*Warren: age 25 when joined, a graduate
of Stanford University, explained his
experience this way: "When I entered
Stanford in 1964, I was a Catholic and
quite conservative politically. But
after a couple of years at Stanford, I
became increasingly aware of social in-
justices and joined the radical student
movement, as the people of the left
seemed more concerned about social in-
justices in the world. Then, I got disillusioned with the radicals, as I could
not trust the leadership. They were not
really committed, not really dedicated.
They would talk about revolution, and
then they would drive home in their
fancy sports cars. . . . Later, I began
to read and study mythological works,
the Upanished, etc. . . . Upon graduation, I was accepted at Columbia and at
Berkeley law schools and decided to go
to Berkeley. Then, I found out that
nearly 95% of the graduates went into
corporate law, and I really did not want
to be a lawyer. I did not see how I was
going to help others by becoming a
lawyer. So, I wanted to go abroad to
study more and to find a meaningful
life. Then, I met the Unification
Church . . . ." (Interview, 2/9/76).*

So, Warren has been drifting away from the mainstream of American society in search of a new meaning of life. He could not feel any sense of satisfaction in life even after being educated at one of
the finest institutions in the States. He could not
feel any meaning and direction in life even after
being involved in radical movements for creating
social justices. He is now working full-time without pay for the Unified Family, saying: "Now I

20

332

have found a real happiness."

> *Laura: age 20 when joined, spent three*
> *years in the movement, said: "I was a*
> *secretary at an airline company in L. A.*
> *but could not stand the shallow life of*
> *a secretary. I always had to worry*
> *about my physical appearance in order*
> *to impress others, especially my boss.*
> *I also attended a local church, a*
> *Church of Christ, but could not see it*
> *meaningful, as most of the people were*
> *hypocritical in their everyday life.*
> *One day a guy approached me to intro-*
> *duce me to the Divine Principle. I*
> *went to their center and studied it two,*
> *three times. I studied the Divine Prin-*
> *ciple again and again, and finally the*
> *message changed my life completely. I*
> *now know how to love others fully. I*
> *am no longer worried about my physical*
> *appearance, because now I spend most of*
> *my time for loving others, not myself,*
> *but others. I am happy because I am a*
> *new person" (Interview, 11/7/74).*

In the above cases of Martha, Warren, and
Laura, all of them had had a sense of disappointment
and dissatisfaction with established institutions,
particularly in their religious life. Yet, all of
them professed that they found a meaningful and
happy life in the Unified Family through the Divine
Principle and the teachings of Rev. Moon. They all
stressed that true Christian love is found and
practiced in the Unification Church.

What then is the source of such a negative
feeling toward a total society, especially toward
established religious institutions? As noted
briefly in the beginning of this paper, theories on

21

American Civil Religions (Bellah, 1965, 1970; W. Herberg, 1960) suggested that the fabric of American way of life has been established on the basis of religious beliefs, and the central integrative system of moral value and social order in America was grounded in religious faiths. The established religious institutions, however, no longer provide, in any significant degree, the metaphysical and spiritual grounding which make the value system meaningful in American society. American "civil religion," today, is "an empty and broken shell" (Bellah, 1975:142) and has "lost its pre-eminence" (B. Wilson, 1966:208). Consequently, the fabric of the American way of life has been broken down, and today's youths can no longer find meaning of life in this fragmented, highly impersonal, consumption-oriented, and competitive world.

Some youths, growing up today, feel that they must find a way to reorient themselves and integrate with a meaningful life in the face of fragmented and diffused social situations around them. In the absence of spiritual and metaphysical legitimation of life's purpose, many youths in America are becoming increasingly apathetic, and some feel helpless and directionless. This malaise is the basis of their receptivity to sectarian movements such as the Unification Church, which promises a new direction toward this worldly life affirmation.

The Divine Principle and teachings of Sun Myung Moon seem to give a sense of direction, ability to work with and for others selflessly and disciplined, and positive life affirmation. Those who turn to the ideology of Divine Principle see themselves as "the architects of history" for building the kingdom of God on earth. In the world of selfishness, hypocracy, and impersonal and blase attitudes, the Moonists assert that the Unified Family offers them comfort, warmth, and decisive

22

guidelines of moral principle, a way of meaningful
life in building the kingdom of God on earth.

Functions of Misrepresentation
and Concealment

If Moon considers himself as the "New Messiah"
as his speech indicates, why does he not publicly
declare that he is indeed the true olive tree, the
New Christ, the Third Adam? Why do the Moonists
not admit that they really believe him to be the
Messiah? Is it a barefaced lie and a deception for
effective "brain-washing" as some critics denounce?
After a careful analysis of my documents, interviews
and observation notes, and contents of their worship
services, I came to the conclusion that there exists
a conscious effort to misrepresent the self-identity
of Sun Myung Moon and a deliberate concealment of a
certain portion of Moon's message from public disclosure.

From a social-psychological point of view,
such behavior of concealment or misrepresentation
can be considered as a normal occurrence in our
everyday life. As Erving Goffman (1959) pointed
out, each one of us in the situation of presenting
himself or his activities to others attempts to
guide and control the impressions or reputations
they form of him and uses certain techniques in
order to sustain his performance or to show his
best part. If such control of the audience to whom
one presents himself is an acceptable part of our
daily life, the concealment of some facts by Moon
may also be justified, as it appears that he does
so for the benefit of the audience. The following
conversation that I had with a Moonist may shed some
light on this point:

> I (Interviewer): Who is Rev. Moon?
> M (Moonist): He is a Prophet and a

23

> *great man who is preparing a way for*
> *the Second Coming of Christ.*
> I: *You mean like John the Baptist?*
> M: *Yeh, like John the Baptist.*
> I: *But, some say that he is a Messiah,*
>   *the new Christ.*
> M: *Time will tell. He can be a Mes-*
>   *siah.*
> I: *What do you mean? You are not*
>   *sure, uh?*
> M: *Well, let me put it this way. If I*
>   *say to you everything that I believe*
>   *him to be, you may make a serious*
>   *mistake.*
> I: *What mistake?*
> M: *A grave mistake of misunderstanding*
>   *Reverend Moon!*
> *(Interview with Mike, 8/4/75).*

The above respondent, Mike (27 years old), has been in the movement for three years and became a team leader after going through all of the basic train- ing sessions. Undoubtedly, he is a very loyal mem- ber of the Church, and for him it is only natural to perform the task of a team leader. He firmly believes that his Master "has a remarkable ability to call forth what is highest and best in others." Therefore, to Mike, his misrepresentation of the identity of Rev. Moon is perfectly normal, as it was for me "not to make a grave mistake of misunder- standing Rev. Moon." When the Master spoke at Rowlane Farmhouse on March 16, 1972, it was said:

> *Telling a lie becomes a sin if you tell*
> *it to take advantage of a person, but*
> *if you tell a lie to do a good thing for*
> *him, that is not a sin. Even God tells*
> *a lie very often; you can see this*
> *throughout history. He often says,*
> *"you be patient for a little while*

24

> *. . . just a little while more." So often*
> *telling a lie, God wants to give a far*
> *greater gift to man than man expected:*
> *Perhaps man wants to have national things,*
> *but God wants to give the world.*

The Master often uses such phrases as "now, I reveal secrets" or "I have revealed too much," etc.,
when he speaks to his staff members (cf. Speech,
3/19/72).

In their organizational activities, they use
various nonreligious institutional approaches in
political, industrial, cultural, and academic areas.
While the Church is engaged in the anti-communist
drive mainly through Freedom Leadership Foundation,
a political arm of the Church, Rev. Moon manages to
maintain good relationships with such political
figures as Park Chung Hee and Richard M. Nixon.   In
his speech, Moon said:

> *People may think that President Park*
> *Chung Hee and his regime are not quite*
> *democratic, advancing forward too*
> *strongly; but without being strong he*
> *could not manipulate the nation. It*
> *is done in a way in God's providence*
> *(Speech, 9/29/74).*

Thus, Moon approves Park's dictatorial "manipulation" as he considers it as an order in God's providence to prepare the restoration of mankind.

In the case of the widely publicized "Forgive
Nixon" rally in Washington, D.C., the underlying
motivation seemed to be the proselytization of Moonism. At one point, Moon said, "American history
will have to record my name when the history of
Watergate is written. . . . I have in mind to publish the record of what we have done on the Water-

25

337

gate issue. I might call it 'the Watergate Treasure house' or something like that. We will write many essays and print it in book form and give it to every library all over the world" (Speech, 1/1/74).

Sun Myung Moon later compared his meeting with Nixon at the White House to "the Roman Emperor having invited Jesus and welcomed Jesus in the past" (Speech, 2/14/74). He has specifically emphasized the importance of proselytization among the members of the U.S. Congress. The Unification Church now keeps 16 lobbyists on Capitol Hill, and Moon seems to value the role of women proselytizers in the following way:

> *Master needs many good-looking girls . . . 300. He will assign three girls to one senator . . . that means we need 300. Let them have a good relationship with them. One is for the election, one is to be the diplomat, one is for the party. If our girls are superior to the senators in many ways, then the senators will just be taken by our members (Speech, 5/7/73).*

It is, therefore, evidently clear that in their proselytization process, the Moonists cleverly infiltrate political institutions, mostly by means of their anti-communist drive and maintenance of cordial relationships with the political figures in power.[15]

In the cultural and scientific areas, the Church is very active in indirect proselytization through many "front" organizations, such as international cultural foundations which operate a number of international conferences (e.g., International Conference on the Unity of Science), New York Symphony Orchestra and Ballet Company (Han Son Ballet and Little Angels). They also operate a karate

26

institute and sponsor an athletic festival under the auspices of FLF. All of these cultural, scientific and recreational programs are, in fact, aimed for proselytization of Moonism.

The purpose of such a misrepresentation of the self-identity of Sun Myung Moon, keeping some secret messages from public disclosure and indirect proselytization through "front" organizations, seemed to be designed for those who do not yet understand the Divine Principle, as they think that undisclosed facts make no sense apart from an acceptance and understanding. Or, perhaps, they simply want to avoid the controversy or accusation of being "heretic" by the established churches. As John Lofland observed in his study, Doomsday Cult, they "wanted the entire world to know and accept their ideology, but only certain parts were felt to be appropriate for disclosure to the outsider" (1966:14).

But, if we look at the phenomenon of misrepresentation and concealment more closely from a sociological point of view, we can note that such behavior of shared secrets has a significant function for a group life such as the Unified Family. Such behavior can produce a strong bond of relationship among the members, thus making a united front for an effective proselytization, fund raising and maintenance of their faith. How does it work for such purposes? As George Simmel (1950:330-376) and Goffman (1959:77-105) suggested, an effective bond in a group life is usually produced as a result of "reciprocal dependence" and "reciprocal familiarity." When each member is pressured to rely on the good performance (concealment in this case) of his fellow teammates, they, in turn, are forced on him. "There is then, perforce, a bond of reciprocal dependence linking teammates to one another" (Goffman, 1959:83). Moreover, accomplices in the maintenance

27

339

of a particular secret, they are forced to define one another as persons "in the know." The members of the group in such a situation then tend to be bound by rights of what might be called "familiarity."

The misrepresentation of the identity of Rev. Moon being their New Messiah and the concealment of secret messages of the Master spoken only to the core members of the Unified Family can serve for the formation of a strong bond among them and mystification of the Unified Family. Tightly guarded knowledge shared only by a few financial staffs on the sources and amount of the capital holdings accumulated within the Family and various indirect proselytization tactics furthermore enhance the bond-formation. Such a strong bond of the Moonists and mystification of the life in the Unified Family, in turn, function as a point of attraction for new members when they see the warm, cohesive relationship of "brothers" and "sisters" banded together with deep commitment in the Divine Principle.

Proselytization: Access to the Divine Principle

Obviously, such a general argument on youths' receptivity to the Divine Principle or the functions of misrepresentation and concealment does not explain specifically how each individual becomes a Moonist. Thus, I now turn to a discussion of the specific process of "indoctrination" each recruit goes through from the time of introduction to the Movement to the point of conversion. The data show that generally two different stages are built in the process of indoctrination: induction to Moonism and formal training. Each stage is carefully designed and its contents are laid down according to the formula suggested by Sun Myung Moon and his staff. Various phases of each stage are operation-

28

alized through authoritarian channels of command
which are controlled by Rev. Moon himself.

Access to Moonism is made through many channels, yet most of the Moonists have first been contacted through street proselytization or "witnessing" and contacts with friends. The following
cases of introduction to Moonism may summarize what
usually takes place in the initial recruitment
process.

> Warren: One day while walking in Golden
> Gate Park on my way to school, this Chin-
> ese-American girl came up to me and said,
> "are you interested in a meaningful way
> of life?" I said, "yes." She said, "how
> about an international community where we
> get together and study Principles of Liv-
> ing? Why don't you come over and see?"
> So, then I went over to their center . . .
> The atmosphere was really nice there, I
> could sense it. Then, I went back to the
> center almost every night to hear the
> lectures on the Divine Principle. After
> eight days, I thought, "hmm." I better
> listen to this once again and then I
> really thought that the Divine Principle
> showed me something I was looking for.
> . . . I was interested in truth, in
> meaningful life, and getting together
> with different nationalities transcend-
> ing my own cultural background to become
> a more universal person. It seemed to be
> that God was guiding me to this place, so
> I thought that I better put my effort in
> here. . . .

After three weeks of studying the Divine Principle
at the center, Warren was finally convinced that he
found the "truth" and a meaningful way of life and
moved into the Unified Family.

29

341

*Sam: I was born in a Jewish family. Right
before graduation from Delaware University
with a B.A. in Theatre and Speech, I met an
Austrian girl who attracted me. She said
to me, "Would you want to know about the
science of religion?" Although I was not
so much interested in Judaism, I liked the
movement of Campus Crusade. . . . So, one
day I went to the center where I heard
for the first time about the Divine Principle. But I did not like what I heard
then. This Austrian girl kept calling me
every evening asking me to come back to
hear the lecture again. I went back again
and again without knowing clearly what the
message was about. . . . Then, one day she
persuaded me to attend the three-day workshop where I learned the "truth" and a new
life.*

Sam left home to live in the Principle Family and
now works there full-time as a choir member since
May 1973.

*Lorri: I was studying at Columbia Univer-
sity for my doctorate for about three
years when a friend of mine, an acquaintance who lived in the same dormitory,
stopped in my room and started talking
about this interesting philosophy. . . .
She told me about this interesting
teacher and also that she really liked
the people who were involved, small
groups at the time. . . . I did not go
right away when she asked me, and later
I went and listened with a degree of de-
fensiveness that first night, and much of
that was said was pretty familiar to me--
the interrelationship between God and man
and the universe. I knew all of that from*

30

342

my background (as a Catholic nun). So, I
kind of realized that there was probably
something here. At that period of my
life, I used to think that there had to
be better answers to the questions and
the problems of the world which were get-
ting more and more complex and the churches
were having less and less impact. So, that
was what made me open up and listen. So,
I went there, about twice a week, to listen
to the lectures on the Divine Principle.
It took me for about three months to be im-
pressed by the teaching of the Divine Prin-
ciple--the whole question of the mission of
Jesus, why the world is like this 2000
years later since the coming of Jesus.
The explanations on these questions seemed
very logical, and not mystical, everyday
kind of an understanding. . . .

The above cases of Warren, Sam, and Lorri show
that the primary aim of street proselytization and
contacts with friends is to attract and persuade the
recruits to attend the induction lectures. Yet, as
discussed earlier, the friendly and cohesive interpersonal relations of the Family members usually
impress the recruits most, as they (recruits)
"really liked the people who were involved" (Lorri),
and felt the atmosphere "really nice" (Warren). The
above cited cases indicate that induction lectures
are not immediately effective, but impressed them
as "something worthwhile to listen to again." As
Terry described it, the induction lectures have a
strong appearance of logical explanation on the
universal history. The lectures are usually divided
into three parts: the Principle of Creation, the
Fall of Man, and the History of Restoration. They
use charts and graphs for numerical illustrations
and quotes from various sources ranging from theological figures like Schweitzer, Barth, Brunner or
other scientists especially who have participated

31.

343

in the International Conference on the Unity of the Sciences.[16] Those who have attended the lecture series described above usually receive telephone calls, greeting cards, and various kinds of published materials, urging those potential converts to attend the formal training sessions, services, and crusades.

Although a major recruitment of potential converts is made through street proselytization and contacts with acquaintances as discussed earlier, various channels of access to Moonism are also provided through organized activities in the political, cultural, and economic institutional settings.

Perhaps, one of the most significant indirect proselytization efforts is made through "street peddling" or "fund raising" activities. Although fundraising is primarily for economic self-sufficiency for the Unified Family, most Moonists I interviewed indicated that it is a form of "witnessing," while ex-Moonists and the critics accuse Moon of exploiting the youths by means of "street peddling." The meaning of such an activity perceived by the Moonists may be summarized by the following statement of a Moonist:

> When I am assigned to go out for fund-
> raising, I do the job gladly. I usually
> make about $120 a day working for about
> 10 to 11 hours. I am happy to earn money
> for the center or whatever project we work
> for. At the moment we are trying to raise
> money for setting up a university at
> Terrytown. I do not receive any salary
> or spending money, because I don't need
> any money. When I need some spending
> money, I can always ask for it. But I
> never keep any money, because I am very
> content with what I have now. You see,

32

344

*I can actualize my own self without
selfish motivation. Fund-raising is
one way of showing others that I love
them selflessly (Interview, 10/7/76).*

While they are engaged in fund-raising activities,
mostly by selling flowers, candles, and other small
items like candies and Gin-Seng tea, indirect proselytization as well as their reaffirmation of commitment to Moonism become intensified. When potential converts are recruited, then they are encouraged to participate in more structured programs of
the formal training sessions.

Formal Training and "Brain-Washing" Controversy

The Unification Church operates a system of
seven stages of formal training programs: 3-day,
7-day, 21-day, 40-day, 120-day, 6 months, and 12
months. It also established a theological seminary
to train 55 future cadre of the Unified Family who
were carefully selected by Rev. Moon himself from
500 candidates. These various levels of the formal
training sessions are designed for the purpose of
"correcting the ways of thinking" on the basis of
the Divine Principle (cf. Moon's Speech, 5/7/75).

A typical first-level training, three-day
workshop usually consists of lectures (about eight
to nine hours a day), constant songs, prayers (about
five hours), and other controlled group activities
from 7 a.m. to 11 p.m. The lecture is entirely on
the Divine Principle, an endless monologue of the
lecturer who does not allow participants to inter-
rupt for questions or clarification. It is like a
non-stop drill of listening to the lectures filled
with various concepts used in the Divine Principle
such as "indemnity," "restoration," "grafting into
the Father," "spiritual parents," "True Parents,"
etc. Undoubtedly, the workshop leaves a strong

33

impression of a tightly controlled programming of a religious experience.

In the training sessions of longer periods than the three-day workshop, the trainees are required to go out for street proselytization and "street peddling" or "fund raising." These activities are very significant as they serve for the trainees as a mechanism of commitment to the Unified Family. While they are out on the street for "witnessing," they also learn how to perceive their experiences in the appropriate frame of reference of the Divine Principle.

In the final stage of short-term training (120 days), "deeper" knowledge of the Unified Family is instructed by Ken Sudo[17] as follows:

> *Life in the Unification Church is far different from Christian life or life in the Old Testament Age--because we have the Messiah living with us. . . . In Korea sometimes those who were in a responsible position equivalent to regional commanders sometimes, gave the same sermon that Father gave in Seoul at the same time on the same morning without any information (without prior notice?), because they had a sudden revelation. . . . We must know that we must witness, we must raise money, many things. . . . Therefore, be obedient to Father's desire and do more than he requires. . . . The fact we can attend (or serve) him must be the most precious event in our lives. . . . We can be a true son or daughter of Heavenly Father, not an adopted son or adopted daughter, but lineal son or daughter of True Parents and eternal joy will be given to us.*

34

It is, therefore, clear that in the advanced stage
of the training the Messianic authority of Sun
Myung Moon becomes a focal point of the instruction.
According to the director of the formal training
programs, Ken Sudo, all of the contents of the
training sessions are designed in accordance with
the "decision of the Father." He described it as
follows:

> Then Father said, "make a pattern of edu-
> cation and revitalize America." . . .
> Next I asked Father, "what should I do?"
> We talked about many things; the key
> point was to give advice on how to estab-
> lish new tradition, heavenly tradition.
> . . . Then, based on Father's words, I
> began to think and pray. And 3-day
> workshop, 7-day workshop, 21-day train-
> ing session, and I am planning the 120-
> day training session even now. I am
> planning the administration of the 120-
> day training session. It's a terrible
> one, a terrible training session. You
> will be scared. When you pass through
> this course, then you will be the
> strongest leader in America (p. 154).

While one-third of the 3-day workshop participants
are usually advanced to the next stage, once you
reach the 120-day level, nearly all of the trainees
become full-time staff of the Unified Family. They
will then be selected to be further trained to become leaders--regional commanders or Seminarians.

Is it then a process of brain-washing or mind-
controlling? Recently, Sun Myung Moon has been accused of "brain-washing" or "mind-controlling" of
young people by some parents of the Moonists and
the critics of the Unification Church. A Baptist
minister, for instance, charged that his daughter

35

was "under the 'hypnotic mind-control' of the Moonies for six months" (Star Ledger, 10/1/75). A former lecturer of the workshop, who left the Family, stated:

> They give four or five hours of lecture on the Principle every morning and afternoon. It is not really to teach the Divine Principle, but to empty your brains out and confuse you. They are trying to make you see that their picture of the world is real, and the former picture (of yours) is unreal. This is an absolutely intentional design. It wears you down, and at the same time it builds up your pride; that is, they want to build up a sense of pride that you've gone through this. It's like a primitive initiation rite. The more intense the initiation rite is, the more that the people who went through it tend to be bound to the group (Interview, 3/27/76).

The critics point out that isolation of the participants from the past life situation, mingling them with the smiling and kind Moonists, exposing them to a new authority figure, wearing them down physically and mentally, and then lecturing them with new beliefs all produce effects of "mind-controlling" among those who are not emotionally and physically strong enough for resistance. Some panic-ridden parents even hire a "deprogramming expert" named Ted Patrick, willingly paying $1,500 plus expenses for the "recovery" of their children (The Record of Bergen County, 1/28/76; NYT, 2/11/76).

To these allegations, the Unification Church officially responded, stating that "Reverend Moon's messages have <u>inspired</u> so many intelligent, creative young people to joyfully dedicate their lives

36

to serve God and their fellow men" (NYT, 2/19/76).
In an official newsletter of the Church, they
stated:

> *Because of the dramatic transformation in
> the lives of his followers, some people
> have accused Reverend Moon of using tech-
> niques of mind control or brainwashing to
> gain disciples. No doubt racial stereo-
> types of Orientals play a role in these
> allegations. However, the success of
> Reverend Moon does not lie in such tech-
> niques. Indeed, when opponents of the
> Church tried legally to prove such ac-
> cusations (Helander v. Unification Church,
> Superior Court of the District of Colum-
> bia), their case against the Church was
> dismissed! In that sense, the Court
> ruled:*

> *". . . the evidence of record is insuf-
> ficient to establish the application by
> respondents (the Church) to Miss Helander
> of any techniques substantially different
> from those which are used by other re-
> ligious organizations for purposes of
> converting or proselytizing."*

Whether becoming a Moonist is a result of
"brain-washing" and "mind-controlling" or "inspiration" by the message of Rev. Moon, one thing is
clear; that is, a significant number of the participants in the workshop are being converted to
Moonism.

Conversion here is broadly understood as a
radical change of an individual's world view, resulting in an abandonment of his previously held
perspectives of the world or reintegrating of one's
self. It is a fundamental change of one's self-

37

349

identity, thus making him confess, "I am a completely new person." What then is the process of such a conversion? The problem of how an individual experiences a conversion has been previously discussed in the works of Lofland and Stark (1975), Lofland (1966), Gerlach and Hine (1970), Tokie S. Lebra (1972). John Lofland, for instance, suggested a model of seven accumulating conditions in his study of a "millenarian cult" as follows (1966: 7-8):

> *For conversion a person must:*
>
> 1. *Experience enduring, acutely felt tensions*
> 2. *Within a religious problem-solving perspective*
> 3. *Which leads him to define himself as a religious seeker*
> 4. *Encountering the D.P. (a religious ideology) at a turning point in life*
> 5. *Wherein an affective bond is formed (or pre-exists) with one or more converts*
> 6. *Where extra-cult attachments are low or neutralized*
> 7. *And, where he is to become a deployable agent, he is exposed to intensive interaction.*

While Lofland's model is useful for a micro-analysis of individual converts, it is very difficult to generalize that all of the seven conditions are, indeed, "necessary and constellationally sufficient" for the Moonists to have conversion experiences. Most Moonists I interviewed, in fact, denied that they had any "acutely felt tensions" or "religious solving purpose." Whatever conditions one is faced with, the potential convert usually develops a state

38

350

of receptivity to a sectism. Then, after going
through a preliminary process of introductory lectures, he begins to attain a conversion experience
in specific, formally organized training sessions.
Perhaps, such a process may best be described in
terms of "desocialization" and "resocialization."

According to William Lambert (1964:9), "to
desocialize a man to the point where he can be
fundamentally changed requires control of the great
social structures that help keep him what he is."
The process of "desocialization" then is to neutralize or eliminate the effects of the previously held
beliefs or the previous socialization in general in
order to "resocialize" him by making him internal-
ize a new set of values and beliefs so that he can
formulate a new self-identity. Unlike the process
of brain-washing which is constantly relying on
coercion, confinement and compulsory techniques,
"desocialization" and "resocialization" can take
place in the absence of such a coercive method.[18]

No evidence of use of coercion or compulsory
techniques was found in the Moonist training sessions. The recruit voluntarily complies with a
tightly organized training session and subscribes
to a new set of beliefs by individual decision. Of
course, one might argue that, from a psychological
point of view, the effect of compulsory techniques
can be resulted from such a tightly controlled
training session of the Unification Church. It is,
however, clear that any process of conversion to
religion or political ideology employs such latent
techniques of "desocialization" and "resocialization."

Rituals and Communal Solidarity of
the Unified Family

The ultimate mission of the Unification Church
movement, according to Sun Myung Moon, is to restore

39

351

mankind from the "fallen nature" and to build a unified, harmonious Family of God. Sun Myung Moon explains his role in the Unified Family this way:

> *So far in the universe, no central parents*
> *have existed. We have only had false par-*
> *ents, who brought the elements of distrust*
> *and betrayal day in and day out. There-*
> *fore, there have been no true brothers and*
> *sisters, and no true husband and wife.*
> *True parents were not there, and true sin-*
> *less children were not there. In other*
> *words, the heavenly family was lost. . . .*
> *Mankind, throughout history, has been*
> *blind, not knowing why they lived, where*
> *they came from, or where they are going*
> *. . . Why? Because they did not have one*
> *central point--true parents as their true*
> *ancesters. You now know the central point*
> *of this universe, the True Parents; from*
> *this central point, as an axis or start-*
> *ing point, you cannot only understand, but*
> *you are given the power to win that past,*
> *present, and future with yourself as the*
> *central dwelling point. You inherit the*
> *True Parents. Since you have True Parents,*
> *you have models to imitate. The True Par-*
> *ents are in the position of models of per-*
> *fection. . . . So you are receiving and*
> *sharing the perfection as the True Parents.*
> *Look up Father saying, "Everything that he*
> *does, I am going to do; I am even going to*
> *look like him, walk like him, and smile*
> *like him" (Speech, 3/24/74).*

The above statement of Moon makes it clear that a
communal solidarity in the Unified Family under the
True Parents is, indeed, the "central point" of his
movement. As discussed earlier, the alienated
youth, without being yet fully integrated into the

40

occupational sphere, tends to develop an intensi-
fied need for communal living. Thus, they join the
Unified Family, pledging their loyalty to the True
Parents, Sun Myung Moon and his "Heavenly Bride."[19]
Since Moon emerged as the Spiritual Father of the
Unified Family, an absolute authority was firmly
established for the fallen men to be fully restored.
The Spiritual Father is the source of unity and
harmony of the Family of his spiritual children, the
Moonists. The communal solidarity under the True
Parents is intensified and maintained through group
prayer and singing which are constantly repeated in
the form of liturgical ritual.

Solidarity Through Praying
and Singing

As the Moonists pray and sing, the theme of
"Father" is most frequently repeated. In a group
prayer, for instance, they start with the word
"Father" by the leader, and then it is repeated
loudly by the followers in an anguished unison,
sometimes repeating more than fifty times in a
prayer, as illustrated in a prayer given at a meeting by Mrs. Won Bok Choi, an interpreter for Rev.
Moon, the Father. In her prayer,[20] Mrs. Choi
called "Father" 52 times mostly to express gratitude (11 times), to ask help (6 times), to affirm
good works through Father's love (5 times), to
recognize Father's work (8 times), to ask help for
others (4 times), to pledge to fight for Him (5
times), and to express a complete trust in Father
(2 times). Frequently, the prayer is closed by
saying, "in the precious name of our beloved True
Parents, Amen."

The concept of "Father" is also clearly expressed in many of their hymns and group songs. The
following song is most frequently used in the formal training sessions:

41

353

> *Father, make me a rainbow to bring old and*
> *new,*
> *Father, make me a gateway for many to come*
> *through.*
> *Father, you are the sunlight in a very*
> *dark land,*
> *Father, make me a prism held in your hand.*

This song is a liturgy for them to ask the Father
to make them a beautiful rainbow for togetherness
of the rainy past and sunshining present, a gateway
for successful proselytization, sunlight in the
dark world, and the Father's hand works as a useful
"prism."

In most of the Moonists' gatherings, either
for a formal service or informal proselytization
meetings, singing together of such liturgical songs
is usually repeated several times for about one
hour. The songs most frequently used in their
group activities are all clearly expressing a reaffirmation of their beliefs in the Divine Principle
and their loyalty to the True Parents. In Durk-
heimean sense, it is symbolic representation of the
social reality of the Unified Family. The following song is the most popular and very frequently
sung in all sorts of meetings:

> *The Father's dwelling place is the foun-*
> *tain of our life.*
> *Drawn to the light of eternal day, we*
> *abandon the darkness.*
> *May the word of God in my heart resound-*
> *So, eternally, to receive- His love.*
> *We shall be His pride and delight, Child-*
> *ren of the living God,*
> *Into the World of Eden regained, Let's go*
> *marching together!*

Whenever the Moonists sing this song together, it is
usually repeated several times continuously with

42

354

rhythmical body motion. Each verse ends with an emphasis of "togetherness"--Let's go marching together/Let's go singing together/Let's go dancing together! These were repeated again and again.

The most recently published song book, Holy Song, of the Unification Church includes two Korean songs among 56 highly selected "most inspiring" songs. They are Tan Shim Ga (Song of Heart's Pledge)[21] and Urie So Wonun Tongil (Our Wish is Unity). Tan Shim Ga is one of the most widely recited sicho poems written by Chong Mong Ju (郭夢周) in expression of his undivided loyalty to his king. Urie So Wonun Tongil[22] is a most popular Kuk Min Kayo (People's song) which is included in the public school song book. The theme of the song is the unification of the Korean peninsula, yet the Moon church adapted it to inspire unity of the Principle Family.

Undoubtedly, singing of the above song is intended to enhance the communal solidarity. The verses do not indicate religious meaning, yet they serve the purpose--Unity and Solidarity! As noted earlier, the songs like "Rainbow Song," "The Father's Dwelling Place," "My Heart's Pledge," and "Song of Unity" are all used in the Unification Church as a form of liturgical ritual, for they all clearly express the idea of unity of the Unified Family. Repeated practices of such liturgical singing produce emotionality, dramatic symbolism of unity, and living immediacy to the ideology of Moon. Through the ritual of prayer and singing in group, a communal solidarity becomes intensified, thus creating a solidifying atmosphere for the Moonists to be influenced and remain in the Unified Family.

43

Solidarity Through "Holy Matrimony"

One of the most widely publicized events the
Unification Church had was mass wedding ceremonies.
Since their holy marriage in 1960, the True Parents,
Rev. Moon and his Heavenly Bride, have successively
conducted mass weddings for 3, 36, 72, 124, 430,
790 and 1,800 couples in Korea, the motherland of
the New Messiah. Being blessed in holy matrimony
by the spiritual Father and Mother, according to
Moonism, signifies the final stage of restoration,
the way of "grafting" into the true olive tree and
sharing the richness of the true olive tree--the New
Messiah (Speech, 3/29/72). The process of such a
restoration through holy matrimony is based on the
explicit guidelines set forth by the Father on the
proper relationship between man and woman, the
spouse selection, and post-marital abstinence of
sexual relations. I shall now briefly summarize
each of these guidelines leading to holy matrimony
and elaborate specifically the function of the ritual of mass weddings.

In the man-woman relationship, sexual purity
is a very important character one should have in
order to be "blessed" by the spiritual Father.
Moon said, "If you have any rumor or scandal between man and woman, you will never be blessed together. . . . You must be thorough and absolute
about that. I am strict about this because the
Divine Principle teaches us that" (Speech, 5/20/73).
Those who have lost virginity before joining the
church, Moon teaches, "must repent and try to keep
purity from then on." If one fails in keeping his
or her purity by "being distracted and set eyes on
other males or females, they can never be for-
given." In the Unified Family, one should follow
or promise to conform to such a rigid guideline of
the man-woman relationship in order to be "blessed"
by the Father. Such a guideline is firmly grounded,

44

according to Moonism, in the Divine Principle which explains how Eve fell by having sexual relations with the Archangel and later with Adam, as discussed earlier in this paper.

If one can prove that he or she is capable of following the guideline by serving in the Unification Church for the period of a minimum of three years, then he/she is qualified to be matched with a spouse by the Father himself. The procedure of Rev. Moon's match-making has been consistently explained by the following top leaders of the Church.

> *Mrs. T. S. who was matched by Rev. Moon with a man whom she did not know well said:*

> *I think this is the way the match-making generally works for most people. They had been in the church for the required period of time, three years, with some exceptions. Through prayer, self-examination and confrontation with others, they decide to take on the additional responsibilities and opportunities to go into a marital relationship. Then, go to Rev. Moon to be matched with an ideal spouse. In my case, Rev. Moon knew me well because I had been in the church for a while. One day at a meeting, Rev. Moon called me aside and introduced this man (my husband) whom I hardly knew, saying, "It would be good for you two to marry!" So, we thought about it and decided to get married (Interview, 2/2/76).*

Mrs. T. S. was married to the man Rev. Moon matched, being "blessed" along with matched couples (a total of 1,800 couples) by the True Parents in Seoul in February 1975.

45

M. W., also matched by the Father with a woman
Moonist whom he hardly knew, explained the process
this way:

> *First of all, I think, each situation is*
> *different. Generally, those who were mar-*
> *ried in Seoul last year had been matched*
> *by Rev. Moon through the following proced-*
> *ure. They had to be members of the Church*
> *in good standing. They all, first of all,*
> *had to want to get through marriage as Rev.*
> *Moon described. Then, you fill out the*
> *forms and records. Finally, when the*
> *people who filed the forms got together,*
> *Rev. Moon matched them on the basis of his*
> *knowledge of them. What shall I say, a*
> *market-place of match-making? Of course,*
> *he did not match them all, the 1,800*
> *couples, at the same time at the same*
> *place. If some individual wanted to get*
> *married with any particular person, Rev.*
> *Moon would say either "good" or "it's*
> *not so good." Then, he would say, "How*
> *about this one?" In each case, the*
> *matched couple was asked to go in a room*
> *to talk it over and returned to report*
> *to Rev. Moon how they felt about the*
> *match. If the couple did not like it,*
> *then he would suggest another match, and*
> *so on (Interview, 2/2/75).*

The above described match-making process is regarded by the Moonists as the most ideal form of
spouse selection, because they have complete confidence in Rev. Moon's judgment.

Once couples were matched, the ceremony of holy
matrimony took place without delay, thus completing
the unity with the Unified Family. Moon said, "for
those of you who are blessed, you are not in the

46

position of the dead Jesus now, because you are blessed. You are in the position of Jesus having come again to restore the tribe" (Speech, 12/27/72). Although those who were "blessed" are considered to be in the position of the Second Messiah, the guideline further requires a certain period of abstinence from sexual relationships. In Moonism, a sexual relationship has two sides--spiritual and physical. After being blessed, a couple must first restore a clean spiritual relationship before a physical relationship takes place. The "blessed" couples, therefore, are required to observe complete abstinence from a physical relationship while they purify their spiritual relationship. The guideline also indicates that if a bride is 35 years old or older, the period of separation is 40 days (a perfect number!) and all others have to go through a 21-month separation. Why is such a rigid rule of separation imposed on young married couples? A Moonist leader who is now in the period of separation explains it this way:

> Our marriage is for God. First thing is then I have to learn to respect my wife and she has to learn to respect me. I have to see her not only as my wife but as a daughter of God. She has some mission for God. She has to see me in terms of that, not just that she is good for me and I am good for her. . . . Through this separation, we can really build foundation of family spiritually on which to value our marriage. I am sure at the end of this difficult period of separation there will be a more solid foundation. . . . The point is Adam and Eve had a sexual intercourse prematurely and became sinful. What we are doing (through this separation) is indemnifying. So, now what we are doing is making up for the mistakes of other

47

359

*people and setting a spiritual condition
(Interview, 2/2/76).*

To this Moonist, holy matrimony is not only a vehicle of his own restoration, but also a way of paying an indemnity for the mistakes of other people. Marriage is, therefore, considered as a mission for God rather than for the happiness of individual couples.

Holy matrimony is, undoubtedly, a ritual process through which an individual member publicly reaffirms his faith in the unification ideology and his loyalty to the True Parents of the Unified Family. Accordingly, such a public affirmation can also promote his in-group status in the Unification Church. Moreover, the mysterious experience of being "blessed" by the True Parents in such a mass wedding could be taken as personal evidence of Messianic authority. It is also in a way the rite of passage to the final stage of restoration of himself as well as fulfilling God's mission.

In sum, the ritual of group prayer, liturgical singing, and holy matrimony is a basic human language by which the Moonists maintain their meaningful interaction with one another. When the Moonists felt frustrated by contingencies beyond their control, rituals functioned to purge them of divisive motives and conflicting roles within the Unified Family. Such ritual symbolism "can unite the organic with the social moral order, proclaiming their ultimate religious unity over and above conflicts between and within these orders" (V. Turner, 1969:52). The rituals, then, represent the whole cosmic order recognized by the Moonists in its harmony and balance, "wherein all empirical contradictions are mystically resolved" (Turner, 1969: 55).

48

Summary and Conclusion

The central ideological foundation of the Unification Church is the Divine Principle of Sun Myung Moon. For the Moonists, the Divine Principle is the only ideology which can unite the world and fulfill the restoration of mankind from the fallen nature. The ideology of the Divine Principle is basically a combination of some Biblical sources, especially from the book of Revelation, the Oriental philosophy of Yin and Yang (陰陽), Korean ethnocentricism, and a mystical element of a Korean legend in Chong Gam Nok (鄭鑑錄), and the appearance of a logical or scientific explanation of world history. The Moonists firmly believe that Sun Myung Moon, born in Korea in 1920, is, indeed, the Messiah, the Second Coming of Christ who can unite mankind and bring about the complete restoration of the universe. They believe that together with their spiritual Father, they can build the Kingdom of God on earth, the Unified Family of the world.

Such an involvement of youths in the Unification Church may be understood in part as reflections of their social relations to the larger society. Religion in America, which used to provide the metaphysical grounding for the fabric of American society, is now "a broken and empty shell." It no longer serves as a central integrative system of moral values and social order in America, and the result is a radical secularization of the overall meaning system and a disillusionment with and the loss of faith in the established institutions. Consequently, youths today in their social marginality are increasingly being apathetic, disappointed and frustrated, feeling helpless and directionless in a milieu of fragmented society. But they also realize that somehow they must find a way to reorient and integrate themselves toward a

49

meaningful life in this world. Thus, some of the youths turn to Moonism, which promises that the Unified Family can offer them a new way of life, true meaning of love, a sense of life's direction, with a set of explicit guidelines and this worldly life affirmation in building the Kingdom of God on earth.

In what is perceived as the world of selfish competition, hypocrisy and impersonality, the Unified Family indeed offers the youths a shelter of selfless loving kindness, warm interpersonal relationships and a positive outlook into the future. Such an attractive offer is made through systematic and well-organized proselytization programs of street witnessing, fund raising, lectures, formal training and other cultural and academic activities. Undoubtedly, the process of indoctrination resembles the process of "brain-washing" or "mind-controlling," because the formal training sessions are conducted on the tightly controlled schedule with endless lectures, praying, singing and "witnessing" and "street peddling," coupled with physical and mental fatigue. It is, however, clear that an absence of coercion and confinement by force makes it a process of "desocialization" and "resocialization" like any other process of conversion into a religious belief system or political ideology.

Once they accept the Divine Principle as the way of meaningful life and become members of the Unified Family, they share the "family secrets" regarding the true identity of Moon as the Second Messiah, the Lord of the Second Advent, secret messages of their Master, and, for some, the sources and amount of the enormous capital accumulated in the Church's financial organizations. Such a sharing of secrets and concealment of their secrets can

50

serve for strengthening the communal solidarity,
making their effective proselytization and faith
maintenance possible.

They also engage in the ritual of prayer and
liturgical singing, reaffirming their loyalty to
the Father and confirming the behavioral guidelines
set forth by the Father. Those who are in good
standing can be matched by the Father to be
"blessed" in holy matrimony, thus completing the
process of grafting into the good olive tree--the
Messiah. These ritual behaviors significantly contribute to the communal solidarity of the Moonists
in the Unified Family. Once such a strong bond of
"brothers" and "sisters" with the True Parents was
solidified, it is, of course, extremely difficult
to break away from it.

Fear of being isolated from the warm fraternal
group, the memory of frustration and disappointment
in their past relations with the total society, and
a constant barrage of words of condemnation towards
those who left the movement make the Moonists stay
in the Family. For some doubtful Moonists, faith-
maintenance could also mean simply a patient waiting for "something better to come" or for the
spiritual growth which enables them to understand
the Divine Principle better. An ex-Moonist put it
this way: "I have waited and waited and waited for
the day when I can grow fully in spirit so that I
could understand the Divine Principle more clearly.
Yet, the 'day of growth' never came and I gave up
after seven and a half years of hard working for
'indemnity'" (Interview, 3/27/76).

Today, the Unification Church in Korea is only
one of 302 religious sects flourishing in South
Korea.[23] But, the uniqueness of the Unified Family
movement with 300,000 Korean adherents is in its
"church-type" organization and utilization of

51

scientific knowledge and technique of propaganda
and public relations for proselytization of their
ideology of Divine Principle. Such an effective
proselytization of the Unification Church is backed
by healthy financial foundation and political institutional support. Therefore, while it is very
difficult to predict what will happen to the Unified Family movement in the future, one thing
seemed clear, that is, the Unification Church as a
social institution with such a well organized, systematic approach in educational, cultural and economic spheres of life will not die away easily.

52

<u>Notes</u>

1. The first missionary of the Unification Church
    in the United States was Young Oon Kim, who
    started her proselytization of the Divine Prin-
    ciple in 1958 in Bay City on the Pacific coast
    (See Lofland, 1966:4-5). Rev. Moon visited the
    United States in 1965 and 1968; yet, the first
    speaking tour in seven major cities was con-
    ducted in 1972, followed by a 21-city tour in
    1973, a 32-city tour, and an 8-city tour, com-
    mencing in Madison Square Gardens in the fall
    of 1974.

2. For a detailed chronological description of the
    Church's development from its foundation, see
    <u>Information</u> (案内), a booklet published by
    the Unification Church of Korea in 1975.

3. The Unified Family, sometimes called the Prin-
    ciple Family, is the fundamental structure of
    the Unification Church. It represents a uni-
    versal family of mankind who is saved and re-
    stored by uniting with the Second Messiah, the
    "true olive tree." See, <u>What is the Principle
    of Unity?</u> (統一原理란 무엇인가?) published
    by the Department of Evangelism, the Unifica-
    tion Church of Korea, 1975, p. 2.

4. The Council of the Christian Churches of the
    City of New York, for instance, twice turned
    down the membership application of the Unifi-
    cation Church, stating that "Mr. Moon's doc-
    trines--particularly those concerning Christ
    and salvation--were too far removed from ac-
    ceptable thought" (NYT, 6/23/75). In Korea
    and Japan, many notable theologians severely
    criticized the Unification doctrine as "heretic"
    and "false" (See Sin Sa Hoon, 1957; Tak Myung
    Kwan, 1972; Arai Arao, <u>Madness of Japan</u>, 1975).

53

5. Those who criticize the Unified Family usually call the members of the Unification Church "Moonies," which, I think, has a connotation of deviance in the cynical sense of the word. I use the term "Moonist" to refer to anyone who publicly admits that he or she is a member of the Unified Family, just like any other religious believers are labeled "Methodists" or "Buddhists," etc.

6. Sun Myung Moon and his wife, Han Hak Cha, are called by the Moonists the True Parents. The identity of Moon and his wife being the True Parents came into being in the year 1960 when the then 40-year-old (a perfect number!) Moon married his 18-year-old "Heavenly Bride," a pure "lamb," Han Hak Ja. Moon speaks of his own "Holy Matrimony" as follows:

    Fourteen years after I began my public ministry in 1960, I performed the holy wedding--the wedding of the Lamb, that the Bible predicted. There the first heavenly family was established upon the earth. That was equivalent in significance to the very moment of the crucifixion of Jesus. . . . I consummated the heavenly plan. This was the most historical day in the history of God. This was the day that the Heavenly Son came to earth, restored the base, and welcomed the first Bride of Heaven. . . . Jesus died on the cross before he was able to restore his bride. Therefore, the base was not found upon the earth--this was restored in 1960 by having one Heavenly Bride restored on the earth (Speech on 7/1/73).

7. "Master" is the term frequently used by Sun Myung Moon when he calls himself in the third person.

54

8.   "Father" refers to Sun Myung Moon.

9.   I had a great deal of problems in obtaining
     reliable data, in being accepted as one of the
     "well motivated" without disguising my iden-
     tity as a researcher, and in interpreting con-
     tradicting sources of data. All of the data
     used in this paper, however, were confirmed by
     other reliable observers or participants.

10. Sun Myung Moon himself stated the significance
     and importance of the Divine Principle this
     way: "The Divine Principle is the measure of
     the way--the guide--that will take us through
     the way to reach God, and to the original po-
     sition. Without going through this way, the
     fallen man cannot reach the original position
     . . . in light of the Principle, we know the
     relationship between God and ourselves and
     ourselves and the universe" (Speech, 5/17/73).

11. The fact that Moon considers himself as the
     New Messiah was spoken in the following speech:
     "In the New Testament there is the parable of
     the wild olive tree and the true olive tree.
     Of course, the wild olive tree is a symbolic
     expressing for the fallen generation, and the
     true olive tree is the coming Christ. . . .
     Therefore, it is our destiny to be grafted to
     the true olive tree--the Messiah. . . . In
     Korea, many levels of restitution have been
     made: individual level, family level, tribal
     level, national level, and international
     level. The expansion of this level is now be-
     ing done, and the process of grafting to the
     true olive tree is now being done just at this
     moment on a world wide scale" (3/19/72). As
     discussed earlier, Moon's marriage in 1960 is
     the first level of grafting and then many

55

couples were grafted into the New Messiah
through the mass wedding.

12. In the Korean version of the Divine Principle
(原理講論), Moon revealed that Korean language will become the universal language in
this way: "What then is the unifying language?
The answer is obvious. It is natural that
children learn the language of their parents.
If it is correct that the Second Advent of
Jesus takes place in Korea, the Second Jesus
definitely uses Korean, and it will be then
the mother tongue. Accordingly, all the
people in the world will have to use this language of the mother land of the Second Jesus.
Then, mankind will unite into one people using
one language" (Wolli Kangnon, pp. 555-556).
Strangely, this verse was omitted from the
English version (1974).

13. I interviewed a total of 72 Moonists and observed and had discussion with more than 300
youths in group meetings. Most of them were
18 to 30 years of age, except a few staff members. Nearly all of them had some college,
although not many of them graduated. Most of
the Moonists from abroad were Japanese and
Western Europeans; strangely none were Korean
except those who belong to the Han Son Muyong
Dan (one of the two famous ballet companies
the Church has). The Korean dancers came especially for the event to be held in Yankee
Stadium on June 1, 1976--the Bicentennial God
Bless America Festival.

14. All the names in this paper have been changed
for the purpose of anonymity.

15. It was reported that a girl named Susan Bergman

56

the daughter of a Westbury, L. I., dentist and
a graduate of Cornell University, had been
assigned to Speaker Carl Albert. She usually
visited him several times a week, bringing him
flowers, serving teas, and discussing "universal questions" with the Speaker (NYT,
12/18/75).

16. The Unification Church held the International
Conference on the Unity of the Sciences four
times. The stated purpose of such a science
conference was "to provide an opportunity for
the world's most imminent scholars and scientists to reflect on the nature of scientific
truth and to discuss the relation of science
to a standard of value" (A Bulletin of the
International Cultural Foundation, 1974, p. 6).

17. Ken Sudo is a Japanese Moonist who heads all
of the formal training programs of the Unified
Family. His instruction manual was obtained
through an ex-Moonist and verified by two
other sources.

18. In a classic study of "brain-washing," Edgar
H. Schein (1965:149-172) interviewed many
Americans who were POWs during the Korean conflict and who have gone through "brain-washing" sessions conducted by the Chinese team of
military psychologists. Those who went through
the Chinese "brain-washing" sessions stated
that they were individually isolated and then
forced to listen to constant propaganda lectures, explaining the bad side of what the
American soldiers have come from. It is clear
that in the Chinese case, unlike the formal
training programs of the Unified Family,
tactics of coercion and confinement were
used.

57

19. Moon described his relationship with his Heavenly Bride as follows: "During my first seven-year course, I had to educate Mother, to recreate her. It took God 7,000 years to locate the bride for me, so during the seven-year course I had to indemnify all those things (his sufferings in North and South Korea). . . . I have been able to recreate Mother. From her part, she must be absolutely obedient to me. She must be different from the fallen Eve. . . . So, when you are blessed in marriage, you women must be absolutely obedient to your husband" (5/20/73).

20. Mrs. Won Bok Choi, one of Moon's English interpreters, led the training session participants in prayer at the closing of Moon's speech on 2/23/73.

21. The Unified Family uses the following translation of Tan Shim Ga: "Although my body perishes,/ And yet one thousand times dies;/ My bones becoming ashes,/ Even my soul vanishing./ Still all my love and all my heart,/ Unchanged, remain with Thee."

22. Urie So Wonun Tongil was translated this way: "Our cherished hopes are unity/ Even our dreams are for unity/ We'd give our lives for unity/ Come along, unity."

23. Among 302 religious sects in Korea, a Christian sect called Pak Changno Kyo (朴長老教) has characteristics most similar to the Unification Church. The Pak movement now possesses an extraordinarily articulate organizational system. It has its own village called Sin Ang Chon with 20,000 Pak followers residing in it. It operates factories and industrial firms, and their

58

370

products are labeled "Zion." Pak, like Moon,
claims to be the "true olive tree." For a
detailed information on Pak Changno Kyo, see
Tak Myung Hwan (1972) and Felix Moos (1967),
Transactions of the Korean Branch, Royal
Asiatic Society, Vol. XLII, Seoul.

59

References

Anthony, D. and Robbins, T. "The Decline of American Civil Religion and the Development of Authoritarian Nationalism: A Study of the Unification Church of Rev. Sun Myung Moon." A paper presented at the 1975 Annual Meeting of the Society for Scientific Study of Religion.

Arai, Arao (荒井荒雄). Madness of Japan (日本の狂気). Tokyo: Seison, 1975.

Becker, Howard S. "Becoming a Marijuana User," American Journal of Sociology, 590:235-242, 1953.

Bellah, Robert N. "Civil Religion in America," in Robert Bellah (Ed.), Beyond Belief (New York: Harper and Row, 1970), pp. 168-192.

_____. The Broken Covenant. New York: Seabury, 1974.

Berger, P. and Luckman, T. The Social Construction of Reality. New York: Doubleday, 1966.

Cohn, Norman. The Pursuit of the Millenium. New York: Harper, 1961.

Coleman, John. "Civil Religion," Sociological Analysis, 31:2, 1970.

Divine Principle. Washington, D. C.: Holy Spirit Association for the Unification of World Christianity, 1974.

Divine Principle. Korean Version (原理講論). Seoul: Sono Hwa Sa, 1975.

Douglas, Jack D. "Watergate: Harbinger of the New American Prince," Theory and Society, 89-97,

59-A

373

1974.

_____. American Social Order. New York: Free
    Press, 1971.

Goffman, Erving. Frame Analysis. Cambridge, Mass.:
    Harvard University Press, 1974.

_____. The Presentation of Self in Everyday Life.
    New York: Doubleday, 1965.

Gerlach and Hine. "Five Factors Crucial to the
    Growth and Spread of a Modern Religious Move-
    ment," Journal for the Scientific Study of
    Religion, Spring, 1970.

Hargrove, Barbara. The Reformation of the Holy.
    Philadelphia: F. A. Davis, 1971.

Heenan, Edward F. Mystery, Magic and Miracle: Re-
    ligion in a Post-Aquarian Age. Englewood
    Cliffs: Prentice-Hall, 1973.

Hobsbawm, E. J. Primitive Rebels: Studies in Ar-
    chaic Forms of Social Movement in the 19th and
    20th Centuries. New York: W. W. Norton, 1961.

Kim, Young Oon. Unification Theology and Christian
    Thought. Washington, D. C.: Holy Spirit Asso-
    ciation for the Unification of World Christi-
    anity, 1974.

Lofland, John. Doomsday Cult. Englewood Cliffs:
    Prentice-Hall, 1966.

Lambert, W. Social Psychology. New York: Norton,
    1964.

Lantenari, V. The Religions of the Oppressed: A
    Study of Modern Messianic Cults. New York:

59-B

Alfred A. Knopf, 1963.

Lofland and Stark. "Becoming a World Saviour: A
Theory of Conversion to a Deviant Perspective,"
in Religion in Sociological Perspective.
Glock (Ed.). Belmont: Wadsworth, 1973.

Lebra, T. S. "Mollenarian Movements and Resocialization," American Behavioral Scientist, Novem-
ber-December, 1972.

Moon, S. M. New Hope. Twelve Talks by Reverend
Moon. Holy Spirit Association for the Unification of World Christianity, 1973A.

_____. Answer to Watergate. Washington, D. C.:
National Prayer and Fast for the Watergate
Crisis, 1973B.

_____. Speeches of S. M. Moon in Master Speaks,
1971-1974.

The New York Times. 12/18/75, 1/11/76, 2/11/76,
2/19/76.

Petersen, W. and Armand, L. M. "The Cross and the
Commune: An Interpretation of the Jesus
People," in Charles F. Glock (Ed.). Religion
in Sociological Perspective. Belmont, Cal.:
Wadsworth, 1973, pp. 26-280.

Rice, Berkeley. "Messiah From Korea," Psychology
Today, January, 1976, pp. 36-47.

Richardson, J. T. "Causes and Consequences of the
Jesus Movement," Social Studies: Irish Journal
of Sociology, 2:5 (October-November), 457-474,
1973.

Schmidt, Joy. "Three Days at the Capitol," The Way
of the World, VI:7(Aug.), 110-137, 1973.

59-C

Simmel, George. The Sociology of George Simmel.
Glencoe: Free Press, 1950.

Sin Sa Hoon (申四勳). Paganism and Present-Day
Criticism, and Our Life Direction. Seoul:
Kidok Kyo Moonhwa Sa, 1957.

So Nam Dong (徐南同). "Critique on the Divine
Lectures of the Unification Church," Kidok
Gong Bo, May, 1970, pp. 92-100.

Stauffer, Robert E. "Civil Religion, Technology,
and the Private Spheres: Further Comments on
Cultural Integration," Journal for the Scientific Study of Religion, 12:415-425, 1973.

Swanson, Guy. The Birth of the Gods: The Origin
of Primitive Beliefs. Ann Arbor: The University of Michigan Press, 1964.

_____. Religion and Regime: A Sociological Ac-
count of the Reformation. Ann Arbor: The University of Michigan Press, 1967.

Szymanski, Albert. "The Decline and Fall of the
U. S. Eagle," Social Policy, 4:5 (March-April):
5-15, 1974.

Tak Myung Hwan (卓明煥). New Religions in Korea
(韓國新興宗敎). Seoul: Sinchong Sa, 1972.

Turner, Victor. The Ritual Process: Structure and
Anti-Structure. Chicago: Aldine, 1969.

Witcover, Jules. "The Political Legacy: A Climate
of Cynicism, An Atmosphere of Distrust," in
The Fall of a President, the Washington Post
staff. New York: D. C. Dell, 1974, pp. 107-
117.

Wilson, Bryan. Religion in Secular Society.
    Baltimore: Penguin, 1966.

Zaretsky, Irving and Leone, Mark. Marginal Re-
    ligious Movements in America. Princeton,
    N.J.: Princeton University Press, 1975.

59-E

CULTS AND NEW RELIGIONS

1. SPIRITUALISM I
   SPIRITUALIST THOUGHT

2. SPIRITUALISM II
   THE MOVEMENT

3. THE BEGINNINGS OF ASTROLOGY IN AMERICA

4. ROSICRUCIANISM IN AMERICA

5. THE ORIGINS OF THEOSOPHY
   ANNIE BESANT—THE AETHEIST YEARS

6. THEOSOPHY I
   THE INNER LIFE OF THEOSOPHY

7. THEOSOPHY II
   CONTROVERSIAL AND POLEMICAL PAMPHLETS

8. JEHOVAHS WITNESSES I
   THE EARLY WRITINGS OF J. F. RUTHERFORD

9. JEHOVAHS WITNESSES II
   CONTROVERSIAL AND POLEMICAL PAMPHLETS

10. MORMONISM I
    EVANGELICAL CHRISTIAN ANTI-MORMONISM
    IN THE 20TH CENTURY

11. MORMONISM II
    PRO-MORMON WRITINGS OF THE 20TH CENTURY

12. CHRISTIAN SCIENCE
    CONTROVERSIAL AND POLEMICAL PAMPHLETS

13. THE EVANGELICAL CHRISTIAN ANTI-CULT MOVEMENT
    CHRISTIAN COUNTER-CULT LITERATURE

14. CULTS AND THE JEWISH COMMUNITY
    REPRESENTATIVE EXAMPLES OF
    JEWISH ANTI-CULT LITERATURE